More memories of a Didcot Steam Apprentice

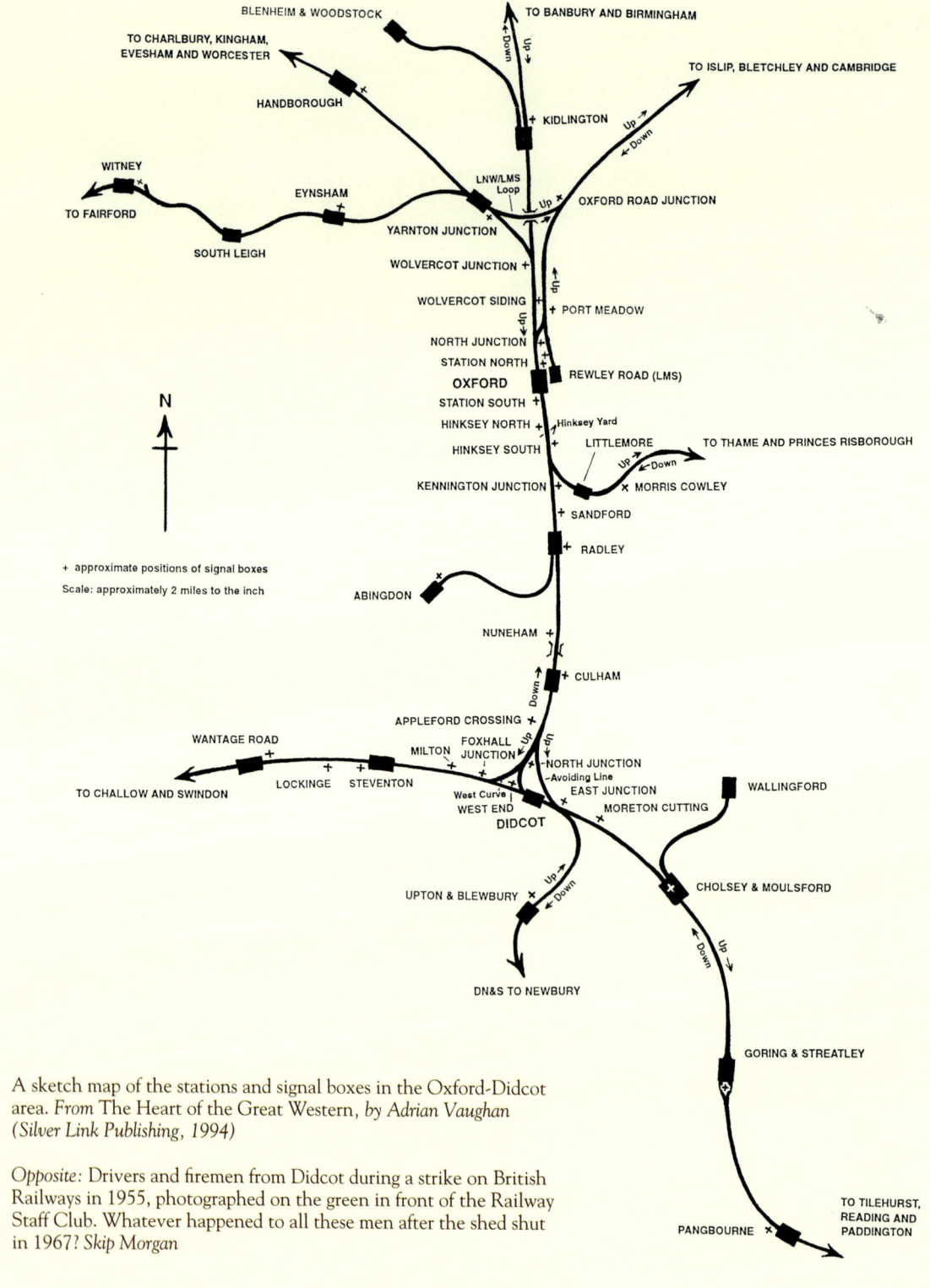

A sketch map of the stations and signal boxes in the Oxford-Didcot area. *From The Heart of the Great Western, by Adrian Vaughan (Silver Link Publishing, 1994)*

Opposite: Drivers and firemen from Didcot during a strike on British Railways in 1955, photographed on the green in front of the Railway Staff Club. Whatever happened to all these men after the shed shut in 1967? *Skip Morgan*

More memories of a Didcot Steam Apprentice

The home and work diary of an apprentice fitter, 1960-1966

Patrick Kelly
Edited by Will Adams

Silver Link Books

© Patrick Kelly 2022

All rights reserved. No part of this publication may be reproduced, stored in a retrieval system or transmitted, in any form or by any means, electronic, mechanical, photocopying, recording or otherwise, without prior permission in writing from Silver Link Books, Mortons Media Group Ltd.

First published in 2022

British Library Cataloguing in Publication Data

A catalogue record for this book is available from the British Library.

ISBN 978-1-85794-572-0

Silver Link Books
Mortons Media Group Limited
Media Centre
Morton Way
Horncastle
LN9 6JR
Tel/Fax: 01507 529535

email: sohara@mortons.co.uk
Website: www.nostalgiacollection.com

Printed and bound in the Czech Republic

Old money
1 old penny was written as '1d'; 2d was 'tuppence', 3d was 'thruppence', or a 'joey'. 6d was a 'tanner' or a 'kick', so '1 and a kick' was 1s 6d. ¼d was a farthing, ½d a 'ha'penny'. 1 shilling (now 5p) was a 'bob'; 2 shillings was a 'florin'; 2 shillings and 6 pence (2s 6d) was 'half a dollar', and 5 shillings was a 'dollar' (roughly equal to an American dollar back in the 1960s). There were 240 old pennies in a pound (£1).

Acknowledgements

I would like to thank Tony Groves, former BR fireman, for his help with the manuscript; the late Alan Caulkett, proud to be a Berkshire man; Ted Abear, former fireman at Old Oak Common, for his story and pictures; Richard Denny, for pictures; John Pritchard, former Didcot driver, for his help with my story; Peter Sedge, for information and help; David Marsh, for information on Harwell; Bill Wright, for information; Derek Everson, for the story of Wilf Diamond; Garth Porter, for information; John Crighton, NHS Estates Electrical Officer, friend and work colleague; Jean Goodall, daughter of Didcot driver Jack Goodall; and Mrs Jennifer Kelly for helping me with the English.

Contents

Introduction	6	
1 Life at home	7	
2 First day	14	
3 Sky hooks and pistons	24	
4 Routine	32	
5 Saturdays and safety valves	42	
6 Charlie Caulkett	51	
7 Initiation	57	
8 Pay day	63	
9 First trip to Swindon	71	
10 Front of shed	80	
11 Paperwork, pipes and pilots	88	
12 Ladies, old and young	95	
13 Mishaps	105	
14 'Warships' and washouts	112	
15 Pistons…	118	
16 …and piston valves	125	
17 'Bloody children!'	131	
18 Fire irons	137	
19 *Purley Hall*	144	
20 Shunting – and Oxford again	150	
21 Christmas and New Year	158	
22 Table lamps and tantrums	170	
23 Something up	178	
24 Revenge	185	
25 Sal … and Adolf	190	
26 Happy birthday!	197	
27 Moving out	206	
28 A 'Castle' in trouble	213	
29 A fishy tale	220	
30 A lesson learned	226	
31 Snowbound!	232	
32 Reading transfer	241	
33 Old Oak Common	247	
34 Ultrasonic fatigue testing from Reading	256	
35 Fireball	262	
36 A brush with death	269	
Epilogue	278	
Appendix 1 The fitting crew at Didcot, Running and Maintenance Department	279	
Appendix 2 Didcot's locomotive allocation in October 1959, October 1960, November 1960 and 1961	281	
Index	284	

Introduction

This book is an attempt to recapture the happy days of 'home and steam shed life', some of which was described in my first book, *Didcot Steam Apprentice*. However, I would like to point out when I wrote the earlier book I had to leave out a lot of true stories and rude items. But in this manuscript nothing is barred, and this is the true account of the men who worked in the Running and Maintenance section of Didcot shed – I was fortunate enough to serve with a most Honourable Company of Gentlemen. Three names have had to be changed to replace their real names.

From the year 1960 to 1966 I was an apprentice fitter at the main-line shed of Didcot, in the London Division, also being transferred to Reading diesel depot, two tours at Old Oak Common and Swindon 'AE' workshop, finishing at Old Oak Common, as a skilled fitter and turner. I was transferred to Oxford shed in 1966 – the worst mistake I made.

I always wanted to write an epic story about shed life at Didcot and the men I worked with, some very two-faced. This is that story, a true account with a little fiction helping along the way. I enjoyed writing it, and I hope you will enjoy reading it. I felt while writing this story that I was inside the text looking out, I was so engrossed in it. I put my heart and soul into the story, sometimes even crying at what I went through. One story I have left out still gives me nightmares, and I did not want to go down that road. I have left out some of the other apprentices for my own reasons.

Myself at 19 years of age, standing next to a linesman's hut on the East Loop line. *Author*

I've never told anyone about the Didcot 'initiation ceremony', which is a true story and the reason why my nickname came to be 'Wobble', which I kept throughout my working life. My mother was as she is described here, and if it wasn't for my Dad I would have left home.

1. Life at home

The first place the Kelly family lived in Didcot was the prefabs on Mereland Road, where I was born. My parents and two brothers came from Dublin. We were then allotted a council house, one of many situated in Sinodun Road that had been built by Italian and German POWs, who lived in Newlands Avenue, opposite the Cornet Picture House. Ours was No 28. When the prisoners went back to their own countries after the Second World War, people started to come from the outskirts of big cities to live in Didcot as work was abundant. I remember people living in the former POW huts opposite the picture house, OK in the warmer weather but in the cold the poor people were freezing and walking mud onto the floors of the wooden huts, with no heat in the building apart from a small stove.

The houses were built as quickly as possible to get families out of the huts and into their new homes – the council did everything possible. After the war money was very tight, with wages from the railway being low, and food and coal scarce; water and ice ran down the inside of our windows and made a pool on the window ledge. In 1956, when I was 11 years old, I contracted pneumonia. There was only one cure for it – I was smothered in goose grease and had brown paper wrapped around me, tied with string. I was very poorly, and outside the snow fell. Both my Mum and Dad worked on the railway, together with our neighbours and others living in the same community; we were all in the same boat. The railway was the main employer in the Didcot area at that time.

We children found our own entertainment. For fun we would go down to the three-cornered field near the Didcot to Newbury line, which led eventually to the

The Prison of War camp for the Italians opposite the Coronet picture house, 1945. *K. Caulkett collection*

docks at Southampton. All the boys and girls would play together and go out looking for sticks, pieces of wood, or anything that would burn as we tried to stay warm for the winter. The three-cornered field was protected from the line by two strands of wire held up by concrete posts. We children would climb over it, or through the strands of wire, and just walk along the track on the sleepers, or place pennies on the rail so that when a train came along it flattened them. The pennies were much bigger than now – today's pennies would not hold the same fascination. These were good times.

Newlands Avenue, Didcot, showing the Prison of War camp for the Germans. *K. Caulkett collection*

There was a crossing to the other side of the track; it had a hedge, a few trees and a ditch. This crossing, with its double-handed gate, was mostly for the movement of cattle to access the next field. The farmer would herd the cows across the railway line; they would make an awful mess when they crossed. We tried to avoid this area.

Once in the field we would play 'footy', hide and seek and rounders – carefree, enjoyable times. I remember once as we played together we saw a lad walking up and down the track putting something into the expansion gaps between the lengths of rails, holding it in with a stone. We looked at each other and said, 'What's he at?' Thinking no more about it, we split up and went home for our tea.

Our home was well known to the local police, and the local 'copper' would ride his bicycle to the house (neighbours in the road thought the police lived at our house, with all the comings and goings). Leaning his bicycle against the wall and the handlebars in the hedge, he would remove the bicycle clips on the bottom of his trousers, walk up the path and knock on the back door, seeing as he was a regular visitor. The neighbours, looking through their curtains, would say, 'What's happening at the Kellys' again?'

I had not been home long when the copper came into the kitchen area and spoke.

'Good afternoon Mr and Mrs Kelly.'

Dad stood near me with Mum as they replied to his pleasantries, and Dad was removing his belt, not for his own comfort, but to use across my backside.

The question the copper asked was, 'Were you in the three-cornered field today Pat?' I was known by that name. He knew I had been and I answered 'Yes.' He wanted to know if I had seen someone playing on the track, and had I seen what he was doing. Not wishing to get involved, I said very little, pleased to see my Dad buckle up his belt again.

The copper told my parents and me that the boy had caused an amount of trouble with the ball bearings he had laid in the rail gaps, telling us that when a locomotive ran over them they embedded themselves into the locomotive's tyre. As the engine went down the track after such an incident it caused indentations in the steel rail, the result being that a new piece of track had to

Life at home

St Birinus school cricket team. In the centre is Jack Luckett, with Mr Robinson standing on the left-hand side. Sitting on the left is Roger Evans (nicknamed 'Parrot'), then Len Barclay, and in the centre Louis Moulsford, then Mr Page and Albert Nutt. Standing on the right might be Ken Shorter, the metalwork master.
John McNamara collection

be replaced. Also, the engine would be out of service for months at a cost of £350. My God, that was a fortune!

I learned later that the boy concerned, the son of driver Bert Brown, eventually joined British Railways as a cleaner, then went on to be a fireman.

I enjoyed school at St Birinus in Mereland Road. The teachers were OK – some were a bit hard on other pupils, while some just took it day by day. The science master, Mr Page, was sheer evil – he must have been into Bunsen burner rubber tube, or the smell of it. I didn't like it, as it hurt when he swung it back over his shoulder and crashed it down onto my back with all his strength. I didn't give him the pleasure of knowing that it bloody well hurt, and I never cried in front of him, being a new boy. Yes, I had been talking in class very quietly, and the master crept up behind me. I never did like science after that.

My form tutor was Roger Evans, who was nicknamed 'Parrot' because of his long nose. He was my teacher in 3C and was very good at throwing a board duster or a spare leather plimsole at me at the back of the class. I was then moved to the front of the class in front of his desk. When the sun came through the huge windows I fell asleep – nothing could wake me. When break time approached everybody quietly crept out of class and left me. 'Parrot' wrote on the blackboard in big white chalk letters '500 lines to be in by next morning: "I MUST NOT SLEEP IN CLASS".'

Mum went mad. 'Do you have to sleep at school? I know you can sleep on a clothes line.'

Swimming started on 1 May 1955 at the big boys' school, in open-air swimming baths that were open to the public. Two road coaches came into the school to collect the swimming classes to be driven the 7 miles to Wallingford every Friday morning. We all looked out of the coaches' windows at the scenery as we trundled through the countryside before coming to a stop near the River Thames at Wallingford.

The teachers would shout, 'All out, you lot – into the changing rooms and get undressed into your bathing trunks!'

It was freezing cold and we had to get into the icy-cold water and do what the teachers told us – they of course were warm in their tracksuits with towels round their necks and bobble hats on their heads. A lot of the boys had their first bath here, being dirty little sods, and when the water went yellow it was too late to go to the toilet.

As the years progressed I went through the stages to gain my certificates. When the last year arrived, 1959, we had a swimming sports day at our favourite open-air pool. Anthony Groves won the medal for breast stroke, achieving the distance on his own. There was some confusion with my teacher telling me off, as I seem to get nowhere with him.

'Keep your hands down at your sides before diving into the pool, or you will get 500 lines!'

'Yes, sir.'

We had to wander across to the grass verge and the water's edge of the River Thames. First off, Roland James went off the spring board at ground level with a huge bounce and crashed into the river with a belly flop. Everyone sniggered, and he came up half drowned. I saw the distress in his face and I ran though the crowd and dived into the water, turned him over in a life-saving position and brought him back to the bank, helping him up the steps to be pulled out of the water by the teachers, who then resuscitated him.

Now my turn, and I thought for a moment what I should do. As well as the spring board on the ground, there was a second one a little higher up, then a third and a fourth. I had been practising this for weeks before the school sports. I climbed to the top of the fourth board, stood on the edge of the flat wooden frame next to the handrail balancing on my toes but not touching the diving board, composed myself and jumped off. Unfortunately I hit the third spring board and sprang into the air, coming down in a swallow dive into the river water with no splash. When I came to the surface, everyone stood amazed as I swam to the steps. Roger said, 'Forget the 500 lines – what a dive!' and we were friends again.

Roger must have thought I was good as he awarded me the school's Prefect honours. All the boys who were made up had to be in the school colours, a uniform of black blazer, grey flannels and green tie. But there was me in blue jeans, white shirt, no tie, and two-tone 'winklepickers', the smartest one there. The chosen boys had to go on stage and have the badges presented to us by the Headmaster, Louis Moulsford. He looked down his nose at me, but I had some power now with that badge – I wanted to be Head Boy, but that never happened. Les Summers got awarded with it. I was glad really as I could not crawl to all the teachers, but I did

1959 Schoolboy Champion for the Corinthians' Team, and Prefect. I am on the left with a USAAF Officer from Greenham Common, Newbury, in the centre, then the Headmaster, Louis Moulsford.

Life at home

achieve something better – I was schoolboy champion for swimming for the Corinthians' team and I was Captain at St Birinus Boys School also.

I designed the new tie as the old one was rubbish, and it never did anything for the boys' appearance. Mr Moulsford agreed and put it into action ('Good at something, Mr Kelly').

When Roger got married I slid under his sports car and tied up empty beer cans. He always left his car in the infants' school behind the hedge. So I gave a little present back to him. I bet he thought, 'That bloody kid again – *Kelly*!' (500 words!)

I enjoyed school. It was the best time of my life, and the teachers were good, except Taffy Davies, the PE teacher. We saw him beat Bob Butters and punch him in the PE lesson. There was trouble as a result, and he was dismissed, with the incident on his record.

Some years later after I left school, one weekend when I was 17 years old, sitting on the bank at Wallingford by the swimming pool, a shout went out that someone's little boy had fallen off a motor boat into the river. I ran down to the water's edge, through the stinging nettles, dived in and swam to the boat. The mother pointed out the position and I saw the small boy go under the water. As I saw his arms raised in the air I swam and grabbed him and pulled him up out of the water, turned him over into the life-saving position, took him back to the bank and sat him down. He was crying and I put my towel around him, as well as my arms, to keep him warm. The motor boat came across the river and moored. The boy's father jumped down and came across to me and thanked me for saving his son's life. He climbed back onto the boat and I handed the small boy to him. I said he should get a life jacket for him, or the next time he will drown.

In 1980, many years later, when my youngest daughter was five years old and my eldest daughter 9½, we were on holiday at Wareham in Dorset, and were sitting by the river, which was a backwater from Poole Harbour from the sea and some heavy sailing ships were tied up at the quay. Two little boys aged about 8, in short trousers, wearing wellingtons and carrying fishing nets, strode down the concrete steps to the water's edge, while their parents sat on the metal seat eating ice creams and taking no notice, just taking in the sunshine. I started to get jumpy as both stepped into the water and their wellingtons started to fill up. Soon they got worried too, and went down under the water. I stripped off my clothes and jumped into the water from the concrete quay, grabbed one at a time and pulled them out. Still their parents took no notice – they were in another world. I led the boys back as they were crying, having lost their wellingtons and fishing nets, but the parents didn't even care. My wife was shocked at what I had done.

*

At the back of the houses in Didcot there was a high bank of earth on either side of the Newbury and Southampton line. Every morning around 5.30, lying in our beds, my two elder brothers and I would hear the two 'Moguls', Nos 5327 and 5380 in tandem, thumping with the strain of the goods freight behind them, pulling up the incline from the East Junction signal box towards the Downs and Upton & Blewbury station, the steel rails wet from the night before. The leading engine's fireman would no doubt be stooping down on the floor to grip the sand-lever with cotton waste in his hand and pulling it backwards to open the slotted tube inside the sandbox. This would allow sharp sand to flow down the feed pipe onto both rails in the path of the driving wheels, giving the 5ft 8in-diameter iron tyres some grip. With the steam pressure at maximum – 200lb per square inch – the fireman would be sweating as he shovelled the Welsh marine coal into the firebox. The black needle on the gauge would be pounding in time with the steam pumping into the cylinders.

The smell of hot oil and the warmth

from the boiler would keep the men warm on the footplate. The driver would be holding the regulator lever wide open, looking through his quarter-light window. He would feel the vibration coming through the centre of the locomotive through his hand, in time with every piston movement, forcing forward. He would also be looking back to see the other 'Mogul' doing the same – those Great Western drivers knew how each other worked.

The noise was electrifying. So much was happening in the early part of the dark morning. As the engines passed under the road bridge and out into the open, they started to draw into the cutting. One of the men on the footplate of the second engine would climb up onto the tender and throw lumps of coal over the side. Later one of the men on the lengthmen's shift would walk along the railway line with a sack, feeling for the lumps of coal that had been dropped along the way to take home for the fire. If caught with the coal, he would be sacked.

*

When Dad was at work on the railway, Mum would be either downstairs in the kitchen or cooking or cleaning the house. There would be an eruption if her three sons starting teasing her. Mum was Irish and very fiery. She would grab the frying pan off the cold gas cooker and make a dash towards the three of us – we honestly thought that if she got hold of us she would have killed us. That was our Mum. Anyway we would run upstairs. Paul was the instigator and the eldest; Dick was trouble, always niggling behind Paul, and I just got in the way.

We would run into the back bedroom, which was Dick's and my bedroom, and larger than Paul's, because he had his own bedroom at the front of the house, which was tiny – no good getting into Paul's.

As we ran though the door it was impossible for us all to get through together, but our lives depended on it, as Mum was in a killing mood. Two hands came out behind Dick and pulled me into the room to keep me safe.

We hid behind the door. There was a lot of shouting and screaming – whatever the neighbours thought God only knows. Mum shouted out that she was going to kill us three, and she meant it, believe me! We couldn't stop laughing, which made her worse. Bejesus, Holy Mother of God! She went raving mad. The worse thing was Paul opening the door a little to see her waving the frying pan at the door. Now the Irish was coming out of Mum's mouth, some I couldn't understand. When Paul shut the door again, Dick wanted to play, so he opened the door just a crack to peep out. Paul

My Mum with my best mate Mick Howard in 1961.

My Dad.

Life at home

was saying, 'Easy, she'll have a heart attack. Come on, let's try and stop her raving.' I had no say in the matter, as I was a squirt.

'Mum, let's have a truce. Come on, let's talk about this.'

'Never, *never*!' she shouted. 'Jesus Mary and Joseph!' she screamed at us.

Dick and Paul shouted together, 'Come on, Mum, settle down – let's all come out and settle down. We can all go downstairs and sort things out.'

'Bejesus, Holy Mother of God! I'll have to say 20 Hail Marys!' Then she simmered down, smiled and burst out laughing, seeing the funny side it. It went quiet as we all went down the stairs, as friends, with me carrying the frying pan. Jesus Mary and Joseph, it was heavy!

*

In February 1960 I had to report to the Careers Office in Edinburgh Drive before leaving Didcot Boys School in Mereland Road that Easter, as I was 15 years old, but it was a waste of time as I knew what I wanted to do. My Dad and I had spoken about it often enough. However, deep down I really wanted to be a make-up artist, but I did not have the heart to say so to my Dad, as I guess he would have thrown a wobbly, as well as my two older brothers – they would have thought I was a pansy potter or a poof and wouldn't give me any rest.

I was going with a girl called Annie (not her real name). We were strongly courting at the time, and I made her up with lipstick and powder, with magic eye mascara and eyeliner, but it was better kissing it off than washing it off. (Later in my career I would use a lot of paste – not on the human face, but the graphite paste used for steam gasket joints. I would slap it on – I was good at it.)

Dad went to make an appointment with the duty office assistant with a request to see George East, the Didcot Shedmaster, after his shift hours were ended – Dad worked on the coal stage, 6.00am to 2.00pm – to enquire if there was opening for a apprenticed fitter within the shed. He knocked at the Shedmaster's door and it was opened by Mr East himself. They exchanged pleasantries, and he was shown a seat in front of Mr East's desk. Also sitting in the same room was Arthur Brinkley, the running and maintenance foreman. I was discussed – what experience I was interested in and what were my ambitions and prospects with British Railways, and when would I be leaving school. I was to leave in 1960, being 15 years old in February of that year.

Dad came home from work one evening with the biggest grin on his face, and in front of the family at teatime he told me that I had been accepted to work on the railway at Didcot shed as a fitter's boy. I was given a start date and had to report to George East, who would introduce me to my foreman, Arthur Brinkley.

Soon came my last morning working for Don Avery as a paper boy. I had to show a new boy the ropes; he was a bit slack, but that was down to Don to get him up to standard. All the people I delivered to came out and said their goodbyes.

It is only now, with the urge to write about those happy days, that I can begin to appreciate what the old Great Western Railway was all about. I became part of that family, together with the many fitting staff all over the Western Region, and followed my two brothers as a skilled fitter and turner, as the railway drivers knew us.

As I look back now, I knew I was a Great Western man and I still feel a pride knowing that I was taught properly, and that I was following the men who had made the Western 'Great', though now all gone.

2. First day

It was February 1960 and I had instructions how to get to where I had to go, as this was the first time I had gone to the station by myself. At 8 in the morning my career was about to start. I ran up the stairs to Platforms 4 and 5 to the paper shop at the entrance to the platforms and got a paper, the *Daily Sketch*. As I left the platform and walked down the concrete steps to the undercroft suddenly a heavy train came roaring through the station. The noise was terrifying to my ears, with the wagon wheels pounding over the rail gaps.

I walked down, pushing my bike, to the end of the undercroft, then climbed the steps with my bike on my shoulder. When I reached the open air I saw for the first time the locomotives and carriages moving up and down. I lifted my bike down from my shoulder, and an engineman told me to follow him across the sleepers, making sure I didn't get my bike wheels stuck in the rails.

He asked me if I was new.

'Yes, I start today as a fitter's boy.'

My first instinct was that this was a very frightening area with the sound of the steam whistles and coaches moving up and down.

Below: Didcot shed when new in 1934. *British Railways*

I left the engineman and rode on down towards the shed along the cinder track that many men had walked since 1934, when the shed was new. When I came to the entrance of the shed I was amazed to see the amount of steam engines gathered around, facing in all directions, and railway lines spread over the area. Didcot was set within a triangle with main-line trains on all sides It seemed like a Pandora's box of steam engines.

I looked at the huge clock on the main office window; at the time I did not know it was Mr East's office. Only twice had I ever visited his office – today and once years ago for being very naughty.

Above: Didcot shed under construction in 1934. Note the steel water pipes lying on the ground.

First day

I placed my bike in a slot in the bike shed – I never locked it as no one would ever pinch it. I then walked across another set of tracks past the clock and noted the time – plenty of time to go yet. Then I entered the shed. Oh my Lord, I had never seen so many locomotives in one place, and how close they stood next to me. The smell was so wonderful – it filled my nostrils. I was in a daze with the smell of engine oil mixed with steam.

I saw the nameplate on the door of Mr East's office and knocked. The Shedmaster opened it and welcomed me into his office. I sat down facing him, shaking like a leaf. He told me about the shed and what my status would be as a fitter's boy for the first year, working within the shed. Then a lady entered the office and handed over a brass disc, which was to be my pay number while I worked at the shed. The number was 388, which she explained has been my brother Richard's work number when he had been an apprentice there. Mr East introduced me formally to Mrs Bray; she was the time clerk and Mr East's secretary and PA. We shook hands. She lived in Swindon and came down on the train when on duty.

I was told how the system worked and my working hours, which were 7.30am start and 5.30pm finish, with an hour for lunch, 12.30 till 1.30, five days a week, plus working a Saturday morning from 7.30 till 12 noon, with two weeks holiday per year and bank holidays off with pay. I was told that every year after completing one year's service I would receive a pay rise of £1. At that time the pay was £1 10s for a 48-hour week. I was taught the safety side of things, like not to jump the pits, always stop, look and listen for steam locomotives, especially whenever the weather was bad, to be on my guard for the sound of engines moving, and never cross the railway line until you were sure that it was clear.

I was given a safety book to read (which I still have today). I was then introduced to Arthur Brinkley, the mechanical foreman, who was in the same office waiting for me

Mrs Bray, PA to George East.

to arrive. He shook my hand and welcomed me to his department. Arthur was the mechanical foreman in our department. I subsequently found him to be a rather solitary character; he had no one with whom to share his sadness and thoughts, and nobody with whom to share any blame should he ever fail. His superiors were in Westbourne Terrace in Paddington.

He stood 5ft 6in tall, small and round, with his hair thinning, but he stood his ground in an argument or when someone had done something wrong. We all thought very highly of him.

Every now and then he would reach into the pocket of his dark blue smock, pull out his tobacco tin, open the lid and roll his Old Virginia baccy and cigarette paper between his small thumbs to make a roll-up. Then he took his lighter from the other pocket and lit his cigarette, drawing a mouthful of smoke into his lungs. He would then rub his eye with his right index finger just like a little boy. I would study him, sitting on a loco footplate on No 2 road opposite his office, or standing outside his office door, deep in thought, level with the metal lockers so he would be in no one's way. Then with a determined look on his face he would march off as if he was still a sergeant in the RAF Regiment, his first step coming down heavily on the floor.

Arthur took me out of the pay clerk's office and we both walked down towards the lifting shop. As we walked along he explained the running shed to me, showing me his office, and the mess cabin where I was to have my meals. I met all the staff who were on duty. I was shown where to put my clothes and issued with a locker with a key for my personal items; this was also the place where I would keep my teapot, cup, sugar and tea. The locker room was very cold in the winter, as there was no heating.

Outside in the lifting shop there was a long ceramic trough; this was the hand basin with overhead pipes feeding hot and cold water into the taps to wash our hands. I had to supply my own soap and towel.

I reported for work at a meeting in the manager's office, collected my working details and was given the opportunity to

Didcot's lifting shop in more recent times.

learn a trade. Frightened? Yes, I was blinking terrified, but I had to stand on my own two feet and get on with life – there was no running back to Mummy and Daddy.

My overalls were supplied by my Mum. She found no end of them in the airing cupboard that Dick would have worn, washed and ironed and waiting for someone else to wear them. She was a good Mum, looking after her little soldier (that was me). She would wash them every week with my Dad's and my brother Dick's; Dick was older than me, while my eldest brother, Paul, had joined the Royal Navy, as the call-up was in place. When Dick received his letter from the War Office with his call-up papers he was worked at Oxford railway depot; after leaving Didcot for call-up, having served his apprenticeship, he joined the Irish Fusiliers in Northern Ireland.

My boots I had bought when I was an Army Cadet at Wallingford Regiment; they were studded and strong leather. They became very handy for working within the shed until I needed another leather pair with a steel toecap, as my toes were still attached to me!

I came out of the changing room fully dressed and ready to see who wanted me (or possibly who had drawn the short straw out of all these fitters). This big man walked across the wooden block floor, shook hands with me and took me under his wing. Mr Brinkley introduced me to him; his name was Jimmy Tyler. We had a chat then both walked off to the rear of the locomotive shed. Between the lines a set of steps led down into the depths; Jimmy told me to keep my head down as we went under a locomotive. He encouraged me down, speaking to me as I crawled on my bended knees with the oily metal frame close to my head. I kept my head down, looking up at the same time sideways, until we came to a space were the wheels and axle should have been. I stretched my legs upwards while Jim explained the system and what was about to happen.

First day

I had started my career, and my first engine was No 6953 *Leighton Hall*, waiting for its driving wheels. Getting out of the pit, crawling the same way as I had gone in, I looked around the engine, seeing that the wheel arrangement was different; it should have been a 4-6-0, but was a 4-4-0!

Jim took me round the shed and explained everything to me, how things worked in general., what the shed boiler did and how it provided the hot water for the sinks and boiling water for the steam pipes around the inside the shed when loco boilers were washed by placing high-pressure steam into the tubes when the side plugs were removed. This allowed the scale from the hard water and bad coal to be flushed away into the pit; this was why we used good marine coal from South Wales.

Tools for smelting and handling tongs when working on the forge.

He also showed me how the forge was used and the controls for the blower, because every morning it had to be lit up, the same way as a domestic fire had to be laid with

A general view of the shed during a Great Western Society Open Day in September 1971. The tall building at the far end of the shed is the fitting shop where I worked with Jim Tyler. The small building at the near end of the shed is the timekeeper's office. *Ray Ruffell, Slip Coach Publishing Services collection*

sticks and paper, or paraffin with cotton waste and a few sticks with coals from the night before.

The engine that had the wheels removed was shunted outside the fitting shop with the smokebox pointing towards London. A steam shunter came into the shop and pushed the buffers together to couple up. I was bewildered to see it happen on the very first day of my new job as a fitter's boy.

The fitters' cabin was situated next door to the foreman's office. There were two long wooden-framed wooden benches and a metal tin-topped table; one bench was against the wall, its end next to the ceramic sink with a cold water tap in the corner. In another corner of the room was a huge wooden trunk with a lock, containing overalls for the men.

On the left side on the wall were notice boards behind glass doors, with instructions for safety. Five feet from the door was an iron potbelly stove with the chimney pipe rising up through the ceiling and an iron kettle on the top steaming away. The room's warmth took the chill off from being outside. Behind the stove a window looked out across the carriages, with green scrub and weeds. There were plenty of stories from the men who had been stationed there during the war, and the daily jobs they had done.

I was told to go into the cabin as it was time to have a morning tea break, so I took my teapot and mug, with my grub bag over my shoulder. Being slightly shy, the most frightening thing was meeting the men having their food and drink. I walked in, they all said hello and I introduced myself. Each man told me his name; some were on nights, others were coming in for the afternoon shift. As I sat down Mr Brinkley appeared and asked if I was OK. All the men stated that I had done well, so it was not so bad really and broke the ice. The tea break was 20 minutes, and after half an hour I went to get up and was told to sit back down, and to take my time. They all asked me different questions, about school, whether I was a Didcot boy, and was it my Dad working on the washouts with Trevor May. They remembered my brother Dick too.

Back in the fitting shop Jim, my mentor, was waiting for the shunting engine that was bringing in an open wooden wagon, because the spares for the 'Hall' engine had arrived. Jim reached up to unlock the pins holding the side door and let it crash open. Two other men came into the shop with overalls on and helped. One was Jim Hale, who got into the wagon with me, while Dave Davies stayed on the ground with Jim Tyler. All four of us struggled to get the wagon emptied by using the block and tackle, a small crane used by engineering. I was given the job of operating the pulley block and chain, with the swing-away iron boom.

The set of driving wheels was hooked onto a straight lifting bar, with the ends turned upwards poking through the spokes. This was hooked onto the swing-away crane, which lowered them down onto the floor by running the chains through the pulley block. The swing-away was then brought back to the wagon, and Jim Hale repositioned the chains round two huge axle boxes, and I helped by hoisting them up from the wagon floor. They were then swung out and lowered down to the ground, then the block and tackle with the chain was put away in its place and secured.

My mentor explained that we had to go to the stores. There I was introduced to the storeman looking through the hatch window, and stood around to listen to the chatter while we waited our turn. The enginemen talked about their experiences working their engines, but every time I went to the stores hatch it was always the same drivers. Those first few hours on my first day involved shaking hands with some of the fitting staff that came on shift at 2 o'clock, working the afternoon shift till 10.00pm, and finding out who were the fathers of sons and daughters I knew from school. It was hard for a boy like me to take everything in, discovering the procedures as I started my new career with British Railways, being shown over the coming years how to go on with the ordering of the stores and writing out the request

First day

forms for parts, mostly paraffin or cotton waste and graphite paste, with the fitters' signatures. So when I was sent to the stores I would have a small black notebook in my pocket for taking notes.

I had to collect a bundle of 2lb of cotton waste and a new galvanised bucket of paraffin, holding 2 gallons, then walk back to the fitting shop. Jim explained to me what our next job would be, to carry the bucket to the middle of the fitting shop near the axle bearing. I was shown what I had to do – pull the cotton waste apart by ripping it away from the bundle, take a handful, dip it into the paraffin, then spread the oil across the journal and take off the preserver, the sticky brown oil. Jim came over with a crowbar and lifted one axle box at a time by jamming the crowbar into the wooden floor blocks and screwing upwards so the bar took the weight and each one flipped over; I then washed the other inner bearing's casing. It was getting near dinner time, 12.30pm, so he told me he would see me at 1.30.

I went to my locker and got the Lifebuoy soap out with a small towel I had brought that morning. I washed my hands in the ceramic sink with hot water generated by the outside steam engine boiler. Everyone started to appear now from their jobs in the shed, doing what I was doing and chatting to me to see how I was getting on with my first morning. I walked up to the Time Office, taking my disc and handing it over to the time clerk, Mark Thomas.

Coming back to the cabin, I ate my sandwiches and drank some tea because I had to have some sustenance as I was as dry as a chip. Everybody was talking about something or other as I got up, walked to the cabin's ceramic sink and washed out the teapot and mug. Saying 'See you later,' I walked from the cabin by twisting the huge iron door handle that had rattled in the door since the shed was built in 1934. I headed back to the fitting shop to put my teapot and mug back into the locker, then shut it and locked it with a key. I walked out into the shed with a smile on my face, and bumped into Dad. He said that he just coming to see me to see how things were going.

'Let's talk in the shedmen's cabin, son, and I'll tell you about 1945 as the war was coming to an end in May of that year.'

At that time my Dad had gone back to Ireland to visit his parents in Killester, a small residential suburb of Dublin on the north side of the city. He went into the bungalow and they welcomed him home, but then he saw two tall men wearing long, grey waterproof coats walking past the side window. His father told him to get out the back door and run and not to stop. Get back to England, and tell no one where you are.

These two grey-coated figures were IRA killers and they wanted my Dad dead for joining the British Army during the war, as they were German spies. My grandfather told my Dad that they had been hanging around for days waiting for the right moment; under their long coats they carried revolvers.

Dad got in touch with his parents to say where he was, and sent money to my Mum and his family in Dublin to bring them to England. He also sent free railway passes for the train and boat across the Irish Sea. He waited at the station at Didcot for the family to arrive, then took them to lodgings at Aunty Molly's next to the fire station until they received a prefab from the council in Mereland Road. That's where I was born in 1945. It was Irishmen that built the roads and railways that we know today.

Dad's job consisted of 12-hour shifts, days, nights and afternoons. He got one weekend off in six weeks, being part of a four-man team within the area; all the other men were from Ireland as well, and were called Paddys, which pleased my Dad.

Didcot shed was the village's employment area for the young men starting out on their first day when they left school. Young cleaners would be asked to go to the coal stage and help with unloading the coal from the wagons, which built up strength in their arms and the backs of their legs. They were given a No 8 shovel, pointed in the correct direction and shown the main principles of the job by the men who worked in that area.

The coal stage job consisted of loading tubs from the 10-ton No 1 coal wagons, which came in different sizes and shapes, wooden, metal, drop gates and open gates. The worst ones were wooden, as the nails that held the planks of wood into place were 6 to 12 inches long, and during movement on the road they would stick up between the Welsh marine coals. The shed foreman was contacted verbally from the coal stage to have six more wagons full of the black stuff, which would be shunted up the slope six at a time, while a fire dropper worked on the lower stage on the waiting engines.

Some men shared their work below on the ash road, with a 2-foot-square iron-bladed shovel on a 12-foot iron handle reaching into the firebox, still very hot from standing on the ash road the night before. Even to pick it up the shovel could be felt within your stomach, and a small cough with a pleasant English short word. There was an art to getting the ash from the firebox with the 12-foot shovel through the small firebox hole. There was not much room standing on the footplate to swing it around and chuck the ash and clinker into either an empty iron coal wagon, or out on either side onto the concrete floor like some dirty men did, leaving someone else to shovel it up in heaps, then load it into the iron truck. But it was easier than on a 'tankie' or a pannier tank, as they had no room at all. You had to keep the shovel down to the wooden floor and shorten your hand grip down the iron shaft till the skin on your arms started to burn with the hairs crinkling up and smouldering.

Didcot's coal stage is prominent in these views taken during Great Western Society Open Days in 1978. In the second one the chute can be seen in operation, coaling preserved 0-6-2 tank locomotive No 6697. *Ray Ruffell, Slip Coach Publishing Services collection*

The pricker would come in useful to move the ash and clinkers to one side of the firebox in a heap, then changing the pricker for the shovel to push the ash into a heap right in the corner and lift it clean out of the firebox without twisting or dropping the long-handled iron shovel. If you had a itch on the end of your nose, there were more old English words (as a quiet young boy at

First day

Didcot, working on the railway, I learned plenty after leaving the boys' school).

The worst job of all had to be the shed fire dropper going under the engine, making sure his head was kept low, very low, to clear out the damper, knowing there was always the chance he would find a leg inside with the boots still tied to the foot, and a splash of blood around the motion with some cloth from a trouser – but normally the job consisted of just raking out the damper with the fireman's No 8 shovel into the pit, with no mask over the nose and mouth, and coming out blacker than you went in.

On the footplate the firebox was cleaned out, then the coal tub tipped coal over into the tender. Then the last job – drawing the short straw – was going up front to undo the smokebox door by pulling the bar that held it tight in its groove, and pulling open the door. A lot depended on which way the wind was blowing, especially if it was coming across the East Loop line with any force. The ash in the smokebox might be as high as the blast pipe. The ash man threw out the ash into the air, where it swirled around the coal stage area and came back to him as he threw it down into the pit, choking and spitting out the black smuts and gritty bits. But it had to be emptied and cleared away; he never wore a mask over his mouth, as they weren't heard of, and were not shown to be in the stores.

With the coal tipped and the tender filled, and enough steam on the gauge – 80lb was enough – the engine went down to the turntable and shunted back into the shed for the next day's washout with the boiler men. Then look out, because no one must get in their way or all hell would be let loose. We were a friendly bunch!

Above: The inside of a '94XX' smokebox. *Les Summers collection*

Right: It was odd being so close to the towering engines. This is the fitting shop with the 'A' frame of the crane in 1966.

After we spoke about how I had got on that morning, and who I had started with – Jim Tyler – Dad said he would see me at home.

'But I think it's best that you call me Cess while at work, son, instead of Dad, but when we are at home please call me Dad, especially in front of your Mum.

Back at work, after picking up my brass disc from the office and Mrs Bray, I took my time walking back to the fitting shop, with that odd sensation of being so close to the metal frames of the engines and feeling the half-moon rivets holding the metal plates together, and smelling the hot oil and fumes coming from the engines' chimneys. As I carried on down the walkway towards the fitting shop I saw Jim standing next to the forge, drinking from a cup and talking to Arthur Brinkley. They waved to me to come and join them. Arthur asked how the morning had been, and I smiled and replied, 'Yeah, it's OK – it's only the first day of many.'

Arthur said, 'If you have a problem you are welcome in my office, and we can talk it through together.'

Jim said, 'Can you wash the journals on the driving wheels, Pat, and run that castle-nut off the thread on the outer con-rod journals? Be careful not to cut your hands.'

So I washed the thread and replaced the nuts. I collected the galvanised bucket, went over to the centre of the driving wheels and did as I was told, scraping off the oil and dirt from the inner bearing journals where the axle boxes were going to be put into place. They were both ready now for the next stage.

Dave Davies came on hand as I was told to smear orange engineer's paste thinly over the inner bearing with my finger. They had already been split, so Jim and Dave lifted the split axle bearing onto the inner driving wheel journal, then the bottom half of the bearing was lifted up towards the other half, then huge bolts were dropped into the holes and the nuts slipped on with the help of Jim Hale's fingers. The nuts were screwed up tight with a spanner, then revolved by twisting the axle box bearing around the inner journal. Releasing the nuts while the men held the boxes, the bolts were knocked away and the split box fell apart onto the ground. They wiped their brows with cotton waste taken from their overall pockets. I felt a scratch on the palm of my hand, and looking into the waste I saw a piece of ragged metal. After that I always felt within the cotton waste first.

As the sweat ran down their faces, they looked at the orange paste for any signs of markings that showed on the white metal bearing. The other axle box was done the same way. Four halves had to be scraped out with a scraper to release the white metal bearing at the high spots. Two half axle bearings were stamped with the letter A, with the other set the letter B, so they didn't get mixed up, the other half bearings being stamped C and D.

It was getting close to the afternoon tea break at 3 o'clock, so I was told to go and have my break. As I entered the cabin I met the afternoon gang, Bill Clark who worked with Bob Looms, 'Belgian Bob'. We shook hands and they welcomed me into the fitting gang. I felt privileged and honoured.

Bill Clark called a meeting, as he was the shop steward, the union representative, within the mess room, and he asked me to leave. Some of the men argued about it, so I made a drink and walked out back to the fitting shop, met up with Jim and we had a chat. He asked me why I had come out of the mess room, so I told him. He said he had a son called Dennis, who started on the railway at Reading as an electrical apprentice, and I said that I knew him from school.

He asked me about the day, what I thought, and had I enjoyed it. It had been good and interesting with heavy work, but I was young and weak.

He said, 'You'll soon build up your muscles, and I'll give you a tip. Do not lift anything with cotton waste or a cloth in your hands, as the item might slip and you'll get hurt.'

'Thank you,' I said, 'I'll remember that.' (And I still do it today. I learned a lot from him all those years ago.)

Then he told me a story about when he was a boy living at home in Monmouthshire. He had two older brothers and a sister, and six younger brothers – ten in all. One day he went out and someone older grabbed him and punched him in the face. When he got back home the brothers asked him how he got the black eye. He wouldn't say, but the brothers kept on at him, so he gave up and said who it was. The brothers went out, found the person, grabbed him and dragged him against a brick building, rubbing his face against the rough brick wall so it was in a mess when they had finished.

I asked him how all the glass windows in the shed had holes in them.

'Ah yes. Your brother Dick was stupid, and he turned a piece of round iron on the lathe and made a cannon, with a truck and wheels. He took a detonator, opened it carefully, took out the gunpowder, poured it into the cannon, rammed it down and put a small ball bearing down the barrel. He anchored it on the bench and set a match to the fuse. Everyone who was in the fitting shop that day dived to the ground, with their hands over their heads. We all went bloody mad!'

'The next time he got two long bolts with a nut in the middle to hold the bolts together, then scraped the heads from match sticks and put them in between the nut and bolt, just touching. He then climbed the frame of the 32-ton crane and dropped it onto the concrete floor in the pit. It hit the ground and exploded, and shot through the glass window. It went off like a rocket.'

The rest of my day went quickly; I was still scraping the half axle boxes on the wooden blocked floor. Then I got myself washed up and away home. It was 5.25pm as I went to the Time Office and handed in my disc 388 to the timekeeper.

'Off you go. Good night,' said Mrs Bray. 'I hope you had a nice day.'

Pulling my bike from the bike rack, I started off up the cinder track at a slow pace, watching the coaches being pulled out of the sidings by a 'Hall'. It was all clear across the smelly oily sleepers, so I walked across them pushing my bike and down the concrete steps into the stairwell and undercroft, emerging into the station into the fresh air and riding home, shattered!

Mum and I talked about my wages. She told me she was having a quid and I had 10 bob, but she bought all my clothes and whatever I wanted. The deal was done.

3. Sky hooks and pistons

My big adventure had started. Next day I was up early because my Mum and Dad had already left for work, walking together down the road towards the station. Every morning when they got up, Mum would put the porridge on the gas cooker and start stirring it till it came to the boil, pour it out into two bowls and sprinkle a little salt over it with some milk. They would sit and enjoy it together with a cup of tea then, noticing the time, they would get their coats on and walk out of the house after shouting upstairs for me to get up and get ready for work. I would then have breakfast of either porridge or cornflakes, and leave about 7.10am. Mum and Dad would be down at the station at 5.30; they would give each other a kiss, say what they had to say to each other, and walk off their separate ways.

Mum worked in the Carriage Department, cleaning and dusting the coaches before they left for their new destinations. When the coaches came back into the sidings dirty she had to go with the other members and clean them. Sometimes there were 12 in a train, sometimes 11. Shunting was done by the station pilot, which would be either a 'Hall', 'Grange' or 'Mogul' (2-6-0), pulling the coaches out of the carriage sidings to make up passenger trains for the following day's work. Sometimes when a stopping passenger train came into the station from Oxford or Swindon, the pilot would shunt extra coaches on the rear to allow for extra passengers and their baggage.

Dad had a transfer from the coal stage away from the shift work to the shed. He would start by getting all the steam hoses connected to the overhead steam pipes with Trevor May, his partner, then they would go around the engines taking out the all the washout plugs, throwing the joints away and refitting the oval plate with a new joint, either lead or graphite. They even went under the engine and let the water drain down, with the yellowy scale running into the soakaways and down the drains. Five engines a day were booked, with three on a Saturday morning, and one Saturday every month they would clean out the shed stationary boiler that supplied the steam and hot water for the shed. This was the dirtiest, wettest job in the shed.

Their shift ended around 2.00pm. But here's the thing – if anybody was working within that area those men would turn the hose on you, even me, but Dad always shouted, 'Move, Pat!' to get me out of the way. They had to get the engines finished for the boilers to be refilled, then the firelighter – men like Mike Gleason, Frank Marshall and Lofty O'Connor – would come out of the shedmen's cabin and open his list to see what engine was next to light up. He would proceed to the stores to collect the square blocks of firewood nailed together with soggy wet cotton waste and paraffin wedged in the middle, place some coal in each corner of the firebox and leave the centre free. He then lit the paraffin-soaked cotton waste, placed it on his No 8 shovel and put it spot on in the middle of the firebox. Removing the shovel, he placed more coal around the four sides of the sticks and a few lumps over the cotton waste and shut the firebox door, leaving them just ajar to draw air into the firebox. By this time all the firelighter would see was the fumes coming out of the chimney. Ever hour or so would return to check the fire and top up the coals.

During the 1960s Didcot people working on the Western Region thought themselves superior to others, and one such staff member was Ernie Alder. His position was looking after the parcel section at the entrance of the station. One day an express train made an unscheduled stop at the station; it was a boat train bound for Fishguard. The station master summoned Ernie to stand at the very front of the station where the locomotive came to a standstill at the water column.

The driver and fireman of the 'Castle' came off the footplate and examined the whole of the engine with the station master. They found only one item, which Ernie placed on his shoulder and swaggered down the platform, showing everybody on the express, then walked down the platform stairs to the undercroft and straight across to his domain, the parcel stores.

When the Fishguard express left Paddington only a few stops were scheduled – Reading, Swindon, then fast to South Wales. After leaving Reading a person had laid down on the lines and committed suicide. All that the station staff had found was a complete leg.

Ernie took it into the parcel office and covered it up, then, without washing his hands, opened his sandwich box, made a cup of tea, and bit into his sandwich.

I made it to the middle platform and into the undercroft, leaving my bike against the wall, ran up the stairs two at a time and paid the lady for my paper, the *Daily Sketch*, then with great strides I leapt down the concrete stairs, grabbed my bike and carried it up the stairs on my shoulder, thinking of all the men who had walked up those stairs over the years – maybe tens of thousands. I stopped to look both ways and waited for the coaches to shunt back into the sidings – I caught them every morning at that same time. Across the other side locomen were waiting to cross as well and we all met in the middle. Someone said, 'Morning, Pat.' He told me he was a friend of my Dad, Skip Morgan. We shook hands and suddenly a whistle blew for the two of us to move on a bit sharpish. We parted and waved to the fireman on the footplate.

I cycled on down to the shed along the cinder path that had been spread to a depth of 25 feet deep all over the complex when the shed was built in 1934; the cinders came from all over the Great Western. There was no one about so I started to act a bit foolish and zigzagged. I nearly fell off the bike with a skid, and never attempted it again. I was a silly sod. 'Grow up,' I said to myself. Those ciders hurt if they stuck in the skin. I came to the bike shed, pushed the bike into a slot and walked into the shed. As I went into the Time Office to book on, heading towards the counter, Lenny Head said, 'Who are you? Pat Kelly? Ah yes, a new apprentice fitter.' He reached over and presented me with my brass tag, 388.

I ventured down the walkway running between the locos and came to the mess cabin, opened the door and looked inside, wishing good morning to the men having a cup of tea. I shut the door and went down to the fitting shop to put my grub bag into my locker. Every morning for the whole time I worked in the shed I would do this ritual.

*

Ted Gallagher lived in Newlands Avenue in Didcot; I went to school with his son Brian. We were in the same class, and they were a big family. Ted worked as a mate with Norman Brogden; he was a new fitter just out of his apprenticeship, and Brogden was not a very nice person. He played silly jokes on people, and I fell into the trap. I was easy prey to practical jokers, having just left school – yes, I was taken in, but he paid for it later. 'Gullible' is the word I was looking for.

I was asked by the men, and given permission from Arthur Brinkley, to leave the area and walk across to the station through the undercroft and across the road opposite the platforms with a list of goodies for the men. I was sent to Midwinter's shop for a quarter-pound of tea and a half-pound of sugar, as well as some skyhooks and a tin of vacuum. I remember that when I left the cabin I heard a shout and laughter from Brogden. The shop at the time was full of people purchasing their provisions. The owner, Mr Midwinter, kept telling me he hadn't got anything like skyhooks or vacuum in his shop. He also told me that I'd been had. So on my way back to work I found an old tin by the side of the track with years of dirt and grime ingrained in it, the top missing and crawling with ants and grubs. I couldn't find any skyhooks, so I found a piece of iron rod.

I had the mickey taken out of me something rotten, but I gave the tin to Brogden and told him that the vacuum had already been sucked out of the tin, and here were some rods to make his own sky hooks. All the men clapped and cheered that I had got my own back on him. He didn't like it, having the piss taken out on him, but if you give it, you've got to take it.

Ted Gallagher was a nice guy and very pleasant. He came from Northern Ireland. One day he came into the cabin, opened his lunch box and found a plastic spider in his sandwiches. Well, if Brogden had been any closer to the food table, he would have killed him. Ted went for him full bloodthirsty, shouting and screaming. Brogden couldn't get out of the cabin quick enough. Ted picked up his food tin and threw it at him with full force, then he threw his food away, because Brogden had opened his bag and fiddled about with his grub. I am sure that Ted went into the office to see Arthur Brinkley and quit his job, explaining what had happened. Brogden was fly and lazy, and he was trouble. My brother Dick told me to stay away from him, as they had been apprentices together in the shed and he disliked him.

However, what goes round comes round. Brogden drove a car with a full driving licence, but got stopped by Didcot police motorbike patrolman Mr Brown, and was given a ticket to produce his documents

A cast-iron piston cover with the steam safety valve, all very heavy and awkward to lift.

Accessibility for oiling and maintenance was good on Riddles's 'Austerity' Class 2-8-0s. This picture shows the bushed ends of con-rods with white metal bearings.

at the Police Station within seven days. He went with his insurance and MOT certificate, and I knew he was crapping himself because the licence was actually a provisional, which he'd coloured in with red ink to show he was a passed driver. He went to court and was fined and banned. In 1961 he lost his job on the railway, as British Railways was strict about police and court cases.

Ted Gallagher eventually quit because of Brogden, and got a job at Harwell at the Atomic Research Establishment (ARE) on the tools as a fitter's mate. We kept in touch over the years; he was a very nice man, and his family too.

*

That second day I entered the steam shed and walked into the Time Office to collect my brass tag 388. As I said my name and said the number, Mark Thomas said, 'Nice to meet you. May I call you Pat?' He told me that 388 had been my brother Dick's old number.

'Yes,' I said, 'I was told that by Mrs Bray when I came in yesterday to be a member of the fitting gang.'

I walked out past the enginemen's notice boards, kept behind glass to keep their dirty hands off them, and walked down the concrete pathway. I noticed that there was an engine sitting on No 2 road in the shed, 4-6-0 No 6868 *Penrhos Grange* (No 1 was mostly kept clear into the fitting shop; if there were locomotives on that road they were ready to proceed out of the shed with a full head of steam or to be worked on overnight.)

There were two teams, one on either side, racing to see who would finish first, but the funny thing was that they were racing between themselves, as Bob Looms just carried on as normal smoking his heavy

The cylinder and steam chest, with connecting rods on trestles.

The central driving wheel with white metal sprayed around the journal.

tobacco while Bob Warwick worked away beside him. Both sides had stripped out the connecting rods, or con-rods, and moved them away from the wheels, slightly back towards the middle of the concrete floor; they had also removed the linkages for the valves on both sides, and had taken off the piston covers after removing the ring of nuts. The crosshead was ready to be pushed towards the outer piston housing, so someone had to help push it to its final position onto the gland before letting the piston head drop. I am sure Jimmy Tyler helped Bob in the correct way to complete this side of the job as the other two never helped anyone.

The other two raced on, having dropped the piston head, cleaned the carbon from the piston ring channels, and fitted new rings into position. But Bob Warwick trundled on – no rush, and not a care in the world. Still got two more days, he thought, until Arthur Brinkley approached him and said 'Ready tonight, Bob?', walking away with a grin on his face. Bob's knees nearly collapsed – they wanted this engine out, so he started to get worried, passing the stress onto his mate. The piston was pushed totally out of the cylinder, and rested on a block of wood that came from the fitting shop. The piston gland and cover were removed to give more space for the shaft to enter the cylinder and the piston assembly to be lifted out onto the ground. Now getting the old rings out of the grooves became hard work, so they would jam in a small chisel bar to lift the first ring out slightly and place a crow's-foot bar under the ring, breaking it – they were cast iron. Hitting the second and third rings with a hammer and chisel did the same, then they scraped out the hard dirty carbon from the channels, taking it in turns.

Jimmy Tyler had to take the measurements of the inside of the cylinder with a extended micrometer, then he went to the stores. Jim could only spare some of his time as he had a fitter's boy in the fitting shop at the time – that was me! Anyway, a couple of hours later they got the new rings in and with bars started to lift the piston upwards so that the edge fitted back into the cylinder. They pushed and heaved it – they were both knackered – but they wanted this engine out of the shed. The piston shaft entered the gland and Jim pulled it through

A cutaway of the cylinder and valve chest of a Southern Railway 'Merchant Navy' Class, on display at the National Railway Museum, York. *Author's collection*

and held it with a crowbar while Bob fiddled with the piston rings with the two thin bars that Jim had given him; they slid between the cylinder and piston rings while the other Bob hit the piston head with a lead hammer. Suddenly Jim felt the piston judder and slide into the cylinder. Then they conquered the next rings while Jim placed the crowbar into another position, jamming it into the spokes of the leading wheel as well as putting the crosshead key into its slot while they pushed the rings together.

Hearing the shout, 'That's enough mate' in Belgian, with the crosshead shaft in position Jim drove the steel wedge into its position with a short 2½lb hammer and a new cotter pin through the wedge.

'Right,' he said, 'now you can get on and don't bother me again as I have my own work to do.'

Bob said, 'Thanks mate.'

The other Bob was smoking, blew out a cloud of smoke and said, 'Cheers, Jim.'

The other side were just finishing up, oiling the bearings on the con-rod by pulling out the corks. Dave Davies and Jim Hale were inseparable and wouldn't help out others in the shed. I found this out from my second week, and I always called them the twins. There's more about them as we go along, as they only did services with the mileage sheets and helped Jim and me, but during my time in the shed I never saw them work at the front of the shed.

Dave Davies taught me a lot about engineering and making things, and I couldn't fault him. However, he was very bitter and twisted and the fitting crew had a nickname for him – 'The Toad' – as from behind he looked as though he had no neck and was bunched up. It's funny that, although there was a lot of contentment among the fitting staff, there were niggly moments, and they always seemed to involve me.

In came the twins, happy with big smiles on their faces and piss-taking – 'We done our side' – all swanky like, cats' claws out. I remember it started with them all the time.

Dave Davies is standing at the back. He died at the age of 90. In front are, left to right, Bob Looms, Ted Powell and Frank Dowding.

Bob was still plodding on as I walked past the organised chaos going to the stores to collect some more paraffin and cotton waste with a chitty signed by Jimmy. I brought the sack full of cotton waste, and Ted Powell said that we'd got a big job on. I'd had my tea break, and now I was going for the midday break.

I wanted to see what the outside of the shed looked like, so I walked up to the Time Office, passed over the brass check, crossed the front of the shed and wandered down outside the shed on No 5 road, then crossed over to No 6 and walked between the rusty engines – this was the sad side of the shed. Coming back to my locker and opening the tin door, I lifted out my RAF shoulder bag with teapot, sugar and a tin of tea leaves, and wandered back to the mess cabin. I helped myself to hot water from the iron kettle and went out of the cabin and across the railway lines outside into the fresh air. As it was a nice day I sat on a bench leaning against the outer wall of the shed and watched the trains go by, without a care in the world.

Suddenly a goods train come down on the loop from the East Junction and stopped at the signals opposite the shed. I couldn't believe my eyes when men dressed in Army uniform got down from the footplate into the '6 foot' gap between the lines. Further down the freight, at the guard's van, the Army unit started to check the axle boxes on either side and the wheels, then suddenly the engine's whistle blew. Now, you will always remember a Great Western whistle from miles away (I might be biased but I only thought of the Great Western – I never believed in any other railway companies – they didn't exist!).

The men pulled themselves up into the guard's van while there Sergeant climbed up onto the footplate and the engine pulled away. Each box van had written across the side 'EXPLOSIVES'. I never saw another train like that ever again. I had to shut my mouth as it was open in a amazement, catching flies!

The hour went quickly, and I got my brass disc back, put away the food bag in the locker and went back to what I had been doing earlier, on the 'Grange'. The bearing had been fitted on the axle on the rigid 6-foot driving wheel and Jim threw the dregs out of his cup into the forge fire. We waited for the shed tankie to come through to the fitting shop and connect up to the engine; it was then pulled through to the shop and out into the shed, while we had to get the wheel sets onto the rails a bit quick. The block and tackle, with the wheels held by the cross bar, was lifted up just off the floor and swung around onto the rails, then the wheels were rolled back to the shop doors, blocked with wooden scotches and held there till Jimmy was ready.

The shout went out for the tankie to come back into the shop, while Jimmy eyed the centre of the heavy overhead crane with the chains lowered down. The 'Hall' came back, and up went Jim's arm: 'OK, stop there!' The tankie's coupling was disconnected and it proceeded back out of the shop and we started to get to work. Jim asked me to climb up on the footplate and pull up the half-moon fallplate between the engine and tender while he took the strain on the overhead crane. Then he said to come down and stand back. The engine started to rise off the rail and rolled backwards until it came into line with the overhead crane. Jim stopped the motor and put the brake on. One of the front bogie's 3-foot wheels was still on the rail, while the other just came off and was hanging in the air. Jimmy had to operate the crane again as we needed the clearances to get the axle under the engine frame. Jim said, 'Go the other side, Pat, and I will stay here, then we can roll the 6-foot wheel and axle into place.'

He went to the crane and pressed the green button that started the motor. He put the low-ratio gear into place by manually

Left to right, Jimmy Holmar, Reg Warr and my mentor, Jim Tyler.

moving the cogs in the gear box, then started lowering the engine. Jimmy Holmar came into the fitting shop at just the right moment and gave me a hand while Jimmy kept an eye on the bearing boxes on his side as they fitted into the engine's frames. Jimmy Holmar stayed at the other side and I went around to my mentor's side. While he operated the crane I kept an eye on the lowering engine frame sliding down the bearing guides and the grease in the slides oozing out as it came to a rest on the axle. The chains were removed from the footplate and they clattered together; they were then raised back up to the top of the 'A' frame in the housing. Jimmy stopped the motor and put the brake on.

He thanked Jim Holmar and we both went underneath the engine with Jim's tools laid between the wheels ready to start work again, showing me what we had achieved. I was so impressed with it, and he told me to go and have a cup of tea, as it was 3 o'clock, and I was as dry as a chip; I needed a drink of some sort, even just 'Adam's ale'!

I stayed up near the engine we were working on, then he said, 'Are you ready? Shall we crack on, boy?' We both went down underneath again and he showed me what had to be done. I was plastered in black grease and muck from being within the frames and working side by side with my mentor Jimmy Tyler. I felt a growing sense of trust and esteem towards this man I had known for such a short time, with just a willingness to help. What was more, there was not a word of blame or criticism from his mouth.

The rest of the afternoon shot by and

Jimmy Tyler, my mentor and friend. I went to his funeral when he died at the age of 92.

soon the time came for me to get washed up and get home. As I walked by *Penrhos Grange* the two Bobs were still at it trying their hardest to get the engine finished for the night; they had till 7.00pm, when their time came to sign off shift. As I walked up to the Time Office and handed over my disc, they said, 'You're running late, Pat.'

'Yes, but I've had a cracking day working. Good night.'

When I got home Mum had made bubble and squeak for tea with a fried egg placed on top. I was starving.

4. Routine

Next morning it was same routine. With my newspaper stuck into my RAF bag, I walked across the sleepers and noticed the time on the clock outside Mr East's office window – 15 minutes before 7.30am – same routine. Having collected my disc, I walked down the shed to the cabin and, looking across to No 2 road, there was the engine full of steam, ready to go out, all fired up. Now our Bob and his mate had put all the parts back on, as they thought, correctly. Bob had oiled up all the bushes and replaced the little corks in the con-rods, the shed firelighter Frank Marshalll had got the locomotive fired up overnight and had kept going back to top up with Welsh marine coal every hour. With a full head of steam the shed driver reversed the locomotive out, but it went out with a limp (like a person walking on a curb with one foot on the road). A shout went out to stop the engine, and as he was stood nearby Jim fixed it, and then it went out the correctly.

The service team were never asked to do repairs such as valves and pistons, as they took too long. Jim Tyler was the lifting shop fitter, and had all his correct tools to do his job within the lifting shop, but I never heard him take the piss out of any of the fitting staff. However, Bob Looms's temper simmered beneath the surface and erupted every now and then like a volcano if someone said the wrong word to him. When he was raging he only spoke in Belgian. I called him 'Belgian Bob' because in the Second World War he had been a Spitfire pilot or technician – well, that's what he told me. He always wore the RAF badge on his sports jacket pocket. He was quiet, and always drank his tea strong and sweet. He lived in the Railway Hostel near the Railway Staff Club and kept himself to himself, and he was always dressed smartly. I never saw him shopping in the Broadway.

On Thursday morning I was up at a crack of dawn, had breakfast and was out early. It was a great day to ride down to the shed; I never felt miserable about going to work as I was a happy chappie, knowing I would have six years doing what I enjoyed the most.

Same routine again: paper, then ride down the cinder path, exchanging greetings with everyone, bike shed, note the time at the Time Office, walk down the shed to the cabin, pop my head around the door to wish good morning to whoever was on shift having their breakfast, walk down to the fitting shop, get my bag into the locker, walk to the forge and speak to my mentor. What a life – brilliant!

I was now beginning to see why Jimmy commanded the greatest respect and admiration, working alone in the lifting shop

The brake block assembly of a 'Hall'. The pipe behind is from the sand box to the rail.

doing the thing he knew well. We both got under the engine as he showed me the next job, and how it worked. Bearing blocks were in place with keeper plates and nuts screwed onto the studs in the frame on both sides, and the springs in place on both sides, then we had to fit the brake linkage rods back into position. When that was completed both the brake blocks on both sides had to be refitted; they were not made of a light material but cast iron, and blinking heavy! As each block was placed on the wheel and pushed up into its slot, I knocked the iron pin into the hole while my mate held it; the pin was held by an oval plate with a set screw or bolt into the brake frame. Jim said it was easier to fit them with the con-rods off.

The lifting shop had its own tools, which were standard in all depots. The general arrangement involved a motor, with a lever to move a belt; the lever would slide a pulley into place to drive another belt, which would then allow you to operate lathes, drilling machines and grinding machines. We also had a hoist crane with the maximum lift of 50 tons, built by Royce of Manchester and installed in 1932 for lifting locomotives up at the leading end or the footplate end; this was only done when the tender was removed.

Jim called me to where he was operating the crane controls, and said that I was to be shown how to operate the controls of the lifting apparatus, but first I had to place one of the heavy blocks of wood near the gearbox and climb up and look over into where the cogs were. I asked him why the gear selector was out of the box with the cover off.

'It's broken,' he replied. 'That's why we use our hands.'

The motor was slowing down with the strain from the gearing, so he applied the brake, and shut down the power. In went his hand and pushed the main drive shaft gearing cog across into the next huge drive gear cog. Turning on the power and pressing the green lift button, he lifted the brake and the engine started to rise into the air until the driving wheels could be manoeuvred clear of the frames. Jim shut down the brake and the electric motor, then replaced the cover on the gear box. I wrote down everything in the little book that I carried with me.

Now the heavy work. We had to lift the

The electrically driven belt system can be seen here, operating a lathe, grinding wheel and mounted drilling machine, and further along the forge. Note the 6-foot driving wheel set.

The red handle was the up or down crane control.

3-foot-square heavy oak blocks under the engine to block it for safety reasons. We then climbed into the pit and went underneath to do our work. In later years I was instructed in the use of the overhead crane when I was more experienced and trustworthy.

On Friday morning I got ready for work as usual, breakfasted on either porridge or cornflakes, then left at about 7.00am, riding my bike down to the market square, where I saw Les Gibbss on his stall. He laid out his fruit and vegetables tidily for the buyers; I gave him a shout and he threw an eating apple towards me. I caught it and shouted, 'Cheers, Les!'

Riding through the market stalls and down towards Edinburgh Drive eating the apple, I then stopped off to go into Don Avery's paper shop and get a *Daily Sketch*. I read the rubbish in the tabloid, and sometimes looked at the horses on the racing page in my dinner hour, then stuffed it into my RAF bag.

Same routine, paper, ride down the cinder path, speaking to everyone, bike shed, notice the time at the Time Office, walk down the shed to the cabin, pop my head around the door, wish good morning to whoever was on shift having their breakfast. One day there were only two men, Ted Powell and Frank Dowding. This was strange, but they said there had been a breakdown last night on the main line, so it was best if I went with them today.

'OK,' I said, 'I will sort out my locker and come back into the cabin.'

The engine was still in its same place, so I got ready to head up to the forge and look for Jim, but no one was about, only the call boy. The call boy was part of every engine shed and was chosen from the junior cleaners. He would be on duty during the night hours and when a driver and firemen were required to prepare an engine and commence duty at unearthly hours of the morning, he would go to their homes riding a bicycle to wake them for their day's work. The bicycles were owned by the railway. and stamped 'Great Western Railway'; they were stored in the storeroom with the paraffin and oils.

Sometimes this job was easy, but some men were very heavy sleepers and it was quite a job to wake them without also waking the neighbourhood and becoming very unpopular. Some men would cooperate and try to make the boys' job easier, like the one who would tie a piece of cord to his big toe and leave the other end hanging down from the window. It was a condition of employment for footplatemen that they lived within 2 miles of the shed.

The weather was cold, and the breakdown men had to stay out half the night, so I got the forge alight with some smouldering coals. I turned on the blower and laid some sticks, which caught fire, then I laid fresh coal on the sticks and it started to burn. The fire started to take hold, the blower doing its job correctly, and getting hold of a No 8 fireman's shovel I gingerly scooped up the burnt coals around the edge of the forge and laid them over the fire, then shut down the blower and left it burning just to keep the fitting shop warm.

Ted Powell came into the fitters shop and spoke to me about helping out with his inspection. At the time I did not mind working with him and Frank Dowding – they were a right pair of characters, but very two-faced. We had to go to the front of the shed, because all the fitting shop staff were out, with just 2½ left – me being the half. Frank was knocking hell out of the pipes that fed the sand down onto the rail, using a hammer from Ted's sack. I went to the sand house with the spouted bucket and filled it with sand up to the brim, making sure the sand was cold and dry by feeling it with my hand. Carrying it across to the engine, I lifted the spouted bucket onto the front frame, then with some effort climbed up on to the front of the engine's buffer beam, walked to the side of the boiler and took off the iron covers. I then gently poured the sand into each port hole, filling the box up to its level. Frank was still smacking the pipe until the sand flowed gently down it.

Ted was on the footplate of No 2836 and he asked me to get up so he could show me what he was doing. He was about to replace the gauge glass tube, and explained to me that you should always close the two shut-

The front of the shed with a line-up on preserved GWR locomotives in 1978, occupying, from left to right, Nos 1, 2 and 3 roads. On the extreme left is the sand house. *Ray Ruffell, Slip Coach Publishing Services collection*

off levers, then open the gauge protection covers and remove them so you could get to the glass tube. He undid the nuts holding the tube and got out of his pocket some cotton waste with which he held the tube while he gently broke the glass with his spanner, which splintered across the footplate. He sent me to the stores to get another glass with 'O rings'. This time there was no queue, and the storeman's window was slightly ajar. I opened the sliding window and ask for the item, handing over the chitty in return. When I returned, Ted had removed the top and bottom plugs of the gauge unit and cleared away the old equipment. He slid the new glass tube into the top hole and pushed it into both rubber rings; as it slid into place he tightened the nuts and replaced the top and bottom unit nuts. He opened the bottom lever, then the top, allowing the water from the boiler to enter the glass tube. He explained that this showed the boiler water level, and to always look at the pressure gauge; at that time it was 225lb per square inch. As we worked, I took out my note book, writing out that day's work load.

Then came a shout from Harry Buckel to get the engine off shed, as the prep time was 45 minutes, including the work being done by the fitters. The driver held out his hand to us, shouting 'Thanks!' Then he blew the Great Western whistle and started to move towards the small wooden box marked with yellow and black chevrons on its face; this was the shed exit phone. The fireman, or driver, would telephone the signalman, informing him of their destination, and the signalman would pull the lever for the ground signal to clear, giving permission to proceed. At night, the signal showed a green or red light, from a paraffin lamp.

I returned to the shed with the two men, who asked how I was getting on in the fitting shop with Jimmy Tyler. All I said was that I had been there nearly a week and I was very interested in steam engines and he was good man, strong and knowledgeable. I knew in my own mind that I did not want to give any ammunition to start silly talk, as my brother Dick had told me keep my head down and mouth shut.

Break time came, so out came the tea leaves, sugar, teapot and grub bag, as I was starving, and it was nectar of the gods! Some silly chat came out of Frank's mouth but he mumbled on and I took no notice. Ted had his head stuck in the paper. Frank liked his Erinmore flake tobacco, and opened his round tin to draw out a small black root.

'Here, chew this,' he said.

'I will in a minute after I've eaten my sarnies.'

I stuffed the root into my mouth and started to chew it – it tasted partially sweet. Meanwhile he stuffed his pipe with the tobacco and set light to it, the sweet smell wafting around the cabin. He had to open the window to allow the smoke to escape. He reminded me of the Waltons' grandfather.

Ted looked at his *Daily Mail*, especially interested in the racing page at the back, picking out the winners, sitting in dead silence and marking the page with his pencil. I finished my grub, went out of the cabin and walked down to the fitting shop to see if the forge was still burning. I went outside through the rear fitting shop's door and saw a tender standing there on its own, going slightly rusty. As I walked towards the turntable I was amazed to see how much space and wasted ground there was around the shed area, across to the carriage sidings and buffer stops, and over to the carriage and wagon department.

I was also interested in the main marshalling yard, hearing the whistles of the small 0-6-0 tank engines running up and down with their wagons and trucks banging buffers, and seeing the wagons running along the tracks like ghosts, then suddenly a crash as they ran into each other with great force – the noise was terrible. As I went back to the fitting shop I heard the sound of men starting to wander in to work. Jimmy Holmar came into the shop, waved and walked into the locker room, then his mate Matt Oglesby followed, together with my mentor Jim Tyler. He walked up to the forge and saw it burning.

'Did you set the fire, boyo?'

'Yep.'

'Thanks!' It took the chill off the shop.

Arthur Brinkley came into the shop to tell all the men what time to book off on the breakdown, then said, 'Next breakdown in the daytime, Pat, do you think you could come out with us?'

'Thank you,' I said.

Jimmy said, 'Ready boy? Shall we get started?'

Arthur asked me what I had been doing.

'Ted wanted me to work with him till you came back in.'

'How did you get on?'

'OK, ta. He taught me about the front of the shed.'

As we climbed down the concrete steps to go under the engine my mentor instructed me about the next job. He told me to get oil from the stores for the axle boxes, remove the cork plugs and fill them up to the levels. He went off to do another job. Then he said, 'OK, let's go outside – we're finished under here, boyo.'

We went towards the inside con-rods between the frames. We put wooden blocks under them, drove the pins into the holes, and tightened up the castle nuts. Jim allowed me to fit the copper split pin into each slot and hole, then showed me the correct way to split the pin and bring one half up to the pin head. Three wheels were done the same way. We then went back to fit the outer con-rod. He picked it up and placed it on the crosshead and I held it there with what strength I had in my body. He put the bush

Con-rods and outside motion, the second picture showing the crosshead and piston rod.

end into the crosshead and I guided the other end onto the journal and screwed the big flat nut onto the threaded screw to stop the con-rod sliding off.

As we both got into the job, we tightened down the nut with a huge flat spanner. This would then be fitted with a large nut with two flat sides using an oval spanner, and a sledge hammer to bang down onto the spanner. The oval nut would drive round until the fixing hole came into view, into which a long threaded screw bolt could be tightened up, then a split pin would be knocked into the hole in the bolt and the legs on the split pin opened. This con-rod was then fixed to the middle driving wheel, called the rigid wheel.

Now we had to connect up the crosshead assembly. Jim pulled back the crosshead with a crowbar stuck into the spokes of the leading wheel, until the piston in the cylinder was at its lowest stroke position. We then lifted the con-rod with a bar until the radius and crosshead were lined up. As I held the con-rod, Jim reached inside near the spokes of the wheel and slid the inner journal into the hole, lining up the position of the journal pin, and placing an iron bush that he had made purposely to do this operation.

Jim slid the iron bush over the outer journal with the thread slightly showing, then placed a washer and threaded castle nut onto the thread and screwed the nut round till the journal came through the hole towards him, as it was a tapered cone. He reached in behind the crosshead and hit the end of the flat pin with his hammer, slightly hitting the wheel spokes and, on the rebound, the head of the crosshead pin with a crash. He removed the castle nut to allow the iron cup off the journal, then the steel washer and castle nut were replaced on the thread and tightened up with sufficient force to line up the square on the nut and a small hole.

I was again allowed to re-pin the nut the correct way by splitting the cotter pin with the hammer, knocking the head onto the hard metal surface on the con-rod, holding the legs of the cotter pin together, as the tension was tight, and slipping the legs of the cotter pin into the hole on the castle nut. Tap the head of the cotter pin till it moves through the pin, spread one of the legs upwards and hit it hard with the flat of the hammer so it stays in position between the castle nut and the threads of the journal, then the other leg, with a chisel resting on the cotter's leg. With a hammer in the right hand, swipe it onto the face of the chisel and the pin rests in the nut beneath.

Three hours later we were about to start the other side, but first Jim went to see the shed foreman to call for an engine to pull our engine out forwards so the journals were lower to the ground, and easier to work on. While we waited for an engine to come into the shop we had a brew, seeing I was as dry as a chip. Jim had his black tea, while mine was white – nectar of the gods!

Jim heard a shout coming from the front engine. A chap looked around the buffers and in a squeaky voice asked how he was. Jim's reply was, 'What do you bloody want? Piss off!'

'Hello, Jim!' He swaggered up to the forge where we were both standing. 'Are you busy?'

'Yes.'

'Have you a new boy, then?'

I said, 'Hello, my name's Pat.'

He turned around and spoke to his old mate about what was going on in the world.

Jim said, 'Don't take this wrong way, but we have a lot to do.'

Just then I saw a tankie trundling into the fitting shop, coming slowly to the front of our engine. The fireman got down in the pit and coupled up No 6953. Jim ask the driver to pull out slowly while we kept an eye on the movement of the wheels, till the inside con-rods were low enough to start work on. Once there, we blocked the wheels with scotch blocks. The fireman got underneath and spread his long legs across the open pit, with his heavy boots stuck into the sides of the track chairs, and undid the coupling, letting it crash back to the frame. He shouted out to the driver, 'Move away!' and the tankie slowly pulled out of the fitting shop. The fireman pulled himself up off the buffers of our engine, walked back to the tankie, slipped his foot on the engine's bottom step and swung around sideways, climbing the steps and back onto the footplate. The tankie swept out into the shed and the driver opened the regulator very slightly, allowing it to proceed into the sunshine and back to its duties. The air was clear for now, but before the night was over it would be full with sulphurous smoking engines ready for the next day, which was

Routine

Saturday.

Now we had to complete the same method on the other side as the engine was coming close to being finished. The con-rods were replaced on the journals of the three wheels, screwed down tight and split-pinned. Jim with great effort lifted the con-rod up into the crosshead while I held it and struggled to fit it over the rigid wheel's journal. We had an audience of men standing around looking, while we tried to finish for the night, and the silly banter started.

Jim drove the crowbar into the spokes of the leading wheel and pushed back the crosshead. I had a crowbar jammed onto a wooden block to lift the end of the con-rod, then the bush suddenly slipped onto the journal and Jim Hale, one of the twins, screwed the oval nut onto the bolt. Jim came back with his hammer and ring spanner and did the business, hammering the oval nut tight while I finished it off with the long bolt with the threaded screw, winding it down tight through the oval nut, and fitted the split pin, splitting the legs. Some of the onlookers clapped and I did a bow.

Jim said, 'Clear off you lot of piss-takers! Right, Pat, home for you. Get washed up. See you in the morning.'

I went to my locker and pulled out my bar of red Lifebuoy soap and towel. I washed my hands and dried them, finding after a week's work that the softness was leaving me and the dirt and oil was starting to become ingrained in my palms of my hands. We didn't have special soaps – it wasn't heard of. Dick said to go across to the carriage and wagon department and get some horsehair, which was like wire wool, rub the soap into the hair and scrub your hands under boiling water. I had another idea when I got home later that night. I filled the sink with boiling water, placing the soap in the water, making it soapy, then scrubbed my hands till they were raw, then ran cold water on them and back into the hot-water scrub. It was tedious, but then I rubbed cream into my palms and fingers, and they became lily-white with black streaks in the pores, two-tone like a zebra.

Talking of hygiene, in those days long ago we never had soft toilet paper to just pull off the roll with the fingertips and do the business like wiping our botty or bum. That's why I brought a newspaper daily, to use it in the shed's toilet area. I did not like sitting on the wooden seats that loads of enginemen used; some shed staff and enginemen were a little dirty, and might have a dose of crabs or other forms of infection. I would tear the paper into lengths and spread it across the seat to sit down in comfort, with the smells in the brown water rising in the cubicle area – someone might have missed the hole and messed all over the seat. At home we would cut the paper into squares tied up on a piece of string hanging off the flush pipe or nailed to the window frame. With that magical rip of paper, the operation of bending down and wiping your soft botty left the black print skidded across the soft skin of your arse!

I heard a shout from downstairs: 'Tea time!' Boiled pigs' trotters and bread and butter, with a cup of tea.

On Saturday morning as I got up early at the crack of dawn. It was the same routine as all week, but going into the entrance to the shed it was quiet. Looking around the complex I saw the Ordnance Depot tankies in line over on No 5 road, with just a few engines at the front of the shed. There was no shouting, just the occasional sound of a few men doing their jobs. Dick Bidmead was shovelling ash out of the eerie pits, always with his old wheelbarrow.

I went to the Time Office and said good morning to Ernie Jones, the shed clerk. He gave me my brass disc.

'How you getting on, Pat? Do you like it?'

'Yes, it's good,'

'What do you like about it?'

'Everything really – being close to the engines.'

I went into the cabin to see who was in, having a cup of tea. All of the fitting staff were there except Norman Brogden, who was on nights and had finished that morning.

Dick Bidmead, the shed cleaner, with his wheelbarrow.

I had never seen so many men together in one pack. I shouted a good morning and some raised their hands. As I went into the fitting shop there was my mate drinking black tea in his tea-stained cup.

'Hello, boyo – ready to finish it? Get over the other side of the footplate and we will lift it up together.'

I could see that the footplate floor boards were up and stacked in the corner near the boiler. We greased the three pin holes and cleared away the old coal and rubbish that lay everywhere. The men were starting to come into the shop now. Jim asked for help to move the tender into position. This is where the fun would start. I was told to climb on the tender, and that I was the brake man.

All the fitting staff that had some muscles would be at the rear pushing, while the rest had crow bars and lever bars. I unwound and released the hand brake.

'Right, let's go!' shouted Jim, as all the men heaved together. The tender started to move, then as it gathered speed a shout went out to screw down the hand brake slightly. I felt the brake blocks grip the wheels gently. Then Jim shouted to put the brake on. The brake linkages had to be lined up, and string was put onto them to lift them slightly to 'take off the brake'. As the men pushed the tender again the linkages went into the webbing under the floor boards.

Jim and Dave climbed onto the footplate with crowbars to align the iron linkages, screwing with their crowbars and pulling the linkages towards them in line with the pin and hole. Everyone was told to heave on the lever bars under the wheels of the tender a little bit. More movement was all that was needed to drop the pins into the linkages' elongated holes; the middle went in, then the two outside. I screwed the handbrake down tight. Jim shouted out a thank you to all the men who had helped.

We had to add the huge cotter pins and flat washers to the pins that were dropped into place under the footplate. The only way was to put a wooden board across the pit right between the tender and the engine. I climbed up into the webbing of the frame, reaching under the footplate to place a large washer over each pin, driving the cotter pins through the round pin holes. All three were done at the same time, one after the other, with the footplate still opened to allow light from the shop's top windows. I kept my head down at an angle to stop anything getting into my eyes. Eventually I was pulled down back into the pit with Jim and he pushed the wooden board away.

Jim then got on with the rubber water pipe and vacuum pipe. These were not easy to fit as they had wire braiding twisted around them to take the tension between the engine and tender and to stop the hose being rubbed, causing wear and tear. The tender's water valve had been opened to drain the tank, so I turned the big red wheel clockwise and shut the valve. This would be filled up when No 6953 was pulled outside under the water column. Now we had to get a tankie in to pull the engine from the shop. While we

Routine

The front of a tender, showing the three connecting rods that held the tender to the locomotive with pins under the footplate.

waited, Jim checked everything that he had done, but we had forgotten one thing. We climbed upon the footplate and pushed the wooden floor boards back into place with our boots. The engine was now ready, and what a week I'd had! I really enjoyed myself, but I had another year to go before signing my apprenticeship papers to become a fully fledged apprentice.

But for now I had to wash the fitters' tools that had been used, using paraffin and drying them with cotton waste, as this was a fitter's boy's job, looking after his mentor every week. At 12 noon we finished for the weekend, the engine was pulled out and the fitting shop left empty. I shouted out to Jim, 'Thanks, see you Monday morning!' and walked quite quickly to the Time Office. No one was about so I put my disc on the counter and left the shed. As I walked by the clock it said 5 past 12. I got my bike and was away up the cinder path at my normal speed, down the concrete steps with the bike on my shoulder, scooted through the station's undercroft, out into the fresh air and rode home.

I had a hot bath, washed my hair, and had a good scrub with caustic soda in the water. I had to get the dirt out somehow. A change of clothes, a bacon sarnie and a cup of tea, then I said goodbye to Mum and Dad. Just as I was going out of the door the tallyman from Reading came in to see Mum. I asked him if he sold suits, and he said he did.

'Come back indoors and we'll take your measurements. First, what would you like?'

I had seen one in a cowboy film on telly (TVs were almost unheard of then, but we had a small black and white one). 'No way!' he said, showing me the patterns and cut. He could order me one from Reeds of Reading, an Italian-cut three-piece suit for 3 bob a week, 15 quid total.

5. Saturdays and safety valves

I walked down from home where we lived in Sinodun Road, but never got as far as the town as I saw Michael Howard on his knees building a trailer out of shelving angle iron. Mick lived in the same road as me. I said, 'That won't work – it's too flimsy. You get a load on that and it'll buckle.'

'Sod off, Pat Kelly!'

Now the banter started. It went on quite a while; he had his say and I threw a spanner in the works and laughed. He asked me what I was doing

'Off down town, mate.'

'Come in and have a cup of tea and meet Mum.'

So I did, and also met his sister Jenny. She was nice, and we had a laugh. Mick found a record player, placed a vinyl record on the turntable and we started to enjoy ourselves. Mrs Howard went into the kitchen to make some sarnies and tea while Mick moved the furniture and pulled up the carpet to the walls and Jenny and me started jive dancing. She was good. Mick joined in with his sister, twirling her around, then Mrs Howard came to the door and started clapping to the music and laughing. Mick left Jenny to me as we started to jive, and he asked his Mum to jive, so all four of us danced the afternoon away. I never made it to town. Mick and I became mates – we were joined at the hip!

Mick went to Wallingford Grammar School – very high class – but something went wrong within the family, and one day at St Birinus School Mr Moulsford, the headmaster, welcomed Michael Howard to our school. He hoped he would enjoy his stay with us. At first I didn't know him at school as he was 18 months older than me. When he left school he started work in the Parcels Department on British Railways, the main employer in the district.

That afternoon I stayed longer than expected. After the sarnies and tea with cake, Mick said we should go for a walk. I never went home to tell Mum where I was, but she knew I was out enjoying myself. After tea we both went out towards the town, chatting about life. He walked into the White Hart pub on the Broadway.

'Wait a minute – I ain't old enough yet.'

'You would never guess. They can only throw us both out. Come on, I'll pay. You can pay next time.'

It was a bob for a pint, so 2 bob then. Brown ale at 15 years old drinking in a pub – my life had started! We had a couple in there, then walked down Station Road to the British Railways Club near the station. As we walked into the bar area I saw some faces turn and look. Mick approached and ordered two pints of brown ale. We sat down in the corner and chatted. We saw some of the fitting staff come in, but they never said anything, just nodded and grinned. Mick was 16½ years old.

'I get paid next week, Mick,' I said. 'It will be my turn.'

That's OK,' he said. 'It's nice to go out with someone from the same road and be a friend.'

We spent Sunday together walking round Didcot, really eyeing up the crumpet. At the time he was going out with Diane. She lived in the prefabs in Mereland Road down near the stream, and he went calling for her to go

Mick Howard with his Mum.

Saturdays and safety valves

to the pictures on the Sunday night, asking me to go along as well

'No, I ain't doing it – you want to be on your own.' I didn't want to play gooseberry.

'Come on,' he said, so he called for her and the three of us walked to the 'flea pit'. He paid half a dollar each, two and a kick, seven and a kick in the top row middle. I sat beside Mick in the middle, with Diane the other side, with her coat over her legs.

'Do you want me to look after your coat?' I asked.

Mick looked round and said, 'Watch the film.'

After a while the intermission came, and down came the girls with ice cream trays.

'Go and get the ice creams, Pat. Here's ten bob. We'll have tubs. You have what you want.'

I came back to see that Diane had gone. I sat down, and Mick turned to me and said, 'Do you know nothing – that coat was there for a reason, as I had my hand up her skirt playing with her private parts.'

I started laughing. 'Sorry I was green.' It was all new to me. Then Diane came back and sat down again. The lights went out and the coat went back into position. I giggled to myself. 'You rampant bugger!'

We walked her home. She ditched Mick after that, but I knew different, and we laughed all the way home. Now we started the battle as to who would get the birds first. We got on like a house on fire, him and me. If the truth was known, he taught me a lot about life, and I bloody worshipped him and his family. (He died on 18 March 2007, never reaching his retirement as he was only 64 years old.) There will be more about Mick as we go – he was full of life and I thought the world of him.

Monday morning came quickly, and I checked in for work with the same routine, picked up my 388 disc and signed on with the Time Office clerk, Mrs Bray. We exchanged our normal pleasantries, and I walked down to the cabin, opened the door, stuck my head in and said good morning to the men

'Had a lot to drink Saturday night, Pat?' 'Belgian Bob' had me to rights. 'Never thought you drank, as a underage person!'

I never replied, but walked out and down to the fitting shop, which was clean and empty. Jimmy was at the forge talking to Arthur Brinkley, the foreman.

'Got a minute, Pat? Today we are short of a fitter's mate and Jim has very little to do as we are waiting for another engine to come in for pistons and valve rings and new bushes on the con-rods. Would you mind working with Dave Davies on a few repairs on a tankie?'

'Yes, OK.'

'Go and get changed and meet him here when he comes back to the shop.'

I went into the locker room, opened the locker door and placed my clean cup inside, got out my over-jacket from the RAF saddle bag and went back to the forge. I pricked up my ears when I heard the foreman say to Jim that I was OK and keen to work and learn.

Dave walked in. 'We'll have to go to the stores and collect the battery-operated torch and lead light. If you like you can strap it around your waist as yours is smaller than mine.

'Where are we going?' I asked.

'To the coal stage. I'll get a red board so we can put it on the tender.'

'What's the job?'

'Ah, yes, you're not frightened of human bits, are you?'

'No, as long as they don't jump out on me.'

The board was placed on the lamp peg on the rear of the tender where normally paraffin lamps were positioned. Dave climbed the steps to the footplate of No 4959 *Purley Hall* and screwed down the tender's hand brake tight, then climbed down and led me to the open pit. It was half full of ashes and coal dust 'Right,' he said. 'Look for bits of blood and clothes and if you see bits of body tell me.'

So, with the lamp shining under the engine we scrutinised every possible inch of its motion. I even crawled and got up into the motion, climbing over the axles and looking, then under the springs I suddenly found a cloth of some sort, but flashing the light at every point nothing more. Then in the beam of the light I saw that the whole of the underneath was covered in blood. When I looked inside the ashpan – bingo! There were two boots with the ankles still inside and the socks on. Turning round, I called Dave. I crawled up between the tender and engine and found an arm hanging over the pipe from the tender. Now I felt a bit queasy, and sick in my stomach. I shouted to Dave, 'More here!' still crawling under the tender. Parts of body and clothing were over the axles and strewn everywhere.

'Right, off you go. I will get Arthur and a black bag and we will sort it out. Go back to the cabin and have a drink.'

I offered to put the battery and lamp back in the stores, but Dave said, 'No, leave them here please – see you later.'

Over the years there were many suicides, and drivers or firemen who saw what had happened were relieved of their duties for several months. The main areas were Goring, Streatley, Pangbourne and Cholsey. They would hide behind the bridge supports and walk out in front of the engine. Oxford was worst of all.

Back to the tankie in question, No 3751 was standing next to the toilets. Dave said he would get a clean sack from the stores and a 'Smokey Joe' lamp – they stank with the yellow flame. I had to get inside the motion, with dirt and grease everywhere, and sit astride the sliding crosshead bar while Dave handed me the sack to keep my bum from getting dirty and preventing the cold from the steel from rising up my bottom. I worried at the time and hoped there was a red board on the rear to stop anyone doing anything to the engine. Luckily there was, so I felt confident.

Dave handed me a spanner and hammer with the stinking 'Smokey Joe'. I put the lamp away from me, and with the 'Snail' brand spanner held tightly in my left hand and the hammer in my right hand, I tapped the spanner upwards on each of the two nuts in turn to release the pressure behind the piston gland. I undid the nuts with my fingers and removed them, placing them on the other crosshead bar to my right. Now I had to remove the gland, pulling it back towards the crosshead out of the way. The gap around the piston rod was as little as half an inch, but then a hand appeared across the frame with some sort of small bar with a twirled corkscrew at one end and a tapered eye at the other. I rammed that into the gap and twisted out a short piece of graphite packing. Three times I had to do this until the job was achieved. Then the black hand appeared again with the new graphite packing. I dropped one, so Dave went under the engine in the pit, found it and handed it up to me from below. I placed it where it was safe.

'Now, he said, 'wrap one packing around the rod when it comes together at the cut-off point and knock it in with this tool.' In came the same black hand with a special tool he had made – a three-eighths square block of steel flat at one end. 'Push the bar onto the packing and tap it around the piston rod.' As I got the other piece of packing, he said, 'Do the same again but this time turn the packing around slightly so all three packing pieces do not line up together.' I pushed all three graphite packing pieces into the hole and pushed the gland back into its slot. I then placed the nuts onto the thread and started to do them up together.

A head appeared over the frame. It was Ted. 'How are you doing? Just leave off the gland slightly – don't apply too much pressure, OK?'

I came out into fresh air and felt as though I had been down a coal mine for a few hours.

'We'll go and have tea now,' said Dave.

I washed my hands in the ceramic sink with the soap from my locker, got out the grub bag and walked into the cabin, sitting down among the men. I made the tea.

Dave said. 'Do you take sugar in your tea?'
'Loads,' I said.

Saturdays and safety valves

'Why not leave it out? Bet you can't for a month.'

'I'm game,' I said. 'I'll give it a try.'

After morning tea break we went back to the engine and had to adjust the brake blocks. Dave went and got the spanners, not something you would keep in your tool box – they were huge and heavy. As we both went under the engine again he showed me the correct way to take up the adjustment on the equaliser. As the hand brake was wound off we both struggled with the locking nuts, and plenty of oil was used mixed with paraffin to make a light oil, spreading it across the threads after I had wire-brushed the adjusting screws. It worked and the nuts loosened off. The equaliser was measured either side and we both checked the brake blocks to make sure they had enough gap on each wheel.

Dave went onto the footplate and wound down the handbrake wheel till the brakes took hold, while I went round testing to see if they were tight on the wheels. There was plenty of 'meat' still on the blocks, but sometimes they would need replacing; metal to metal never lasts long. We went underneath again and tightened up the locking nuts, then came out into the fresh air.

Up on the footplate we now had to repack the regulator gland. I was told to go the stores with a chitty and get some graphite string. I walked up to the stores, edging my way in front of the engine crews chattering about their beloved football or horse racing. The storeman, Jim Parsons, went off and came back with a foot length of graphite string. Back at the engine I handed it to Dave, and he showed me how to pack the gland. He had removed the regulator ready while I was away; that was easy as there was no high-pressure steam in the boiler to scald us. The repairs seemed to be wrapped up now, so in the cabin I was shown how to fill in the brown card, looking over Dave's shoulder as he explained why we had to complete the repair cards and sign them off. It seemed that if anything happened or something went wrong out on the line, perhaps causing a derailment, the documentation would be collected up and taken to a responsible person and checked for faults, then heads would roll and maybe the sack from British Railways.

It was dinnertime, and as I was in the vicinity of the Time Office I walked straight in and handed over my disc. The clerks had come to an agreement that there would be no need for the fitting staff to put their discs in at dinnertime, as they were always on the shed, but if anyone had to leave the premises they would have to hand over the disc. I went down to the fitting shop, washed my hands, got my grub bag and cup, went into the cabin and made a mug of tea, then walked outside to sit in the sun on the bench against the wall on No 5 road watching the trains thunder by as I ate my grub. I was in heaven – it was peaceful and warm and I started to nod off.

Feeling the bench move slightly as someone sat on it, I woke with a start, and looked around. Dave had come and sat down away from me.

'How do you feel about making some tools, Pat, for your tool box? Then you could keep them and use them when required. We have nothing to do for the rest of the day, so after dinner come into the shop and we can sort things out'.

'Sounds good, Dave.'

Dinnertime over, I walked into the locker room to put my gear away, then looked over to Dave's tool box locker as he opened it. These tool boxes were 7 feet high with loads of shelves and an open cupboard to keep heavy-handled tools in, including a spare pair of blue overalls.

'Come on then, we'll go over to the carriage and wagon department and see what they'll give us.'

We rummaged about in their store area, coming up with some flat iron three-eighths of an inch thick, and a couple of nuts and bolts, Whitworth screw size, copper pipe and a lamp shade that had come out of a carriage. 'That won't be missed.' I was looking at a new side of life, finding what to look for in certain areas, borrowing but not taking back. 'Unless it's nailed to the floor it's mine.'

'Right,' said Dave. We – let me rephrase that – you are going to make a set of dividers, and a set of inside callipers. We have enough metal. Let's draw out the profile on the metal and the shape.'

I drew out two lengths of identical legs approximately 8 inches long and left a square for the end of the legs. He gave me his hacksaw as there were no cutting hand tools in this workshop.

'There's the vice – go careful and cut out your design.'

Now, I know this might be funny to most of you, but I really enjoyed working with iron, or copper, and making instruments was an art to me. Placing the flat iron in the vice with some newspaper in between the vice grips, I started to use the hacksaw, cutting the iron roughly from the main body, sawing straight down the length and squaring off. Having done the same with the other set of legs, I took back the hacksaw and asked for a half-round file. I found some vice grips in another vice and placed the two bits of iron together. I then started to use the file, Dave instructing me on the proper way to handle it, making sure first that the wooden handle was tight into the file spike with a knock down onto the vice handle – always be afraid that the handle might come off and the spike be driven up into the arm. I placed the two bits of metal together within the vice, wound the vice tight shut and started to file until the legs took shape. Afternoon teatime came and went – I never bothered, I was enjoying the work I was doing.

I smelled sulphur coming into the workshop and looking outside the shop I saw that the tankie had been fired up. Arthur came into the fitting shop and asked how I was doing.

'Enjoying myself,' I said. I enjoyed the work, and could not wait to start my apprenticeship in less than a year's time when I would be 16 years old in 1961.

I could have used the grindstone but I never trusted it as it was too lumpy and it seemed that no one ever refaced it with the special tool, so the file was a better tool and gave me more experience. I enjoyed working with my hands.

Now it was time to get washed up and start to get home. I waved to Jimmy and Dave and put the metal into Dave's tool box with his file, thanking him. I wished them both good night.

I rode home, calling at Mick's house.

'What are we doing tonight? How about the pictures?'

'OK, I'll call for you about six.'

I rode home halfway up Sinodun Road and went into my house, straight up to the bath with soda crystals, then down for tea, bangers and mash with gravy.

'Mum, any chance I could borrow some money off you. I'll give it back this week. A dollar, five bob. I want to pay for the pictures and popcorn for me and Mick.'

As we walked up to the picture house two girls were in front of us.

'Hello, darling,' I said. 'What you doing

The three amigos: Graham Wilde, myself and Mick Howard.

Saturdays and safety valves

Graham Wilde, Mick Howard and myself in less formal attire!

on Saturday night about 7 o' clock. I'm free – are you two, for me and my mate?'

Mick laughed. 'Shut up,' he said.

'Let's get into the pictures – my turn to pay, mate.'

We had a good night, and after the pictures finished we walked across the road and got fish and chips from Goodenough's mobile fish and chip wagon – he lived in the prefabs in Mereland Road. 'I'm paying – you got a free night, Mick.'

I left him at his house. 'See you tomorrow night if it's OK.'

On Wednesday morning, back at work, I walked down towards the cabin and, poking my head around the door, said good morning to the men. Dave was in having his tea break.

'Can I have a word with you, Pat?' There was no one else was in the cabin. 'When you packed that piston yesterday why did you leave those nuts loose?'

I tried to avoid the intensity of his gaze, which put the shits up me.

I told him that Ted Powell had told me that was the correct way to do it, leave the nuts loose. Christ, he went livid. I said I wouldn't lie about such a thing. 'You were missing and he poked his head into the frame of the tankie.'

Dave went straight into the office and told Arthur Brinkley what I had said, but I never heard another word about what had happened after that. Now it was my turn and I didn't for the life of me know that there was back-biting within this community in the Running and Maintenance section, but it opened my eyes. I would never trust men like these again, I thought; I only had to work with them and, as Dick my brother had said, keep your mouth shut. As I walked into the shop my head was held low, and I put up my hand to Jimmy. He called me to him – no one else was about. He said, 'Just ignore it and don't trust no one, Pat.

I said I was disgusted with the likes of men in this shed, but he said, 'It will be sorted. Dave will do it. It's called jealousy and they know you are getting on well so far with the skills that we are teaching you for your career.'

I nodded several times and thanked him for his advice. I wiped the tears from my eyes.

Later I was called to Dave's locker and he said that we had to change the safety valve gasket on No 6910 *Gossington Hall* inside the shed on No 3 road, so we would have to keep our heads down as the smoke chute was low and full of ash from the engines. 'Here, carry this sack,' he said, and brought some tools and the gasket that he had withdrawn from the stores that morning. I said I was sorry about the earlier incident. 'Trouble is, Dave, I'm not sure at the moment about men either lying to me or telling the truth.' But what good would come out of it, as I knew who had stitched him up as well as me, and again I was easy meat, but I had noted it and I logged it in my notebook for future reference

– but it was not going to be easy working with the pair of them.

Arthur called me into his office regarding the incident and said he would keep me away from them as much as possible. 'But sometimes you will have to work on inspection, either with those two, or Jack Dearlove would be better, as he will teach you the correct way of doing things.' I thanked him

Dave was looking for me up and down the shed while he stood on the engine's frame holding onto the boiler handrail. I waved and put up my thumb, shouting that I was just coming. I walked to the engine and, climbing up the steps and hanging onto the footplate handrail, I swung out onto the ledge outside the cab and reached out to grab the boiler handrail near the quarter-light window. I heaved my body across close to the boiler side and shuffled on top of the frame then climbed up on to the handrail, still keeping my body weight over the top of the boiler. I took the sack and tools from Dave and placed them on top of the cab roof where the sliding hatch was situated. There wasn't much room to do the delicate manoeuvre as the smoke extraction chute was low over the engine.

As I slid over the top of the boiler and down onto the handrail on the other side, Dave gave me a spanner to start taking the bolts out of the safety valve cowling. Doing as I was told, I worked around anti-clockwise while he went clockwise. I collected up all the small bolts and placed them in the corner of the cab and boiler together with his.

I next got on top of the boiler into the depths of the smoke chute and lifted the cowling off the safety valve, then gingerly walked over to the roof of the cab, knowing that there were support struts inside the chutes. It looked like I was ready to do a vanishing trick with just my legs and feet

No 6910 *Gossington Hall* in Didcot station.

showing. Turning round, I went back over the boiler top, digging my toes inside my boots trying to get a grip on the metal covering of the boiler.

I now sat down astride the boiler, and Dave handed me an open-ended spanner and a length of steel pipe. I positioned the spanner on one of the nuts. He said to jam the open pipe over the end of the spanner and put some pressure on. While he climbed on the boiler and pulled, I held the spanner down tight with the end on the hammer shaft. The nut started to turn slowly, squeaking. I asked Dave if he had any oil over on his side, and he gave me his squirt oilcan. I gently wet each nut in turn around the safety valve.

Now we were in business as we proceeded around the base of the safety valve. All the nuts started to move until we had loosened them all. We had no sockets or bars, or ring spanners, only 'Snail' brand open-ended spanners; being thick metal they took a lot of weight.

We started to undo the nuts, being careful that the heads of the nuts had no rough burrs on them. The spanner was handed back and forth until we had removed all the nuts from the ring of the valve's base.

Next Dave handed me a small crowbar with a flat edge and a small block of wood.

Saturdays and safety valves

From sitting astride the boiler I got up and knelt across it. He stuck the flat edge between the valve and its base frame and held it while I pulled myself up to a standing position, inside the chute looking down. I put my foot on the bar and pressed it down hard. Having the grip now, he got a lead hammer and whacked the valve with force. Suddenly the valve moved. I stepped over the valve and we did the same thing with wood and the crowbar jammed in place. I put my boot heavily down while he whacked the valve again, and this time it jumped up as my boot went down.

This was my first encounter standing on top of the boiler. I bent over to miss the struts in the chute, then Dave and I picked up the safety valve together. He walked backwards and I followed, walking over the gap in the boiler top, with the studs sticking upwards. I could see the tubes inside the boiler and felt the studs poking into my feet, praying that I would not let go of the valve. My feet inside my boots were blinking killing me something rotten, while my toes dug into the soles of the boots and the outside of the boots dug into the rounded top of the boiler.

We made it to the top of the cab roof, but as I got up and stretched I cracked my head on a chute box strut. It blinking hurt, and years of soot came down all over my head.

The old gasket was in shreds, so it was easy to take off the metal face if it hadn't been for the 1-inch studs sticking up. I started to drop the chisel, but held it until it hit the gasket, which was fragile and broke away easy.

I looked into the sack and found a file. It was slightly better now as I could use the file to scrape away on the metal face between

This view shows the overhead smoke exhaust chutes inside Didcot shed. There was not much room to move when working on a safety valve on top of an engine.

the studs until I made the radius face shine, dusting away any old joint. Bits fell into the tubes, and were picked out and thrown down onto the concrete floor below. I looked across to Dave, asking him if he wanted a hand with the valve.

'No, I can manage, Pat. There's a tin there – open it up with this hacksaw blade and spread the manganese graphite paste over the face, please.'

Firstly I'd never seen a hacksaw blade that big – it was huge, and the teeth had been ground down and sharpened like a knife. I stuck the end of the blade in the tin, then it hit me that I had wanted to be a make-up artist before I started on the railway, and here was my chance to train. I had the blade in my hand and I gently started to layer the black manganese paste over the metal frame, filling in the gaps and thinking what a spotty face this person had! I gently manoeuvred around the studs sticking upwards and filled in the cracks with the sort of muck people put on their skin! Dave came to see how I was doing, and was amazed how evenly I had spread the paste. I had the knack to do the job well.

He laid the gasket over the studs and told me to carry on what I was doing; he was impressed, as once again I worked the paste into another wrinkle and smoothed it over the gasket on my imaginary face. Now Dave said, 'Ready to walk backwards, Pat?'

'As long as you guide me over those studs.'

Again my feet dug into the boots that were like magnets digging into the metal covering of the boiler as I shuffled backwards with my head down looking at my hands holding the safety valve with the tightest grip. If I fell sideways both of us would fall 15 feet to the ground.

Now I felt the studs jarring the inner soles of my leather boots. I had to step over them, still holding the safety valve. I was ready to do the splits and pulling Dave, but he was OK – he was old, I was young. We lowered the valve onto the gasket successfully – thank you Lord! Dave climbed down off the boiler onto the frame.

I stayed on top as a hand came from nowhere with a few nuts. I started to screw them on finger tight, moving around the valve doing the same until he passed the spanner up to me as I stood on the boiler-side handrail. The spanner in position, I started to tighten them down as instructed. Then I crossed to the other side, then back again. The metal tube now appeared, and we were near the end; all we had to do was start again really tightened them down from one across to the other diagonally, then with the tube really going to town with all the weight we both had. The cowling to cover the valve was the last to be put into position, and that was done with ease. When it came to sign the job off on the brown card, he put my name down as well as his. I was chuffed. (At least Ted bloody Powell didn't climb up and whisper that it was the wrong way!)

6. Charlie Caulkett

I was with Dave for the rest of the week as his mate took a week's holiday with his family and went to the seaside. Dave said that we had finished the heavy job on the 'Hall', and now the other team of 'Belgian Bob' would cover the light work.

Now we had some free time on our hands to get on with the callipers, continuing where we had left off. As Dave walked over to Jimmy I was happy filing the legs to shape with a half-round medium file, opening the vice with the screw handle slightly so that the jaws came apart, then repositioning the metal legs, again lifting the file and placing it into position with my left hand holding on the far edge and pressing it down while my right hand held the wooden handle, pushing it away from my body. I was getting into the rhythm now, twisting the file as I pushed it away, and the metal was starting to take on the shape I wanted. The filings from the metal were spreading across the bench, and I was pleased with myself, then a visitor tapped me on the shoulder and said, 'Its teatime – come on, Pat.'

I went into my locker and as I pulled out the bag of tea I did not realise that I had caught my hand on the spout of my teapot, and it fell to the floor with a crash. Sod it! I put half a spoon of tea leaves in my cup and walked into the cabin, pouring boiling water from the iron kettle on to the leaves – what a mess! I poured some milk into the cup, then I threw it away, drinking a cup of water instead. I sat down at the table with the rest of the crew, hearing their chatter about what they were doing. Dave looked at me and nodded his head to get me out of the cabin. I nodded too, and got up. I held the iron door handle to open it upwards, feeling the years of metal and gears and the locking system rattle within. It's funny, but I always remember that door handle – something that always stuck in my mind.

When we got outside he said, 'Let's go and sort out some more metal so you can make the inside callipers, and keep you busy away from this lot.'

Putting my cup in the locker, I caught up with him at his tool locker. We went out of the small top door and across the rails, making sure they were all clear, then walked near the red breakdown van and across to a long line of coaches standing at the buffer stops. I asked Dave what those black tanks were for between the coaches and the fitting shop, and he told me they were for the oil used in tenders instead of coal; Didcot had oil-burning engines during the war, as Welsh marine coal was in short supply. But the tanks were empty now.

We headed for the carriage and wagon department. Dave tried the door and it opened, then a voice came from the corner of the workshop. 'What do you bloody want again, Davies?' He told the person to shut his big mouth, then he said that he wanted some more flat metal like before. 'What else you got in here we can have?'

'Help yourselves.'

So we both had a look around. I found a glass shade and some copper pipe in one of the tool boxes, as well as some wire and plugs, a three-pin for the mains; now we needed the sliding on-off connection switch for the shade. Dave looked at me. 'What have you got in mind, Pat? Making a table lamp?'

I knew where to come now for bits, but he said, 'Only with me, or they'll sack you.'

'Point taken – thanks.'

It was getting closer to home time as I went to wash my hands.

'See you in the morning, Dave, and thanks for a good day.'

I wished him good night, and also Jimmy.

*

Charlie Caulkett was one of the old firemen who shared his memories with me. He said that he found the best drivers to work with at Didcot were Ron Durman, Archie Davies, Mick Slade and Wilf Butler. Pilot work during the day became boring with not much to do, only pulling a train to Culham and onto Moreton Cutting yard and shunting; then there was the station pilot, and the Ordnance Depot. Charlie got out of the pilot work, and started working the all-stations Swindon passenger trains, especially the 7.05am; then he turned at Swindon on the turntable and came back to Reading station pulling the same number of coaches.

The Newbury to Southampton trains were quite nice to work unless you had a Dean Class '25'. They also had No 3030, and old 'ROD' engine, which would always work the Newbury and Reading 'fly'. The 'fly' turns were working all stations to Reading, shunting coal wagons at Cholsey and with cattle wagons picking up and dropping off at the cattle docks for the farmers, then taking the empty wagons away back up to Reading yard. They then finished for the day, travelling home light engine.

The footplate pay was good, £3 12 6d per week. Some days they would work the Banbury train with cattle, or the sugar beet trains to Kidderminster. The 'Castles' were quite hard to work, and you would need the exhaust injector on most of the time to keep steam up. The 'County' Class 4-6-0s were a bit shy for steaming, but Charlie enjoyed the '6800' 'Granges', which were very easy to work and fire. However, the 'Hall' Class engines were the top of the grade, and the best, pulling 11 coaches with no trouble. After transferring to Reading shed, Charlie enjoyed the Southern engines, the 'King Arthur' and 'Lord Nelson' Classes, as they steamed freely and were better to fire.

In his loco box, which he carried everywhere with him on the footplate (he had purchased it in 1954 for the sum of 7s 6d) was a sight glass with two rubber rings, a flare lamp, a pair of leather gloves, an empty billycan (after he had drunk his tea), a tube with both ends separated for sugar and tea, several journals, speed restriction notices and, the main item, his Rule Book.

A typical day's work would start with booking on at the desk with the office clerk, reading the notices and checking the number of the engine that would be designated for that turn; it might be a 'Castle' or 'Hall' Class. He was allowed 45 minutes to prep the engine.

No 3033, a First World War 'ROD' 2-8-0, at Didcot. These engines did all the 'fly' turns.

A general view of Reading's Southern steam shed on 8 February 1960, with three 'N' Class 2-6-0s and 'Schools' Class 4-4-0 No 30903 *Charterhouse*. *Ray Ruffell, Slip Coach Publishing Services collection*

Another view of *Charterhouse* a few days later on the 19th. Above the shed yard can be seen the Great Western main line and one of the Reading signal boxes. *Ray Ruffell, Slip Coach Publishing Services collection*

There was usually 101lb per square inch of steam on the gauge, with the water bobbing in the gauge glass. He would then go out looking for engine tools off other dead engines, or from the oil stores – the fire irons, shovel, prep pipe and the fire shield or ring, if it was not placed back after the fire and ash had been thrown out. A Western shovel was a man's shovel!

Charlie filled the tender with water and filled the lubricator on the footplate as the steam gauge started to rise, then left the footplate to walk along the frame by the boiler and check the sand boxes in turn, replenishing with fresh sand where necessary, the driver helping by passing the spouted bucket up to him.

While standing on the frame, he walked to the smokebox door and tightened down the handle, making it secure; this stopped air being drawn into the front of the engine, affecting the steaming. He returned to the footplate along the frame, checked the detonator tube for the correct amount and replenished where possible from the oil stores. He made sure the flags were together – red and green – pulled the coal down from the tender and broke the heavy lumps with the pickaxe, sweeping the coal dust off the side of the footplate – making sure first that no one was walking by – then connected the prep pipe to the steam water valve and washed down the footplate.

In the meantime the driver would oil the motion bars and glands and any other pots that required oil.

Before leaving the shed they needed to get permission through the booking office, after which they rang the signal box. The driver always blew the whistle before leaving the shed and moving off the front forecourt, then moved into position in the carriage sidings to collect the coaches. The signalman was informed and the points and signals set.

Part of 'the Lawn' at Paddington, seen in April 1960. *L. W. Ibbotson, Slip Coach Publishing Services collection*

The driver blew the whistle and the train then proceeded out onto the main line, the driver shunting the train down to the platform in the station.

Charlie would then make sure that everything was ready, with both billycans on the plate above the firebox door to warm. The crew both had a cup of tea from the top lid of the billycan, resting a while before the off and until they got the guard's whistle and green flag. It might be an all-stations Paddington job, arriving at their destination by the huge platform area called 'the Lawn' beyond the buffer stops.

Old Oak men then relieved them. Passengers would greet the locomen, but the passenger guard would ignore the fireman because he was dirty, and had dirty overalls on, only speaking to the driver because he had a gold badge on his hat.

Leaving Paddington the driver opened the regulator, then shut it down, winding the cut-off lever backwards slightly, then again lifted the regulator as they passed Wormwood Scrubs. Charlie opened the exhaust injector on the driver's side and kept it open till Twyford came into view. The driver then eased the regulator as they arrived at Reading, on time.

There they had to refill the tender with water from the column at the end of the station. Hanging the canvas bag over the filling hole, the driver wound the handle open and Charlie watched until the tender was full, then shut the metal cover.

After Reading it was first stop Newbury, then Pewsey, Westbury and on to Taunton and Exeter St David's. Reaching there, both driver and fireman were thirsty, so went into the buffet for two cups of tea, saying 'O.C.S.' – On Company Service – a relic of the GWR days, meaning they got a penny off each cup, paying threepence in total.

Then they travelled back in a compartment for locomen only, sitting on cushioned seats. These were for the men in dirty overalls, not the passenger guards, as they too dirty.

Working goods trains was much more pleasant. Goods guards would be salt-of-the-earth types, very friendly, and treated the fireman as part of the train crew.

One night, when working a heavy freight train of iron ore on the Worcester line, and coming to the steep ingredient at Blockley and Campden, just before entering Campden Tunnel the goods train was brought to a halt. Charlie had to leave the footplate with a shunting pole and peg down the brakes on the ten leading freight wagons, which was hard and heavy work. The guard at the other end of the train pegged down the same amount, and wound the brake down on his van, making it secure so that all the blocks were on the wheels. Climbing back onto the footplate, Charlie wound the tender brake down tight and placed the chain over the handle.

Eventually the guard waved his paraffin oil lamp, colour code white, from his balcony, giving the driver permission to proceed. The driver opened the regulator a couple of notches and they sailed through Campden Tunnel at a fair pace, then down the 1 in 100 gradient, the brakes staying on, helped by the driver also applying his vacuum brake on the engine.

When they reached Honeybourne Junction station they stopped to release all the brakes, then set of again to Worcester, where they were relieved by two new enginemen. The driver called Control using the internal 'omnibus' telephone system, the guard travelled back in a passenger train, and Charlie and the driver travelled back on a '28XX' Class loco, tender first, to Reading, getting the road straight away. It was a cold and frosty night, and both Charlie and the driver agreed that they wanted an early finish. The engine steamed well, and Mr Jackson the driver had his overcoat on, but they only had their overalls on. By the time they got to Kingham they were frozen stiff, and the wind blowing over the tender brought great lumps of coal and dust into their faces.

When they arrived at Oxford they asked if they could go on the turntable and turn this beast around to travel on smokebox-first. They were both covered in frost and freezing cold, and needed the heat from the fire, hugging the boiler back to try to stay warm. It was a bad experience, but they continued their journey in comfort, not tender-first.

One day they worked the Fairford branch. They started at Yarnton, shunting at every little station along the line, which had once been the East Gloucestershire Railway. Charlie's driver had come to Reading to get his driver's position, and his uncle was once a driver and owned Arkell's Brewery at Swindon, but Charlie never met him.

They used to shunt the Black Mills at Witney; in the yard was a bridge over a stream, and they noticed it was full of trout. They therefore saw the boilerwasher, as he used carbide for the lamps when working inside a firebox, and obtained a large amount, keeping it dry in a sealed tin.

They had the same shunting duties the next day, so brought a few empty lemonade bottles along with them, stored in a cardboard box on the tender. They half filled the bottles with iron nuts, then the carbide, then water, and screwed the tops back on tight. Then Charlie and his driver threw them from either side of the footplate over the bridge into the stream; they sank, and they gave the mixture time to work. Suddenly there was a huge explosion and water erupted high into the air. Walking along the bank of the stream, they found a couple of large trout, and shared them with the goods guard.

A boilersmith's carbide lamp for working inside a firebox. Carbide was mixed with water to produced a gas – they always 'popped' when working.

7. Initiation

The Didcot initiation ceremony happened to me one morning when I came out from the toilet and walked into the fitting shop. I was caught from behind by two great hands holding me tight – that was Dave Davies. I tried to get free by kicking, but his mate Jim Hale whipped down my trousers inside my overalls and slipped a length of string with a slip knot on the end on to my genitals. They were now out in the fresh air, and a loop at the other end of the string carried the biggest steam nut I had ever seen in my life. It was heavy, and I was told to walk though the fitting shop with it dangling. I felt ashamed, but everyone was laughing and cheering as they lined up, and I had to walk between them, as they said that it would make my penis stretch. I didn't want it any longer as it was down to my kneecaps now! I went into the locker room and took the string off – it was stopping the blood reaching the head of my knob.

Putting my clothes back on, I smartened myself up, walked outside and threw that nut away in the scrap heap. I should have kept it and mounted it on a wooden board to remind myself what a big boy I was. However, every dog has its day, and mine would come. I was totally ashamed, and I have never spoken about it or written about it till now. After the initiation ceremony I had a nickname given to me that has lasted to the present day – 'Wobble'. It's funny, but I am very proud that it has stuck to me for ever.

A bit of wet soot never hurt anyone – it was nothing that couldn't be removed with hot water, and with carbolic soap dipped in the sandbox and a drop of paraffin using a good stiff brush. But if you weren't careful there were always plenty of helpers to hold the victim down on the table in the mess room, and he finished up with a red chest just as if he was sunburnt. It was a good clean fun to liven up the duty, and you could always pay them back, perhaps by placing a fog detonator under the loco wheel while shunting in the yard – or if someone laid their cap down for the moment it would be placed under the loco wheel and neatly cut in half as soon as the loco moved.

Young lads joining the railway and going to the loco shed were given a reading and written test. It was very basic. They were given a free pass to travel to Parkhouse, at Swindon. The Medical was very strict with two company doctors. Having passed the fitness, they were supplied with two pairs of overalls, and a grease peaked cap with a BR Western Region badge. The following week you reported to Didcot shed and Mr Tom White, who was a lovely old man. He was the cleaner foreman and had 20 cleaners, 15- to 17-year-old lads, working under him, but he couldn't control them.

When a 'Hall' or 'Castle' came in there would be two cleaners on the boiler with two lads on the tender. The cleaners' cabin was filthy, with lumps of oil waste on the table. We used to play jokes with the cleaners. When someone went to the toilet and had a wash, we got a lump of axle grease and smeared it under the handlebars of their bikes. Or if they were working inside the smokebox shovelling ash out into the pit or onto the floor someone would close the door and lock it; the only way out was through the chimney, if you were slim enough. On Mondays to Saturdays young firemen and cleaners were cleaning copper pipes all day; everybody dreaded that shift.

Skip Morgan's main-line career started a long way from the main line. It began in the dark confined to the shed as a member of the cleaning gang. To become a fully-blown member of the cleaning gang meant acceptance, and as in all industries where adventurous young men worked in a gang, full membership meant that an initiation ceremony had to be carried out. It was short but not so sweet, and not a bit like a wedding; yet in its way it was very serious and a memorable part of life, for it was one of the first steps towards manhood, sorting out the men from the boys. Some young lads would leave when their time drew near; it was too much to face because there was no help at hand, as firemen, drivers, foremen and shed staff kept well out of the way. The boy was about to become a man, and when it was over he would be addressed as an equal by all.

It began when one of the lads walked into the cleaners' cabin and mess room on a Monday night at the start of the week on night shift. When Skip looked at the door next to the gents' toilet at Didcot shed, he still remembered that first night. He walked in through the big wooden door and the 15-watt bulb was switched off, and two 'Smokey Joes', the flickering flare paraffin lamps smelling of pungent oil, came at once into the sacrificial chamber. His clothes were removed – he had not a stitch on – and was lifted up by many hands, carried through the open room and laid down on the mess table. Many hands held him down while the senior cleaner began to pour a pint of heavy lubricating oil over his body. The senior cleaner climbed onto the shoulders of another cleaner, who was standing on the bench. Therefore from a great height, and with a leer on his face and much concentration, he poured a pint of heavy lubricating oil all over the victim's private parts. It would have been better if they had warmed the oil up first.

When it was all over the men's gentlemanly instincts came to the forefront. It was time for the cleansing ceremony. They all trooped out, leaving the cleaning materials consisting a pint of paraffin, and handful of dry sand with a bucket of hot water. If you could clean the oil off with that, you could clean a locomotive. But as a full-blown cleaner one now took a step towards better things. He was no longer addressed as 'Boy' – it became 'Hey, you'!

*

The enginemen's cabin was full of waiting men, either having just coming off duty or awaiting their orders from the management. But if nothing seemed to be moving from behind the time clerk's desk, and with more coming into work, they would overflow around the store area. Some men might have been in work since the early morning.

In the cabin was a frying pan, 30 inches round, and the fat must have been in the pan for years, as it was never replaced with new; it just lay on the seat by the iron pot-belly stove. When there was no one about at night mice and rats would fight each other to climb up the stool legs, clambering into the pan for a feed. They left their droppings, little bobbles, all around inside the frying pan like raisins. Then someone would come in the next morning bright and early, a driver or fireman, pick up the pan, put it straight on top of the hot stove and crack an egg into the fat with bacon and fried bread, cooking everything, even the 'raisins', and scraping it onto a plate with salt and pepper – nice and tasty!

The storeman had a busy time dealing with chitties from the requisition pads, which got smaller as each man signed for his requirements, cotton waste and oils of all grades, lifted onto the counter in gallon spouted jugs. Trying his hardest was the fitter's boy, approaching and trying to pass the hoard of men mingling outside. He carried a heavy hammer and a large open-ended spanner to adjust the braking system on the defect engine No 2849, on which the brake blocks had seized, while his fitter carried some other tools that might come in handy in a dirty old sack. He walked with a limp, weighed down on one side. He told his mate to collect some cotton waste from the stores, using a chitty that had just been signed.

The rain lashed down outside on the front of the shed and the team wore dirty old raincoats that had been around since the days of Noah's Ark, covered in grease and dirt; they were stored in the fitting shop for this sort of day. The fitter's boy's coat was so big as he walked along it dragged on the concrete floor, wiping it at the same time.

There was a procedure for handling the braking system. We shouted to the driver to release the vacuum and blow off the brakes, then the fitter with the huge hammer hit the check nuts with so much force that it shook the rest of the connected rods. The rain was now pouring cats and dogs, soaking into the ash surface that comprised the base of the shed when it was built, 25 feet deep, and the rivers of rain came off the boiler and slithered down the frame, collecting dirt on its way and becoming a waterfall, splashing down under the frames where the fitting crew were working – 'Bloody typical!' we thought. We were under the ashpan now and the trailing axle. The two locking nuts on both rods were unscrewed half a turn either side, with the main adjusting screw also unscrewed with the same revolution, while the fitter's boy went outside to check the brake blokes one side and the fitter's mate doing the other side. The driver was then asked to apply the brakes and release them again, as they had to be checked again. If they were all OK, the fitter tightened up the locking nuts on both sides. The fitter then climbed up to the footplate and applied the brakes again to make sure they was no gap between the wheels and the brake blocks; we checked again all was clear, and that he was happy, and the re-test had been completed.

One day, when someone was on top of the tender filling it with water, I heard a shout to shut down the water column. I had no idea how it worked so I wound the handle round and round. He shouted, 'No, that's the wrong way!' I knew the person – it was Kenny Haycroft. Christ, he did scream at me as he got soaked all down his legs. I was never asked again, especially by him.

The shed fitters were a special breed of men that served the steam engines with love and hate, but always with care, but we didn't like wet weather, especially in the cold freezing snow, with that damn easterly wind driving across the fields from Appleford and Cow Lane, then, after it left us, across the station.

*

After dropping off my pay disc at the Time Office, as no one was about I went across the sleepers to where my bike was, pulled it off the rack and started for home. I heard a noisy rattle in the front wheel, so I went to Bosley's shop on the Broadway to see if they could fix it. 'No chance, mate – it's had it. You need a new bike.' So I left the bike there – if you want it for spares. I walked home to Sinodun Road and asked Mum if she could come down with me to Curry's shop at the top of Edinburgh Drive on Saturday afternoon so I could buy a new bike 'on the knock', as Mum had to sign the Hire Purchase Agreement papers, seeing I was under-age at only 18.

I went to see Mick as we were now very close mates. For both of us it was payday the following day, so what was on the agenda? How about going down the Labour Club, as there was a Union meeting? He said OK, and would see me there at about 7.00pm.

I had an early night as I was totally knackered – I couldn't burn the candle at both ends. Yes I was young with youthful looks and a slim body, but the muscles in my arms started to ache with the heavy lifting. I had a bath, climbed into bed and slept like a log.

Next morning I was up at the crack of dawn as usual and left early as I had to walk to work. It wasn't far, really, about 2 miles and all downhill. With the rain still coming down in sheets, I could hear the engines, then see them as they appeared near East Junction signal box; they were waiting for the points to move and the signals to drop. This was the height of activity on the railway at Didcot; there was much more going on with the railway than I saw on the roads. No cars, no traffic at all, only men dressed in boilersuits, hobnail boots and blue dungarees, the railwaymen with their peaked caps, some picking up waste paper wrappers off the road to keep the streets clean. These dedicated men thought the world of our streets and roads in this large village.

I walked to the entrance of the station and into the subway away from the rain pouring outside – it was heaven for a few minutes. I might be lucky, as I only had the concrete stairs to climb, and in that short time the weather might have turned dry. At that moment I heard overhead the sound of a high-pitched whistle as a freight train passed West End signal box. The clatter of the milk tanks built up into one mighty continuous roar as the engine pounded overhead, followed by the screaming of the wheel flanges as the tanks bucked and swayed, the wheels beating out the pattern on the rail joints, so fast that they almost merged into one sound. Then she was gone as the guard's van rattled away into the distance and the darkness. I had only walked a few paces when suddenly there was another fast freight overhead on the up relief line, each rail joint capturing distinctly the solid weight of 40 tons as the wagons passed from rail to rail. As I walked away I caught the sounds of the lifts moving upwards to the platform and the heavy four-wheeled platform trolleys being pulled along by the station porters carrying parcels for the next train due into the station. I was alone as I walked up the concrete steps to cross over the wet sleepers, watching the coaches and parcel vans stopping as the driver of the pilot waited for the signal to proceed onto the main line once the freight had passed.

I met a few enginemen as I walked towards the shed, hearing the crunch of the ash path underfoot and feeling the wet coming over my boots, and creeping into my sock. The shed appeared around the corner of the hump with the coal stage above, and now it was starting to rain again as I hurried towards the entrance and dryness at last.

The darkness of the sky that morning started to lighten, but there was not the usual glamour or beauty of the steam engine. The office windows were steamed up from the heat within, and the locomotive tail lights around the shed disappeared through the smoke. There was as usual organised chaos, with drivers and firemen getting their engines ready within the 45-minute allowance, getting ready to leave the shed. Fitters ran round eagerly like headless chickens, being shouted at by the shed foreman with his bowler hat and his air of power and authority, asking what else was there to be done. 'Another 10 minutes or so and we shall be done.'

'What?' came the roar in reply.

But the fitter did not wait to argue – he had work to do.

That bowler hat sitting on his head represented power, but when it was removed he was a normal as any other man within the shed.

Then the sound of a Great Western whistle was heard and the shed foreman looked as the engine pulled away, late as usual, with the driver's thumb stuck up in the air and the regulator slightly open as it creaked away, the big side rods pulling on their journals, the oil revolving around the dry metal as the bushes within the con-rods squeaked until the oil did its work, while the rain poured down from the heavens.

*

Whenever a trainspotter came into the shed, taking engine numbers, I would approach him and ask how would he like to buy a spanner with 'GWR' stamped on it for half a dollar.

'Cor, yes!'

'Right, go away and when you have had a look around I will be here.'

I went into the scrap area, found a 'Snail' brand hammer and went into the fitting shop. I pulled out the metal stamps from the cupboard, held them the correct way and with a hammer hit the 'G', then the 'W' and the 'R'. The spotter came back to see me, I handed over the spanner and he donated the money to my fund.

In the shed, men were as always a cross-section of the working community, good and bad, tall and short, cheerful and morose. However, the one thing they had in common was the love of the steam engine and pride in their jobs. The foreman and his deputies, the fitters, boilersmiths, firedroppers, drivers, firemen, cleaners, storemen, clerks, labourers and all the back-up services that went into the running of the shed all made it a privilege to work in the 'company of gentlemen', as you might say.

*

After coming into the shed after a derailment, Jim Hale had to gather all the stock as he was in charge of the breakdown van, but when he was on his holidays Dave and I had to refill the train from the stores. We got a two-wheel barrow, went to the stores and collected the boxes. The sliding door was pulled back to the wall, revealing a shed with so many nooks and crannies. I looked around, seeing the big oil tanks and wondering how they filled them. There was equipment stocked everywhere, and hidden in the corner was the callout pushbike with a little leather satchel under the saddle stamped 'GWR', as well as the bike frame itself.

We collected the stores, signed the paperwork with Jim Parsons, then the sliding door closed quickly behind us, with Arthur Wheatley pushing. We felt like we were in prison, as everything was locked down! We then followed the path out and across the sleeper crossing towards the oil tanks and turned right to the breakdown train's own siding. I climbed between the two coaches onto the buffer, then up onto the first step and swung myself onto the ledge, grabbing the door handle. Dave handed me the key to unlock the door and, pushing it open, I saw for the first time inside the red van all the tools that men required for derailments.

The store at Didcot. The oil tanks held different grades of oils, and the small box on the left contained the First Aid kit. Everything to the right was for the fitters. *British Railways*

I clipped the chain from its hook, heaved the wooden steps to the edge of the van and lowered them down to my mate; I found two slots in the wooden floor boards, and secured the steps.

Dave came into the tool area, explaining to me what had to be done. He showed me the other coach as we walked from one end to the other. It was very interesting, but for now we had to fill the stores in the kitchen area cupboards with provisions, biscuits, tinned meats, tinned milk, and coal and firewood for the stove. Then we walked through into the store area where the jacks and the oils were kept, and the timber blocks were stacked tidily in their own store area and kept secured.

All the lifting jacks and traversing jacks had to be replenished with oil, so we drained the old oil and filled up with new; the jacks sat in metal trays, keeping the overspill away from the walkway. The train was ready now for the next derailment. The last bit of work was for me to walk along the roof of the breakdown coaches, but first we had to remove the double ladder from the van; we put it to the side of the coach, making sure it was safe and secure, then connected it to the roof of the coach to refill the tanks from the manhole in the ground where it was connected to the town's water supply. Dave handed me the rubber hose, I opened the tanks and filled them to the brim, with the excess running out of the overflow pipes on either side of the end coach.

From my vantage point I could see over the whole complex, but heard a shout to be careful and not to slip. It was a smashing day, the sun was shining, and there was lots of steam activity and Great Western whistles; traffic of all sorts filled all the lines to the brim, and further out I could see the West curve. What a sight – Didcot station, the Provender Stores, parcels stores, and the great reservoir lake. I pretended to be a cowboy, jumping from one coach to the other, even though the train was stationary, then heard a shout.

'Come on down – you've had your fun.'

Dave saw him as well as I did in the corner of my eye. Arthur Brinkley, the foreman, was on his way over to where we were standing. I leapt down the ladder and stood ready as he walked around the tool van with his blue smock nearly touching the ground. Dave was in the tool van trying to be busy.

'Everything OK boys – all done? I'll like a look inside before you lock up,' he said.

I held the steps as he climbed into the tool van

'Have you had a look inside?' he asked.

'Yes, Dave showed me, thanks.'

'Come up and I'll tell you what it's all about then, Pat.' Arthur taught me a lot about breakdowns and it came in handy over the years.

Dave and I removed the ladder and replaced it in its position in the tool van, then we trotted over to the shop's small door, climbed in over the wooden frame and walked into the working area.

8. Pay day

Thursday afternoon, 3.00pm – pay day. My first ever pay day of many to come. I was over the moon – 48 hours worked in 5½ days, from 7.30 till 5.30pm with 1 hour for lunch. Nine hours a day and 4 hours for the Saturday morning, 8.00-12.00 (threepence farthing per hour for £1 10s, or 6 dollars, per week)

However, I would have worked for nothing as long as I got through my apprenticeship unscathed for five years, but alas that was never to happen, so here I was, in a one-year pre-apprenticeship, a fitter's boy, a gofer – do this, do that. Well, that was not quite true as I felt like an apprentice and was treated like an apprentice, and the fitter's boy never came into the equation, only on paper.

As I lined up with my fellow members of the fitting staff, in front of us was the riff-raff, the drivers, firemen, shed staff, then someone swaggered in wearing winklepickers and his hair brushed back with Brylcreem, a white grease that smothered the hair and was all the rage then – I have to admit I used it also. Teddy boys were turning into Elvis Presley, with winklepicker shoes that crippled your toes and made you walk pigeon-toed. That must have been me! So Frank Dowding started to laugh and giggle behind me. The firemen turned around and glared. I asked, 'What's so funny?'

Frank returned, 'How do you get your feet in there?'

'The same way as a copper gets his helmet on his head – a little bit of friction,' came a reply from the firemen's side – Tony Neal, if I remember.

When the fireman handed over his brass tag, a few minutes later a brown envelope came out with his disc, then the payment book, which he had to sign. He pulled the brown envelope open with all his might and went off in a huff – not a happy chappy. I was led into place by Dave, to be shown the proper way to receive my wage packet. I went through the same process and the packet was handed over. I thanked the paymaster, and he was taken aback how polite that new boy was.

The wages always came in a bullion coach, stopping at every station from Paddington to Swindon. I remember this because in 1965 I was asked to collect the wages from the bullion coach with Ernie Jones; we went into the coach and the bodyguards, Dave Davies and Jim Hale, stayed out on the platform. I wore a chain bracelet around my wrist and carried the briefcase with Ernie Jones. Silly, really – if there were bandits about they would have cut my wrist off and the guards would have run away screaming. We walked back to the shed as the guards kept looking around to see which way to make their break and run for their lives. Nevertheless we made to the shed office. I never received anything for doing my bit, but had to pay more tax. That was the enjoyment of working.

When I opened the first brown envelope I was amazed at the amount of money I received, and all the paperwork inside. I had never seen one of the old green £1 notes for a long time, and the 10 shillings in change – whoopee! Roll on 1961, as I would get another quid for my birthday and every birthday after that, but London was the best place as you got London weighting, extra cash. I paid Mum a quid for the housekeeping, and the 10 bob was mine. I was rich.

On Thursday night Mick dressed up and washed up pretty clean, and I scrubbed up too. We went down to the Labour Club, the meeting place for all union members. As we walked into the establishment we heard the noise coming from upstairs. There was a racket going on: 'Brother this' and 'Brother that'. Not me – we went to the bar, but my head sunk as I saw Bill Clark, the fitter's mate, who was secretary of the club.

'You're under age.' He never spoke

quietly, but shouted out so everyone heard. 'No, I am not serving you!'

Mick said, 'Two pints please.'

'One pint for you, not for him, the *underage boy!*'

I had to cross his palm with silver.

'So what's your poison, Bill?

'Tot of Lamb's rum, please Patrick.' I handed over a shilling for his tot. Then he spoke to Mick: 'Cheers – and now I will get you two pints, young man.'

There was a fruit machine in the bar area. We started to play, and Mick said, 'Shall go 50-50 shares?'

I agreed, but as I put the tanner in the slot and pulled the handle the machine's cogs all went click and the dial on the three discs all stopped at the same point one after another. Jackpot! Out it poured – some fell on the floor. Mick went down and picked it up – I was handed a round serving tray, and we scooped the coins onto it. Bill Clark looked at me and was about to say, 'You're underage!' when I said, 'Have a drink on me, Bill.' That shut him up. We split the winnings, 5 quid each, finished our drinks, and said, 'Good night, brothers.'

We went outside and walked across Station Road to the Railway Staff Club. Mick went to the bar and ordered two pints of brown ale at 1 shilling a kick. I had a few tanners left in my pocket, and Mick came back to the fruit machine, put his tanner in and pulled the handle. Two cherries – a couple of bob. I put a tanner in. One bar, then another, and jackpot! Someone came over and started to accuse us of taking his place, and that the money was his. We had a word in his ear and told him piss off, or go away politely. Mick got a clean glass ashtray, raked the winnings into it and took it to the bar. We split the winnings again, then someone shouted out that we had won the jackpot in the Labour Club as well.

Mick asked for half bottle of Lamb's Navy Rum for half a dollar, two and a kick, and stuck it in his pocket. We had a good night – 4 quid each plus 5 quid, about six months' money to me.

We walked home and when we got near the fire station on Mereland Road across the road was Dr Green's surgery, Mick went around the back, cracked open the cap of the rum bottle and drank some, offering me a mouthful. It tasted quite nice, but the trouble was that I was now merry, as I never drank alcohol. We sank the bottle and threw it away empty, then both staggered home happy as two Tom Boys.

On Friday morning it was back to work. I walked down to the booking office to book on and collect my disc. 'Good night last night? I hear you won both jackpots. Lucky sod!' As I appeared around the cabin door I shouted a greeting, then someone shouted out, 'Jammy sod!' The word was out – it was all over the shed. I went into the shop and slid quietly into the locker room. 'You don't need to hide in here, jackpot king! Do you feel OK to work? How much did you have to drink?'

'Very little.'

'Right, come on then, Wobble.' My nickname was out, and I took it well.

The metal was inside Dave's tool box ready to make the inside callipers to the same design as before, only with thinner legs this time and the two ends bent inwards. I cut the first leg with a hacksaw, shaped it and finished it off with the fine half-round file, giving me the shape that was needed to work on the second leg. Placing it onto the flat metal, I scribed around it close to the edge of the metal so I didn't need to use all of it. Now I gently cut it with the hacksaw around the markings, leaving a small amount of free to play with. I then place the existing leg onto the frame and placed it in the vice with a cloth to stop it marking the metal and started the same procedure until both legs were the same.

Now I had to drill the legs with this big humongous belt-driven drilling machine that had gone out with the ark; it was OK for use on the steam engines. I turned on the motor and operated the controls to drive the drilling machine. I had to find a drill small enough with a taper sleeve to come down to

Pay day

the size I wanted, which was three-eighths of an inch. I clamped the legs into the huge vice, which took about an hour to set up. I pushed the pillar frame over the vice where the job was positioned and with the huge wheel manoeuvred the pillar taper sleeve down to the legs until the drill bit started to connect with the metal where I wanted to drill the hole. Still winding the huge wheel a little at a time, the drill went through the metal in one prize swoop.

I always felt as though I was in a First World War submarine pulling up the periscope as the drilling machine was withdrawn and I shut down the motor. The fun wasn't finished yet, as I had to remove the tapered sleeves – not easy if there was no tool on the end of the string supplied. The next best thing was a file, the tapered end put into the slot on the pillar drill and whacked with a hammer. If you were lucky you did not split the file and the taper dropped out.

Now I filed off the rough edges of the hole, and fitted in a nut and bolt slightly tighter than normal, rounded off the bolt head and the nut, and job done – Fanny's your aunt!

I cleaned all the pieces I had used and placed them back into the tool box of the mate I was working with. Dave called me over at break time, so I got my cup and RAF bag and we went into the cabin. Arthur came into the room and spoke to Dave, asked if he would go into his office after he was finished. The room was full of men: Ted reading the racing page, Frank drinking his tea with a slurp, Belgian Bob supping his strong brown tea (the spoon stood up in the middle with the amount of sugar in the cup), Jimmy Holmar talking about work with Matt Olgesby while he ate his grub of onion sarnies and drank his tea, Norman Brogden sitting quietly reading the paper, and Bill Clark smoking his Capstan cigarettes.

Belgian Bob suddenly said out of the blue, 'Had a good night last night, Pat?' All ears

No 6983 *Otterington Hall* in the passenger sidings some time in the 1960s. *Skip Morgan collection*

pricked up and papers were dropped onto the table with everyone trying to get a word into the uproar. 'You jammy sod!'

After grub was finished I was called into the shop by Dave. We had another job to do, and it would take us into tomorrow morning to get it finished. We were going to help two other men, Norman Brogden and his mate Bill Clark, to change the brake blocks on No 6983 *Otteringham Hall*. She would be in the shed soon, so we got a barrow and collected the new brake blokes from the corrugated shed outside the fitting shop – we needed six, three each side.

We loaded three at a time, as they were very heavy, pushing the two-wheeled barrow and dropping them at each wheel, then going back and getting three more. They were not made of a light material – they were rough and horrible to handle and blinking heavy, being made of cast iron, with nowhere to grip them. With the red board ready to hang on the tail lamp bracket, Dave had got the collection of tools ready, including a long crowbar and adjusting spanner with engine oil mixed with paraffin. I was sent to the stores for 2lb of cotton waste.

We saw the engine coming in on No 2 road. She had been outside in the parcel sidings pulling coaches out into the station ready for a passenger train when the engine failed on her brakes. What brake blocks? She had not much left on them, so Dave instructed the driver to come in steady, ready to stop him at the right moment when the con-rods on both sides were level as near as damn it. The red 'DO NOT MOVE' board was placed at the rear of the engine on the tender.

I was glad it wasn't the tender brake blocks, as they were a pig of a job to change, although the loco's were hard enough. I was now getting into the swing of the various jobs and interacting with the men and machines within the shed. The fire was still in the firebox and I could feel the warmth coming from the ashpan as the sweat ran down my neck, but the fire had to be kept in overnight. I was told to undo the two bolts that held each clamp to the pin and pour some oil over the area; I did this to all the bolts, leaving them on top of the frame. We had to block the engine wheels with wooden scotch blocks as the driver blew off the vacuum brakes. I was then asked to go under the engine with Dave and help undo the locking nuts on either side of the adjusting rods under the ashpan. With a wire brush I brushed off the muck accumulated over many years of running, from the sleepers and what was dropped from the trains' toilets, which covered the threads so that the nuts could be undone. They were spread with more oil over the threads, then we started to screw off the long adjusting nuts. But first we had to hammer them to shake them and release the dirt trapped in the nuts, so they became easier to move.

Now the fun started. Dave jammed the spike end of the crowbar into the frame as I pulled on a small crowfoot bar jammed behind the brake frame, heaving on the bar till the pin started to ease out of the brake block. I spread oil over the pin and Dave said to knock it back in a little and extract it again. It seemed easier this time and out it came. 'Two more to do, Wobble.'

We followed the same sequence on the middle rigid wheel, then the leading wheel, but this was a little harder. We both struggled and the sweat ran down our backs, but the pin started to move slightly as I knelt down on the concrete floor and hit it with a hammer to shake off the years of dirt and rubbish. Dave again told me to oil it and knock it back in, then pull it out, and it nearly fell out of its frame. The wheels, being 6 feet in diameter, gave us both a little bit extra height to fit the new blocks.

First I was asked to make sure the pins went back into the same holes. Out came a round file from Dave's sack and I cleaned out the holes on the brake blocks on the side we were working. If there was too much of a rough edge I used a hammer and chisel to knock away the rough excess. It sounded as though Norman was doing OK, for the time being anyway. I got into the pit now, and

Pay day

held the block on the wheel. God, they were bloody heavy and awkward! I lifted the block up to the frame till Dave shouted that he could see the hole appear in the frame and jammed the spike of the bar into it. At that moment I had muscles on my arms like I had never seen before! He got the small bar and gave it to me so I could stick it into the rear inside of the frame and lever the block up and position the holes' radius, as he pushed the pin into the hole in the frame and the hole in the brake block. He put some oil onto the pin and told me to move away as he hit it with a white metal hammer.

We did all the others in the same way, but I had to rest for a while as my arms ached. We then went back knocking the rest of the clamp brackets into position so we could fit the two locking bolts onto every frame and screw them down.

Dave went around the other side of the locomotive and asked how they were proceeding. They were OK. 'Well, give us a shout when you're ready and we can adjust the brakes. Come on, Wobble, collect up the tools.'

'What about the old blocks?'

'They said they'd finish off.'

But I wondered if they would.

We went off and had a cup of tea together, then I washed the tools up in paraffin and cotton waste left over from the job, and Dave put them away. 'How's your arms? he asked.

'Sore.'

'Go out the back and have a rest. We're finished today.'

As I sat watching the loop line and freight traffic, I heard a train going by outside near No 8 road, which was the Reading to Oxford loop, bypassing Didcot station. I ran out to watch what sort of locomotives they were and see what the freight train was carrying. Everything went by rail, and often there would be a long flatbed vehicles with a double set of wheels at each end. These were called 'Macaw' bogie bolsters, and there might be a whole train of them carrying heavy equipment. They were designed to carry steel girders, although a lot carried army vehicles, including tanks, and army trucks being carried on their own freight trains, and sometimes the locomotive was from the supply stores carrying their own livery.

If it was an oil train it would have a box van or the guard's van connected up behind the tender. The loaded crude oil tank wagons were always marshalled at the rear of the train as far away as possible from sparks from the locomotive.

The fullest freights were banana trains, extra-long goods trains with banana vans running regularly from London towards Birmingham, where Fyffe's had their own warehouse. Some other trains were the old 1950s red Underground trains being towed by a locomotive either for private companies to repair in a private yard or, if too old for repair, ending up on the Isle of Wight, replacing steam trains there.

The shop doors were closed at each end of the building as we had another engine inside to have its the rigid middle driving wheels removed. These took most of the strain at every revolution, which is why they frequently had to be rebushed and new white metal bearings fitted into the con-rods. This time it was No 6910 *Gossington Hall*. As we were taking our time, Dave came over to talk to Jimmy. I was back in the shop with Dave, as his mate had returned from holidays. I asked a question that had bothered me for several days. Had they ever seen a '61XX' pannier tank with a ball bearing…? I never even got to finish the sentence – they all jumped on me at once. 'Was that you?' cried Dave.

I had to shout, 'No, no, no! I was just asking…'

'We know what you asked. Again – was that you who did it?'

'No. I only brought it up as I was there when it happened, and I had a visit from the Old Bill.'

'Yes,' they confirmed. 'It took weeks to repair. The ball bearing was embedded in the tyre. Do you know who did it?

'Yes – he lived in Hagbourne Road. It happened on the Didcot, Newbury & Southampton line.'

We went back to doing what we all knew best – stripping the con-rods off the middle rigid driving wheel and with them the piston rod. The axle had to be removed and sent to Swindon in a wooden wagon nailed down with wooden blocks and iron linkages together with the axle boxes. However, the hard work had to be done first.

Everything had to be removed from both sides before getting to the axle. First we removed the outside con-rods to the crosshead on both sides, as the engine had to have every bush replaced with new white metal bushings, remoulded by us in the shop. The old bushing was removed by splitting the white metal bearing with a hammer and chisel, splitting it into two halves and pushing it out with a lump of wood manhandled with the white metal hammer. It was put on one side so it could be used to make another soft hammer at our leisure.

Jim got the forge raging with extra coal placed over the old coals; he put on the electric blower under the forge, spreading the fire. Now he placed two iron ladles in the middle of the flames. I was sent up to the stores for the white metal ingots, with his signed chitty and a two-wheeled barrow. There was no one at the stores counter, which made a change, so I handed over the chitty and was allowed inside the store room while the storeman loaded the barrow. I brought back six ingots, then had to go back for another six, leaving them by the forge. Looking at the ladles I saw two ingots had been laid inside the half cup, melting in the heat which by now was a red glow turning white hot. I went back to the stores and got the other six ingots, bringing them back to the forge. When I returned the ingots had become white-hot molten lava swimming around in both ladles. Jim had a long rod with a bend at the end, and I saw him scrape off dirty floating deposits from the white lava, throwing them into the fire. I was taught how to mix the moulding clay, not too wet, then I cleared a space on the forge corner.

White metal ingots.

Jim looked into the locker in the corner of the shop near the forge, taking from a shelf two iron metal templates of different radiuses. He walked over to the engine and slipped one over the connecting rod journals, then the other into the connecting rod where the bushing was originally right. He said, 'That's the connecting wheels journals sorted.'

Again using two more iron metal templates of different radiuses, he measured the main rigid wheel and con-rods the same way, as well as both crossheads. He laid the templates on the forge, knowing what had to be done, then bending down he pulled out from under the forge a solid piece of flat iron plate and laid it on the anvil. Taking the template for the connecting rod journals, he put one inside the other and measured the inner sizes with his callipers. Now the clay was ready, after I had mixed it to his spec, and he neatly started to put the clay around the base of the template. 'Right, Wobble, stand clear.'

With the ladle full to the brim, he put on a pair of leather gauntlet gloves, which had seen many a day, and, picking up the ladle, touching nothing around the area, he poured the molten lava into the gaps between the radius templates. He then replaced the ladle in the fire.

With the tongs he gripped the new ingot

and laid it in the ladle till it ran like molten lava. Using a flat iron bar. Jimmy scraped the waste off the top of the melted white metal, also to stop it blowing back at us. More clay was now required – 'Not too wet,' he said.

The templates had to be reused as the white metal was required for three bushes on one side of the loco and three the other side; we constantly felt like we were on a production line, just making bushings all day long. As soon as the first one had cooled down enough to fit over the journal, we had to make another five the same way. The rigid wheel bearings were slightly larger and heavier, so out came the templates, to be checked against the con-rods and journal. Again the templates were placed on the metal plate and the gap measured, clay placed around the base, then out came the ladles. He poured in the white metal and let it cool, then at just the right moment pushed it off the anvil. Two were required, and two crossheads also.

Then we measured the size of the journal on the axles of the wheel with the outside callipers, or odd legs. Jimmy had some iron radius round bushing spare in the lifting shop cupboard, especially made in Swindon for the work that had to be done. Soon it was all done, and we were both dry as a chip and slurping our tea.

After the tea we carried the con-rods away from the engine and got two huge 3-foot-square wooden blocks with years of oil ingrained in them. We laid the con-rods sideways across them, so they would be easier to work on, as we never had a hydraulic press to use, only a long threaded bolt with two nuts. Jim placed a radius 'top hat' cap on the outer part of the con-rod with the white metal bush in the middle, ready to enter the centre. With the threaded screw bolt through both bush and con-rod and the outer side of the con-rod, he put the other 'top hat' plate in place and screwed the nuts down. He positioned the bush, added some oil, and wound the nuts tight till the white metal bush pulled itself into the con-rod. All the others were done the same way. What strength that man had, and knowledge, as we went through the con-rods! Out came all sizes of squashed 'top hats', as we got on lifting and placing and rebushing till that side was done. Then we turned the con-rods upwards and removed the oil corks. Jimmy got his electric hand drill and, with the correct size of drill, he drilled out for all the oil holes.

Now we had to turn all the con-rods over, and with a ruler and pencil I marked the line across the oil hole to either side of the bush – this was for the oil run. With a small half-round file I started to gently file the white metal bush channel. Jimmy was quicker – he used the drill bit to scoop out his own channels where I had marked the line. Finally all the equipment used was replaced in the cupboard, but the ladles stayed out, hung up near the water trough.

Jim went out to the toilet and Norman Brogden appeared. He started to say something, got hold of a ladle and put it into the forge's fire. 'Here, Pat, see what I am doing?' He place a block of white metal bush into the ladle. I thought at that moment he wasn't half the ticket. He got the ladle with the lava and poured it into the water trough, with steam shooting upwards and outwards. He got burned, I giggled, and he shouted out a word that I was not familiar with in the English dictionary and was new to me. I replied, 'Oh dear, have you burned yourself?' He screamed and shot out of the shop. At that moment Jim came in.

'What's going on, Wobble?'

I had a big grin on my face and had to tell him.

'Silly bloody sod!' he replied.

Now we had to split the tender away from the engine. Jim was on the footplate with his crowfoot bar. He drove the end into the wooden floorboards and lifted two out of the metal frames. He showed me the pins that connected the tender – three in total, but the middle was the biggest. We lifted up the tender fallplate and he climbed down to go under the engine. He got a brush from the corner of his toolbox, handed it up to me and told me to sweep the footplate. After I'd put the broom back where it belonged, I went under the tender into the pit. This pit was spotless, as it was swept regularly. Keeping my head down, I saw Jimmy with his beret on his head. He had a torch in his hand and a pair of pliers, with which he squashed together the huge legs on the pins that held the tender's tow bars, and with a 45-degree rat's-tail bar he placed the hook into the eye of the pin and hit the end of the bar with a hammer, and the pin shot out onto the footplate. Later we retrieved it, and went onto the next pin, doing the same. I had to get the pit board under his feet as he could not hang on for much longer, so I legged it out of the pit, found it by the door and pulled it back under the pit, positioning it under his feet. 'Thanks, Pat.' He grinned and I heard something spoken in Welsh.

Now, standing on the board, he removed all the cotter pins and tapped his 2½lb hammer head upwards to see if the pins would move. They only moved very slightly, so he asked me get him a huge crowbar and go on top and put a rope through the eye of the pins.

'When I say pull, do it, and pull your guts out!'

I found the rope in his toolbox and handed the crowbar down to him through the gap.

'Ready?'

'Yes,' I shouted. I pulled on the outside pin with all my might and felt it shudder away up through the metal frame, then suddenly it shot out. Then we did the other side. Rope in ready, I took the strain as he hit the pin. It shot out onto the footplate. However, the middle one would be harder.

At that very moment the twins came into the shop.

'We could do with some help,' said Jimmy. 'Can you push the tender against the engine as I release the tender's brake?'

They got a crowbar with a fat lip on the base and placed it under a tender's wheels, one on either side, and started to take the strain. I held the rope, pulling with all my might. Jimmy hit the bar dead centre and up it came.

'Wobble, put some oil on the pin and knock it back down.'

I rubbed some oil around the pin from a driver's oilcan I found in the toolbox on the tender, and hammered the pin downwards with the pickaxe.

'Right, do it again.'

I pulled upwards, with the twins heaving on the tender's wheels. Jimmy hit the pin and this time it shot out clear onto the footplate. The tender brake was wound down tight.

It was getting close to home time now, so Jimmy told me to get washed up and get away home. 'You've done well today – earned your bread and butter today, boyo.'

'See you all in the morning,' I said.

9. First trip to Swindon

I called at Mick's on the way home and we talked about what was on tomorrow. I told him I had to work in the morning, and at midday I had to meet my Mum at Curry's to buy another bike as the old one had given up the ghost.

'Got any ideas about the weekend? What are we doing tonight?'

'We could go and have a have a pint in the White Hart and have a natter.'

'OK, see you about 6.30.'

I went home, had a bath, and scrubbed my hands and arms; the grease was ingrained in my palms and skin. After tea I got dressed and went downstairs wearing an open shirt with jeans and my two-tone winklepickers – casual wear – and Brylcreem in my hair. Tea was spuds, tinned tomatoes and fried bacon, with an egg cooked over the spuds – good food!

Mum asked me what I was doing that evening, and reminded me that my suit was coming tomorrow, so I had to be there. We arranged to meet at Curry's the following day at midday, then we could walk home together. I enjoyed walking with my Mum; she always told me to walk on the outside of her. 'That's the correct way to keep the women from getting hit by a car, Patrick. It's a gentleman's correct way to walk.'

Mick was ready when I knocked at his back door. Mrs Howard was standing at the sink and Jenny was wiping the dishes and putting them away.

As we walked he lit a ciggie and asked what was happening tomorrow.

'Well, there's only the pictures or pub. Maybe next week there's some talk about Pat O'Brien running a coach to Reading to take a few guys and girls to the Oxford Ballrooms.'

We decided to go to the pictures for a change – some sort of cowboy film was on. We agreed to meet again tomorrow.

On Saturday morning there was no lay in. I was up at the crack of dawn and when I got to the shed that morning the weather was starting to get better. I entered the shed, the engines stood around and men were working on them. Some cleaners were rubbing down the paintwork of the mainliners, and I noticed the smokebox area had been cleaned. When I went into the booking office Lenny Head was at the counter with my brass disc ready in his hand.

'Morning Pat. Are you ready for the morning's work?'

I called into the cabin and shouted 'Morning' as usual, then headed for the shop. Jim was up at the forge. 'Hello, boyo!'

I went to the forge. I was wearing my overalls and ready for work. He threw his tea dregs into the fire, and put his cup in his tool locker. I noticed that the pit was wet, and he said that they had drained the tender last night, so we only had to undo the services and get it pushed outside by the boilersmith's hut. But we had to get the engine's rigid axle out.

The tools were ready on the outside of the pit as we both went under the engine. We split the services – brake vacuum and water. I held the rubber pipe in its twisted wire casing and he undid the couplings – all was free now and the tender was ready to push out of the shop. The big wooden doors were open, so I got up on the tender's plate and unscrewed the handbrake while Jim placed a huge crowbar under the tender's wheel and started to lever the bar. I came down to the ground, got another bar and did the same. We both heaved on the crowbars and the tender started to roll away towards the buffer stops. I dropped my bar, climbed back up the tender's steps, got hold of the lever and wound the brakes on so the blocks just touched the wheels till it stopped dead.

We came back into the shop, after smelling the fresh air from outside the building, and with his tools ready in a sack Jimmy and I went underneath and he instructed me to unscrew the nuts on the spring hanger studs, but to only take the leading ones off. First I had to remove the split pins.

'Go outside, Pat, and near my toolbox you'll see two blocks of 4-inch-square metal bars. Put one on either side of the wheel we are working on.'

I did as I was instructed, then he put the crane motor on and put his hand inside, moving one of the cogs to give slow gearing. I waited for the chains to be lowered to the level we wanted them to be, then walked on the wooden board still laid across the pit and placed the hooks into the webbing. I held them in place as Jim operated the crane, and as soon as the hooks got hold of the engine's webbing and took the strain I let go and the crane started the lift, just high enough to put those solid metal blocks under the rigid driving wheel axle. Jim went one side and me the other side and we slid the metal blocks under either side of the tyre of the wheel; he then lowered the engine onto the blocks, with the hooks still tight in their holdings.

Now it was time to undo the spring hangers. We knocked out the pins that held them under the main bearing boxes on one side, then the other, and the weight was taken off the axle. We then undid the long stud bolts that held the springs, two on either side of the axle, and did the same on the other side. Getting out of the pit, the crane was put into operation again, and as the engine went up on the chains suddenly with a crash the springs fell into the pit. Now the engine was lowered again onto the rails, with the hooks still tight.

The last job, and the worst, was to remove the keeper plates under the axle boxes, fixed to the engine's frame – sweat was now dripping and running down my back like rivers of black coal. Holding the bolt head between the frame and axle, and standing up on top of the axle, Jimmy started to undo the nuts with his huge spanner. Then we moved onto the other one; I slipped over the axle and held the head as he undid the nut, then the same with the last one.

'Right, let's get out and get this engine sorted.'

For the last bit he operated the crane and all the frame and other wheels went upwards, leaving the rigid wheel on the rail, high enough to push out. Then he lowered the frame again. But it always amazed me that when the engine was in the air the bogie's leading wheels were the only wheels still on the rail – I wished I'd had a camera.

We now pulled the pulley block and chain crane over, with its lifting bar still attached from the last time, and connected it up. I operated the chain and lifted the rigid wheel axle off the rails and over onto the wooden-blocked floor, leaving it still on the hook. Then we unhooked the wheels and scotched them. The bottom plates had to be removed on either side to allow the top bearings to fall out into the pit.

It was now midday, so Jim said, 'You'd better get off home, Wobble. See you Monday. Have a good weekend.'

'You too, mate.'

I had a quick wash in paraffin then washed my arms and hands in Lifebuoy soap together with my face. I was as black as the ace of spades. Putting my disc into the Time Office, I legged it up through the station. I had to walk quickly to meet Mum at Curry's, running through Edinburgh Drive and up the hill. We picked out a new bike with drop handlebars, derailleur gears and my favourite colours of black and yellow. Mum signed the papers and I had to pay the shop 3 bob a month; that was going to be easy. At least I'd got wheels now.

Mum and I then walked towards North Hagbourne and went to Mr Dale's shop as I wanted a billycan. They seemed to be the new thing in the 1960s. I bought one for a bob, so I had a good day. On the way home I bought Mum an ice cream in a tub, and I had a wafer. The shopkeeper placed one wafer inside a square box, then scraped the ice cream into the centre of the box like a brick and placed the other wafer over the top

First trip to Swindon

and handed it to me. Then we walked home together, me pushing my new bike.

The tallyman came from Reading that afternoon so I had to try on my new Italian three-piece suit; he waited while I went upstairs to change into it. Mum was shocked at the sight of me when I came down. I was as skinny as a rake and had lost more weight, so he took the sizes and measured me again. He asked Mum what she would like to do. She looked at me in amazement and said, 'We'll have it and I'll pay for it for you, Patrick.' I thanked her.

I looked the business – suave, after wearing blue jeans and a shirt. Now all I had to do was shine my winklepickers. Later that evening Mick and I went to the pictures and sat in the one and a kick on the left-hand side with all the yobs. As we got into the film, an usherette came down the carpeted walkway with someone and flashed her touch around the yobs. Someone said, 'That's him,' pointing at me. The usherette asked me if I could come out into the foyer. I was surprised, and all the Didcot boys shouted, 'Will I do? Can I come as well?'

As I walked towards the foyer a girl stood in front of me and said that I had not been at the meeting place outside the pictures. I looked in amazement as she introduced herself as Annie. I was about to say my name, but she said it was OK: 'I know your name – it's Pat Kelly.' She made arrangements for next week. I said, 'OK but Friday night might be better.'

She reached up and kissed me on the cheek, then ran off home and I said to bring a friend for my mate. I went back to the crowd sitting in the cheap seats.

Later Mick and I went over to Goodenough's mobile fish bar opposite the Coronet's front doors across the road and had a portion of chips with a huge fish each, and bags of old batter, with vinegar and salt twice, so it ran out of the newspaper. I am sure Mr Goodenough used beef fat instead of lard as the taste of the fish and chips was great. As we walked home eating our food I said about the two girls we were meeting at the flicks about 7.00pm. We said our goodnights, then arranged to meet tomorrow at Mick's at about 10.30 for a coffee.

We met as planned next morning at my 'second home', as I partially lived here. I only slept at my home up the road. We were mates for many years.

There was talk on the railway about a coach going to Reading on a Saturday night, picking up at the Post Office, as there was nothing different to do in Didcot at weekends. It was a dead boring place to be.

Until Pat O'Brien and his holiday company with his coaches took people away on their holidays, he came up with the brilliant idea of running to the Oxford Ballrooms at Reading on Saturday nights only, to help out the young people with some live music and big bands, and he arranged everything. All the firemen in their best suits were there, and girls would meet at Didcot Post Office and catch O'Brien's coach, there and back for the small fee of half a dollar. This went on for a few years every Saturday. In the ballrooms there was jive, swing, waltzing, something for everybody. We paid the driver as we got on the coach, and seeing that I never had a girl with me I sat in the front 'riding shotgun' with the driver, in my new Italian suit and waistcoat – I scrubbed up quite well! As we were going along the girls would sing a rock and roll song, then we lads would sing the other lines of the song and we all joined in together, the coach erupting into laughter. The dance hall had some good drinking bars, too, so we had a drink or two, or more, but all the party had to remember the correct time to get back on the coach, which sat in the alleyway where the driver had dropped us all – it was a long walk back to Didcot! A load of girls and boys who could not hold their drink stayed on the coach. It opened my eyes when I saw the hanky-panky going on on the back seat when I had to bring Mick's sister Jenny back to the coach, as she was out of her mind with booze! Mick asked me to look after her while he went back to have a good time with Diane Washington of Mereland Road, the one who had chucked Mick in after the pictures.

We used to go out dancing every Saturday night, until we found the village hop tours supplied by Pat O'Brien to Benson one night, with the 'two hombres' side by side to see who could pick the best girl. This time I won, and Mick drew the short straw. My girl was game, but he wasn't so lucky that night; mind, she was a smasher and good looking with blonde hair – a beauty.

*

My first few weeks had gone by quite quickly, but with the end of Saturday and Sunday it was back to work on Monday. As I came into the station area I saw two drivers getting into the back of a Swanborough taxi. They were going to work in Wallingford on the 'bunk' branch line to Cholsey & Moulsford station on the main line in Berkshire, which saw some stopping trains covering Reading and all stations to London, and the same the other way to Didcot, Oxford and Birmingham, or Swindon, Bath and Bristol Temple Meads. You had to cross the main line on the level, with a porter escort. When the locomen's shift was over they came back to the station at Didcot and went down to the shed Time Office to sign off.

I wondered if No 6910 *Gossington Hall* would still be there where we had left off on Saturday morning. Fresh now, it was back to the grindstone, riding through the undercroft on my new black and yellow bike. I rode into the shed area and placed my racer in the bike stops under the bike sheds – it put the rest of the bikes to shame! I walked across the sleepers to the shedmaster's office and, looking at the clock, saw I had 10 minutes to walk in and collect my disc, and see what was in the shed. Standing outside at the front, I was nosey that way, as I really enjoyed what was happening in my career, and took note of the engines standing outside and in. Sometimes when rain hit the tops of the boilers, little spits of steam jumped up into the air – it was a joy to stand and watch before going into the dark shed.

Same routine: call in to the cabin to see who was on shift, walk down to the shop with my new billycan in my bag and my *Daily Sketch*, place my bag inside the locker and wander up to the forge ready to start work. Arthur Brinkley approached me to have a chat.

'Let's go somewhere quiet, Pat, in my office.'

God, I always got the feeling I was in for a right bollocking from management, but I had done nothing, anyway. Arthur only wanted to know how things were progressing and was the work too heavy for me every day, was I fitting in with the running and maintenance crews, and had I had any trouble with any of the men. My reply was, 'No, but have they with me?' He said that sometimes he would like me to go with some of the men when their mates took off on their holiday leave. Then I twigged it. I bet Jim's on holiday next week. I wasn't far wrong, for he was finishing Friday evening for a week in Monmouth, South Wales, with the family.

'So, after this next week I would like you to start with Jim Holmar, as Matt is on leave. You will be on the front of the shed.'

I agreed, he thanked me for my time, I got up from the chair and walked past Sam Morgan, who had his head down doing brown service sheets. We exchanged greetings and I proceeded out of the office towards the shop.

Sam lived three doors from away from the Kelly family in Sinodun Road and he was very quiet man at home, but at work, my God, he put me to shame, and always talked about how big his manhood was, shaped like a banana bent upright. I was a virgin when I started work, and the things that came out of those men's mouths! But that's what makes the world go around. One other thing about Sam – he could knock off the table eight half-crowns in a line with his manhood, and he bet anyone they couldn't beat them. I saw him one day with his penis out of his trousers and, with the eight half-crowns in one straight line on the mess room table,

First trip to Swindon

he proved what he had said was true, and boasted about doing it. The other men, with their manhoods out, bet with loads of green pound notes in a heap with the fitting staff to see if they could beat him. I had never seen so many two-and-a-kicks in one go; I managed four, someone else did six. These guys were married, while I was single, but there was no hiding behind the walls to do what they did.

I went back into the shop after washing my hands in the ceramic sink and giggled, shaking my head at the same time. As I walked over to Jim he told me he was on leave next week. 'That's why we must get this engine out and have another come in to start a small job.'

We were waiting for the shed tankie to enter the shed to remove *Gossington Hall* outside to No 6 road to be stored until the spares came in. Waiting for the tankie everything changed, as into the shop came a single-car diesel unit with Tommy Edwards driving. Hearing the roar of the diesel, it sounded very nice; the same AEC engines were made at Slough for red buses. I went there in 1963 from Reading Diesel Depot to collect one with a Reading driver, and even saw the wet skid patch – a brilliant day out for BR!

Tommy Edwards shut down the engine because of the fumes, and Norman Brogden was summoned to go to the fitting shop. Tommy said he had heard something rattle underneath when picking up passengers in Newbury to run down to Didcot on the Didcot, Newbury & Southampton branch. Jim and I stood while Brogden went underneath. I was asked to go under as well, which I was keen to do, and he showed me the engine and exhaust system with the gearing and drive. He was the only person qualified to work on these engines and cars. All he said to Tommy was that the exhaust was rattling. They were a new thing for Didcot drivers to play with, and when their shift came they would hear the slightest noise and report it, being new toys.

The diesel then started up with a bark from the exhaust – a brilliant sound! I wished I could work on these engines. Then it went out as quiet as a mouse. All the shed staff stopped what they were doing and watched it leave, driving back to the station.

Jim told me what was going to happen, and at that precise moment in came Arthur with his big feet striding across the wooden flooring blocks straight to where we both stood.

'Pat, tomorrow morning can you catch the train at 7 o'clock from No 3 platform to Swindon and go to the works stores? I understand that when you come out of the station you turn right and walk straight down the road, keeping the railway line to your right. You will come to a tunnel on the right – walk through there and ask someone to direct you to the Work Stores Department.

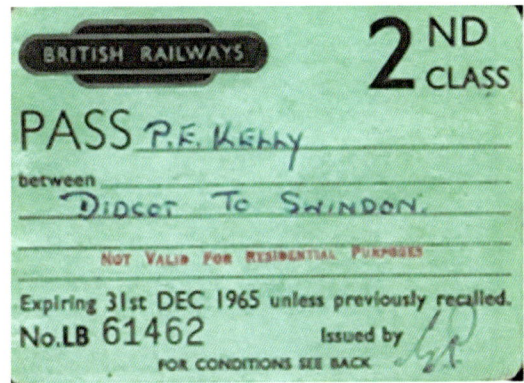

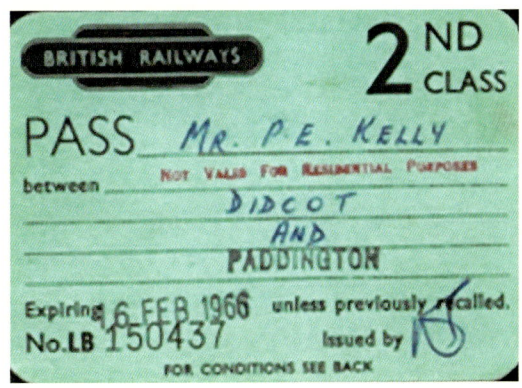

Workmen's six-monthly passes enabling me to travel for work purposes from Didcot to Swindon and Paddington.

Here is the information and address on the envelope, and all the papers you will need for the stores request are inside. Take some food with you as you could be out all day. Here is a free workman's pass to travel.'

It was a travel permit. I had never seen one of these, but there was a lot I was to see in the years that followed.

At dinnertime I went and handed in my disc, and walked across the marshalling yard while it was quiet, taking my time to keep a lookout and stepping over the points. When I came to the main lines out from the station I stood and looked at what trains were in the vicinity. As I stepped over the rails I was still very scared and moved quickly across to the path near the Provender ponds, which fed the water columns around the Didcot complex; it was pumped from the pumping station, a small brick building near the West Curve.

After a year of cleaning engines some young lads were promoted to fireman. This was mainly pilot work and shunting at Didcot. There were four tankies in the depot, two for the Army, and three more for the Milton RAF depot, all fitted with spark arresters or 'busbys' over the chimney. There were also two pilots at Moreton cutting, and two in the 'Dardanelles' and Provender Stores, doing shunting duties all day long. There was also a Culham pilot, No 1502, a short-wheelbase engine that could negotiate the sharpest bends, and used to shunt into the siding at Culham yard to the RAF, which was a Supermarine Spitfire squadron.

Having watched the activity I then walked around to the Provender Stores, and called in to see Mick, who worked in the Parcels section. He introduced me to the men on the platform, and as I strolled along the wooden platform he showed me the great green crane that stood at the end of the adjoining platform, and explained to me what it had been used for in the old days. This was the end of the line for Isambard Kingdom Brunel's 'broad gauge', introduced in 1838 with a gauge of 7ft 0¼in, and the track on the opposite side of the platform was the 'standard gauge' of 4ft 8½in. Everything had to be transferred for onward travel to Oxford and beyond. He said that as the old wooden carriages came into the shed, anyone too big to walk about would sit in a lifting frame and the crane would lift them out of the seating compartment high enough to clear any object that might have been in the way. The crane was then rotated to the standard-gauge line, and the person was slowly lowered into his or her seat.

We both spoke about what was on tonight. Mick said, 'I have to ask you something, but not here, as there are too many ears twitching.'

'See you about 7 then, OK?'

I walked back the same way, watching for any main-line diesel multiple unit (DMU) passenger trains. As I crossed into the main marshalling yard, my eyes were everywhere and my ears as well, as I did not want to be crushed in the yard, where the tracks seemed to be closer than normal. Some years later, in 1964, I nearly got killed in the 'Dardanelles', and even today I still have dreadful nightmares.

I got back in time to collect my disc from the Time Office, where I had left it on the counter, and as I went to pick it up a hand came out from nowhere and frightened me to death. I shouted out, but then heard a laugh – it was Stan Barten playing the fool.

As I proceeded down to the shop I met Jim.

'Where have you been, boy?'

'Been to see my mate over at the Provender in the Parcels Depot.'

'Which way did you go?'

'The safe way,' I lied.

'Arthur would like to see you in his office, about tomorrow, and give you some paperwork or something.'

I went back to the office, knocked on the foreman's door, then wandered into the abyss! I found Sam Morgan at his desk.

'Hello, big boy,' I said, grinning. 'They should name you donkey.'

He gave me a sly look. Arthur sat at his desk attempting to take control of his baccy

First trip to Swindon

tin, making roll-ups. He wet the fag paper and placed it within the machine with two fingers of Virginia tobacco; he then laid across it the fag paper, closed the lid and the rollers inside did the rest – out popped a roll-up. Now he was ready to speak to me.

'Here's your workman's pass, and you've got the paperwork. Go directly to Swindon – I've given you directions.'

'OK, Arthur, I'll find my way.'

'What are you doing now, besides standing here?'

I said, 'Are you finished with me, as I think Jim has got something to get on with.'

'Wait a minute. You can do me a great favour.' Here we go I thought. He continued, 'I'm always after someone to take measurements of the tyres and record them on a brown card, with the engine number and the shed's identification – like 81E is our shed, on the small oval plate under the smokebox door. Get Jim to show you how it works.'

I was pleased to be trusted, and Arthur said he would tell me when I would be doing this job.

When I went back into the shop, I asked Jim to explain how to take the measurements of wear on the tyres. He showed me the correct way, and said, 'Before you start any job always put a notice board on the engine. In that way someone will know that the engine is being worked on. Come on, I'll show you outside in the shed.'

We ventured out and saw an engine being worked on, so he took me under it. He placed the gauge inside the wheel with the left-hand edge looped over the wheel's flange, and the outer oval inside the wheel, measuring the depth of the tyre. Although still only a fitter's boy, I was proud to be trusted and happy with what I was doing and the men I was working with – better than walking the streets looking for a job.

*

On Friday morning I was up early, had a good breakfast, got out the bike from the shed and rode down the market to say hello at Les Gibbss's fruit and vegetable stall. Gibby threw an apple my way and I caught it like a professional baseball player. 'Cheers, mucker!' Now I had to speed down Station Road at a great rate of knots. I entered the station and the Parcels Department was open. I asked Ernie Alder if I could leave my bike there. I leapt up the concrete steps towards Platform 3 to catch the 7.00am stopper to Swindon; this was a workmen's train, and I had my workmen's free pass and paperwork in a BR sleeve stuffed inside my RAF bag. I found a carriage with no one in and sat down, looking out of the window. I felt as though I was going on holiday – all I needed was an ice cream and my bucket and spade.

Some young Didcot firemen who did a few turns to Newbury and Winchester also had the small passenger job on the 7 o'clock to Swindon, stopping at all stations and halts. Three bands of Didcot men were known as 'Hagbourne men', because North Hagbourne was the heart of Didcot in the early days. When joining, if you were lucky you would still get an overall jacket with a 'GWR' emblem on it, or still get cleaners' overalls with the 'GWR' emblem on the lapels; that was the only pair of overalls that was ever issued.

We stopped at every station to Swindon, picking up and dropping off passengers. The journey only took 35 to 40 minutes. Some people wanted to sit with me and chat, but all I wanted was to look out at the passing greenery and cows in the fields. I even remember seeing the fuselage of a USAAF plane in a field near Shrivenham used as a shed; the markings could still be seen.

So here I was in Swindon for the first time. I did as I was told: walked out of the station, turned right and walked down the road. As I got nearer I noticed all the motorbikes and sidecars stacked along the side of the road – I must be near, I thought. Arriving at the Works I walked through the tunnel entrance. A train passed overhead, building up to one mighty continuous roar as the engine pounded by. Beyond the tunnel there was so much to see, and so much going on. There were three-wheeled Scammell lorries pulling trailers loaded with stores. I had to keep an eye on where I was going, with all the high offices around the perimeter. I had to be near the office, the one I was after, then I saw someone come out of an office door. I asked for the Stores Ordering Department, showing my paperwork. He pointed across to a door; all the buildings looked the same, but if I got lost, I could come back again.

I found the door, then had to walk up some stairs. At the top was the magic sign, 'Stores Department for Enparts'. Well, I had cracked it – I was here. I knocked on the door and someone came and opened it. I went as red as a beetroot from shyness. The whole department was full of young, good-looking girls typing; when they saw me they started grinning, and I went quiet. They all looked at me, and bang beetroot shyness came over me. I showed the paperwork to a manager, and he pointed to an office.

'In there.' He was so rude.

I knocked at the door, and a person opened it. 'Come in,' he said. 'How can I help you?'

I explained where I had come from.

'Sit down there and we will sort you out. Would you like a cup of tea?'

'Yes please.' I was gasping and dry as a chip!

He took the paperwork and sorted through it, organising everything. He asked my name.

'OK, Pat, we will send it out on Enparts in a special box wagon for tomorrow morning. The driver can shunt it off the rear of the Enparts train at the station at 6.00am, but for now you can return to the station with a sack of light spares if you want.'

'Yes, I might as well.'

'You've not been here before?' I shook my head. 'OK, come with me – I need to get out of this office and breathe some fresh air.'

He took me down the back of the works where the steam hammer was situated and pointed to where it stood.

'We will stay here outside.' Suddenly a loud noise rattled the building.

'Blinking hell!' I said. 'What's that? I've never seen one before.'

He opened the door and showed me. 'Let's get out before it comes back down.'

The men inside the building beckoned him to stay and chat, but he said, 'Come on, run for it.'

We legged it out of the area – I didn't want to wait and be deaf for the rest of my life.

As we walked through a lot of stores, men started to joke with my guide. He explained that he had started as a boy working in the stores areas, and now he was in charge of these men, and the banter was real. He came to another store area and introduced me to the storeman. He offered me a cup of tea. 'Yes, please.'

The manager said, 'Look after Pat.' As he went back to his office I thanked him, and he said, 'I will more than likely see you again, Pat. Stay here – these men will get your order ready and then direct you to a quicker way to the station. But be careful when you cross the rails near the station as the trains stop for no man!'

I opened my bag and had a sarnie with the tea the storeman made. He was chattering to me, and said that he was off to Devon on Saturday and did I know what train he should catch at Reading, and when he had to change. Did he think I was a walking timetable for trains or something? I apologised, explaining that I knew nothing about travelling to places, as this was my first trip out of Didcot.

He went off and collected my order and put it into a sack. I asked him how I should get back to the station. He said to turn left and stay on the tarmac road, then I would see the station. I did as I was told, taking my time to get to the station and head home. Suddenly a scream came from a pit, and I saw a crowd of men rushing to the area

First trip to Swindon

where there was a crane and chains hung onto a coach. A man shot by me and ran, screaming down the tarmac road towards the offices. I went to see what was happening. Some men were trying to help underneath the coach, and I could see what had happened. A man was trapped between the coach's underframe and a steel trestle, and the poor man lay dead. However, all the men rushed to help and to get the crane working, lowering the chains and placing the hooks into the lifting eyes, then a works ambulance came into view. At that moment I felt tears rolling down my face – I had to leave the area quickly.

I came to the rail sleeper crossing and waved to the signalman to see if I could cross. He shouted that all was clear, I put up my hand to thank him and walked to the station platform. I looked back, and because I was slightly higher now I could see the ambulancemen remove the poor man from the area on a stretcher, covered over and in a body bag.

The next train to Didcot came in just as a porter asked me what was happening over there. I told him, and he felt sick. I got into the coach – first stop home. Trains to Didcot were very few and far between – every 2 hours for a stopping train. I made it back at 4 o'clock. I walked down to the shed and straight into Arthur's office. There I handed over my free pass and the sack of items. I explained that the Swindon Stores Department had asked if it would be possible to take the box van off the Enparts stores train. It would be the last van; could the Didcot 'fly' shunt it down into the fitting shop directly from the station at 6 next morning to be unloaded? Then ring him to say that they have done the deed – ask for Phillip, as that was the manager's name.

Jim was nearly finished as he was on leave in Monmouth on Saturday till the following Monday week. 'Get off home – see you in the morning, Pat.'

'Thank you,' I said. 'Actually you don't look well,' I told him.

Arthur went to the Time Office and said I could go home, and they signed me out for 5.30pm. I walked up the cinder path to the sleeper crossing and down the concrete steps towards the Parcels Department, but I had a shock as the door was closed, and no one was about, not even Ernie Alder. I went around the back and found several bikes; mine was on the top, so I pushed it out into the entrance and scooted along on the pedal, then my leg went over the crossbar and I was away home.

10. Front of shed

When I got to Mick's he was indoors. I knocked at the back door.

'Are we OK for the pictures tonight?' he asked, then added, 'While you're here can we have a word?'

He told me he was a diabetic, and had to inject himself every day. He asked me to carry some sugar knobs in my pocket, in a brown paper bag wrapped up tight. He carried them with him with a Mars bar as well, and when he was hungry he had a bite out of it. 'What are you doing Saturday afternoon?' he asked. 'Can you give me and Pete Brown a hand, say 1.30. We'll pick you up at your house, OK? It might turn out to need finishing off on Sunday as well – I'll tell you tomorrow. But we're going to the flicks tonight – I've got two nice girls to meet. See you about 6.30.'

'OK, are we wearing suits?'

'Let's – why not?'

I called for Mick as planned and we walked to the flicks. I said, 'Do like my suit? Three bob a week on the knock – Mum's paying for it.'

'You scrub up quite well,' he said.

We headed for the pictures and waiting for us were the two girls, all done up like a dogs' dinners – but good-looking as well.

'What seats are we going in?'

'One and a tanners.'

We were the big-time spenders, down where we always sat on the left with the yobs of Didcot – but this was Friday and quiet, so we had the left side to ourselves.

Mick was away with his bird walking down to the seating area. I went into the next row behind him. All anyone could see was two couples sitting as a bunch of four low in the seats. While the picture was showing I sat there cool, then I sort of slipped my arm around the girl's head and she came closer to me, quick off the mark – no good hanging about, is there?

'What's your name?'

'Annie.'

The place was in darkness and I wanted to touch her red lips with my mouth. Well, we hit it off. She was a smashing girl with a cracking figure and long black hair down to her waist. When the film was over we went over to the small green parkland opposite the Coronet picture house and sat on the metal bench. Mick was over by the trees, and we were all kissing and cuddling. Suddenly there was a scream from Mick's end. It was a cold evening, and her hands were cold, so Mick undid his flies and said, 'Stick your hands in there – that will keep them warm.' But she walked over to her mate and said, 'I'm going home – are you coming?' and they both went off.

But Annie said, 'Can I see you again? Where did you work?'

'In the railway shed, and Mick's in the Parcels Depot.'

Mick told me what he had done, and I laughed my head off. 'You never change, do you? Let's go home.'

'See you tomorrow, Pat – 1.30.'

Next day I went into work and Jim had left his toolbox key with me so I could wash his tools with cotton waste and clean paraffin I collected from the stores with a chitty he had signed before leaving the day before. I had to be gone at noon.

As arranged, the station pilot shunted in the box wagon into the shop, then the fireman uncoupled and drew back out to the station. Dave said, 'Give us a hand, Pat.' We opened the big wooden van doors, and had the paperwork in a folder ready for Arthur. We pulled around the pulley chain to lift out a set of axle boxes and a rigid axle, these being the spares that I had gone up to Swindon for the previous day. We lifted out the bearing boxes and laid them on the floor away from a walkway. The rigid driving wheels then had to come out, but much more slowly, an inch at a time. Dave slung a rope around the wheel and anchored it to the wagon's frame. We kept out the way as

I lifted it up, and it went out of the wooden doors like a rocket. Suddenly the rope took the slack and it started to twirl round, then I let it down onto the ground and we secured it. All the sacks were lifted out and put next to the wheels, ready for Jim when he came back off his much-needed holiday.

I finished washing the tools with the clean paraffin and cotton waste, and Dave opened his toolbox and I washed his tools as well to help out. It was getting near the tea break so I made a welcome cup of tea near the forge. Arthur came into the shop and Dave handed over the paperwork. He then asked about Monday, and who I would be working with

'Pat's working with Jim Holmar on the front of the shed.'

'Pity,' he said, 'as I could have had him with me.'

'Sorry,' said Arthur, 'but he has to be with everyone each week to get familiar with the way they work.'

Then he mentioned to Dave about the man I had seen yesterday when walking back towards Swindon station, and the crowd of men helping with a crane to get the coach onto the trestles. 'He saw a man cut in half – be gentle with him, please.'

Twelve noon came and I got washed up and rushed out, placing my disc on the timekeeper's desk and flying out to get my bike. I raced up the cinder path, through the undercroft into the fresh air and away home.

No more than 15 minutes later I was home. Mum had bacon and eggs in the oven, and on the table a plate of bread and butter slices. I poured some HP brown sauce over the plate of food, and it wasn't long before I was wiping the plate clean with the last piece of bread.

'What's on today?' asked Mum.

'I'm working with Mick and Pete Brown.'

Pete drove a lorry, and they earned a few bob working together during the week whenever the railway driver required help delivering parcels to houses and businesses. The Parcels Depot had a contract once a year to move some bales of Irish peat from Upton station to Johnson Houghton Horseracing Stables at Blewbury, on the Downs. In the sidings at Upton there would be two box vans full of peat. Pete drove the BR Bedford parcels lorry and trailer so we would load and deliver it all day long.

'Be careful and have a good day.'

'Yes Mum – and I'm at it tomorrow as well.'

'Are you out tonight?'

'Yes – Mick and I will be going to Reading dancing at the Oxford Ballrooms.'

She shook her head. 'Be careful – don't burn the candle at both ends, son, or you'll do yourself in.'

I heard the lorry's horn outside in the road, so said goodbye to Mum.

'Enjoy yourself, Patrick!' My Mum always called me by my full first name.

I climbed into the cab, Pete and I shook hands and exchanged pleasantries, then he told me what the Department had set up on Friday morning, with No 2201 working a goods train of mixed wagons up the Newbury branch, stopping at Upton yard first. The two special deliveries for the stables were a priority, and the two box vans had been on the rear of an express passenger train from Ireland. The 'fly' engine had been waiting for the train to stop at Didcot, and the vans were uncoupled with the help of Harry Andrews, Bert Betteridge with Albert Smith, together with Mr Goodall – these men were always together on the station. They then helped to shunt them back into the main marshalling yard, where they were incorporated in a mixed goods train up the DN&S line, stopping at all stations to shunt full wagons in and remove empty wagons out, and bring everything back to Didcot marshalling yard.

We drove to Upton station, and Pete said that when he was a boy he remembered that the GWR parcels service was a horse and cart. Then the Provender Stores were full of horse feed to feed all the 4,000 horses in that department. He said they had their own stables, and they used the horses to move good trains in the yards, and even on the branch line. He said he used to drive those horses and carts for the Department, collecting around the vicinity of Didcot when it was still a large village, not quite a town yet.

When we got to Upton station Pete reversed onto one of the vans, leaving enough space for Mick to get the box van's doors open. I jumped out as well, then we both sorted out the doors. I gave my mate a lift up into the wagon, then Pete reversed with the lip of the lorry just touching the wagon. We pulled up the concertina roller door of the BR trailer, and inside was a two-wheeled barrow, a load of sacks, a fork and spade, and a good heavy brush – everything on hand and in its place. I looked at the delivery note on the side of the railway wagon and saw from the ticket that it had come from Southern Ireland direct.

We emptied one van, which was filled to the top with sacks of peat, and made several runs to Blewbury. It was around 3 miles away, and as we passed through the village of Blewbury I noticed the village's garage on the corner. 'We'll stop for some refreshments coming back.'

Pete put the lorry into low gear and trundled around the corner, indicating the hill that we had to tackle. It looked like 1 in 6, and we went straight up as slow as the gearbox allowed. Mick and I could have got out and walked faster. However, we reached the top and I saw the stables spreading all around. Pete shunted the lorry into the yard. The owner said, 'OK, you know where to put it, Mr Brown.'

We unloaded the trailer, Pete in the back and Mick and I moving the sacks and stacking them undercover in a barn. It was either used for the racehorses to bed down on, or spread over the trotting track. We had just finished the first load when Mrs Houghton came out with a tray of fruit drinks. We were gasping – as dry as a chip!

Thanking her for her hospitality, we pulled up the trailer's tailgate, then the three of us got back in the cab and drove back to the sidings. Four trips, and we had finished for the day. It was about 4 o'clock, and when I was dropped off at home we made arrangements for the following day. Meanwhile, Mick and I arranged to meet later as we were going to Reading.

That evening Pat O'Brien's coach was waiting outside the Post Office. I had a dollar for the two of us in my pocket next to the brown paper bag with the sugar knobs in – I ate the Mars bar as I was hungry! Mick stood next to me in the queue – all the railway boys got on first with their girlfriends paying as they went. I think we were the only ones that stepped up into the coach to pay the driver on our own. We found some seats and Mick looked out the window hoping to see Diane. Then the driver closed the bus's door and we were on our way. I shouted, 'Are we there yet, Dad?' and the whole coach erupted in laughter – that broke the ice. We had to travel around 18 miles to Reading, so I got my head down and crashed fast asleep.

Mick was also dead to the world when we reached our destination, and came round, rubbing his eyes like a young boy with his index fingers, both eyes together.

'Come on,' I said, 'let's go and have a good time.'

He said, 'Why not go into the ballroom for a few moments and see if we can do a waltz?'

We went to the bar and ordered two pints of bitter. Looking across the dance hall we noticed two girls sitting by themselves. We drank the beer and Mick said, 'Come on, let's see if they want to dance.'

As we walked across the dance hall, Mick said, 'She's mine.'

'OK, you win.'

We asked in tandem if they would like a dance. Both girls got up, one for Mick and one for me. The live band started up a waltz, so I held the girl and put my arm straight out. She connected, but as I started to waltz I kept treading on her feet. She wasn't that bad looking, I would say about 22 years old. After the dance we all sat down and chatted, then Mick wandered off one way and I went the other. We kissed and cuddled, then went back inside and just talked about life in general. It was quite a while before the other two appeared, all over each other.

The evening went quickly and we had to be back on the coach for home. The girl I was with said, 'Are you here next week?'

'Yep, could be.'

She gave me a kiss, and I got on the coach. Mick came running towards the coach and got on – he was only half dressed. We waved at them, then we drove away. Quietly I said, 'How did you get on?'

'She had my trousers off and was gagging for it.' I bet his sugar levels shot through the floor!

We got off the coach, shouted goodnight to all, and walked up the street and home.

On Sunday morning, a bit bleary-eyed, I was standing by our gate in Sinodun Road, waiting for Pete. The lorry arrived, I got the door open and said, 'Where's Mick?'

'We'll pick him up as we drive down near his house. As we got closer Pete blasted the horn, and out came Mick, his hair all over the place – the poor boy was still asleep! He got in, we all said 'Good morning', then he put his head on my shoulder and we never heard a sound from him till we got to Upton.

It was the same routine as the previous day, and we worked flat out and got cleared by dinnertime. Both box vans had 'MTY' – 'empty' –written across their doors in large chalk letters. I filled about six broken sacks with loose peat material, and when I was dropped off at home the boys helped me unload them into the shed. Pete slipped me a 10 bob note and thanked me. 'OK for the same next week, Pat? Same time pick-up?

'Yes please!'

I walked in and Mum was laying the dinner on the table – a good Sunday roast. I had timed it right, as I was starving and could have eaten a scabby cat! I washed my hands and sat down for dinner with Mum, Dad and Dick – it was a long time since we had sat down together, since I'd started work.

After dinner I had a bath and washed my hair, put on some clean jeans and a shirt, and told Mum I was going for a walk up the park, taking my bike.

As I rode away from Park Road into Norreys Road, I remembered that most of the enginemen lived up here – the likes of Bert Paice, the shed fitter, Mel Davies, a driver, and Charlie Clanfield, who was part of the engine crew but came over to the fitting side later; his son John was an apprentice fitter at Oxford, and they all lived in the same close. Then sitting on a wall I saw her – Annie. She got up and ran into her parents' house, but as I came to a stop and got off my bike she wandered back out.

'Shall we go for a walk? I want some different air.'

We went towards Edmonds Park, named after a driver who had been killed on duty at Didcot shed. I am sure it was his own fault. Finding a metal seat away from the 'madding crowd', I stretched out and was half asleep from exhaustion, after working straight through the seven days.

'When can I see you again?' she asked.

'I'm only free Wednesday or Friday.'

'Where do you work?'

'Railway shed.'

'And your mate in the Parcels Department.'

We agreed to see each other on Friday. I walked her back home, then went home myself, had some tea, and went to bed, crashing out, dead to the world.

*

On Monday, as every day, it was the same routine. I always looked across the front of the shed to see what was going out. 'It'll be my turn out here today,' I thought, as I collected my disc from the Time Office and walked down the path between the engines and the wall of engine staff's lockers to the cabin.

Then came Arthur's voice. 'Pat, wait please. I know you are working today on the front, but we are going to get you to go with Bert Paice, if that's all right.'

'Yep', I replied. 'Anyone want to buy some Irish peat for their gardens?'

But there was no reply; they went back to reading their papers and drinking tea.

When I walked past the shedmen's cabin I poked my head around the door – I must have had a thing with poking my head round doors – and asked if there was anyone wanting Irish peat. The shed's fire-raiser had the best show of roses he had ever grown, so he took two sacks off me, and kept coming back for more. I sold it for half a dollar for a huge sack full. I said that next week I should get the last of it. 'I'll have it all, Pat!'

Arthur instructed me to work on No 6 road with Bert Paice as he needed help to remove the safety valve from a Churchward 'Mogul', No 5380, then when I had finished I was to come back to the front of the shed. Unbeknown to Bert the men were still name-calling, and very jealous behind their backs; I was told that 'the Colonel' was his nickname. He was a very nice, quiet person.

I met Bert getting his tools from his cupboard (the men had tool cupboards against the wall) and helped him carry them in a sack to the cold engine outside, overlooking the Eastern loop line. It was slightly raining still. However, the sun started to break through the clouds and 'shine on the righteous', albeit with an early morning chill coming from the east.

I climbed up to the footplate, and walked out onto the 1-inch ledge just below the cabside, holding the handrail all the time. I then made a dash for the other handrail on the boiler side near the driver's quarter-light glass window. On the 'Mogul' it was 6 feet down to the ground, and I was balancing on the metal frame ledge above the 5ft 6in rigid driving wheel.

Bert handed the tool sack up to me from the ground while I knelt down on the frame reaching for it, then he did the same thing as I did to get on the frame. I had to lift myself up onto the boilers' handrail, with one foot holding onto the cover of the safety valve. I then lifted the other foot up onto the handrail pulling my body onto the top of the round boiler top. I stood on the curve of the boiler, balancing and walking along the top with my feet at 'quarter to three' and my toes tightened to the soles of my leather boots. Looking towards the chimneystack, I sat down on a sooty circle – if someone had a bow and arrow I was a prime target when I bent over! I took in the wonderful view across the open fields eastward towards Appleford. I was approximately 15 feet above ground level as I waved to the firemen as they came to book on for their shifts.

Bert was now ready to climb onto the top of boiler, and he once again handed the sack of tools up to me, and I placed them on the cab roof.

I was looking across the passenger sidings, over to the fields, and it was brilliant. Bert finally crawled up, hanging on for grim life, as I walked to the cab roof to open the sack of tools that we required and started to take off the cowling that covered the safety valve. I must have been the king of safety valves, as it seemed that was all I had ever done – so, useful for something!

Sitting opposite each other astride in the wet – it had rained that morning – with our legs dangling, we started to undo the ring of nuts, with Bert standing back on the handrail and setting up an open spanner with a metal tube in the jaw of the other end. I then started pulling on the tube, taking the strain, until each nut in turn loosened off. Then after one side was done I stood over on the handrail on the other side doing the same. Then the heavy bit came – lifting the safety valve off its base, as the gasket held the two faces together tightly. Between us we knocked the valve with a soft white metal hammer to loosen the gasket and the dried graphite paste jointing compound between the valve and base.

I pulled from the tool sack a small crow's-foot bar, placing it on the lip of the base and valve and, prising it upwards, it started to come free. Then came the difficult bit. We had to lift this very heavy valve straight up in the air, me standing at the chimneystack end on the curve of the boiler, Bert at the cab end. He had to walk backwards and I had to go forwards and over the open hole and the screw studs proud and upright where the valve had been located. I was afraid of slipping off the boiler with my feet in heavy metal boots at an angle, gripping with my toes and walking over the studs, while at the same time carrying the weight of the safety valve.

We both held onto the safety valve – there was nothing else to hold on to – crouching with our backs bent over our knees with the weight of this thing until we both laid it on the cab roof. (I wonder to this day how men never fell off those boilers doing what we had to do in all weathers.)

Kneeling on the cab curve, lifting and turning the valve on its side, I started to scrape off the dried manganese joint with a file. Bert did the same on the safety valve base frame, most of the joint having been blown out with the steam pressure into the atmosphere, as the locomotive's working steam pressure was 200lb per square inch.

After completing the cleaning, from the sack came the tin of manganese or graphite paste with a knife made from a large hacksaw blade. Bert ran the paste over the frame then I put the joint over the studs and again he ran the paste on top of the gasket.

We then both lifted the valve. I was walking backwards, crouching, and he was following, shouting to me to watch where I was walking. We placed the safety valve gingerly over the studs and levelled it onto the metal face. We retightened the nuts in the same order and method as before, making sure that every one was tightened down. Cleaning our hands with cotton waste and paraffin, I washed up Bert's tools. I jumped down from the handrail to the edge of the frame, Bert handed the tools down, then he came down slowly while I guided his foot with my hand to the edge of the frame. We did the same in reverse to get down from the side of the cab and frame. As we walked into the shop Bert said, 'I saw you in Norreys Road yesterday. Are you courting Annie? She's a nice-looking girl.' I was really pleased to hear him say that.

I then had to report to Jimmy Holmar on the front of the shed. I guess he was hiding as Arthur Brinkley, our foreman, came out of his office looking for him. It was his turn to be on the front of the shed with Matt and me.

We had to get a spanner and go underneath to adjust the brakes on a 'Grange' Class 4-6-0. Matt and I went under the locomotive with the huge spanner – not like the spanners of today, but three-quarters of an inch thick and 3 feet long. We also had a hammer. Jim climbed up on the footplate to blow off the vacuum brake. We did sweat, and although the water dripping from the locomotive kept us cool the ashpan was warm, so we couldn't win. Matt and I adjusted the brakes and checked the brake blocks for free play. We also made a report that when the loco came back into the shed again new brake shoes would be needed. What a pig of a job that was going to be!

Didcot only had four 'Granges' at that time: No 6849 *Walton Grange*, No 6868 *Penrhos Grange*, No 6874 *Haughton Grange* and No 6824 *Ashley Grange*, which was at present away at Swindon Works.

Packing pistons on both sides of No 6868 *Penrhos Grange* was part of our job, Jim on one side and me on the other. We removed the two nuts that held the piston and valve glands; these had to be removed and with the corkscrew-like rod. It was pushed into the old graphite packing, twisted and removed. This had to be done three times, with the rain pouring down – I got under the engine's frame for a bit of cover. I had to pack the valve gland as well, and that was leaking steam.

Now I had to put the packing around the piston shaft, measuring it by eye. Holding it in position with my fingers, I measured the length I wanted, placed it onto the sliding bar frame and with the hammer belted it hard until it broke. Twice more I had to complete this, then push one graphite packing into the gland at '12 o'clock', knock it into the gap with the flattening bar, another at '3 o'clock' and the last at '6 o'clock', so there was no gap between each piece that would allow the steam to escape. Having completed the packing and allowed the gland to compress, the nuts could be placed back on the threaded studs and tightened up properly. I hoped Ted Powell wasn't about looking over my shoulder. Matt ran to the stores like a headless chicken for the spares.

Sometimes a driver or fireman left the metal cap off the sand pipe on top of the frame and the rain water flowed into the sand box. To clear the sand pipes people frequently hit them with a hammer and flattened them. The best way was to remove the cap and get your hand and arm into the box, scraping out the wet sand in handfuls and throwing it out onto the concrete floor. I went to the sand hut and refilled the box with clean warm sharp sand. The result was much better than smashing the pipe with a hammer. Some fitters couldn't fit shit in a bucket. The new sand would be tested and proved on icy or greasy rails if the locomotive was slipping on an incline with a heavy train. Slipping might mean that the axles would need a visit to Swindon Works, and an entry against the driver on his records.

We worked continuously, one engine after another. Now 'Mogul' No 5337 was ready to proceed out of the shed and the driver shouted that the gauge glass has broken. I went down to the stores and asked for a glass boiler gauge tube with rubber 'O' rings. Jim looked up at me on the footplate and asked if I could manage. I said I could. 'Yep, okaayyy mate,' he replied in his native Hungarian tongue.

I shut down the gauge valves and opened the blowdown pipe so the boiling water was flushed away. With the bottom valve closed, I took off the gauge glass safety cover. I had a spanner in my pocket so I held some cotton waste over the tube and hit the glass; the bits flew into the cotton waste. I undid the top and bottom gland nuts, removing the broken glass and the old rubber rings. As I removed the very top nut it was still very hot to hold in the hand – I was jumping about like a jack-in-a-box until the driver handed me some clean cotton waste. The new glass tube slid down through the union with the 'O' ring glands and two nuts, and found its place. The bottom union was tightened up, the glass tube nuts replaced and all the other parts tightened up, then I opened up the safety shut-off levers and watched the boiling water flush through the tube. I then shut the flush pipe, looked at the boiler water bobbing in the glass, and replaced the safety cover.

Changing the tube gauge only took a matter of minutes. The shed foreman wanted those two engines off the front of the shed – my 'Mogul' blew its Great Western whistle, so I got off the footplate a bit smartish or I would have gone for a ride.

Now it was dinnertime – I had missed breakfast as we were so busy, running around like headless chickens, but believe it or not we railwaymen loved our steam engines despite all the moaning and groaning. We never wanted it any other way – we were quite jolly really and dedicated men, and a boy. We three looked at each other and Jim said, 'That's it – we're going to get something hot and some food inside us.' The shed foreman came by so Jim said we were going for some grub. 'Shout if you want us.'

'OK,' came the reply. 'At least you got two off shed.'

The time flew by. We sat resting for half an hour, then Harry Buckel, the shed foreman, came into the cabin and said we were wanted out again. More brake adjustment was required on No 4939 *Littleton Hall*, and packing piston glands on both sides. And the superheater was leaking. The shed foreman was stomping around impatiently. 'How much longer?'

'Two hours.'

He was outraged, and like a jack-in-the-box, or a rocket with the fuse lit, he flew up in the air and stormed off in a huff. That got rid of him – now we all got on with what we had to do, but the next instant he came back with Arthur Brinkley. 'What's going on?'

Jim said, 'He keeps annoying us and leaning over our shoulders, really aggravating and rushing us. We haven't stopped from when we came in this morning, even when we went to have a break, as we missed the timed tea break.'

Arthur took Harry Buckel aside. 'Leave them alone and they'll conquer the front shed without you getting in the way.'

The engine's smokebox had to be opened to get to the superheater. Kenny Haycroft struggled as he climbed up to undo the levers. He put his foot on one of the levers and held onto the handrail on the side of the boiler, then he kicked it and it moved. He could then undo the levers. He pulled open the door and saw the heaped ash, nearly up to the blast pipe. The fun had gone out of the engine as he had to get the ash out before it left the shed. He called the shed foreman over, and he went off like a rocket again as they both walked away. I got into the back of the smokebox with Jim and a 'Smokey Joe' 'Aladdin'-type oil lamp. Jim told me to ask the driver to open the regulator slightly. I felt the blast pipe get warm near my bum. Jim put the flame under each of the gaskets and joints of the superheaters, and when the flame disappeared he marked it with a cross of chalk he carried in his pocket. He went through every gasket and found no more leaks.

Harry Buckel came back and we shouted to the driver to shut down the regulator. Climbing up on the front of the frame and looking into the smokebox, Harry was shown which superheater element it was that was leaking. I shouted to the driver to open the regulator slightly and Jim again put the 'Smokey Joe' under the joint area. Harry said, 'That looks OK – we'll let it go.'

Jim said, You'll sign off the card then?'

When we had finished our work Jim took the brown card to Harry for him to sign off the superheater. Now we were clear and, having finished the work, we had a rest back in the cabin after washing our hands. I got my billycan, put a spoon of tea leaves into it and poured in the milk ready for the boiling water. With the fresh tea I ate my sarnies; we took the full hour for dinner as we had become very hungry.

The hour up, and having taken all the dinner items back to the locker room, on my way out of the shop Dave stopped me and asked if I was OK. I said I was, but was missing working in the shop, and getting on with the lamp I was going to make, but people wanted me to work with them. He pulled me aside and asked if I had been working on No 4939. 'That was a pig of a job! Keep it quiet. Ted Powell was on nights and he never found the leak.'

I shouldn't wonder, as the fireman had a job to get the smokebox door open as it was jammed tight. I told Dave that Jim had found the leak, and it was not found on the brown card – nothing was said. Dave went on about Ted Powell, and I went away and kept my mouth shut, as instructed by my brother Richard.

We went back on the front again and saw a mess spread over the ash pit. Dick Bidmead, the shed cleaner, was a very quite person; he swept up the ash, shovelled it into a wheelbarrow and dumped it. The front of the shed was empty with no engines to shout about. Dick kept the rest of the front clean, sweeping and shovelling.

Jim said, 'Let's go in the mess room,' then as he entered the cabin he grabbed me. Playing the fool, he grabbed the middle finger on my left hand and went to punch me, as I thought, so I swung round while he held my finger. I heard the most awful crack and thought he'd wrenched the finger off my hand. I let out a scream and shouted at him, 'What are you playing at?'

'Why did you move? I was only playing.'

I said, 'Honestly I thought you were going to hit me.'

I put my finger under the cold tap and let the water run over it. Cor, it didn't half hurt! We had to put it into the record book for accidents. I told Arthur and he sent me to the doctors in Mereland Road.

Next morning I went back to work with three fingers strapped together with sticky plaster and had to wear a glove on my left hand. Luckily I wrote with my right hand. Jim had a telling off from Arthur about playing pranks with a young fitter's boy.

11. Paperwork, pipes and pilots

Arthur Brinkley asked me into his office to talk about me helping him and training me to write out daily report sheets and the weekly reports. Not having a fitter or mate coming out of the system, we were short of manpower. He could also keep an eye on the situation and make sure my finger got better. My office job was to keep records of locomotives and next-day repairs; I also had to pull out the cards and check each record on each locomotive. No 4939, for example – I noted who had signed off the job and gave it to Arthur. The superheater fault had failed the engine out on the main line. The inspectors came to look at the maintenance record and saw that Harry Buckel had signed it off. However, the engine had originally failed before leaving to go off shed, and Jim Holmar and Matt Oglesby had gone under the engine and tender and found that someone had never secured the pipe properly and it had been rubbing from side to side. The appropriate clips must have been left off when someone had done another job earlier.

However, the engine was checked over by the night shift men before with the inspection men team and Ted Powell. Why hadn't they picked it up? Someone's head was about to roll. All the brown cards and reports were gathered up and placed in a special packet and sent directly to Paddington, with a special seal.

Most of our engines were 'Halls', 'Moguls', pannier tanks, 'Greyhounds', '28XXs' and small shunting tankies, as well as 'foreign' locomotives that came into the shed for repairs. Their cards all carried fitters' remarks and what had been signed off. I had also kept my own records for the future in my black book. I had to walk around the front of the shed mid-morning and take note of the dead engines, and the numbers of the engines that had been left overnight on the East Loop side. In the afternoon I had to write everything out and make phone calls to other sheds. I then went out again and make a note of the shed codes on the oval plates fixed under the smokebox door – for example, Old Oak Common was 81A, Slough was 81B, Southall 81C, Reading 81D and Oxford 81F. Didcot shed's code was 81E.

The phone was on an 'omnibus' system and rang from Didcot station, which was the exchange. I sometimes had to take a message with a report from other depots, including foreign sheds as far away as Doncaster or Leeds, or Westbury shed on the Western Region. I had to take the person's name and telephone number and send back reports. It also worked the other way, when I had to ring them about their engines that had broken down, and had to be repaired. Everything I did had to be Arthur's decision – I would wait for his opinion and orders. Really and truthfully he had a brilliant filing system down to a month in advance with the brown cards. I enjoyed working in the office.

I had to pull the cards for the next day's working for the fitters, looking at Arthur's worksheet that he had prepared; he kept it in his drawer, and I was allowed to see it. I pulled out the brown cards and thought about which teams would fit which job. I wanted to get my own back for Ted Gallagher, so fitter Norman Brogden drew the short straw; I don't know how Norman finished his apprenticeship. With his mate Bob Warwick they carried out the 24,000-mile planned maintenance (PPM) work on No 4939 *Littleton Hall* after I added the extra work of a superheater change, which took five days to complete, replacement engine and tender brake blocks and all the shitty jobs that were required, even down to what Jack Dearlove had picked up on his repair test sheet when the engine had come in off the road the day before. The boiler had to be washed out by Trevor May and Chris Kelly, my Dad, and if Brogden or Warwick got in the way of the boiler washout men they would shout at them and spray the hot water at them if they were working in the

Paperwork, pipes and pilots

pit – my Dad would soak the men with the steam pressure hose to move them away. Dad also stood in the pit listening to the men quietly talking about someone – he would reach between the wheel spokes undo their boot laces and tie them together. When they tried to walk off they would fall to the ground, and Dad would burst out laughing.

They had five engines a day for boiler washouts, and refitting new lead joints to every washout point as the water used on the Western Region was very hard. Good Welsh marine coal was the best, but the water was the worst as it was hard and caused scale in the boiler.

I started to grin and burst out laughing to myself over what I had done to Brogden as I sat in the office with no one else there – whoever walked by must have thought someone had cracked a dirty joke. The two other fitters had 6,000-mile planned maintenance jobs, and worked together side by side – Bert Paice and Bob Looms were a good pair of nice men and worked well together.

While Dave Davies and Jim Hale were the breakdown train keepers, having the door key, being on nights they had to work on the front of the shed and do very little repair work. And I knew they got their heads down. However, being outside the shed the breakdown coaches were the only ones having a fire in them to cook their food, and kept the chill off them while they slept warm. They would know which foreman was on duty with them, and I knew what was going on; then at 5.30am the alarm clock sounded and they went back into the shed and looked busy. They waited for the 6 o'clock men to come in so they could pass on what had been done overnight, then could get home to more comfort.

Six o'clock was Ted Powell with Frank Dowding's time, but they came in at 5.45pm

Left to right, fitter's mate Matt Oglesby, fitter Bert Paice and fitter Bob Looms.

to cover the inspection tests, and get the two night men away home, while Jack Dearlove covered the afternoon shift, 2 till 10, on a roster system. Jimmy Holmar was on the front of the shed with his mate Matt Olgesby, and the only person on holiday at that time was Jim Tyler. Alan Membury was on nights working with Johnny Cooper; Alan shaved with a soft pastry brush to get more soap on his face.

Arthur got out the MP11. Every fitter's boy upwards as well as apprentices had to read this manual, in between the brown services being issued and the telephone ringing, and when the shed foreman came into the office. It was the fitters' routine maintenance manual. A nightmare! It was bigger than an encyclopaedia and heavier, and contained the instructions on how to inspect all moving parts on the locomotive – linkages, safety valve, pistons, valves, gear linkages, and wheel and tyre measurements, together with examinations and work sheets for services every 3,000, 6,000, 12,000 and 24,000 miles. Every driver would fill in a repair card after his shift and pass it through the appropriate channels to the Time Office clerk, then to Arthur Brinkley's office.

I was also at the railway's request to go anywhere that eased the workload of a fitter's mate, and was the spare person to go to Swindon for spares for the engines. I also had to travel to Reading depot and Oxford shed with iron pipes that had holes worn in them from continual rubbing from side to side with the motion with the engine. I got fed up in later years as I wanted to stay in the shed and work – I was a conscientious worker with a photographic memory and loved what I was learning and needed lathe work to be trained properly.

Another problem involved the vacuum pipe on No 3211. Jim and Matt started to remove the pipe clips and unions at each end of the pipe. The fitting crew were not very happy about the situation, as the last driver never reported the fault and he was hauled over the coals in front of the shed foreman; this would go on his report card, which was located in the shedmaster's office. The engine had failed and was towed back to the shed. The vacuum pipe had the biggest gash I had seen. It was wrapped in sacking, and was 8 feet long. I was asked to pull out the brown card to see who had serviced the engine and see who had signed off the card. I handed over the card and placed it in Arthur's private drawer for him to inspect when no one was about.

The next day I was asked to go to Oxford shed mid-morning to get the pipe fixed. I was given a workman's free pass with instructions how to get there. I was told how to proceed

No 6927 *Lilford Hall* stands at the north end of the down platform at Oxford. Beyond the bridge can be seen part of the loco shed complex. *Gerald Adams, Slip Coach Publishing Services collection via John Stretton*

Paperwork, pipes and pilots

when I got off the train at Oxford – walk down to the end of the platform, go across the River Isis by a steel bridge, then, when I saw a wooden structure, stay the same side until entering the shed; I was told to be careful as I would be very close to the main line. I was told to walk across the entrance and look for the fitters' shop – the welder knew I was going so would keep an eye open for me. 'Catch the stopper on Platform 5 – it will be in shortly.'

I made my way towards the station holding the old pipe with its ends downwards and away from passengers, as it had years of dirt and grime over it. When the DMU came in I went to the guard's van and put the pipe in his cage. I found a seat near the guard's van, as I did not want to leave the area and walk along the whole of the train. As it was an all-stations stopper, I was happy as I saw loads of different parts of the landscape and the pretty stations along the line – things you don't see when driving along the main roads in a car.

As the train approached the outskirts of Oxford I saw Hinksey marshalling yard, which interested me a great deal – goods trains were shunting over the hump and I saw the brilliant way the tankies shunted and let the wagons run until they stopped at the buffers. Soon the train entered Oxford station: 'All change, all change!'

I returned along the corridor to the guard's van and collected the pipe. The platform was clear, so I could step down safely. I followed the instructions, and eventually found the fitting shop. The foreman introduced himself as Bill Miles. 'And you are Pat Kelly,' he said. 'Any relation to Dick Kelly?'

'We're brothers.'

'So you must be the youngest. The welder is waiting for you in there. Go and have a cup of tea in that wooden shed.'

I left the paperwork with the welder, then walked to the shed, which was full to the brim with all sorts of trades, chatting away. As I entered the room it went deathly quiet. 'That's what I must do to people,' I thought.

Someone said that the kettle had boiled, so I pulled out a mug from the sink and asked if I could use it. 'OK,' came answers from all directions. 'Here's some tea, sugar and milk.'

'Has anyone got anything to eat?' I grinned.

'Give us some sand on the floor and we'll do the desert dance for you as well.'

'Ah, that will be nice. Where do I get the sand?'

'Sit down and have your tea.' Then I saw who had spoken. It was Paddy Driscoll from the bottom of Sinodun Road.

'Well I never – I wondered where you worked when I saw you ride off about 6.30 every morning.'

Bill Miles entered the mess room and told me the pipe was ready. Then the sly remarks came out: 'Oh Pat your pipe is ready.' 'Oh, Pat's got his feet under the table – only been here 10 minutes.'

'Have you got a problem?' I asked the person.

'No,' he said.

'Well keep your fucking mouth shut or I'll shut it for you.'

Everyone looked. 'Sounded like your brother talking then – and he meant it.'

'Yes, and so do I. Thanks for the tea, Paddy, and the hospitality.'

I walked away from their childish ways and closed the door behind me. I went to see the welder and thanked him.

'Might see you again,' he said. 'Did you get a cup of tea?'

'Yes thank you, and some foul remarks with it as well.'

'Friendly lot, aren't they? That's why I have my tea here in the welding bay.'

I walked back to the station, and this time had to go over the sleeper crossing to the far platform to catch to train back to Didcot. Today the pipe was urgent, but next time I decided I would venture into Oxford and see the sights, as I had never been by myself before. My train came into the platform, Didcot and Reading only. I once again walked to the guard's van, and stepped up inside.

'What are you at, young man?'

I showed him my pass, then put the pipe in a corner out of everyone's way. I walked through the corridor, found an empty compartment, shut the sliding door behind me and sat down.

*

As the rain approached Didcot I saw the various tankies at work. The job they all enjoyed was the station pilot, but the other was the horrible 'fly', of which more later.

The station pilot was provided to deal with main-line passenger trains by either adding or removing coaches, horseboxes, milk tanks, etc; making up coach sets in sidings and taking them to the bay or main-line platforms; and acting as a standby engine for any main-line failures. If they had an old 'Mogul' as the pilot engine, the foreman always had a 'Hall' in steam on the shed just in case, but as a rule they did not have many failures at Didcot, for somehow the top link men would struggle on to Reading or Swindon. They would spot the 'Mogul' on the up or down trip, and to a 'Castle' man, even if she was rough, another 20 miles was preferable to changing over engines at Didcot. Bert Edmonds of Old Oak Common said that he would rather jump over the river bridge at Goring than run into Paddington with an old 'Mogul' on the front.

There were some compensations for being on the station pilot. They would stand in front of Didcot East Junction signal box on a spur waiting to 'tail' trains, and on a Saturday they had a 1st Class seat to watch Didcot Town football team in action. Any goals scored for the home team would be accompanied by a series of short blasts on the Great Western whistle, and as half the team were railwaymen this encouragement was as good as another goal. In the evenings, particularly in the summer, the education of the pilot men was further enlightened by the antics of some of the courting couples behind the bushes in the fields, but they were gentlemen enough not to blow the whistle and disturb them.

When Annie and I were in that situation, but on the ground opposite the North Junction signal box, I never thought at the time that anyone could see me and my companion in the long grass – I forgot that the engine was high above us and the driver enjoyed himself pulling on the Great Western whistle as though he had suffered a stroke and couldn't take his hand off the whistle chain! Both of them partially naked and wrapped up in what was happening, while the passengers had their heads pressed against the windows trying to find the best view!

Bert considered that a great step forward in steam power was the 0-6-0 pannier tank, at which the Great Western excelled, possessing by far the largest collection of standard locomotives in the world. The men were quite rightly proud of them, for they were utterly reliable, economical and, with the Stephenson slide valve motion, easy to maintain. Some were very old rebuilds from old saddle tanks, but age did not matter. They would be found hammering away in every shunting yard on the entire system.

Every driver and fireman was weaned on the little tank engine, and to lift a 60-wagon coal train out of a yard for remarshalling was the basic training for all the main-line work to come. The tankies had a sharp characteristic 'bark' when exhausting, except those fitted with a spark arrester, which emitted a 'whoof' from the chimney, but in no way at the expense of power.

With the firebox doors were open the amount of air sucked into the firebox was very considerable, and bicycle trouser clips were favoured by both driver and fireman, not to keep coal dust from flying up inside the legs, but for comfort, as the construction of the male is such that a vacuum in certain quarters is not appreciated.

Another hazard from this movement of air at speed was a very serious one. The most mouth-watering and succulent meal on a footplate was bacon fried on the shovel, and to receive a whiff of that beautiful tang

Paperwork, pipes and pilots

drifting from the cab of a pannier tank on a frosty morning was to create a craving so strong as to completely obliterate all other thoughts. It would start the nostrils twitching, recalled Bert, and the lips and tongue searching in anticipation, and this was the most dangerous moment. It was known that to open the large ejector on a big engine to create a vacuum was a quick way to remove the bacon from the shovel, but to open the regulator on a pannier tank when your mate had his bacon on a shovel in the firebox was to see if your reflexes were as good as you thought they were. That bacon would disappear up the chimney so fast that it took a moment of thought to realise it was no longer there.

Every railway company owned some fine locomotives but, more important, they also had the finest collection of men in the country to man them. No matter how well the engines were designed, it was only as efficient as the two men on the footplate. The designer could produce figures on paper showing the total output of any given type of locomotive but, without the skill of the fireman swinging his shovel with all the artistry of his trade, keeping the engine on the boil so that the driver could exercise his skill with the regulator, cut-off and braking, all could be lost. However, with two men working together in such unison, output figures could go far beyond those of any designer. Bert said that he hoped he was not biased in any way when he said that the Great Western engine was one of the most handsome-looking locomotives anywhere in the world, and could outrun and out-steam any comparable locomotive, class for class, and all based on a standard design begun by Churchward in 1903.

Western men were proud of their locomotives. Just compare the USA Transportation Corps 2-8-0 freight locomotives imported during the war with any Great Western locomotive. The US engine, like many of the other companies' engines, fairly bristles with bits nailed on. There is the Westinghouse pump projecting from the smokebox door, exposed valve gear, oil pipes, steam pipes, sand pipes, and bits of plumbing twisting and snaking their way all over the boiler – but the Great Western engine stands clean and proud. The US engines had a great deal of influence on the future British Railways 'Standard' designs because of accessibility for oiling and maintenance, as seen in Riddles's 'Austerity' Class 2-8-0s.

*

I got back to the shed with the 8-foot pipe intact. I laid it down next to the wheels for the fitter and his mate to replace it, as the engine was all fired up and would be ready to go off shed, but I was asked to find the fitting crew first. I found them in the cabin having some grub, and told them where the pipe was, ready for them. I then went back into the office with Arthur and handed over the workman's pass

He gave me a job out in the shed, measuring up the wheels with the tyre gauge, so I went to get my overalls on, and stuffed the scraper into my pocket; I had been given a tool locker with a galvanized bucket and many of my tools I had started to make, taking them out from the stores on a chitty signed by Arthur. The engine was No 6937 *Conyngham Hall*.

I took the empty bucket with the signed paperwork to the stores to collect 2lb of cotton waste and 2 pints of paraffin. I handed over the bucket to the storeman, Arthur Wheatley, to be filled with the paraffin, then armed with a pencil and paper I sketched out the engine's wheel arrangement. I found a 'Not to be Moved' red board and placed it on the tender's rear lamp bracket; as it was positioned over the pathway on No 1 road it could be seen from any approaching locomotive. I left the bucket and cotton waste beside the engine, then went under the front frame, climbing down into the pit at the smokebox end of the engine, holding onto the buffer then the coupling linkage and lowering myself down. Then on my bended knees I crawled to the engine's leading front wheels and started to scrape the oil and muck off the sides of the tyres and washed them down with the clean paraffin, pleased to see the muck disappear. Taking the tyre sizes didn't take long, as I knew exactly what wanted doing. I wrote all the measurements down on a scrap of paper, then climbed out of the pit, picked up my bits and walked into the fitting shop. I left my boiler suit on, rolled up my sleeves, got washed, put all the tools back in the tool box and went back to Arthur's office to write up the brown job card and sign it off complete.

I stopped for a cup of tea, which I brewed for the foreman, using his tea things.

'Help yourself to sugar, Pat,', but I declined as I had stopped using it for a bet between Dave and myself. I found there was no difference with or without sugar, and sometimes I even drank just 'Adam's ale'. Very cagily I asked what happened over the clips from the pipe. I'd seen the paperwork for the job, just a squint, but never got the detail.

'He'll be coming in to see me after you've drunk your tea. So please wander off and say nothing to anyone Pat, OK?'

I got up and left his office and wandered outside to watch the trains go by – plenty of Bournemouth and country engines coming from and going to Oxford with their green coaches, then came the freights that made my day, especially the bogie bolsters with Army lorries and tanks covered over with canvas sheeting heading towards an Army barracks somewhere up north, with its own 'Austerity' engine on the front and engine crew. Brilliant! I just sat looking and counting the vehicles

I think to be honest I missed Jim Tyler when he was away.

A modern-day view of No 1 road. The shed is now part of the Great Western Society's complex at Didcot.

12. Ladies old and young

I looked over the site and saw cold dead engines with sacks over their chimney stacks. There must have been at least 20 engines going rusty. Then I looked towards the fitting shop to the fired-up boiler of a Great Western steam locomotive, representing the very beginning of steam at Didcot shed. The stationary boiler was the spare fireman's burden, so far removed from the glamour of the mighty 'Kings' and 'Castles' but nevertheless a steam engine. All sheds needed power for tube blowing, boiler washouts and pumping within the complex, but only the Western could come up with a boiler house like that. It was a masterpiece of improvisation, so simple, and looking back on it now I can see the wisdom of it all.

From time to time, as a Collett '22XX' 0-6-0 replaced an old Dean engine, Swindon would find that it had a perfectly good boiler mounted on a worn-out frame, so the cab would be removed, the boiler lifted off the frame, and the frame scrapped. The boiler then went into the boiler shop for a small modification in addition to an overhaul. The regulator would be removed and replaced with a large steam valve, then the coach steam heating valve would be blanked off, and the steam brake vacuum gauges and fittings removed, together with the lubricator. The stationary boiler was now ready to be lifted onto a wagon and transported to its last home.

At the shed the boiler house would be completed except for a side and roof, ready to receive the boiler. The best example of this can still be seen at Didcot at the bottom of No 3 road next to the lifting shop. All that was needed was a pit to be dug and concreted, and a brick cradle to be built at each end of the pit. When the boiler arrived it was lifted onto the cradle, the pit now becoming the ashpan, then the side of the boiler house was bolted on and a roof added, with the smokebox protruding outside. A 30-foot chimney was added, supported by stay wires – but for all this, it was still unmistakably a Dean goods engine. All that remained was to couple up the main steam valve and lay on the town's water supply to the injectors. She was now ready for the spare fireman's enjoyment, and if there was no spare fireman, one would be booked on for her. To be booked on the stationary boiler led to the unhappy man scouting round for a duty swap, going sick, having a grandmother pass away, being called for jury service or tempting some young sprog of a fireman into thinking that it was a wonderful experience to work on the 'old lady' and that he would learn a lot about steam.

But he soon found that the 'old lady' could be just a demanding as a main-line run in with a rough old '43'. Her fuel was coal, of course, but in the loosest sense of the word. It consisted of the pit sweepings, coke ovoids, coal dust, old paper, overalls, mouldy food, oil-soaked cotton waste, the foreman's bowler hats and, now and again it was said, an old engine cleaner or two. However, her steaming depended a lot on the direction of the wind. An old-hand fireman would use his loaf, and supplement her diet with some Welsh marine steam coal purloined from the nearest engine, and on this borrowed coal she would perform. On washout day an old-hand fireman would always booked to fire her. Somewhere there was some collusion between the boilersmiths and the shed foreman, but there was always plenty of steam when it was most needed.

Firing her was as much a work of an art as firing a mobile locomotive. The firebox was chest high, and with no exhausting from the chimney the 'little-and-often-all round-the-box' rule did not apply. She thrived on a good thick bed of fire, with the blower half on, dampers and boilerhouse door wide open, a bracing north wind, and both hands put together in a prayer, until washout started. Then seeing the speed with which the water level dropped down the gauge glass was to make one forget all about the Promised Land and start using some basic words. It was I think the nearest to the cleaner lads. Perhaps they believed she fed on young cleaners, as was possible in the dark inferno, and the old shed cat found another home.

With the day's work over you could run the water level down. The boiler pressure was 165lb but at this she was only on a 'titter', so we would give her a good pull through with the pricker until she began to roar through her safety valve and rock on her cradle. On went the injector, and the dirty work began. Her fire would be blacked in with the slop one could find, then it was off with the blower, shut the dampers and firebox door, then go outside and look at the 30-foot chimney. The smoke would roll out of the chimney, slow and thick, oily and so heavy that you could almost carry it up past the coal stage, until it spread out in one great all-encompassing blanket over the station.

*

On the notice boards within the booking office there were notices about 'Not to be Moved' boards to be placed in position at all times and every tender brake had to be wound down tight, and no one should leave anyone on their own because of what happened to a old Great Western man. It was 1954, and Mike Bosley had just graduated from being a cleaner to a fireman, but there was no position for him in Didcot. His nearest transfer would be Worcester shed.

On his first day he was shown around, told what his duties entailed and where he would stow his belongings. Checking the roster, he found which driver he was to be with – but at least he had a job doing what he enjoyed most.

The driver and Mike were oiling the engine and tender working side by side, then the driver went looking for a board, placing it on the rear lamp bracket on the tender so it could be seen clearly. He asked Mike if he would mind climbing into the motion to oil all the oil pots – taking out the cork plugs, replenishing with oil, then replacing the cork plug tight in the hole. Unbeknown to both men there was another locomotive creeping up behind the tankie they were preparing. Mike was inside the frames with his legs hanging between the con-rods and lying over the rest of the motion – only a very thin person could do this work as it was a very tight place to be.

Suddenly the other locomotive's buffers touched the tender buffers and moved the 0-6-0 forward by 2 feet. Mike rose up as the con-rods started to drive the pistons inside the cylinders, then the rods came backwards towards the underside of the boiler, with Mike's back pressing against the frame. He was screaming and shouting with fear as he was being burned through his overalls. He was stuck with his body and legs, conscious of what was happening. The driver went crazy against the other engineman, calling for the shed supervisor and shedmaster, and the first aid people. They knew that the only way to get him out from the position he was in was for the tankie to travel to move the cranks through 180 degrees back to their original position. Mike was driven to hospital in an ambulance; and never went back on the railway again. Alan Caulkett and a few other cleaners that knew him visited him in Worcester Hospital.

*

Another Thursday came, and pay day. 7.30 till 5.30, nine hours a day, one hour for lunch, then 8.00 till noon on Saturday morning; 48 hours worked in 5½ days, £1.10s. That was 3¼d an hour. But the money didn't bother me – I was playing with a full-size train set, albeit getting a pittance for it.

I stayed in the office being given a load of work by my foreman, so I never saw much, only an engine passing the swinging single window; the driver knew that I would be inside the office so waved as he steamed by. It was good to see engines going down to the turntable and coming back, sounding the Great Western whistle and slowing down – there was a sign on the office wall that said to sound the whistle. There had been many an engineman or shed staff nearly run over for not noticing what was creeping up along the office wall, an almost silent engine moving slowly towards its next victim stepping out onto the wooden sleepers.

The telephone never stopped ringing, message after message, from all parts of the Western Region. I wrote them all down, taking their numbers and saying that I would get the foreman to contact them as soon as he reappeared. As soon as I replaced the receiver there was another telephone call, and a voice asked if there was anyone in the office with me.

'It's me, Mick.'

'Cor, bloody hell – what do you want?'

'Come over at dinnertime. I want to see you. I have a surprise for you.'

All that morning the brown service cards were stacked in a pile and report sheets the same, with the list of telephone messages form Ebbw Newport, South Wales, Westbury Running and Maintenance Depot, Old Oak Common – a Mr Diamond – and Tyseley, Southall, Shrewsbury… I had just finished when Arthur walked in his office. I explained about the list and said that I had done all tomorrow's service cards. He looked at me bewildered.

'If it's OK may I have a early dinner? I've got something planned. I would like to see my mate over at the Parcels Stores.'

'Which way are you going? Not across that main line?'

'No, I'm going to the station and will walk towards the West End box into the Baltic sidings near the Provender Stores area.'

'Go careful – see you after dinner.'

I walked the route I had told Arthur, keeping my eyes fully open and my ears the same. I walked by the signal box and headed for the Parcels Stores. I found the office and a set of stairs, and as I walked into the rest room I trod on something and my boot started to smell of burning rubber. Mick pushed me off, then told me to watch this! He would put an old penny on the belly stove to get it red-hot, then slide it off onto a shovel and onto the concrete floor. He would then walk out onto the platform and load up the covered vans, waiting to hear someone scream when they tried to pick up the penny!

'That'll stop him,' he said. The culprit would have a penny mark on his fingertips.

'Before you go, come out onto the parcels decking and look up there on the railway bank behind the wire. Those girls waving and shouting to us are the two we met in the flicks last week. They want to see us Friday night, same time, same place.'

So we fixed up to meet later on and I walked back to the shed. As I walked along the cinder path I saw three gentlemen on their way towards the shed. They were Great Western enginemen, master craftsmen of the steam age, practising their trade on the footplate of those beautiful Brunswick Green engines. They strode down the cinder path, talking to each, their boots shining and their overalls and jackets brushed, wearing their peak caps with the 'GWR' badge clipped to the braided black band. Each wore their watch chain threaded through a waistcoat button hole, the small medallion and watch key hanging from a small piece of chain, swinging gently as they walked. These were proud men of Didcot Great Western shed. As I passed them, stepping over the railway line onto the wooden sleepers, I said 'Hello' to Jack Goodall, Charlie Skinner and Tom Smith, the 'three musketeers' of Didcot shed.

Jack Goodall was born in January 1917 in Lydalls Road, Didcot. He went to Manor School, and when he came of age he started work on the GWR. He was the only employee at the time, as Didcot had not been opened long, and the brand-new shed was still being built. He sat a small exam in the shedmaster's office, then signed his contract on 5 November 1934, starting as a cleaner at 17 years of age. His father had also worked on the railway at the Provender Stores.

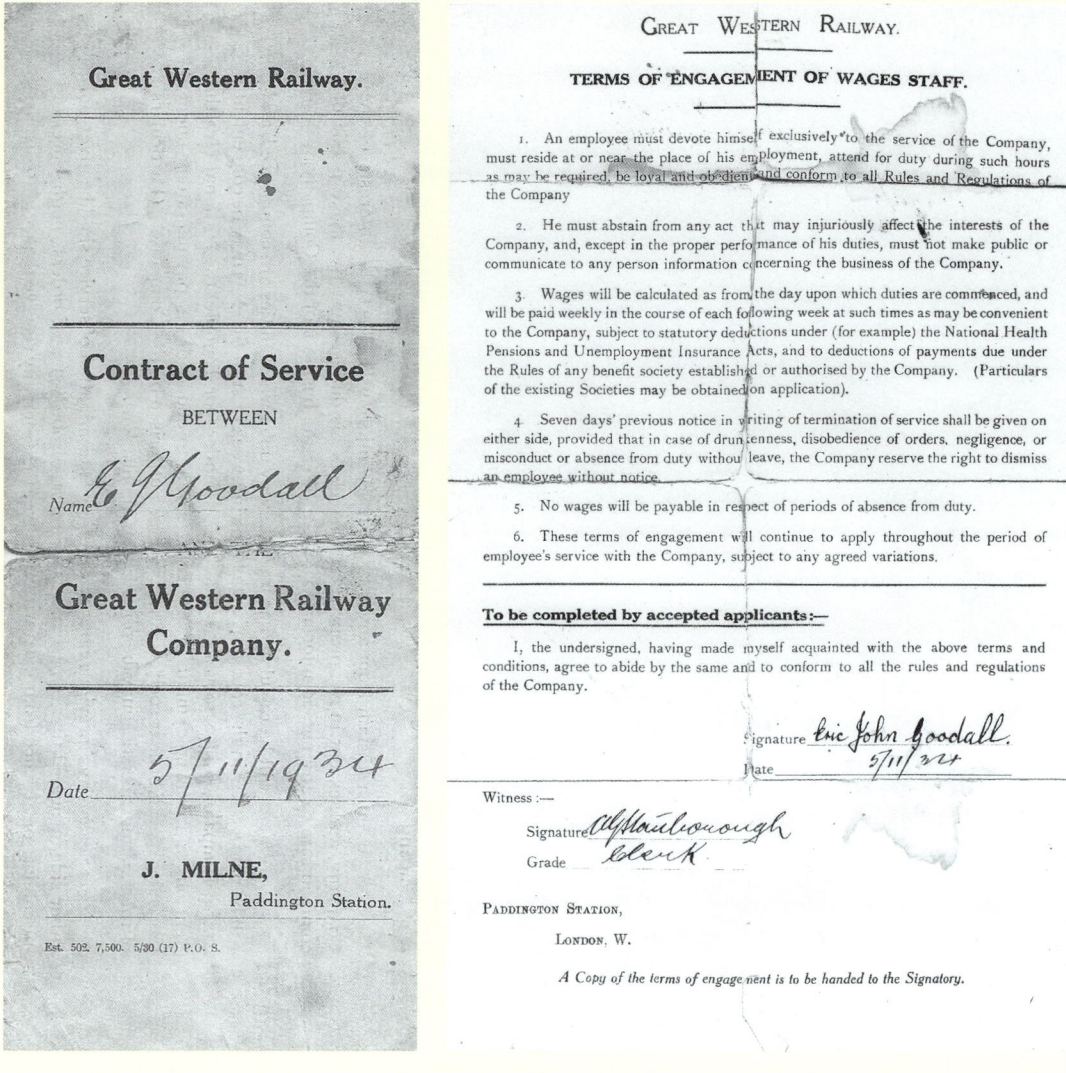

Jack Goodall's Contract of Service, November 1934. *Jean Goodall collection*

Before long Jack was firing, and during the Second World War he fired to his brother-in-law, Stephen Freeman, as they got on well together. (Stephen became a Didcot Parish Councillor in the 1960s.)

Jack never drove a diesel, but often told his family that he had been out on DMUs 'showing drivers the road'.

Jack's daughter Jean recalls that he had decided to leave the railway as he found the shift work too hard and was not sleeping well during the day. This was 1965 and Jean was getting married in February of the following year, so this seemed the right time to leave, as otherwise his wife would have been on her own at night when he was on night shift. She says that Jack didn't talk much about the railway, but he did take early retirement in 1965. She knows for sure that he didn't get a watch for his service. He was offered a job with the Bosley family in their turf accountants office in Didcot, and stayed there until his early 70s.

Meanwhile younger and older men than Jack, who were dedicated drivers and enginemen, went out in all weathers

Ladies old and young

Driver Jack Goodall sitting in the cab of 'Mogul' No 6378. *Jean Goodall collection*

Jean's father. *Jean Goodall collection*

Jack Goodall on the footplate. *Jean Goodall collection*

trying to keep warm from the fire in the firebox on the coldest of cold nights with a long heavy dirty overcoat and their railway peaked caps pulled down over their faces to keep the wind off.

One of Jack's older colleagues was Walter Wells, born on 17 November 1898 in the Row Barge Inn, Wallingford, where his father was landlord. During the First World War he served in France and North Africa, then on 31 December 1917 HMS *Osmanieh*, which had been commissioned as a troopship and was carrying soldiers and medical personnel, struck a mine laid by a U-boat and sank off Alexandria with a loss of 209 lives. Walter survived (as did Jack Cohen, who went on to found the Tesco brand!), and managed to swim ashore.

After the war he obtained employment as a fireman on the GWR, progressing to driver, based at Didcot. He met his wife Mary in Swansea, in between shifts (she worked at the University there) and they eventually settled in Wessex Road.

Above: Jack's daughter Jean, aged 12, with her cousin Peter Goodall (5), on the footplate of No 6378. *Jean Goodall collection*

Right: Driver Walter Wells (left) with his fireman.

He remained with the railway until his retirement in 1963. He was Chairman of the ASLEF trade union branch at Didcot and a popular member of the staff. He was invited to the Railway Club every Christmas, where he was given a bottle of whisky, until he was unable to get there, as his wife didn't like him going out 'at his age'!

His granddaughter Eleanor recalls that 'he used to cycle over to us when we moved from Brightwell to a very old house in Long Wittenham – sometimes twice a week in the 1970s, then later on the bus in the '80s – where he helped my Mum with the garden. He continued to wear his driver's overalls and jacket when he was doing so! He painted, polished the brass hood that covered one of the fireplaces, and did all the odd jobs that my Dad couldn't get round to as he was running a factory in Swindon!

'It was a comforting and familiar sight to see Grandad when we got home from school on Thursdays. He would give us all a Curly Wurly or a pack of Toffees each! He was a strong, capable and kind man whom we all loved dearly.'

Walter and his wife continued to live in Wessex Road until 1994, when they both died at the ripe old ages of 93 and 96; in July 1994 they would have celebrated their 75th wedding anniversary. Walter died in the November and was buried on what would have been his 97th birthday.

*

As I walked into the shed entrance the wonderful aroma of oil and steam rose into my nostrils. Then it was just a short walk down to the cabin, where I waited before going into the office to see what was next on the list from the foreman.

Arthur stuck his head around the door of the cabin and asked for me. We both went

Ladies old and young

into his abode and sat down.

'How do you feel about having another week in here with me? I could do with you, as I am run ragged with the workload and you are a godsend helping out, and it will give your finger a rest a bit more. Then the following week you can go back outside.'

'Actually,' I replied, 'I was wondering about having some leave before going back into the shop. A week's holiday.' I said that I would confirm that, as I was waiting for a letter from my uncle in London.

'Are you out tonight at the Union meeting,' continued Arthur. 'Be careful pulling that one-arm bandit! You jammy sod – two bandits in a matter of an hour. So what else are you doing at the weekend.'

'Working with my mate, moving Irish peat to the stables. Helping out really, using the Parcels Depot lorry and unloading two box vans that have travelled from Ireland.' Arthur couldn't believe it. 'Then on Monday I can have a rest, as I'm in the office.'

When I came out of the office and joined the queue of men standing waiting for their pay, hearing the jolly sounds of them cracking jokes, as happy as Larry, when all week they were walking around with their heads stuck between their legs and as miserable as old women.

I received my wages and went to see Arthur to ask permission to leave the shed. Arthur asked me to get a tin of Virginia tobacco and a quarter-pound packet of tea. 'Go and ask the others if they want anything as well.' In the end I had a shopping list for the fitting staff, but they paid for a chocolate bar I wanted, as I had a sweet tooth.

I walked through the station's undercroft and headed across the road towards Midwinter's 'open all hours' shop. The list was mostly tea and sugar, as well 'French letters'. Where would I get them? 'Try a balloon shop,' Mr Midwinter said. The fitters thought it was funny, but I found somewhere that cut men's hair that sold them.

When I left work that day to go home I made a deal with the proprietor, and he sold

1965 was when we all had a photograph taken together, and nothing was ever mentioned. We just turned up for the picture and went back to work – we were never told anything about the shed's future of the situation. Later we felt we'd been kicked in the teeth – the end of an era after 31 years of Didcot shed. All these men and more besides disappeared.

me four packets with three 'johnnies' in a packet and one for myself as a floater. When I got in hand with the cash it came easy, and all the men in the shed did dirty things with their wives and sweethearts every night or at weekends. I giggled when I saw who had bought them off me, and who would be walking arm in arm around the town. I was on the make again; money came easy, a couple of bob here and a couple of bob there. I was flush.

This went on for several months until a big hand came around my ear with a clap and Dad wanted to know if I was selling 'johnnies'. Cor, my ear hurt, but that was better than his belt, as I could never sit down for a week. 'No, Dad.' I was a good Catholic boy and never got into trouble. He called me a fibber, and said he knew different. It was funny as he never asked to buy any off me.

I paid Mum my rent money out of my wages as we had agreed, and she wanted to know what I was doing at the weekend. All I said was that we were going to the flicks Friday night and working till noon on Saturday. Then I'd be gone all weekend moving the peat in Blewbury. I never mentioned about girls as she was dead against me seeing any and going out with them.

Mick and I met up at the usual place, at his at 6.30 on the Thursday evening. He would drink a pint of milk to line his stomach before going out on the razz and when he came home half cut he would drink a another pint of milk. He taught me a lot as I started to drink the white stuff as well, but when I came home silly I drank 'Adam's ale'.

We both casually walked down towards the Labour Club in Station Road like two studs on the pull, and when we reached our destination I went to the bar and asked for two pints of brown ale. 'And have a Lamb's Navy Rum for yourself, barman.' That would shut him up and stop him yapping about my age.

We both played the one-arm bandit, but not very lucky this week, then wandered across to the Railway Club. Mick got his usual half-bottle of Lamb's Navy Rum, then we walked home and chatted. He told me he was going away for a week's holiday the week after next to Colchester Army barracks to see his uncle and aunt. That was OK, I told him, as I was going to Whitechapel in London for a week to the Kelly family home.

We agreed to meet at 7.00 on Friday night, and would work again over the weekend, one and a half days and the job would be done. Pete was going to pick me up, then Mick about 12.30, but as I finished work at noon it was going to be a rush; but we were all in the same boat, and wherever you were the finishing time on Saturday was noon – the railway stopped for no man.

On Friday morning I rode down towards the market, but Gibby must have had a bad start and told me to piss off, so I never bothered any more. I was looking forward to meeting the girl again as it had been a long week. When I left the undercroft it was impossible to move for the engine movements, and all the railwaymen were stuck. We all had to wait until the coast was clear, then there was a mad rush to get to the other side, the first time I had ever known it to happen.

After wishing everyone on the cabin 'Good morning' I walked by the smithy's cabin, and there was Johnny eating winkles from a brown paper bag with a pin, scraping them out and straight into his mouth. My stomach churned. 'Help yourself,' he said.

'No thanks, John, I've not long had my breakfast.'

Johnny Cooper worked at Didcot as the boilersmith's mate. He originally came from Bristol, where he had lived and had a girlfriend, but they broke up. He was a real character – no one took him seriously. But he would always say 'Hello' to me every day, whenever he was on the day shift.

His eating habits were a bit weird as well, usually pigs' trotters, cabbage and peeled spuds cut into quarters and covered in water with a couple of Oxo cubes stirred together in a galvanised bucket that sat on the pot belly stove in the rest area. When he went

Ladies old and young

off shift he kept the bucket in his locker covered with a galvanised lid.

Every morning while working in the office my routine was to go round the shed and see what engines had come in overnight as I had to make a note of the cab-side number and shed code on the smokebox door. Johnny worked hard like most of the men in the shed, but outside among the cold or dead engines, on Nos 5, 6, 7 or 8 roads, it was hard to find a boilersmith working until I heard the noise of hammering inside a firebox, and the echo of curses coming from that area. Climbing up onto the footplate and waiting for the shouting to stop, I would look over the other side of the footplate and there below me was the wooden wheelbarrow that the smiths used. Seeing what was inside, I realised that the workload consisted of fitting new firebars. Then the shouting eased slightly and someone popped his head out of the firebox – like a guillotine with his head in it ready to be chopped off! It was Johnny Cooper, with a face mask on with rubber straps holding the air valves over his mouth, and rivers of sweat running down his face. He climbed out onto the footplate, wet through with sweat, and cursed how hard those firebars had become moulded into the slots with clinker and burning coal; with that amount of heat the bars would twist.

He asked if I had seen Bill Cox on my travels – he was going to help him but it seemed that he had disappeared, as usual. 'I've got to get back inside, Pat – sorry. I've got to get these bars out as they want this engine tomorrow.'

So I did a quick inspection on the footplate for what was needed and reported back to Arthur with a list that Jack Dearlove would follow up on with his inspection of the engine, which was No 2221, an 0-6-0, the Collett 'miniature' version of a 'Castle' with a tender. The 0-6-0 wheel arrangement was liked by the enginemen and fitters to work on.

I put my leave in to Arthur and requested a free pass to London and on to Whitechapel, returning the following Monday. I was looking forward to getting away, and seeing the cousins with all my Dad's brothers and sister as well as Grandfather and Grandmother – it would be a right shindig. I had one more week at work then I was off.

Within the shed I always looked out for the '22XX' Class of 0-6-0 tender engines. They were allowed up the branch lines, and we had a number of them – Nos 2214, 2221, 2234, 2240, 2252, 3210 and her sister 3211, seven in total. Some had come to us from other sheds, but the others had come directly from Swindon Works when brand new. No 2252 was fitted with an ex-WD tender, and although she steamed as freely as her sisters she ran like a coal tub. In fact, when she was running tender-first one could with good reason think that it was a weedkilling train approaching, it rocked so much from side to side.

These engines were considered a treat to work on by both enginemen and fitting staff. They were just as much at home working freight traffic as passenger trains. The ATC ramp gave the impression that it was there to stop the high smokebox perched on the saddle from tipping forward. They were compact little locomotives, with no front bogie. I enjoyed working on them when instructed to climb between the frames to view the motion under the boiler. Fitted with a 'Castle' cab and towing a small tender with 3,000 gallons of water, they were attractive little engines, painted the Great Western colour of Brunswick Green. The footplate had enough space to work in, and there were pivoting wooden seats.

On a '22XX' it was easy to complete the 45-minute preparation time to get the jobs done and get off the shed. Skip Morgan said he would have liked the full hour, but the foremen were strict about the rules; in fact, he would come in early and start on the engine without booking on, as he found the full hour helpful. With the fire built up in the firebox, he would get the pricker out of the rack on the tender and spread the burning coals around the box, then shovel fresh coal evenly across the box in all four corners. The sand boxes were filled to the brim and the caps replaced to keep the weather out. With the black needle rising up the scale on the steam gauge, the back damper wide open and the blower on just enough to draw air into the firebox, he then shut down the front damper before leaving the footplate. When the driver had finished oiling the con-rods and motion, their jackets would be hung up with their food bags, and the billycans of hot water stood on the shelf above the firebox door to keep warm. When they got the signal from the shed foreman to move off and proceed to the exit stop board, they phoned through to the signalman in the East Junction box to be allowed out onto the main line.

When I went back in the office Arthur had put a note on the desk, folded in half. A driver had come in to tell me that someone wanted to see me at the station at dinnertime. So I got my bike and in no time I was up at the station placing the bike against the iron railings. Then I saw Annie waving to me. I put up my hand, then, seeing that the coast was clear of moving traffic, I walked across the rails and climbed up onto the platform.

'Hi, what's up?' I asked her.

'I just wanted to see you,' she said.

'Well, you've seen me. Shall I go back to the shed?'

'I was being silly – sorry.'

'Are we meeting tonight at the pictures, and what about the weekend?'

'Yes to the pictures and no to Saturday night, but I'll come up to your house on Sunday like last week, if that's OK?'

'I'm working all weekend with Mick. I'll walk you out of the station.'

Then she buried her face in my neck and whispered in my ear, 'I love you.'

I gave her a kiss and said I would see her later. She waved, and I waved back, and went back to the shed walking with my bike.

One of the popular '22XX' Class 0-6-0s, No 2297; a Banbury engine, it was withdrawn in 1960.
Gerald Adams, Slip Coach Publishing Services collection via John Stretton

13. Mishaps

Mishaps and accidents were common round the shed, and there was a lot of larking about that young firemen got away with.

One day there was an engine standing at the coal stage, one of the 'ROD' (Railway Operating Division) 2-8-0s, on loan from the LNER. The regulator was fitted in a horizontal position, and Western men did not like them – they were horrible to work on. Four firemen climbed aboard to drive her down to the turntable, but she was short of steam after the fire had been dropped; she had 90lb of steam, not much for that old engine, and the water gauge was showing just below three-quarters full. They talked between themselves about how they were going to turn the engine and drive her back to the top of the shed, pull the points and run her down to No 6 road. However, it never happened as they planned it. The youngest fireman, a Cockney lad, was elected. He pulled the regulator and nothing happened. Placing one foot on the boiler face and with two hands on the regulator, he pulled with all his might. Suddenly the engine surged forward and slipped with a roar, the chimney spurting black sooty water like a column of volcanic ash out into the atmosphere.

As the engine started to run two firemen leapt off on either side of the footplate, leaving the Londoner standing at his post, not moving or quivering quite yet. Looking out of the side window towards the turntable, he saw another engine, No 2226, a Collett 0-6-0, being turned. The driver and fireman stood in amazement, seeing the 'ROD' coming towards them at a rate of knots, with the turntable sideways on. Suddenly the

Turntable trouble: a Stanier 8F with its nose in the pit.

driver saw two boys jump off the footplate at the last moment as the engine went into the turntable pit with it nose embedded and the steam cocks on both piston housings broken off, steam rising into the air and boiler water surging out into the ballast. Ouch!

All the railwaymen within the vicinity ran down to the table as the bad news travelled, then the laughing started with nudging and shaking of heads. One person said it looked funny with its nose in the ballast and its tender slightly over on its side. There was plenty of advice about how to get her out, but the fitting shop foreman, Bill Young, just ignored them, having his own thoughts on how to deal with the situation. He got his fitting crew, including some of the willing shed crew, to fetch pulleys, block and tackle with hydraulic jacks and blocks of wood. With hard work and know-how she eventually came out, with another engine standing back on the same road to help with the operation. But what about the engine sitting on the turntable sideways? Did she have an appointment somewhere else?

Accidents were quite common on BR in the days before Health and Safety was invented.

Tom Edwards was one of the senior hostel firemen who was on shed duty moving locomotives from one road to another as instructed by the shed foreman. Didcot shed had a slight incline up to the exit stop board, and this incline was used to advantage by driving an engine past the points of the chosen road, reversing the gear and opening the regulator while the engine was still moving forwards, then jumping off, changing the points and jumping back on as the loco passed by.

Tom was performing this dangerous manoeuvre one day, but as the loco was travelling rather fast he stumbled, missed the footstep and his foot went under the engine's wheels. His scream could be heard all over the shed as he lay on the rail holding his foot and tears running down his face. Everyone turned out to see what had happened. Tom was still screaming in agony so one of the drivers, an enormous man called Sam Essex, decided to knock Tom out with one punch. Tom was taken to hospital and patched up – the engine had run over his toes and completely flattened them. After they healed they were all joined together like a duck's webbed foot.

When I was working with Jimmy Tyler our orders from Arthur Brinkley were that when any of the '22XX' engines had a boiler washout in the shed we had to inspect the half-moon slide rods on the piston connecting rods and tighten the nuts and bolts with a torque spanner. We were on No 2 road at the entrance as the whole line was blocked with locomotives having their monthly washouts.

I was up in the motion under the boiler tight against the firebox above the middle driving wheel, sitting astride the con-rods with my legs dangling, as I was the thinnest fitter's boy in the shed. I held a ring spanner on the bolt head while Jimmy stood underneath in the pit with the torque bar; thus we worked together tightening down the locking nuts on the slide rods of No 2201. We were the first locomotive in the shed by the outer door. The track had no buffer stops, only pyramid metal blocks on each rail, and a small walkway on the shed wall side. Suddenly the biggest shout went out to clear the area – on its way in on No 2 road was a runaway, coming in fast.

Jimmy pulled me down into the pit, out from the motion a bit quick, and we both ran keeping our heads and shoulders down under every locomotive, five in total, partly crawling back towards the stop ends on our knees. Then, huddled together, we waited for the crash to happen. We couldn't get out because all the locomotives were buffer to buffer, so we stayed in the pit where we were, under the tender of the last loco near these pyramid rail blocks.

Dave Davies shouted to everybody to wind down the tender brakes on every loco on that road, but it did no good as the line of locos moved towards the blocks and Jimmy and I were both laid down flat side by side.

Mishaps

'22XX' Class 0-6-0 No 2201 at Didcot shed waiting to come into the shop for brake blocks. *R. J. Russell collection*

No 6162, a 2-6-2T 'Prairie' tank, came to grief at Reading shed in 1960 when it was too close to a set of points and was knocked over by a 'Hall' Class locomotive. In the third picture Bill Gibson, fitter, is on the right and Len Collett, crane driver, on the left. Also the underside of the vacuum cylinder can be seen on the right between the rear pony truck and trailing driving wheel. *All Bob Judge collection*

Because of the slight incline down from the exit stop board, the locomotive came in with considerable force and hit the first engine, which was No 2201, the engine that we had been on before we legged it away. The crash shunted every locomotive down to the last over the stop blocks. We were frightened but unhurt. The locomotive we were working on had to have the buffer replaced on the tender, as it broke off with the force of the collision. The buffer trolley ran well, as I oiled it regularly; running down to the end of the line, I jumped on it, having a ride for fun; Arthur could not believe it was in such good running order.

Another story concerned a young fireman named Pat Walsh,

who was shunting dead locomotives into the shed ('dead' meaning no steam in the locomotive, only 80lb pressure and no fire as the fire had been dropped). He drove No 6109, a 2-6-2T, backwards out of the shed, then, driving past the points, Pat shut the regulator and applied the vacuum brake to slow the locomotive. He then pushed the gear lever into the forward position and slightly opened the regulator. He climbed off the footplate and the locomotive went past the points until it caught up with the change of gears. He pulled the points over and as the locomotive went past him he climbed up the steps. However, he too slipped and fell off onto the ground.

It was a runaway, and approached the shed like a 'bat out of hell'. When Pat got up all he could do was shout 'Get clear!' After that shunting in the shed was a two-man job. Pat Walsh left the railway because he did not want to be a driver, and wouldn't take the driver's course with its exams.

*

On Friday night we had our regular outing. I had a very hot bath, washed my hair and was dressed to kill with my new suit on. I went to call on my mate down the road, as we were off to the pictures. We met the girls outside the Coronet flea-pit, but I don't remember seeing the film as I was to wrapped up in what was going on between us. Annie asked if she could see me tomorrow, but I explained that we were going dancing at the Oxford Ballrooms at Reading. What about Sunday? No, sorry, we were working till afternoon.

'I'll try and get up Sunday evening like last week,' she said.

'It's better if you meet me in Edmonds Park,' I said. 'There's a metal seat over near Samor's canning factory. I'll wait for you there, about 4 o'clock.

On Saturday morning I worked till midday, then had to report to Arthur, who asked me to pull out all the cards for the following week's work as I was not going to be there. In fact, I pulled out two weeks' worth of cards:

First week
Bob Looms and Bert Paice – 12,000 mileage servicing brown cards/repairs

No 5985 *Mostyn Hall* at Didcot shed on No 6 road with the rigid driving wheel out. 9F 2-10-0 No 92227 alongside is one of the double chimney fitted variants introduced in 1957 *R. J. Russell collection*

Jimmy Holmar – assist with 24,000 mileage servicing brown cards; No 6868 *Penrhos Grange*, tender and engine blocks change
Norman Brogden – assist with 12,000 mileage servicing brown card repairs
Dave Davies – 24,000 mileage servicing brown cards at front of shed

Second week
Dave Davies – 12,000/24,000 mileage servicing brown cards/repairs
Bert Paice – 12,000/24,000 mileage servicing brown cards/repairs
Norman Brogden – 12,000/24,000 mileage servicing brown cards, DMU and No 6868
Jimmy Holmar – 12,000 mileage servicing brown cards/front of shed repairs
Bob Looms – 12,000/24,000 mileage servicing brown cards
Jim Tyler – refit wheels to axle boxes on No 5985 *Mostyn Hall*, as all the parts were waiting for him

Arthur came in with my free pass for my week's leave. I explained about the cards and he couldn't believe what I had done. Everything was laid out on my desk for him – all he had to do to keep the office running. Anyway, Sam Morgan would be back on Monday morning from his holiday.

At the mid-morning tea break I sat in the office making notes about what I had done over the last two weeks; my finger was much better, and I was thinking about the journey to London. When should I leave? It had to be done on Sunday, after the Blewbury job. Arthur asked me what I was thinking. 'When to leave to go up the smoke.'

'Give me your brass tag and get yourself home. You've done well – have a good holiday, and when you get back go with Jim.'

I got my bike from the bike rack and rode up to Norreys Road to explain to Annie that I would have to cancel the afternoon in the park, as I was going to London for a week's holiday. She wasn't pleased. I could see now why she went with other boys, although being true to me.

I got back home and explained to Mum that I was going to London on Sunday. She OK'd it, and made me a huge sandwich with fresh bread and loads of boiled hock bacon and mustard, as I had plenty of time before Pete picked me up. We then went down to Mick's, and as he climbed into the cab I asked if we could finish early on Sunday, at midday, and explained why.

'Can't see why not. But we are out tonight dancing?'

'Yep.'

'Well, let's all get stuck in and have an easy day tomorrow,' said Pete.

On Saturday night we caught the coach outside the Post Office, paid our travel money, half a dollar each, and climbed on board. I shouted out, 'Are we there yet Dad?', and a roar of laughter went up. When we drew up at the front door area there were two girls and two guys standing by each other. They were the girls we'd met before – and their husbands. Mick said, 'Let the others go, then hang back and ask the driver to shut the door.' This he did – like a good 'un he knew what was going on, and he stayed in the coach with us. The four people stood around for a while then walked away. The driver got out of the coach and went walkabout, then came back and told us all was clear. We gave him a dollar and thanked him, then ran into the dance hall. We kept our eyes open all evening and had a great time drinking and dancing with other girls.

When the time came to go home everyone got on the coach, and we saw the two guys hanging about. The driver counted up the number of people he had brought and everybody was on board. As we left Mick and I waved like royalty to the two men and they chased the coach down the road, banging the sides with their fists. Everyone on the bus saw and waved like us as we sped off back to Didcot.

After a good night's sleep I was up at the crack of dawn on Sunday. I had a good fry-up with a cup of hot tea, which would last all day. Pete picked me up on time and we drove down to Mick's. As usual he came out with his hair all over the place – the poor boy was still asleep. He put his head on my shoulder and we never heard a sound from him till we got to Upton station.

The two box vans were left in the same place in the yard against the buffers. Pete backed up the trailer to the loading ramp on the box van, and we shifted the sacks of peat into the trailer. We loaded as much as we were allowed, and it didn't look as though there was much left, but it certainly fooled us as there would be three trips to do, back and forth to the Johnson Houghton stables.

After two more runs we were finished. We swept the floor of the box vans and the same with our trailer, leaving it all tidy. I wrote 'MTY' on the box vans.

Mick said, 'We were lucky last night. If those men had got hold of us we would be half dead today. The one you had was married?'

'Yep, and so was yours.'

I must have had something she liked then as I was only 15 years old. Pete listened to us two studs, and told us to be careful. I told Mick I was not going again as it was so close, and anyway we would have to give it a miss the week after next as we are both away on hols. When I was dropped off at home Pete stuffed a 10 bob note in my hand.

I had to have a bath as I was covered head to toe in peat dust, then I changed into jeans and shirt with my winklepickers, and carried my leather jacket. I sat down for some dinner with the family before going to the station; Dad said he would drive me there. Mum had packed a few things into a holdall. 'Take care – have a good time.'

I caught the 2 o'clock fast train to Reading and Paddington, showing my free pass to the ticket collector on the train; he gave it back to me without punching it.

Paddington was really quiet, being a Sunday afternoon. I proceeded down the Underground entrance and looked at the map to see which way to get to Whitechapel. I got there a little late in the evening, found the address and knocked at the door of my Aunty Betty and Uncle Michael – Aunty Betty was Dad's sister. They were going to put me up for the week; they spoke pure Irish, and I had a job to understand them.

I was dead knackered and asked them if they would mind if I went to bed. I crashed out fast asleep like a baby, then early next morning I heard the milk cart coming down the cobbled street. The next few days were good, as my cousin took time off work to stay with me. Her name was Addie, and she was lovely girl. We went everywhere together and enjoyed ourselves, laughing and joking and playing the fool. Addie introduced me to her friends' family, who were Jewish – great people. The father called me into his sitting room – he said, 'Come in, my boy,' like Fagin in *Oliver Twist*! I went to take off my shoes. 'No need, my boy – come and sit here next to me.'

Addie walked into the room and he shouted at her, 'You can bloody well get out and take off those bloody shoes!' The carpet was at least 10 inches thick with a deep pile – I could have rolled on it like a dog on heat! We supped tea with him and ate cakes. He glared at Addie.

'What you are doing for work, my boy?'

I said that in six months I would begin training as an apprentice fitter and turner on the old Great Western Railway at Didcot.'

'Well done, my boy! It's very nice meeting you, Patrick.'

I thanked him for his hospitality and wished him and the family well, and we left. The next time I went back in Whitechapel in 1965 all the Jewish families had left to be replaced by Asians.

Addie and I went to London Bridge, we rode the Underground, had ice creams, walked around the markets and bought honeydew melons, cutting them in half and eating them as we walked along. We had a smashing time together. We were getting closer to each other every day and friendlier, holding hands, and when we went back to the flats we both kissed each other in a corner. Unfortunately her little sister saw us and told her Dad, and I was kicked out of London. We were first cousins, and my uncle wrote a letter to my Dad banning me from going there again.

I travelled with my cousins to Paddington. I had my railway pass, but my cousins knew the system and hopped on and off the Underground trains like no one's business, and never paid a penny. The Didcot train was waiting in the station and we all sat in the carriage. Then a Didcot fireman, Vic Laity, walked by with his billycan – I slipped up there, as I could have ridden the engine to Didcot, but being young I never thought about it. I introduced my cousins to him and he was pleased to meet them.

I asked them how they were getting back to Whitechapel. 'The same way we came, on the Underground.'

I offered them money for the train fare but they declined. Addie's youngest sister said to me that she was sorry, and shouldn't have told her Dad that I had kissed her sister. They were upset that I was going home; it was Friday, and I was supposed to have stayed till Sunday.

The engine's whistle blew and Vic ran up to loco, and my cousins got off the train. As it pulled out of Platform 8 bound for home we waved to each other.

A letter had arrived from Dad's brother, Uncle Billy, and Aunty Jean, who lived just across from my Uncle Michael and Aunt Betty, in the same flats. I was expecting a telling off, with Dad's belt. But he screwed the letter up and threw it in the bin, then had a quiet word in my ear. 'You cannot go with first cousins, Pat.'

I had a quiet time at home for a while with Mum and Dad, then I wandered down to Mick's place to see when he was coming home from his holiday. I seemed to be lost without him, walking around with my tail between my legs. His Mum offered me a cup of tea and said he wouldn't be home till Sunday morning. Then she asked what I was doing home so early from London. I replied that I was banished as I had kissed my cousin Addie. 'Old-fashioned people you have – they're silly.' I thanked her for the tea and left.

I went home, got my bike and rode up to Norreys Road to see Annie. She was dumbfounded to see me and I was welcomed into the house to face the same questions, but I never told her. We went for a walk to the park and sat together on our favourite seat. I asked her if she would like to go to Reading with me tomorrow, and we arranged to meet at the station at 11 o'clock. I rode home and had a early night, telling Mum that I was going to Reading to buy some records – another fib. She didn't like me being with girls – she only wanted to mollycoddle me.

On Saturday morning it seemed funny not going to work, as I was still on holiday. I bought a ticket for Annie and showed my free pass, as it hadn't been punched. We had a smashing day out together, and she was thrilled to be with me. The last train home from Reading about midnight seemed OK, so we went dancing at the Majestic, as we both enjoyed it.

We met a man on the station sitting in a wheelchair. He said, 'You two seem in love – be happy, as she looks a million dollars.'

When we arrived back at Didcot we caught a taxi home, riding in style as it was too far to walk after a smashing day with Annie on my arm.

14. 'Warships' and washouts

On the Monday I called in to pick up my brass disc, then walked into the shop. I felt like a new member of staff again. I saw Jim up at the forge having a cup of black tea; when he had finished he threw the dregs into the forge fire, walked to his tool locker and replaced the cup.

'Well boy, did you have a good holiday?'

'Yep, not bad ta. So what's on?'

'I heard you had your finger broken and strapped up, and worked in the office with Arthur for two weeks. Sounds like he was pleased to get you in there.'

'It kept me out of trouble.'

Once again, Frank Marshalll said he'd have my left-over sacks of peat for his roses. Later in the day when I passed the shedmen's cabin there was a cooking smell from it – it smelled nice and I went in to have a nose and there was a young guy in there cooking apples in their skins in a pan over the belly stove. He said, 'Help yourself. There's plenty.'

I looked at him – a walking dustbin, dirty hands and face, and he smelled high. I said, 'No thanks.'

His name was Roy and he lived in the hostel in Didcot, which was named the 'Polar Star'. He had his own room, which stank as well! One day a few firemen burst into his room and grabbed him, took him to the amenity block where the bathroom had a lock on the door and everybody washed and took showers together, ripped his clothes off and dropped him into the hot water in a bath and scrubbed him raw. It left a dirty ring around the bath. He took the hint after that and kept himself clean.

Arthur came into the shop and asked if I'd had a good time. I said it was nice to see the Kelly family in London, but never said a word about what had happened.

'Right, stick with Jim Tyler, Pat – we have some work coming in soon for you both.'

We decided to help out the washout gang. The engines were being towed out by the shed shunter, and when the area was cleared Jim and I washed the pits out. While I pushed the heavy brush he got the fire hoses out and washed out the scale slurry down the waste holes on either side of the pit on No 4 road. When we had finished they bought in the next day's engines. Dick Bidmead, the shed cleaner, came and gave us a hand. While we washed out the pits he shovelled up the sludge from the drains to stop them getting blocked. He put the sludge in his wonky wheelbarrow and took it outside and dumped it, while Jim washed the concrete down clean again.

We went onto No 3 road and washed out the pit there, then again the next day's engines came in, five in total. As we were getting into it my Dad and Trevor May shouted out their thanks to us as they got away early.

The engines that were finished were put into No 2 road and Micky Gleason, one of the firelighters, started to light up the fireboxes with coal in each corner, with the middle left open. Then he got a block of firelighters on a shovel, nailed together, placed dirty cotton waste over the sticks, poured paraffin over the cotton waste, lit the waste and with great care slipped the shovel into the centre of the coal. With small lumps of coal he built a pyramid up either side and enough at all four sides and shut the firedoors, leaving a small gap to allow the draught. He also opened up the ashpan draught plate as the Welsh coal started to take hold.

Frank Marshalll came into the equation and they had two engines each. They both had to go around the engines, to see if the steam gauges were starting to rise, with the black needle fluctuating as the water in the boiler started to boil. The shed's doors had to be wide open as the sulphury, yellowy-green smoke rose out of the engines' chimneys and started to choke the men walking around the shed. They had to keep an eye on them

'Warships' and washouts

for 12 hours for the next day's working till the firemen came in to take over some 45 minutes before the locomotive was required to leave the shed. Sometimes the firelighter brought a shovel of burning coal from another locomotive to start the fire.

Outside the shed there was a small wooden box painted with yellow and black chevrons; this was called the shed signal frame. The fireman, or driver, would telephone the signalman letting him know his destination and the signalman would pull the lever to clear the ground signal to give permission to proceed.

It was a long day and I couldn't wait to get home and rest up before going down to see Mick and swapping stories about our holidays. In the end he decided to come up to my house instead, and sat and told my Mum how he had got on. She spilled the beans and said I had missed him. We had a laugh and decided to go and have a drink in the White Hart on the Broadway. We went to the public bar and had two pints of brown ale, then sat down and enjoyed the chat and drank the beer, one and a tanner a pint. I said that we had been lucky the last time we went to Reading, but I didn't want to go again, and he agreed.

'We'll go to Harwell Saturday evening. We can walk the 3½ miles walk there and home. Let's start at the Kicking Donkey, then up to the Crispin, Merv's place on the corner, and walk up the main street to the Chequers, have a skin full and walk home.'

'Sounds good.'

'And I think Jean's Café is open to coffee lovers – best in town on Sunday as no lorry drivers should be in.'

'Sorted!'

'Now what happened at London?'

'I kissed my cousin and got banished.'

'Did she kiss you back.'

'Blimey, yep!'

He said, 'You're a stud!'

We walked home after 15 pints each and silly as a bag of taters. He then drank milk and I sank a pint of water.'

'Goodnight, mate.'

The following day, Tuesday, I was asked to go into the cabin as Bill Clark wanted to see me.

'I have three pairs of overalls for you, Pat, that you can change into each Monday morning, and put the dirties in on Saturday morning when you leave for the weekend.

'Smashing – that will please my Mum.'

'The men said it was about time you looked like the rest of us, in blues.

They fitted a treat.

Arthur rushed into the shop about 9.30 and told Jim Tyler to get me and go up to the station as a passenger train was coming in from Bristol and the passengers were complaining that it was cold. The train arrived and it was headed by one of the new 'Warship' diesel-hydraulics, No D832. We climbed aboard and tried to get the boilers fired up. In came the spare driver, who said we would have to go with them to Paddington. So off we went, a day out in London – nice one!

We got the boiler working near Twyford – the filters were blocked. The noise in the engine room nearly blew your ears out, as the diesel engine was roaring all the time. We entered the cab and told the driver that it was fired up and would produce some heat through the coaches soon. He said we should go back into the rear cab and sit down for the rest of the journey. When we drew into Paddington we had no money between us, so we left the engine and Jim rang Arthur from the station master's office.

'What you are doing in London?'

'The train wouldn't stop for us.'

So we walked the station checking each engine until we found a Didcot driver heading home. He was driving 'Hymek' No D7078 and we got a lift in the rear cab, still in our overalls. At one point we had a walk through to the front to see the world passing us by. It was a good ride, but it was very noisy in the engine room. We got home mid-afternoon and had to report to Arthur.

On Wednesday the cry went up: 'Breakdown! There's a breakdown!' So Arthur said, 'Come on, Pat, you're coming

Classmate of Class 35 'Hymek' locomotive No D7078, in which the author and Jim Tyler secured a ride, No D7072 is seen in sidings at Didcot on Friday 2 April 1971 shortly before withdrawal.

out with us.'

I got my grub bag, slung it over my shoulder and walked across the rails, then climbed the stairs into the tool wagon and went down to the men's rest room.

There were breakdown limits around Didcot main line. Reading shed's limit was up to Moreton Road Bridge, Swindon's was to Steventon Road Bridge, and Oxford shed's was up to Appleford Road Bridge. Didcot had more to look after than any shed, with the centre marshalling yard and Didcot Ordnance Depot for the Army Stores. Sometimes the Swindon and Old Oak Common cranes crossed the borders to help out, because Didcot never had the heavy equipment to lift items back onto the road.

A few wagons had come off in the centre marshalling yard, so out went the crew with the breakdown van, which was painted red, while the rest room van was black. It was fine day and by mid-morning the sun was coming up good and strong. We got the wagons back on the road and as I was helping with the jacks in the van I smelled bacon being cooked, wafting across the marshalling yard. Just opposite there was a locomotive standing. I climbed up to the footplate and the driver and fireman were there having breakfast. I noticed that Chris Galloway, the fireman, had a shiny clean shovel on which they were cooking their food; it was placed just inside the firebox. On this shovel he put eggs and bacon, which were sizzling away, and a billycan of tea was ready.

What a lovely memory of long ago! This is how the footplate crews lived on these locomotives. She was 4-6-0 No 4950 *Patshull Hall*. Then I came back into the real world and had to go back to the lifting shop. The breakdown van was loaded and on its way back, and a few of us walked across the roads and back to the shed, looking left to right and listening for the sounds of moving trains. We were about to cross over the next set of lines when suddenly No 2836 with a goods train passed within inches of us. I could feel the steam rushing out of the piston gland onto my arms and I turned a funny colour – white with fright! Jim and Dave pulled me back against a box van and shouted to the others to look out. The piston casing just missed all of us by millimetres. In a marshalling yard the lines are closer together and there was not much room to walk and be safe at the same time.

It was good to get home that night and see my mate to arrange our next meeting place and what we were going to do on Friday night. We wouldn't be going to Reading dancing on Saturday night, as we had both come near to having our heads bashed in! We decided to get together again down at the Union meeting and have a crack.

Pay day came around quickly. In fact, the days went by fast as I was kept busy learning everything possible from the men, teaching me how to handle a spanner, how to hit the hammer correctly, what the half ball end of the hammer was for, and knocking out the graphite gasket joint holes with the metal flange in position – it was drummed into me by my mentor.

Suddenly there was a roar of steam escaping from the shed's stationary engine and streaming into the fitting shop. Jim and I went around the entrance on No 3 road and saw what was going on. He went under the frame and shut down the steam valve. 'Get two ladders, Wobble, and bring some tools. You know what sizes we require – standard sizes and a hammer.'

Meanwhile he went to the stores to get a safety valve graphite gasket, and a tin of graphite manganese paste with cotton waste. We met back inside the corrugated galvanised shed, and I put the wooden ladders to either side of the engine's boiler. It was very tight both sides to get near the safety valve, as the galvanised sheeting came pretty close to the engine, and overhead Jimmy struggled with the studs that stuck out holding the roof sheeting together, ripping his overalls and clothes. It was the same with me, and I had just had a new set of overalls given to me – Bill Clark would not be pleased.

Thank God the shiny casing had been removed or we wouldn't have had a chance of reaching the safety valve. Out came the spanners from the sack and we started to undo the nuts from the flange, with hot steam blowing out from where the gasket had blown. A small metal tube positioned in the mouth of the spanner gave support when pushing to undo the nuts. Arthur appeared, asking if everything was all right. But the high-pitched scream of the escaping steam made our ears sing, and was painful. We pressed on undoing the boiling-hot nuts, and the safety valve started to lift slightly. We both ducked down as the steam rushed out with such force into the atmosphere – from outside it looked as though the shed was on fire as the steam found every nook and cranny to escape.

'Right, Wobble,' came a shout. 'Get the two small bars either side.'

We lifted the valve together over the studs and heaved it onto the brow of the boiler, turned it on its side and Jim balanced it, holding it as it jammed onto the wooden ladder's rungs. It was very awkward and heavy, but to lower it down on the ground would have made lifting it back up into position very difficult. We both started to remove the old gasket from both flanges, me on the boiler and Jim on the valve, as he was strong enough to hold the unit with one hand and scrape with the other. I went around the studs with a file scraping off the old gasket, stuck down from years on the job, not having been done properly by someone within the fitting team. We cleared away the mess.

'You can paste up now, Pat.' So the tin was opened and I looked in the sack for the blue hacksaw blade that was used as a knife. I scraped the paste onto the boiler's flange, remembering my magic make-up skills, then put the new gasket over the studs and got more paste out of the tin, smearing the magic mascara over someone's lovely face in the make-up dressing room on a film set! Then, back to earth, we both turned the safety valve down onto the brow of the boiler, and with one lift between us up it went and rested on the studs.

'You OK to lift it?' asked Jim.

I had come this far, so answered, 'Ready when you are, mate.'

We lifted it straight over the studs and it slid down onto the boiler flange. By this time my arms and shoulders ached. We were both still standing on the wooden ladders; I had almost forgotten where we were, I was so comfortable. Placing the nuts back on the studs, I got the spanner out while Jim went around his side doing the nuts up finger tight, then started to tightened them all down, first with the spanner hand tight, then, placing the metal tube into the mouth of the spanner, we went criss-cross all around the valve until we both were happy. We then climbed down off our ladders, collected all the tools into the sack, placed the lid back on the paste tin and hit it with the spanner to fasten it down.

'How do you feel, boy?' asked Jim in his Welsh accent.

'Sore but OK.'

'You done well. Let's take all this stuff back into the shop and have a break. A cuppa wouldn't go amiss.'

'Blinking good idea.' I was gasping for a slurp of hot tea.

Then we went to Arthur to get the shed fireman to get the fire going again. The smokebox door had to be opened up for the shed cleaner to get in and clear out the burned ash as it was causing a problem.

Back at the forge, I poured boiling water into the billycan and the fresh tea leaves. Jim twirled the billycan round in the air and poured out the black nectar into his dirty old cup. 'That's how you drink it, Wobble – black.'

I had cut out sugar since starting at the shed, but not milk yet, because I liked a bit of colour in my tea. I drank my tea and ate the grub Mum had prepared for me while I sat on the anvil with a piece of wood and some cotton waste under my bum – I was at home.

*

After work Mick and I met up. I told him it had been a hard day.

'You must have muscles on your arms by doing all that heavy lifting.'

We went down to the Labour Club, and there at the bar was Jim. He bought us both a drink.

'You worked hard today, boyo, and you deserve that beer.'

I sank mine in one go. Then Dave Davies appeared, and bought another round.

'Cheers, Dave.'

We all touched glasses and said 'Cheers' to each other.

'Right, my turn,' I said.

'Put your money away – you don't earn enough. It's my turn.' Jim Hale had appeared.

'Blimey,' I said. 'The three musketeers! And you all scrub up quite good for oldies!'

'You cheeky little sod! Now do as you're told and behave yourself!'

I felt bad. All I wanted to do was buy them all a pint each. But I was happy now as the beer started to take effect and put a smile on my face.

'Clear off home,' they said. 'We'll see you tomorrow at work.'

Mick and I walked home. He had bought his bottle of Lamb's Navy Rum in the club while no one was looking.

We arranged to go the flicks again the following night, as we wanted to see those two beauties again.

'It seems you're getting serious with Annie…'

We walked home, drinking Mick's rum. He finished it off and threw the empty bottle into the undergrowth. Those bottles must have been starting to mount up!

I drank a pint of water at Mick's as he drank a pint of milk, then we said our goodnights.

The next morning, as usual, I avoided Les Gibbs at the market square as he had a knob on and was grumpy. It had been raining heavily overnight, and at the station I saw that the porters had their socks off and their trouser legs rolled up. The undercroft was flooded with rainwater – the drains couldn't take the water from the heavy storm. I had two choices: ride through it or take the stairs to Platform 3 and walk across the tracks. I chose the second method, as it kept me dry all day.

I had made good time as I always left in plenty of time to get to work. I went into the Time Office to collect my brass disc, and Ernie Jones said, 'I see the water never held you back then. I guess you can walk on water!'

I grinned and under my breath I said, 'You cheeky sod!' as I wandered down to the cabin. Someone said I was always grinning when I came out of the Time Office.

I saw Cess (my Dad) with Trevor May rushing about as normal, as they were on a

'Warships' and washouts

piece rate. They shouted to each other who was doing what. This time Dad had undone the plugs on the bottom of an engine's boiler, draining the sludge and acids resulting from the hard water in the Didcot area. He would run along in the pit with his head low and drain every engine in turn, then get out of the pit on No 4 road and go over to the pit on No 3 road and do the same again. Meanwhile Trevor collected a handful of lead plugs from the stores, placing them at the different places where the old ones were being removed; he would throw the old ones into the corner of the building and place the new ones over the spindle studs ready to be replaced. By now all five engines had been drained down and all the boilers plugs removed, even at the rear of the boiler on the footplate.

Both men screwed on the steam hoses at the highest point of the first engine and opened the steam valve from the stationary engine to flush steam through the piping system while they had a cup of tea. One engine finished, they unscrewed the steam hose and did the second engine in exactly the same way, and so on until the fifth engine had been flushed through. While one man dealt with the steam hose, the other was refitting the new lead plugs with their graphite paste, screwing them back into the boiler. They had a brilliant system going: when one man had finished the steam hose he would go back to the start and refill each boiler with clean water with a hose fitted to the top plug, taking a look at the water gauge on the footplate every now and then to see that the level was correct. The other man would go back and help to fill the rest of the boilers with water until they met, then both men finished by screwing the top plugs into the boiler sides. Their times on the shift were 6.00 till 2.00, but they were good and would be walking out of the shed at noon with clean clothes on after showering and washing themselves. On weekdays they dealt with five engines per day, and on Saturday morning three engines – 28 engines per week. The stationary boiler was washed out on a monthly card, which was counted as part of the piecework system.

God help anyone who got in the way, as my Dad would turn the steam and water hose onto them. I was as bad as him for a laugh: I tied a piece of black cotton onto a 10 bob note and sat under an engine waiting for a fitter's mate to come into the shop. He would put his foot on it, look round to see if anyone was looking, and bend down to pick it up, as I pulled the cotton towards me. On one occasion Jim Hale nearly fell over and hurt his back rushing towards the money; I legged it out of the shop under the tender, laughing out loud and putting the evidence back in my pocket.

One day I lost my chisel when it fell into the open safety valve of engine No 4939 *Littleton Hall* and down through the steam pipes while I was scraping off the flange around the studs. One morning six months later Cess presented it back to me; it had dropped out of the bottom drain hole! (I still have it today in my tool box.)

15. Pistons...

I walked into the shop and Jim was having a cup of tea in his dirty cup stained from black tea.

'It's about time you gave that cup a birthday,' I said.

He laughed and said, 'Right, we have a big job on. No 2819 is coming for piston valve replacement.'

The tankie shunted two engines outside on No 5 road, which got rid of the smelly sulphur coming out of the chimneys. Then the tankie, with the shed driver Ted Brown and his fireman Ernie Paul, came back into the shop with the engine we were waiting for, tender first. Ernie got off the tankie and uncoupled the engine and asked Jim if he was happy where it stood.

'OK, boyo, that's lovely,' he said in his Welsh accent.

I got up on the footplate and wound the tender handbrake down hard, as he knew where he wanted the engine stood to remove the piston rods. But first he told me to go into his tool locker and get a quarter Whitworth size 'Snail' spanner to remove the bolts from the casings on both sides. 'No need to take off the side covers, Wobble, not just the front covers.'

I got down under the frame of the 2-8-0 engine. The front pony truck wheels were smaller, at 3ft 2in, while the four driving wheels on each side were 4ft 7½in. These engines were very powerful when pulling freight trains, only this one had no power as she had to have new piston rings fitted on both sides. I was on my knees now under the front frame where I could tap the bolts with a small hammer to shock them before attempting to unscrew them. It seem to work, and I placed the small bolts in a dish I had found for safe keeping. One side done, I went over to the other side and, once completed, I removed the front cylinder casings in turn, making sure not to bend them.

'Right,' said Jim. 'Go over the other side and take off the piston glands that slide on the piston shaft. I heard you have packed them when working with Jimmy Holmar at the front of the shed. Remove them with the old packing inside and throw them away, Wobble.'

I got the tools from Jim's tool locker. One was a long metal wire with one end that twirled like a wine bottle corkscrew, and at the other end had a loop to hold it with. You screwed it into the graphite packing and pulled it out. We needed space when

Shed fireman Ernie Paul is crouching at the front of this group at the 'Polar Star' hostel in 1962. Standing, left to right are 'Curly', Frank Feast, Pat Walsh and Cedric 'Bronco' Ashmore.

One of the powerful '28XX' Class 2-8-0s, No 2847, heads south through Oxford in 1957.
John H. Eales, Slip Coach Publishing Services collection via John Stretton

pulling out the piston and shaft as it was a cramped, low job, explained Jim. I did as I was told and removed the old packing from both sides of the engine as well as the piston glands, and pushed the glands back to the crossheads.

'Come down with me at the front of the engine and help me, Wobble, by holding the tool bar.'

While he pulled up I held my boot on the bar's knuckle at the socket end, while he cracked off some nuts, going around the circle on the piston cover. I kept replacing the socket on another nut, then he slid the metal tube over the bar and held it while I stuck my boot on the knuckle, pressing myself against the lower frame for support.

Thinking that I was getting better at what I was doing, but knowing that I could do much better, I really got stuck into the work. It had been five months now, working every day with the same man and watching his methods. Without him asking me, I fetched the large wooden block of the necessary height and placed it down near the piston cover as he went to get his small lever bar.

'I wondered where you went to, Wobble. Good lad!'

He edged around the piston cover, poking the chisel-like end of the bar into the gap as it started to ease away. Suddenly with a whoosh the cover fell towards the wheel and frame, and fell onto the wooden block. He looked at me and said, 'You were bloody lucky boyo!' Then we rolled the piston cover out of the way.

I had never seen inside a cylinder before. Jim stuck the chisel end of his bar into the casing and showed me how much play there was. 'See, Wobble, we are going to be busy when we get these pistons out into the open. Well, *you* are.'

'What, me again?'

'Yes, boyo – you've got to learn. I'll show you the next step.'

I bent over the slide valve looking between the spokes of the wheel and the back of the crosshead.

'See that cotter pin? Go around the other side and knock it out while I do the same.'

I had a hammer and the small bar that I had made with a 'rat's tail' that was slightly bent for just these jobs. 'Dave helped me when you were on leave.'

I poked the point into the cotter pin's eye and whacked it with the flat of the hammer, and out it shot.

'Now look – see this metal wedge? It's got

to be hit from underneath, so go back and try knocking it out.'

I did as I was told again, I leaned over the slide bar gripping my 2½lb hammer and eyed up what I had to do. I whacked the wedge upwards on the leading edge and felt it move.

'How are you doing, Wobble?'

'It's moved.'

'Keep at it – it will eventually come out and you'll be over the moon.'

He was dead right. One big hit and out it shot.

I went off again and brought back another wooden block the same size as before and placed it under the piston cover I was working on.

'Right, come and give me a hand,' said Jim, 'then we can get yours done the same.'

We both went round the engine together. He had hold of a huge crowbar, and slid the crosshead backwards a little away from the piston shaft. I saw it drop slightly. Holding the crowbar and poking it into the wheel's spokes, he pushed the piston out of the cylinder. He placed the wood onto the piston shaft's end, told me to stand clear, then with one mighty pull on the crowbar the shaft shot through the gland hole and the piston shot out of the cylinder with a whoosh. We got hold of the piston shaft, twirled the piston round off the wooden block onto the floor, and laid it down.

'Right, let's go round your side and do the same.' This we did, then he said, 'We'll do the pistons first, then we'll have to pull the valves out. That will be harder. Are you up to it, Wobble?'

'Yes, boyo.'

He said that I knew what to do to get the rings out, but to be careful as they have sharp edges and will slice your fingers off. His bled a few times, and that was the only time he would hold cotton waste. I poked a small screwdriver into the channel under the ring's edge. Jamming a chisel under the ring, I forced it up to break it, hitting it with a chisel and hammer while covering the ring with cotton waste, in case it flew back at me.

I had to do this three times. Then I scraped out the black carbon that lay in the channel and wire-brushed the remains out, as clean as I could, with the help of a chisel and hammer. I then washed out both cylinders with paraffin, in case there were any foreign objects resting in either bore. With the piston channels clean, now the new rings had to be fitted.

Jim went to his tool locker and brought back his box of tricks for taking the measurements of both cylinders. We knew that the cylinder bore was 18½ inches, so he put the dial bore gauge indicator in with the micrometer gauge and adjusted it by minute twists of 5 thous. Then he went to collect the correct rings from the stores. Meanwhile I cracked on with the other piston, breaking the rings off out of the channels and scraping the carbon to get them cleaned out ready for the new rings. Then we had a tea break, before refitting the pistons and dealing with the valves.

'That will take the stuffing out of you.'

'Thanks, that's all I need!'

The time flew by and we were still having our grub when Arthur appeared. I went to move but he grabbed my arm. 'Stay where you are – you've earned it. How are you getting on?'

'Good,' said Jim. 'The pistons will be back in today and the valves will be started tomorrow, first thing.'

Then Arthur said he was in a pickle, and did I know anyone with a pipe threader as we had nothing here at Didcot and needed one for our tool list.

'I might do,' I said, 'but it means going off site and talking to some people.'

I asked if it could be left till next week when we'd finished the engine.

At dinnertime I wandered out to the station and walked up to a gentleman I used to deliver the *Daily Telegraph* to for three years when he worked with Station Garage. Would he remember me? He did, and asked how I was getting on. I told my story to him, then asked if he had any pipe fitting sizes in the workshop that could help us out.

Pistons...

Unfortunately he didn't carry the required sizes.

I walked towards Mr Midwinter's shop and climbed the wooden steps to the entrance. The aroma of that old shop was wonderful, and the old floorboards bounced as I walked over them. I bought a couple of Mars bars and a quarter pound of tea, then returned to the shed. I still had plenty of time so walked over the tracks to the East Junction loop. Looking across the sewage pits I saw a small brick building. It had a wooden door but the glass was frosted so I couldn't see inside. I knocked and someone shouted 'Come in'. I entered and the manager asked me how he could help. I explained about the situation and what the shed was looking for.

'Go in there and talk to those men. Say I sent you and they will help.'

When I left that building I had a sack of pipe threading teeth of all sizes and a pipe wrench, coloured red as they wanted to get rid of them. They were heavy and I struggled towards the East Loop line embankment, climbing up on my knees trying to get a grip in the long grass. However, I kept slipping back down as the bank was wet and steep, so I threw the sack up higher, and hung onto the pipe wrench until I made it to the top. Collecting all the bits together and looking to make sure the coast was clear, I crossed the tracks and went into the shop by the rear entrance, laying my booty near the forge and hidden away.

Dinnertime was over and we went back to what we were doing. When Jim came back from the stores he had six new rings on his arm.

'Right, Wobble, look and listen. When you place the ring in the bore and let it close up you will see that the ends overlap. Mark the ring with a pencil, take it out and measure three-eights of an inch from your mark, and scroll another pencil line down below the ring. Place the ring in the vice and close it very tight. Now with the chisel you're going to cut off the waste. Put the cold chisel at the lower mark and hit it with the 2½lb hammer, but covered with cotton waste in case it flies back towards you – the rings are hardened steel and very tough.' He watched me do the first one as he had instructed, looking over my shoulder. 'Now do the next two rings by yourself, and I'll measure the other cylinder the same way with the rings and mark them.'

When all the rings had been cut to size my three stayed with me and the other three went into the cylinder for safe keeping.

Coming back with the oil can I shot oil into the cylinder and wiped it over with a duster I got from his tool box.

'Now let's put these rings on. I'll watch you. Start with the open ring and heave it over the face of the piston and tap it with my soft white metal mallet. Go over to the first channel as I did.' After sliding a screwdriver in the channel the ring proceeded to edge over and into the middle channel. 'Now do the first channel with the new ring that fell in.' He lifted the piston shaft upright, dropped the last ring down onto the shaft at the rear of the piston, and knocked it into place.

Again Jim got his oil can, squirted oil over the ring and spread it around the piston head; he then spread the graphite paste on the face of the cylinder and around the studs. 'Right, Wobble, let's get this one into the bore.'

We lifted the shaft into the cylinder's mouth and eyed up the gland where the shaft had to go. He got his crowbar, stuck it in the spokes of the pony truck wheel and lifted the piston upwards, as I got the 3-foot-square block of wood under it. He rested the piston on the wood. 'Now, boyo, this is going to be bloody hard work.'

We both edged the piston into the mouth of the cylinder and I went to the gland and looked for the shaft, giving instructions which way to move the piston so he could edge the shaft into the gland's opening. When it was in he told me to come and help him. 'Get that soft hammer and hit the centre of the piston hard.' I did so, but it seemed slow.

'Hang on a moment,' I said. I looked

around and saw a block of wood in a corner and ran back with it. Jim was still holding the piston up. I sized up the area and hit the piston full on face; it shot partially in towards the cylinder and against the outer casing.

'Good lad! Go and get another crowbar and take over for me here, Pat, please.' Oh, getting friendly now, are we?

I did as I was told, found a crowbar stuck between his tool locker and Dave's. Bringing it back to where I had left Jim struggling, I took over the bar one hand at a time – as he took his hand off, mine went where his had been. I kept the pressure on – by this time my back was aching – while he went to the rear and put the crosshead shaft key into the slot. He placed his crowbar against the leading wheel spokes and in front of the key and pushed with all his might.

'Stop!' I shouted. 'We have to get the rings into the cylinder. Get the thin bars and prise the rings in while I will keep the pressure on this bar.'

I kept my fingertips away as the rear ring went in first. Jim juddered as the middle ring slid into the face of the cylinder and came to a sudden stop. Now I had to tease the rings into the cylinder bit by bit. Jim's whole body juddered again as they went it, then suddenly a great whoosh of air shot out through the gland's hole.

Just as we were about to take a rest, Arthur appeared and asked how we were getting on. Jim asked if he could have a quiet word with him. Arthur said that now was a good time, so they went off together. Meanwhile I got all the tools together and went to the other side ready to refit that piston the same as the other. I removed the new rings from their hidey hole and started to fit them on the piston.

I did the same routine as before while the boys were away chattering. I got the second ring in the centre channel, then the first, then the last – I lifted the shaft to rest the piston head flat on the floor on some brown paper I had found, then slipped the ring over the shaft and dropped it onto the rear of the piston. With the soft hammer I started to feed the ring around the edge until it slipped over into the channel. I found the oil can and squirted the inside of the cylinder, wiping it around inside the bore, then used the same amount of oil over the new piston rings.

I then waited for the return of my mentor. I walked to my locker, got out my tea things and made tea – I was gasping for a drink. When the kettle boiled I poured the water into the billycan onto the tea leaves, got a Mars bar out of the grub bag, placed a piece of wood on the anvil and sat eating the chocolate bar and drinking tea. I was getting more like Jim, and the way he worked, but I had a premonition that it would not last, and that things would change in years to come.

When the boys came back I asked no questions, just saying that I had made the tea. Arthur asked if there was a spare cup. I cut my other Mars bar in half with the wrapper still on, then Arthur came running back with his big heavy feet and long blue coat rubbing the floor, as if he was still in the RAF. 'Help yourself,' I said. 'There's a chocolate bar for both of you – half each I'm afraid.'

I brought my sack out from under the forge. 'Arthur, have a look around here and see if this is what you want.'

'Where did you bloody get that from?' Even Jim couldn't have guessed.

'Right,' said Arthur, 'tell us what you've been doing when we left you.'

'I took the tools around the other side of the engine and put the rings on the piston, waiting for you to help put this one back in place.'

'So where did you get this stuff from. They never had it at Station Garage, as I know a man there, and they do not carry anything that size.' They shook their heads. 'Unbelievable, you are, Pat.'

'I went to the sewage works and they said I could go back and they will pass on anything I want.' They were both dumbfounded.

However, we had to get on as planned,

Pistons...

as we had to finish off this piston malarkey. We plodded on, placing the shaft into the cylinder as before, but this time we had everything to hand. Jim stuck the rat-tail end of the crowbar into the pony truck wheel as he lifted up the piston head and I went around the crosshead end and told him which way to line up the shaft. Then I came back with the lump of hard wood and bashed the piston head as he took its weight. I got the thin bars and ran them around the rings, lifting and squeezing them together so they slid into the tapered face. Suddenly with a judder the first one went in, then the bars did what they had been made for, edging around the cylinder. With a shudder number two went in, then the third, and the air whooshed out of the gland.

Having placed the oval glands in their correct position on both sides, Jim slid the crosshead up to the shaft and connected it until he saw the wedge's hole line up. Now the wedge was fitted, and he placed his hand in his overall pocket and drew out two cotter pins, finishing off that first side. We did the other side then called it a night – we had done everything ready for Saturday morning.

I got washed up and scrubbed my hands with boiling water, Lifebuoy soap and hair from seats in the carriage and wagon shed, before leaving for home and a night out with Mick. As I had my tea it dawned on me that me and my mate were both comfortable in each other's company, although he was 1½ years older than me.

I was totally knackered now, but knew that I would come alive when I met up with Annie at the flicks; she made my day just walking with me and her arm resting on mine. We could have been a young married couple!

We all met at the flicks, and went down to our usual place. When the lights went out I got down with Annie and started smooching, coming up for some air a little later! She asked me if I would be seeing her this weekend. 'What about Sunday morning, meeting at your house, or if you like at the usual place in the park. Come home and meet Mum and Dad. Then maybe we could meet again that night. Can't I see you tomorrow?'

'I'm working till midday.'

'I'll come down the station and we could see each other.'

'OK, that will be nice, but I'm sure I will be dirty and oily.'

After the pictures finished I walked her home and we kissed and cuddled in her parents' garden outhouse – we couldn't keep our hands off each other. She was a smashing girl and I thought highly of her, although she did come out with some rot about her being more mature that me, but girls are like that. I started to walk home when her father said he would drive me home. We had a long chat in his car, and I thought he was a bit rude, but I could see his point and never argued!

On Saturday morning we had to check that no one had put anything into the cylinders, as some men, whoever was on nights that week, liked to see us mess up. We got stuck in to replace the covers. I had to cover the cylinder flange with graphite manganese paste, especially working around the studs and coating them. I had to do the piston cover as well. Now came the main item, lifting the covers up onto the studs. I found a nice long square crowbar, and we both placed the 3-foot-square block under the lip of the cylinder casing. We lifted the cover up onto the wooden block, then gingerly picked it up, holding the safety valve at the bottom and my hand on the top face, and heaved it up gently while Jim stuck the square of the crowbar under the faceplate. It was blinking heavy! I took the weight and pushed against the cover as Jim lifted it up until it fell onto a stud. I looked down to see if I still had any fingers on my hands. Those covers weighed a few hundredweight.

Believe it or not, the cover fell onto the correct stud and I knocked the faceplate with the lump of wood we had used the day before. Jim told me to get a nut on any stud to keep it where it was, which I did with great relief. Now we placed all the nuts on their studs, but one wasn't going on properly so I turned it over and wound it onto the stud to remove the thread burr, then turned it again and put it back on the correct way. We did up all the nuts then hit the cover again with the wooden block to make sure it was fitted correctly. We soldiered on and put the socket and extension bar on each nut going criss-cross style all around the faceplate.

We then did the other side the same way. We knew it wasn't going to be easy but it had to be done. I then started to pack the glands on one side while Jim did the other.

It was coming up for home time and I had had enough, so we made a pot of tea at the forge and drank it before washing up to go home. While we sat there Jim said, 'Do you want to know what we were talking about yesterday?'

'That's up to you.'

'Well, I'm going to tell you anyway. I want to keep you in the shop and teach you everything as I'm sure you're going to be a damn good fitter when you come out of your time, Pat.'

I thanked him for believing in me, as I still had five years to go.

'You're a conscientious worker and I appreciate you as you are willing to keep going and learn as well, and I think you are privileged with a photographic memory of what you do.'

I washed up and we both walked to the Time Office to hand in our discs. I got my bike and rode up to the station. Jim rode beside me as I saw Annie waving from the station.

Jim said, 'Is she waving at you?'

'No, it might be you, you old sod!' I replied, but he knew that she was waiting for me.

'Nice-looking girl, Pat. What's her name?'

'Annie.'

'Nice name. See you Monday. Behave yourself.'

'Thanks, Dad!'

'You cheeky little sod,' was his parting shot.

16. ...and piston valves

As Annie came off the station I gave her the biggest kiss with my dirty oily face as we walked home to her house, fingers entwined and talking and laughing. She was dressed to kill and very beautiful. When I got home in the afternoon Mum asked where I'd been.

'Went out to see a friend and forgot the time.'

That Saturday night Mick and I went out on the razz at Harwell, 3½ miles from Didcot. We did every pub in the village, six in total, and ended up at the Chequers. There was Harry Bill and Marge, who spent most of their time arguing – I never knew which one was in charge – and over in the corner were the lads, Jim Tyler, Dave Davies, Jim Hale and Bob Warwick. Mick was at the bar, then up came Bob and brought a round of ale for themselves. We were invited over to their corner, but every time I got up to get a round I was told to sit down, as I didn't earn enough. We got into an argument but I was told to shut up. Everyone in the pub was buying tote money tickets. The prize was 15 quid, so we said if we won it we would all have to sit there and drink the pot. Guess what? I won the pot, 15 quid. I was handed a fiver to put into my pocket, then they let me buy the beer. What a good night we had! They caught a taxi home, but we said that we were going to the Crispin place, then walking home.

We went back to Merv and Jean's place for free beer. Merv locked the door, then someone knocked. It was the local copper. 'Time to shut up,' he told Mervin.

'No, this is a private party, officer. Good night.' Mervin shut the door and locked it. 'Nosey old sod,' he said, but if he'd known how old Mick was at the time, 16½, and me 15…. We left the pub and walked home three sheets to the wind. We must have got home around 2.30 – a night to remember, all old mates together. Mick and I walked home happy as two sandboys.

I met Annie that Sunday morning a bit later than I should have, still partially drunk. She was at home with dirty old clothes on. She said, 'Come here and look what I've done. I got permission from Mum to clean out the outhouse, so we can stay in here instead of going into the house and sitting on the stairs, to be alone together.'

I saw her point. When I told her what her Dad had said to me when he took me home, she went ballistic and raised the roof.

'I'll see you later, say about 6, if that's OK, as Mick and I are going out this afternoon.'

Most evenings when I wasn't with Mick I was with Annie, as we were getting very serious, and she was a delightful, pretty girl. She was smashing to look at with her long black hair, and I told her I loved her deeply. I would have loved to get engaged and her Mum would have been overjoyed. I walked in one evening with a ring box in my hand, and her mother put her hands up to her face in excitement as she thought we were going to get engaged. However, I'd bought a signet ring for her, and a couple of weeks later she bought me a gold ring in the shape of a snake with a red garnet, which I treasured for years. Her Mum always shouted to me to come into the house without knocking. I was very close to her – she was a great mother.

Sunday lunch at home was an opportunity for the family to talk together, Mum, Dad, Dick and me, and I'm happy to say we brought up most things together – but not the food! My Mum was a good cook and could put on a good spread. When I'd finished I said 'See you later,' and told her I was going out with Mick.

Mick and I went down to Jean's café near the station to get a coffee, as it was the only place in Didcot to get together, with all the Teddy Boys and yobs, with Mick and I being respectable and smart with our Italian suits and our winklepickers.

We looked the bee's knees and sat in the cafe having a joke with different railway people about work. Looking out of the window we suddenly saw two girls we knew walking up towards Station Road, then someone ran into the cafe and told us that two girls were looking for me and Mick. They came from Reading and had turned up under their own steam.

These were the girls we had begun to meet at the Oxford Ballroom until we found out that they were married, and their husbands wanted to kill us both! Mick said he would go out and talk to them, but when he appeared they ran to him and asked where I was. Mick said I was with my girlfriend. Then Mick told them to go home to their hubbies and forget us. Mick's girl kept crying – she really went for him – while the other one was shouting for me. He stood his ground and told them to leave Didcot, as we had moved on. He was good like that.

We left the cafe and walked home, chatting all the way. What if the girls went to our houses and asked for us? My Mum would have blown her top – her little boy enjoying life and sex with a married woman! Whatever next? But what the eye doesn't see, the heart can't grieve over. Mick said the same as me, but his Mum would allow it as she was more down to earth. It was my Mum who didn't want to let me go out into the big wide world and have fun, so I had to fib now and then to enjoy myself.

I went to Mick's on the way home and was welcomed into the house for some tea. I stayed for a couple of hours chatting, then they pulled the carpet back and we started to jive and dance to the latest records, together with a smooch with Mick's sister Jenny to an Elvis Presley record, *Pocketful of Rainbows*. 'You'll make a lovely couple!' said Mick.

Six o'clock came and went, then I walked to Annie's house in Norreys Road for 7. She was waiting for me, and I had to explain where I'd been.

*

Monday was the start of a new week and workwise we had a lot to achieve. I'd had my fun over the weekend, now I was back, and

that night I would be going to bed early!

In the cabin, Dave Davies and Jim Hale, 'the twins', sat together supping tea and reading the paper. They asked what time I'd got in on Saturday night, and I told them it was Sunday morning, explaining about drinks at the Crispin, claiming that they had left us in the lurch.

I went into the boilersmith's shed to see what was in there; it was where they kept all the bricks and firebars dry, stacked neatly around the edges, as well as superheaters stored out of the wet weather. We had a Technician Officer from Reading two days a week to inspect the AWS (Automatic Warning System) systems on the engines, as the railway was going 'high tech', and sitting on the bricks was a Jamaican having a drink. He said his name was Jimmy and he had travelled up by train to visit the engines that required their ATC boxes on the footplate to be looked at.

'Why sit in here? Why not come into the cabin and eat your grub there?' I said to him.

'I'm happier here, thank you,' he replied. He asked my name, and suggested that I go with him to the Railway Club at dinnertime. We arranged to meet near the station at 12.30.

'OK,' I said. 'Give me a shout if you need anything, Jimmy.'

The men were still having a good laugh about Saturday night – they kept on and on, until my mentor came into the shop. He too asked what time we'd got home. 'We never got home as you lot left us in the lurch!' I lied. Off he went – I'd got him hooked and was pulling him in. I kept a straight face.

It was time to work on No 2819's slide valves. 'Come on, let's do this. I'll get the spanner to undo the rivet nuts under the front side frame so we will pull out the valves. And what do you mean about us leaving you in the lurch?' Then the twins came in with Bob Warwick. 'Come on – what's going on?' they demanded. I burst out laughing. 'We had a good night, though you all must admit it was at my expense – I bought the beers all night!' The rest of the fitting shop crews came in, hearing the laughter, as well as Arthur, who heard it down the shed. Jim told them all and everyone was choked.

'That little sod won the jackpot again at the pub and he ended up paying the beers all night – 15 quid'.

Dave said to Arthur, 'You should lock up your daughter as he's spending more time in Harwell these days.'

Arthur glared at me and asked if that was right. 'Yes, but not looking for girls, as I have a girlfriend. We drink at the Crispin, Merv's place. I even changed a barrel for them.'

'What, you went behind the bar, not just down in the cellar.'

'Got your feet in there!' Arthur was choked.

I got the spanner and hammer from Jim's locker to get the front covers off and press on with the removal of the valves. It was hard going as the nuts must have been there since the engine was built. As I hit the rivet head to shake the stud the nut seemed to get loose. I got the oil can, poured some paraffin in and shook it up, then squirted it in the air. I went under the front side plate near the pony truck wheel and squirted the nuts with this mixture, and it seemed to work. However, some were still tight as a rat's arse, so I got the cold chisel, placed it on the flat of the nut and whacked it. I went from one to another and was getting on OK until I whacked my hand and thumb. The tears ran down my face as I cried out. Jim told me to put it under the cold tap – the tap water was freezing cold and my thumb turned white then a deep purple. I was still hurting and trying not to cry.

Then I got back under the front frame and got a spanner and started to undo the nuts that had come loose and placed them on the top of frame together, but there was always one in a hundred that wouldn't shift. Jim said to jam the chisel between the frame and bracket. I got the spanner and felt the nut shift a little, then it went tight again, so I jammed the chisel in more towards the cover, hitting it with the hammer, then the spanner did the trick and the last nut wound off. I tapped out the rivets and screwed the nuts back on, laying them all in a pot with some oil to keep them moist.

It was easier now, and we could see the valve covers, easy to get to as well.

'What's the plan, boss?'

'Do you want to do your side and I'll do my side, as you've got to learn?'

I concentrated on removing the rear knuckle on the shaft, then undid the nuts so I could take off the gland and slide it off the shaft. I got under the frame, and was now covered in dirt and grime. My hair had more oil and grease in it than if I had emptied a pot of Brylcreem over it.. Jim wore a beret on his head – I will have to get something like that, I thought.

I got the tools from the locker to take out the packing with the 'corkscrew', as it was old and crumbled. I had never seen such old graphite packing.

Now I went to the front and, with the correct size of spanner, I started to undo the holding nuts on the valve cover, knocking the spanner with the hammer as I went around the circle anti-clockwise, but couldn't get to the top ones as the frame was too close.

'Stuck, boyo? Go to the locker and get a bar and socket, and bring the home-made lever-bar with you.' But the top nuts were still tight, so he came around and said we would do it together. When I pressed down on the bar the socket fell off, so Jim went off and came back with a small piece of square wood.

'Hold this on the front shaft, Pat, and I'll press down on the bar.'

He got his hammer and whacked the bar. I felt the block judder and the nut moved. We did the same with those that were left, then went round to his side and helped him. I got under the frame and he placed the socket on the top nuts, pulled the bar and they came off easy-peasy. Lucky bugger, he was.

'Have you removed your knuckle and gland yet?' I asked.

'No, but you're about to do that for me. I'll start it if you go and put the kettle on.' It was time for a drink as I was parched. I went outside towards the tin shed, opened the door and there was Jimmy. 'Would you like a cup of tea, mate?'

'Please. Milk, no sugar.'

'Are you coming in?'

'No, I'll sit out here, Pat.'

When I walked back into the shop Jim gave me an old-fashioned look. 'Where have you been?'

I tapped the side of my nose and said I would tell him later.

I took a cup of tea over to the tin shed, and when I returned Jim said, 'What's going on? Where did you go?'

'I made someone a cup of tea. He's sat out in the shed.'

'Why? Doesn't he want to be seen?' Jim walked to the door.

'Leave it, please,' I said. 'He's the Technician Officer from Reading. He's sat out there because he's coloured and thinks maybe no one would like him.'

We went back to the valve covers. I removed the knuckle at the rear of the valve guide, then the gland, undoing the nuts and placing them on top of the frame. Using the 'corkscrew' I started to pull out the old graphite packing, same as the other side. The old stuff came out easily enough – we needed some free play to get the valve assembly clear. As all the ring of nuts had been removed, the faceplate came off easily with a tap here and there on either side of it. I got the small bar and edged the faceplate away from the cylinder assembly, rolling it around the shaft of the valve, lifting it off and placing it with all the parts that had been removed.

My mate got his soft hammer and whacked the shaft at the rear, and suddenly the whole assembly started to come out of the cylinder into the fresh air, for the first time since it had been built at Swindon Works!

Now Jim got his bar and went to the front of the frame and heaved the assembly into the open. He placed his bar between the valve and frame to give him leverage, then told me to hold the shaft as he went back under the frame at the rear and hit the shaft with the bar, to knock it out of the cylinder. I was juddering backwards standing on the frame, but I still held it, although it was very heavy. He even poked his crowbar with the pointed end into the cylinder bore and knocked it out. With a crash the back shaft came down from the casting. We pulled it away from the frame and laid it down on the front of the engine. My mate jumped down onto the floor and took the weight, calling me down to help. We took it and lowered it into a heavy vice to be clamped.

Looking at the assembly now there wasn't much to do only knock out the cotter pin and undo the huge nut on the shaft. Easily said! I walked to the wall and looked at the assortment of spanners and found the correct one. Everything was huge and heavy. It was a ring spanner, and I placed it over the flat of a nut to see if it was the correct size. It fitted a treat.

But first I had to remove the cotter pin, which was driven into a hole and wouldn't come out. So I chopped off the legs and eye with a chisel, fitted the spanner onto the nut and hit it. It made no impression. I found a 7lb sledge hammer with a long shaft. Now I had power in my hands, so standing back slightly I whacked the metal spanner and saw it move. I hit it again and it started to edge around, then again and again. I saw what was holding the nut – the cotter pin inside the shaft's hole was catching the threads. I just kept whacking the nut, then it suddenly got looser.

Then my small heavy hammer came back into my hand and, laying down the sledge, it really got easier now. I was on a roll, and the nut came off. I slid it off the shaft, then went to Jim's locker and found a small punch to knock out the cotter pin from the hole in the shaft.

Now there was the other side to do, but God must have been on my side as I knocked out the cotter pin with no trouble. This time

...and piston valves

I added a drop of oil to the leading threads, placing the spanner on the far side as I was going anti-clockwise. I hit the spanner with one heavy whack and the nut moved all easy like. As I unscrewed the nut it became easier and I was able to undo it manually with my hand. Two nuts off. Now I asked Jim to give me a hand to remove the ends while I held the other end up. When the weight was taken, he tapped the unit and all the pieces fell out onto the bench.

'I'll hold the other end, Wobble, and you can knock it off,' which I did. I expected it to fall apart, but it seemed to be stuck together. So Jim undid the vice, lifted the shaft up in the air and dropped it down onto the wooden-block floor. Suddenly the whole unit slid down the shaft and separated on the floor. I bent down and collected up the bits and placed them on the bench the way they had come off. Now he showed me the instrument to measure the inside bore. He took off the extension bar, which was too long to put inside the valve cylinder – we only needed a short one.

'Here, come and see. You look through the front and I will show how it's done.' He covered up the valve holes to stop anything from dropping inside the piston cylinder, took the required measurements and wrote them on the metal piston cover with chalk he had in his pocket. Being a standard cylinder the rings were all made the same. I brought new rings from the stores and pushed them into the cylinder. As before, I marked them with my pencil, then when I pulled it out I measured three-eights of an inch and scrolled down. I used a hammer and cold chisel to break off the excess on each ring, doing this eight times – each valve had four rings on it.

I looked at the valve to see how it went back together before stripping out the other unit. I replaced all the spacers and rings, and got Jim over to check what I had done. He was pleased at what I had done on the old unit, as I had used my initiative and rebuilt the valve block, placing the nut onto the shaft and screwed it up to the face of the valve, until the cotter pin came in view, finally hammering the valve assembly block together very tightly. I placed new cotter pins in the hole; I placed the two cotter pins on the vice and hit them one after the other with the hammer onto the eye that spread the legs. Now all I had to do was knock in the cotter pin and secure the legs by opening them and knocking them flat against the nut.

I did the same with the other end, and I had now stripped out the old block and rebuilt it with new parts. I repeated the same assembly with the second valve, again with all new parts.

Now we were ready to fit the valves back into the cylinders. First I got my hand into the cylinder and removed the cotton waste from both ports, and with the oil can sprayed the inner cylinder with oil and wiped it around the bore.

'How you doing, boyo? It's dinnertime. Wash up and I'll see you later.'

When I was clean I walked out of the shed towards the station, meeting Jimmy in the undercroft. We walked towards the Railway Club, talking all the way. I asked him why he wouldn't come into the shop and have a cup of tea instead of being in the shed.

'You know why, Pat – I don't need to tell you.'

'Colour doesn't bother me.'

'No, not you, but in others I've seen it. Come on, let's go inside and have a beer.' He asked was I was drinking – bitter – but then said, 'Can I change your mind? I drink Guinness and tonic water. Have the same and see how you like it.'

It was smashing – the tonic took the harshness off the stout. We walked back to the shed, and Jimmy said he was coming back on Friday. We parted and he walked up the track behind the offices towards the turntable and disappeared back into the tin boilersmith's shed.

Jim and I started again to replace the newly assembled valve but first it had to be lifted up. The two of us struggled. I stood on the cross brackets with my bum in his face as we gently threaded the valve assembly into the bore in the top cylinder. I held it while he knocked it. I pushed and it found its level going through the bore. I got down and went around to the slide bar area. Jim said to look into the bore and place a tube over the shaft – it was about 18 inches long and slipped over the shaft.

I shouted, 'Your end up, Jim ... stop ... hold it!' as I pushed the tube over the shaft. It was a dead fit and not sloppy. This tube was taking the strain sitting on the cylinder face. Jim got his soft hammer and I held the tube centred as the whole unit started to come towards me. My arms and shoulders ached as I was under the frame, then I saw the valve assembly unit block the bore.

'Right, hit it hard, Jim!'

He exchanged the hammer for the block of wood, and whacked the leading shaft. The valve moved into the bore and the metal tube went past my face only inches away. Shouting out for a rest, I placed the knuckle back on the shaft and asked Jim to tap it gently. As he did so I removed the metal tube, putting it on the frame, as he jumped off the front end onto the floor.

'That's it, boyo. Connect up but don't forget to put the gland on first, and fit the packing in afterwards.'

'OK, as good as done, uncle!'

To measure the graphite packing I held the end in my fingers and bent the loop around the shaft till it touched the existing piece of packing, then pulled it off the shaft, placed it over the slide bar edge and hit it with the hammer till it cut the packing. I did this three times, then packed the valve at different angles, not all the same, as the steam would find its way back out of the cylinder.

Now I pushed the first packing into the gap, pressing it all around against the face, then at a different angle, pressing it in with a small bar, then the third piece different again. I then replaced the gland by pushing it hard onto the gland nuts and doing them up equally till tight, and refitted the knuckle bar and tightened up the locking studs.

I removed the tools to the front on the assembly unit and replaced the faceplate with graphite paste, on the bore flange and faceplate, as my magic make-up skills came to the fore once more, then refitted the plate the correct way up and replaced the nuts, as before winding them down in a criss-cross fashion till they became tight. Then I used the hammer to knock the nuts up very tight; I even got a tube on the spanner and checked them over again.

'How are you getting on?'

'Not bad. What are we doing next. I thought the frame, if that's OK with you, uncle.'

'What's this bloody "uncle" lark?'

'Just some silly talk, like you when you say "Pat", then "boyo".'

'OK son.'

I collected up all the nuts and rivet studs and dropped them into an old galvanised bucket of paraffin and dirty oil by my bench, leaving them there as we had a cup of tea. My stomach rumbled for food, so I brought up all the tea things and billycan and the grub in my bag. As the kettle boiled Jim disappeared outside, and next thing in he came.

'Your mate wants a cup as well before he heads off back to Reading.' He went out into the tin shed with a cup, and next thing he came in back with a smile. 'Nice man, that Jimmy. I never asked him when he was coming back again.' I nodded.

17. 'Bloody children!'

Arthur came into the shop as if he was marching in line with his size 12 boots shining, and came straight towards the forge as I was about to drink another cuppa.

'Pat, can you help please? Jack needs a hand and you're the thinnest here. There's a pannier tank, No 6259, just outside here, and Jack's draining the water tank at this moment.'

Jim said to go to the stores and get a battery light rather than use a 'Smokey Joe'. So I walked to the stores and Jim Parsons came to the window. I said what I needed and he invited me to come into the stores, 'so we both can pick out the best one for you. Here, Pat, here's the best one for you.'

'Thank you, Jim.' I was always polite with him, minding my Ps and Qs.

I jumped the pit and walked back to the engine between Nos 1 and 2 roads. Jack was waiting.

'Can you climb inside the tank? Take this spanner inside – on the facing frame you'll see a float and arm attached. Come on the footplate and I'll show you.'

We both climbed onto the footplate and in the corner he showed me the gauge and there were the studs behind it. 'You'll see the inner gauge. The tank is dry – I've checked it.'

I walked to the front of the engine, climbed onto the front step, then the frame, then up on top of the boiler. I was handed the spanner and battery lamp, which I left hanging on its belt, and looked inside the tank. I could see the tank's webbing criss-crossing. This is going to be hard, I thought. To access the bolts I had to get into the side tanks, which was via the filler opening. This was a job for a slim person, an apprentice. I got into the hole, dropped down and switched on the light to see where I had to go. At least the tank was dry.

Inside the tank it was a pickle, to say the least. I had to screw myself around and through the webbing. It was dark and damp, and the bottom was covered in sludge. I crawled to the back and got as comfortable as was possible.

Then suddenly there was this loud banging on the tank. I went out backwards the same way, and lifted myself out of the tank. Bloody Frank Dowding was hitting the tank with a hammer, and his mate Ted Powell. I got down and walked back into the shop – I'd had enough. 'Do it yourself, Dowding!' I shouted to them.

Jack came and apologised. 'No,' I said, 'I'm not going in there with bloody idiots banging that tank!'

I was very annoyed at bloody children playing with a hammer. I walked off, slung the spanner at the engine, and disappeared from the shed. I was gone for an hour, sitting inside a scrapped engine looking out across the fields to Appleford, raging till I became quieter. I heard someone shouting between the scrap engines, but I just sat there on the footplate of No 1502, a short-wheelbase engine that had worked in the MoD sheds, but now with her chimney stack covered with a sack and tied off. Someone had written in chalk 'GOODBYE OLD GIRL' on the smokebox door, with a small bunch of wild flowers stuck in the rusty door.

There were two or three men in between the engines walking down looking for me, and shouting out my name. I came out of my hiding place and met them. They said that it had been sorted out, but I said nothing, walked to the open shed and back to the engine, picking up the spanner from the side of the frame.

Climbing up on the tank, I lowered myself once more into it, holding the spanner and battery light. I had to screw myself around and crawl through the webbing, which wasn't easy on my hands and knees. I reached out and knocked the frame. The nuts and bolts were of poor quality; the nuts were called 'rough' and the nuts 'black'. The seal was made with hemp string, which was prepared before going into the tank. You just prayed that you did a good job and that on filling there were no leaks, as I would not have wanted to go back inside again.

I heard Jack shout out, 'Top one, Pat!' I tapped once, placed the spanner on the nut and started to turn it clockwise to tighten it. I tapped the bottom twice, and did the same again. Before I started I could see that the nuts and bolts were loose and the rubber jointing was flapping.

Once done, I had to crawl out backwards the way I had gone in, flashing the lamp to see how I was going to fit through the webbing. My arms were stretched out in front of me, so I had to push myself backwards. Then I saw daylight just behind my head. I sort of tried to sit down and reached up to grab the frame of the opening, pulling myself upwards out in the fresh air. I pulled myself out of the hole and sat down on the lip of the hatch with my feet dangling in the hole.

Jack came to thank me.

'OK, any time for you.'

Then he went into the pit and I saw him between the wheels lifting up his arms to turn the tank's water valve into the closed position. I asked if he was finished with me. He was, so I walked back to the shop to carry on with what I was doing.

Back in the 1960s there was a young apprentice in the Western Region who was asked to go into a tank the same as me, but the idiots just had to play hitting the side of the tank with their hammers. The lad's body swelled up with fear, and he got stuck. It was not very nice working in those tanks, as I knew. Anyway, they couldn't move him, not even talking to him to release the pressure, and it was getting late in the day.

Management said to cut the tank open with oxygen and acetylene bottles and burner, and that's what they did – the whole side. They got the boy out, and he never went in again.

At the end of the day I rode home and said nothing to anybody. I had a hot bath, got some food into me and went to bed, as I was dead tired.

On the Tuesday morning I felt much better after a good night's sleep, and ready for work after eating a good healthy breakfast, dried-up fried eggs and bacon that had been left on a plate on a saucepan of boiling water, and a mug of hot tea that I made; Mum and Dad had left for work earlier, around 5.30am, and Dick was on nights at Oxford. He would soon be coming home, as his train got in around 7.40am. We would all miss each other that morning, and I never said anything to the family about the previous day's incident – I just got on.

When I reached the shed I ignored the cabin, and went straight to the shop, changed into my overalls and went to the forge. Jim asked me how I felt. 'Great,' I said, as I had had a good night's sleep. 'I'll get on and run those nuts down the rivet studs if that's OK, so I can put back the front plate, unless you want me to help you.'

'No, boyo, you get on with what you want.'

I got a spanner from his tool box and felt in the bucket for the rivets and nuts. I washed the screws on the bench with cotton waste, placed the rivet end in the vice and started to run the nuts down the each screw. I did this for a least 40 minutes, finishing off with the same amount of studs for either side. Back at the engine, I lifted the valve cover and placed it firmly where it had sat for the last so many years and started to slip to rivets into their holes. Then I placed a nut on each one until I came to the last, which as usual wanted to play up. I had a job to get it into the hole. I went back to Jim's tool locker and found a tapered rod, went back to the engine and started to take out one of the rivets after removing the nut. I put the taper into the hole and pulled it towards me, then placed the rivet back into the slot and held onto it. When I got underneath I tried to do up the nut as well as holding the taper; pulling it out, I went back under the frame and poked the taper in the hole from underneath at arm's length. I held the rod and got up level on the outside, then stuck the rivet into the bad hole, still holding the rod. I did up the nuts tight, then released the rod and looked at the free hole. I poked the rivet screw into place by screwing it around with a pair of pliers until I had enough thread on the stud to start the nut. I did up all the nuts with a spanner, placing a tube over the end of the spanner and pulling it towards me. The cover found its place and locked down.

Suddenly someone crept up to me while I was daydreaming. 'How are you getting on, Pat?'

Christ, I jumped! 'Did I frighten you – sorry. You're quiet, aren't you?'

'Yes, I'm staying away from certain people, and just getting on with the work.' There was nothing anyone could do, I told myself; and all I wanted was to get on with what I was doing.

I went around to see Jim and tell him that I'd finished on my side.

'Good, let's go and have a cuppa.'

As I was brewing the tea Arthur appeared again, after a cup. I sort of knew he would be around after a bit of company and a chat. I really didn't want to hear about it, but I knew it had to come out some time.

'Are you OK now, Pat?' said Arthur.

'Yes,' I replied.

'I know they're like kids, and it was wrong to hit that tank with you inside. I honestly thought you'd chucked the job in and walked off the site, and that frightened me.'

'Why is it the same blinking two causing trouble?'

'I've had it with those two,' he said. 'And do you know that you left work early?'

'I didn't realise, sorry. I was as mad as hell, which will lose me thruppence-farthing for an hour's work, out of my wages.'

'Is that all you get?' Arthur said. It was taboo to mention money. 'We're good then?'

'Yes, I'm OK.'

'Thanks for the cuppa. I'd better show my face.' And he left.

I opened my bag and took out a sarnie. It tasted lovely – cheese and pickle with a red onion that I had to peel. I was going to stink the place out!

Jim whispered, 'You're staying with me. As I told him, you're better than that. Right, let's get going again.'

The new valve had to be replaced. I got all the tools that was needed around me, and we both lifted the valve into the cylinder, his face against my backside. I had been eating onions – he'd better watch it! But first I had to check the cylinder, as I remembered the waste in the ports. I reached inside and found an object. Pulling it out it was an empty fag packet. I went to the stores and got the battery lamp, came back and looked inside the bore. I found nothing else, only the waste in the ports, which I removed. The bore was oily and now we were ready to place the valve in the top bore. By this time Jim was seething with Welsh temper, his face as red as a beetroot.

'Come on, let's get this one in then go and have a moan!'

We heaved the valve into the bore. He held it while I got the wooden block and whacked it on the shaft. It seem to go in a little faster this time, as it left the first bore and was in 'no man's land'. I got down and with the battery lamp could check the level of the shaft. I reached down and got the tube placed into the shaft, then rested. He picked up the wooden block, I lined up the valve to the bore, then he hit the shaft with so much force the valve shot straight into its own bore and flew past my face at a rate of knots. He was angry: 'Finish off, Wobble, I'll be back.'

I nodded, took out the tube and replaced the knuckle. It needed no adjustment, so I removed it and placed the gland over the shaft. I had already cut the graphite packing, so I fitted it, then put the gland up to the threads. Two threads were showing, so I refitted the nuts and screwed them both down tight. Now the knuckle was placed into position, screwed down tight and secured.

The front cover was coated in graphite paste and went on perfectly. I then started on the nuts, screwing them on by hand round the whole circumference. With the spanner I went criss-cross until they were all tight. Now for the spanner and tube, and I went the same way in the same criss-cross manner. All done.

I wondered where Jim had gone, as I was all alone. Then Jack came in to talk to me, asking how I was after yesterday. I said I was OK.

'You haven't fallen out with me, Pat?'

'No, Jack, you're OK.'

Then he wandered off.

I got the front plate into position, and started to place the rivets into the holes. Every one went into its hole, and I started to screw the nuts on. I tightened them with the spanner – still Jim was not back. Last job but one – I had to change the steam cocks on both cylinders at the bottom of the steam chest, then replace the front covers over the piston covers and valves. I took the tools back to Jim's locker and came away with a small quarter-inch-size spanner, went under the front plate with one cover and replaced it, then over the other side. As I started to find the hole for the first bolt I heard someone talking on the tool box side.

'Did you do it?'

'Bloody right I did.'

'Why?'

'I wanted to get my own back on them both.'

I stood up and it went quiet. He stood looking straight at me. I pointed straight at him – he knew, and I nodded.

At dinnertime I went to the forge, got the kettle topped up and put it on the fire. I turned on the blower a little, then went to wash up in the ceramic sink. The Lifebuoy soap gave a good lather and the grease started to come out of the palms of my hands. I wiped then clean and went back to the forge, where the kettle was boiling vigorously. I turned off the blower, moved the kettle and went and got my grub bag. Jim had a toasting fork hanging on the side of his tool box, so I collected it and walked back to the forge. I got out my cheese and pickle sarnie and was about to toast it over the fire when the same person I had caught came to me and said, 'You heard what I said. Are you going to say anything to Tyler?'

'Ask him yourself – he's stood behind you.'

'What?'

Jim grabbed him and took him to Arthur Brinkley's office.

There was another incident I heard of when a breakdown was in operation one night, and the men had to carry a railway line out of the breakdown van. All but one person carried it on their shoulders, walking over the wreckage to the broken rail – the person in question never carried it, as he kept low with it away from his shoulder. I think he resigned, as I never saw him after that. I heard he was about to get the sack anyway from being caught breaking the rules.

I got on making the tea and toasting my sarnie, sitting on the anvil.

'Got a spare cup?' said Jim. 'I think Arthur's coming up as well. All right, are you not going to ask me?'

'No, none of my business. It will all come out in the wash.'

'How have you been getting on?'

'All done ready for your inspection.'

Arthur appeared. 'There's plenty in the pot,' said Jim. 'My mate's just topped it up.'

'Got anything to eat, Pat?' asked Arthur.

'Some grub in the bag if you would like it. Mum always make enough to feed the five thousand.'

'Have you told him, Jim?' he continued.

'No,' said Jim. 'He doesn't want to know. I think he's fed up with what's going on, like children in the playground. They want their arses kicked.'

I was daydreaming about seeing Annie that evening, in a world of my own – I just wanted to enjoy a quiet life.

'See you later,' I said. 'I'm going for a walk.'

I went out of the back door and down towards the turntable, and walked across to the main line watching the freight trains, and the light engines making their way down to North Junction signal box to pick up their freights in the marshalling yard. I kept walking, looking across the fields at the same time – I was multi-skilled at doing two things at once – walk and watch! I hadn't a care where I was going, I just needed some fresh air, 'Am I silly to work here?' went round in my head. I was sure I was going to chuck it all in, then with a grin I realised I would miss the thruppence farthing per hour, and suddenly burst out laughing. Big time money! People were getting more staying at home on the dole than I got working. Then again, I will be playing with steam engines for the coming years. I turned round and gently walked back to the shop, taking my time and enjoying the summer's heat, talking to myself and looking for the hairs in the palm of my hands to see if I was really going mad!

As I walked on I looked across to my left, noticing the shunting in the yard. I seemed to be drawn towards the noise, with the yard engines moving backwards and forwards with strings of wagons. It was the closest cooperation between four men working together as one team, with the under-shunter changing the hand points and braking the loose wagons, the head shunter carrying out the actual shunting, and the driver and fireman providing the power. The fireman had a very important task, as he had to judge his boiler pressure to perfection to provide sufficient steam – not too much as to blow off through the safety valve and obscure the driver's vision, as all shunting movements were carried out to the shunter's hand signals. However, in some yards the driver did not even see the shunter as he operated from the fireman's side, so all the signals had to be relayed to him by his fireman.

Daylight shunting with hand signals was a straightforward matter, but at night the driver had to have his wits about him, but the shunter always carried a lamp with him to indicate to the driver what was going to happen, or did happen. The most frightening for the shunter was fog, when a good yard man carried a whistle, and the driver or fireman stood on the footplate straining to hear: one blast on the whistle meant 'come ahead', two was 'go back', and three was 'stop'. The driver would open the regulator slightly and move slowly forward, then hearing the whistle blown three times he would brake hard. Depending on the load to be shunted and the gradient he would sand the road all the way from the end of the yard to the freight train being broken up. Then he would open her up to full gear and full regulator, and the blast from the chimney could be heard for miles around, echoing from cutting sides to the yard buildings, and with cinders coming down like a hail storm. Meanwhile the yard's cat would stretch out in the sun and take no notice.

One young man, fresh up from the country on shunting duty at Didcot yard, decided to wash his coverall jacket while on his tea break. He used the loco bucket that hung on the lamp bracket, and hot water from the engine. The jacket was then draped over the backhead of the boiler to dry, but it was not drying quickly enough. The driver said that it would take quite a while to dry. 'What I should do is roll the jacket into a long sausage, place it on the track and I'll run over it to squeeze out the water.'

'Good idea,' said the young man.

When the mangling was completed, the fireman picked up his jacket and it came apart in half a dozen strips just like ribbons.

When shunters wore white shirts, or maybe no shirts at all, it was time to have a little fun. We would fill the boiler just that little bit too much water in the chalky gauge glass, which was white as the boiler needed a washout, then when he opened the regulator to its fullest it would shower the yard with fine wet soot, resulting in a clean white shirt covered in small black smuts from the smokebox.

I strolled back to the shop and came through the big wooden door to see No 2819 being pulled out of the other end of the shop so that the firelighters could get the fire going overnight, which meant that the shed would be full of that greeny yellow sulphur.

I got the stiff broom out and started to sweep up where the engine had stood for the last four days, while Jim got a shovel and we both cleaned the area while we waited for the next engine to come in.

'Get yourself washed up, Wobble, and I'll see you tomorrow,' said Jim as he wrote up the brown card to report what he had repaired and the extra parts fitted, including the steam cocks; the old ones went back into the stores to return to Swindon.

When I got home I had the usual hot bath to get the dirt out of my pores. We never had smelly soaps – like my brothers I bathed in soda crystals, which were caustic and could have burned, but in those days that's all we had. My hair was washed in Red Lifebuoy soap and rinsed out – funny, I never had nits.

After tea I walked down the road to Mick's house – we were 12 houses apart, and lived in each another's houses. His Mum made me a cup of tea while Mick got out some magazines about motorbikes, which we scoured through picking out the best bike. I liked the Ariel Arrow Leader. We chatted about what we were going to do at the weekend. I wanted to go to Oxford on Saturday afternoon with Annie, although I hadn't asked her yet – I would see what she said.

I then walked up to Norreys Road to see Annie; all this walking was doing me good as it kept me fit and slim, and the heavy work made my arm muscles stronger. I cut across Edmonds Park as it seemed nearer, and she must have had the same idea as she appeared through the top gate. We waved and pointed to the metal seat, where we met. I put my arms around her and kissed her, and asked if she would you like to go to Oxford on Saturday afternoon – we could get the 1.15 train and get some lunch, and go to the pictures. We planned our day and she seemed happy enough, and it gave me something to look forward to, having her on my arm. We sat for a while and she asked what I'd been up to. Just listening to her voice thrilled me – I was really falling in love with her.

18. Fire irons

The following day, Wednesday, I got my new washed pair of overalls out of the box and changed into them, leaving the dirties on the floor next to the box – they could almost stand up by themselves, they were that dirty.

There was no engine in the shop as I walked to the forge to see Jim, as usual drinking from that dirty old cup stained to hell with black tea. 'What's on?' I asked.

'We're waiting for a "Mogul" to come in to have its con-rods removed to bush the rigid bearing later today.'

Meanwhile I could get on with some tool work that I had left in Dave's locker. I wandered out of the shop looking for 'the twins', and heard that they were on No 4 road, but I couldn't find them. I wandered back into the shop and there they were.

'Ah, Pat, you're going to Reading.'

'Am I?'

'Arthur's gone to get your pass and paperwork and the time of the train.'

I could see a long pipe on the shop floor, and Jim Hale was wrapping it up with sacking.

'Do you know how to get there? Well, there's two ways but with this long pipe you better go the road way.'

Jim Hale, Dave and Arthur got their heads together.

'What's wrong with Oxford?'

'The welder's off sick.'

I got the fast to Reading, putting the pipe in the guard's van with his permission and finding a compartment to sit near the window not far from the rear of the train. The compartment was pretty full, with every seat taken. Opposite me was a male passenger reading his paper. I sat with my legs apart and comfortable, taking in the views as we proceeded through the countryside without a care in the world. Suddenly the man opposite started to make faces at me, sort off nodding his head downwards and opening his eyes. We never spoke, as I thought he might be a bit odd, but he kept sort of shaking his head and looking downwards. I shook my head, thinking, 'What's he after?' Whatever it was, he wasn't going to get it.

We reached the outskirts of Tilehurst and the express started to slow down. We were now not far from Reading, and I couldn't wait to get off this train. Finally I got out of the compartment and walked back towards the guard's van and opened the door, waiting a few minutes to let everyone go by. When I got out into the fresh air, carrying the pipe, I suddenly felt a draught of fresh air around my testicles and realised that my manhood was hanging out of my trousers – they had ripped wide open! Now I knew what that guy was looking at and trying to warn me about!

I manoeuvred my way down the station, keeping an eye on the front of the 12-foot-long pipe with a piece of rag tied on both ends to warn people. It wasn't easy as people crashed into me, not looking where they were going. I followed them down to the station entrance, but went the wrong way, turning left. I met a postman and admitted that I had never been to any of the sheds, and was beginning to feel nervous – the damn great pipe I was carrying didn't help! Luckily the postman gave me instructions and pointed me in the correct direction. Turning right out of the station I followed the path towards a slaughterhouse; the railway was above me as I walked along, with the brick arches on my right. I asked someone else, who said I was on the right road and to go to the end of the street and head for Hodsoll Lane and Great Knollys Street. 'When you come to the shop on the corner turn right into the railway yard and you will see the shed area.'

And there it was. I was totally knackered by this time. I made my way towards the fitting shop, which was the same design as ours at Didcot, so I felt a little better, and more relaxed. I made my way across the rails, escorted by fitter Eric Hall into the fitting shop, where I met Johnny McNamara from Didcot (he lived in Kynaston Road), and he took me to Bert Crawford, the blacksmith and welder. I left the pipe with him, and he told me to go and have a walk around Reading and come back in 2 hours.

I walked back towards the town looking at the sights and shops, making a mental note of how to get back to where I was. The area was pleasing and familiar, as I remembered my parents bringing me here many years earlier when I was a small boy, and seeing the trolleybuses running up and down the main street. Of course, that had all gone now. Eventually I made my way towards the station and followed the route back to the shed to see if the pipe was finished. I entered the blacksmith's area and spoke to Bert Crawford, who confirmed that it was ready.

The next train from Paddington came in behind a 'D800' 'Warship' Class diesel-hydraulic. I heard the diesel engines roar past me – a brilliant sound! With luck the guard's van was dead in front of me. The guard showed me where to stow the pipe, then said, 'You might as well sit in here – we will not be long before we will be in Didcot.'

I found the pull-down hard seat and, keeping my legs together, opened my grub bag and had a sarnie. It seemed only minutes before we were pulling into my home station, Didcot.

I walked down to the shed carrying the pipe that was now brazed. I was so pleased that I had got it home in one piece, and in the same dirty state in which I had taken it to Reading. I laid it down on the wooden floor blocks, in no one's way.

'Where've you been?' asked Dave. 'You took your time.'

'Yes, I went around the town sightseeing.'

'I bet your neck hurts.'

'No, why?'

'From looking up at all those high buildings.'

'Ha ha, funny.'

'The twins' took the pipe away to their engine while Jim sat waiting for another one to come into the shop. 'How was No 2819?' I asked Jim. 'Was there any comeback or faults?'

'No, not heard yet, Wobble, as she hasn't gone out to work yet.'

We were waiting for 'Mogul' No 5380 to come in, to have its con-rods rebushed; this might be later, as they had to drop the fire at the coal stage, leaving the shed driver with just enough steam to drive her into the shop. At that moment Arthur appeared at his 'second office', the forge.

'Jim, your engine's coming in tonight, just before 5.30. Can you ask them to turn it on the turntable and come in smokebox first? Nice ride to Reading, Pat? Did you go to the diesel depot and see where you might go in a few years?'

'No, never thought of it really, Arthur,' I replied. 'There'll be plenty of time next time I'm there.'

I went home and asked Mum to sew my trousers, which she did in time for the next day. I never said a word to anyone.

Mick and I went down to the White Hart on the Broadway and sat in the corner. We both were under the legal age of 18. Beer was one and a tanner a pint, brown and mild (nicknamed 'Boilers'), which was all we drank, plus a shot of Lamb's Navy Rum neat, at half a crown.

Around this time, as we came home after a few pints at the White Hart, we met a lovely girl walking home. We knew her as a friend, and she was pushing her bicycle. Mick came onto her and whispered in her ear something or other. I really didn't take any notice as we walked towards the barn in an open field, which is a housing estate now. Mick said, 'I'll go first – you can follow after me.' We walked her home, and kissed her goodnight. It was his nature to share, as we were mates. As I walked home alone I said sorry to Annie, as I should have met her that night.

On Thursday I started coming out with boils on the back of my neck and under my arms, with one on my forearm, with big juicy red and black heads. This was something I was ashamed of, but couldn't help it; the food I was eating at home was greasy, as Mum did a lot of fry-ups, and with the oily conditions and coal, the dirt started to get into my skin.

I heard in the shedmen's cabin the men talking about the same subject, and I listened to their remedy. I walked over to the carriage and wagon area near the empty coaches, where all different-sized bottles lay inside several rusty 45-gallon barrels that had the tops missing, so the bottles overflowed. I sorted out a small whisky bottle from the heap, went back to the cabin in the shed and washed the bottle all over with boiling water, to sterilise it. I then pulled up my overall sleeve, poured boiling water into the bottle, quickly emptied it out placed the open end of the bottle over the boil's head.

It hurt, and when I looked into the bottle I saw my skin rise up. I couldn't stand the pain and ran outside after trying to pull the bottle off my arm – it was impossible as it was stuck on. I whacked the side of an engine and smashed the bottle and the skin sank back into place. I had never felt pain like it. Yes, the boil had gone, but it left a huge mark on my arm. I went into the locker room, brought out the Lifebuoy soap and bathed my arm with frothy soap and washed it over. I was feeling a little better when Jim appeared and asked me what I had done. I told him, and he went to his tool cupboard and brought back a bandage with some ointment.

'Dry your arm, Pat.'

He opened the tin and scooped some paste over the area, then wrapped my arm with the bandage. 'Leave it like that for a few days and we'll look at it then. You silly little sod!'

No 5380 came in, as requested, with the smokebox facing towards North Junction signal box. Jim had already started to disconnect the rigid wheel's huge nut, and asked me to go to the stores and get eight bars of white metal ingots. 'Take the two-wheel barrow and you can write the chitty out, Wobble.'

'Why eight bars? Surely four should do.'

'I've used up my spare stock.'

So I got hold of the barrow and pushed it to the sash window at the stores; it was open and enginemen were gassing, as it was a favourite meeting place. I wrote out the chitty on the bench, signed it and gave it to Arthur Wheatley, the assistant storeman.

'Signing things now are we, Pat?'

He pulled open the door and I followed him in, then I heard from the enginemen moaning about me being a favourite. Archie Davies said, 'Do you make pokers, Pat?'

'Yes, I can make anything.'

'I'll come and see you in the shop.'

Then someone else asked the same question, and all I said was, 'It'll cost you.' It went quiet.

I loaded the barrow with the ingots, handed over the chitty. Arthur Wheatley asked if I could make one for him too.

'OK, after I've done this engine. You will be the first. A dollar for a poker, shovel and toasting fork.'

'OK,' he said.

I went back to the forge with the load and placed four ingots into the cupboard and four on the forge's frame. I stoked up the forge and got the blower on, got a wire brush from Jim's locker, brushed it out and laid it in the fire. I lifted two ingots one at a time into the bowl of the ladle with metal prongs, laying them on their sides, and let the fire do the work to melt them.

Jim shouted to me to give him a hand to lift off the con-rod after he had removed the pin from the crosshead. He didn't mess about, as he knew what he had to do. 'Hold the con-rod at the crosshead end, Pat, while I knock out this end.'

I held it while he jemmied the large end with his small crowbar.

'Now lift it and carry it onto the trestles.' There was no word about whether I could manage it – he knew that I was stronger now than when I had first walked into the shed, and he could trust me more. Before we started the lift together we threw away the cotton waste and held the con-rod with our bare hands.

'You're doing the bushes. I'm leaving it for you to get on with.'

Jim then went round the other side to get the con-rod off, while I cut out the old bush and threw it down in the corner of the forge. Under the forge I found a steel plate and placed it on the anvil, as I had seen Jim do several times before. I collected the iron bushing and placed it over the journal for the correct size, which was the inner, then placed it onto the steel plate. With the bush knocked out of the con-rod, I looked in the cupboard and selected the size that was required, placing the outer with the other one and measuring the inside gap to get the right measurements.

I mixed up some clay from the powder in the tin with a little water and bedded the clay around the outer journal. Now I was ready for the ingots to melt down. I got the scraping rod and scraped the dirt off the white metal, throwing it in the fire and spreading it across the coals.

Now I put on the big gauntlets and lifted the ladle. It was very heavy and I felt my shoulders pull away from my neck. 'Can you manage?' a shout went out.

'Just.'

I poured the 'lava' into the gap around the metal bush till it was full to the top, and replaced the ladle in the fire.

'Christ, boyo, you done well!'

Jim pushed the bushing assembly onto the floor to let it cool. When it was cool, the iron bushing was removed with prongs and it went back to the anvil for the next con-rod. This was repeated twice as there were two sets of bearings to each set of wheels.

Now we had to drive the bushing into the con-rod's brass cones. We didn't have hydraulic pumps or any equipment to help us, it was all manual. I filed off the edge around the radius to give a lead as I levered the bearing inside the brass assembly and placed a lump of hard wood over it and held it. Jim came round the side of me with a 14lb sledge, and hit the wood dead square and the bush went into place; another hammer and in it went, solid.

'What do you want to do, Wobble?'

'Can I work on the other con-rod while you do the drilling and filling?

'OK, get on with it.'

With the 2½lb hammer and cold chisel I cut the bearing out and took it to the forge with the other one. I got the prongs and gauntlets and placed two ingots in the ladle. With the bushings placed in order and the clay mixed with a little water, and pasted around the base, again I put the gauntlets on, scraped the dirt from the white metal 'lava' and threw it into the fire. I heaved up the ladle and poured the white molten metal very carefully inside the bushing, into the gap as before. The fumes came back and hit me in the face, but I kept pouring until the assembly was filled to the top.

As soon as the molten metal had cooled off, the new bearing was pushed off the anvil onto the floor, and the round iron bushing was removed with prongs and put back in the cupboard.

I went down to the locker and got the food bag and billycan and came back to the forge. Jim had put the kettle on – it was rest time.

Tea was made, grub was out, and guess who appeared. I think he smelled that tea and my grub, as he never asked. 'What you got to eat, Pat?' asked Arthur.

'Whatever Mum makes. You got you cup?'

'Yes,' he replied, and pulled one out of his pocket. I giggled and shook my head.

'What have you done today?' he asked Jim.

Jim looked at him. 'I've done nothing. Wobble has built the bushes and fitted them, and we will be ready to get this engine out this afternoon.'

'Well, I guess I'm here all day today working on the con-rods, as it's pay day,' I said. 'When we finish later may I do some blacksmith work?'

'What are you making?'

'Pokers and small shovels, toasting forks.'

'How many?'

'A shed full, I think!'

One of the drivers came into the shop just as I had finished my tea, and I recognised him as he got closer with his peaked railwayman's cap hanging off his head. It was Alec Shand. He and Skip Morgan had been friends before Alec retired earlier in 1960.

'I have a river boat cruiser at Clifton Hampden near the road, Pat, but it's half sunk in the mud. Would it be possible that you could come and see it and give me a hand to raise it? Skip said you might be able to help. What about Sunday? Are you on shift?'

I said I could meet him there. 'I'll bike over there as it's 5 miles as the crow flies and it will give me some fresh air. Say 10.30?'

Continuing with my job, I picked up the white metal bush and knocked off the scrag around the base and with my file rubbed it at an angle to give a lead into the main bearing. I got a crowbar, put the pointed end into the bush area and pushed the bar downwards to turn the con-rod over onto its side. Jim came around just as the con-rod was going over. He stood amazed.

'Couldn't you wait?'

'You were busy,' I said.

Now we had to drive the bushing into the con-rod. The radius looked good and level, sitting ready to be hammered into the assembly. I placed the lump of hard wood over the bush and held it as Jim hammered it in as before. 'Precise engineering,' I said, which made both of us grin.

'While you're here I can show you how to run the groove for the oil channel. I know you file the channels, but this is easier.' We turned the con-rod over to the upright position, took out the cork, and he drilled a hole though the filler point. We now turned the rod over through 180 degrees, and with the same drill bit in the chuck of the electric drill he ran straight across the white metal bearing from one outer side to the other outer side, crossing the hole he had just drilled.

'Now use the file to roughen off the edges.' After I had done so, he said, 'Right, we'll get this on and they can pull this engine out. You do the rigid end and I will do the crosshead.'

We lifted in tandem. I slid the bearing onto the screw while he helped me push the con-rod into place, then wound the oval nut onto the screw. Jim had pulled the crosshead back into position, with the air coming out of the cylinder cocks. I then got the oval spanner, placed it on the oval nut and with a 7lb hammer whacked the spanner around while the nut went onto the screw, repositioning the spanner as necessary each time, until it was very tight against the con-rod. I looked through the pin hole and could see just half a hole, so with the huge sledge hammer I whacked the oval spanner and moved it until the hole was lined up dead. I placed the screwed pin into the hole and wound it down with a spanner until it was tight. I had the right size of cotter pin, held the legs on the pin and hit the eye with a small 2½lb hammer. The legs sprang out and I tapped the pin to pull the legs apart. Jim had finished and the engine was ready to be pulled out of the shop. He went to Arthur's office to ask to get the engine out, and Arthur went to the shed foreman to pass on the message.

It was now dinnertime. I went outside to the scrap area and found some flat tin plate, with some three-eighths square bars, and brought them in to my bench. Thirty minutes later, after having eaten, I went to the forge and poked the square metal bars into the fire until they were red hot. I retrieved them one at a time, placed them on the anvil and with my only hammer I started to shape the ends into 'rat's tails', using the horned end of the anvil to bring the tails around into a tight bend. I placed the metal back into the forge to get it crimson red, then brought it out again and resumed where I had left off, shaping it into a circle with the tail twisting away off the metal. I placed it on the floor to cool.

I completed all the bars the same way and let them all cool, and used a wire brush to brush away the flaked metal around where I had worked. Then I collected them all up and went back to the bench. I went to Jim's tool locker and helped myself to a spanner the same size as the square bar, went back to my bench, placed each bar into the vice and used the spanner to twist it around to the same degree, as I had six to do all the same.

Returning to the forge I poked all six into the fire. I had a visitor looking over my shoulder.

'What are you doing?'

'Making pokers.'

I turned each bar 90 degrees round in the fire, then pulled one out and started to hammer the other end into another rat's tail, but not so fine. I went to the water trough and slowly dipped the poker into the water till it sizzled, then lay it on the floor. I did the five others the same way.

'Who are they for?'

'Drivers, Arthur, whoever wants them.'

'Can you make me one?'

'Cost you a dollar, five bob.'

'What, for one poker?'

'No, shovel, poker, toasting fork, a set.'

'No,' said Jim Hale, 'it's too much money.'

Then go away please, as I'm not familiar with the swear words of the Great Western Railway, and leave me in peace.'

I pushed the button to operate the motor-driven belts for the grinding wheel. I hated this wheel as it was too lumpy to work with and needed facing off. I got on with what I had to do; the ends of the pokers had to be ground to a taper to finish them. All six done, I shut off the motor, and everything went quiet.

The six small shovels used the same method as the pokers, but there were no tapered ends, as they had to be flattened down and bent downwards, ground off, drilled and riveted to the three-sided small shovel, which took me longer to make with the correct measurements and skills to bend. I made my own rivets out of one-eighth-inch steel bar.

The toasting fork again used same idea, but required a bit more precise engineering for the fork end, as we had no welding equipment, but having oxygen and acetylene bottles would come in handy.

I walked up to the pay office window. Most of the crowd had gone, and there were only a few of the fitting staff in line. I handed over my disc, and Stan Barten said 'Sign here, Pat,' then handed my disc back with my pay packet. I stuffed it into my pocket, then put it in my locker. I was parched for a cuppa – working at the forge gave me a thirst – so I made some tea. I shouted out, 'Are you about, Jim?' No reply, so I waited a while for him to appear.

I had to finish off what I was doing. I placed six pieces of square metal in the fire beside the kettle and went to Jim's locker, looking for a pair of pliers. Taking the small prongs, I pulled out each metal bar and knocked one end at right angles, then left it sitting on the coals. I did the same with the other five bars and replaced them in the fire. I then held the first one, took a metal ruler and measured from the inside of the first bend 1½ inches, and placed it back into the fire. Having made the tea, I removed the first bar, held the metal with the prongs and with the pliers made the bend, placed it on the anvil and tapped it with the hammer to straighten it up. I did the other five the same, but still no Jim – blinking gassing again!

Pouring the tea into my tin mug with a splash of milk, I had just put it to my lips when once again he came out of the woodwork.

'Got enough for another cup?'

'Sarnie in the bag, Arthur.'

'What have you got today, Wobble?'

'Arthur, my name is Pat.'

'Sorry, Pat,'

Jim arrived and said, 'Thanks, Wobble.'

Arthur looked at me sideways – you're the manager, he's the boy!

Bread and lard with an onion, and eating it like an apple. Or you can't beat a cheese and pickle butty. If there's a choice, I have the bread and lard – take off the outer skin of the onion, throw it in the fire and eat it like an apple, munching both together.

Arthur, supping his tea with a sarnie, said, 'Your Mum makes some lovely food, Pat. These cheese and pickle sandwiches are lovely!'

'I'll tell her tonight when I get home.'

'What have you been up to today?'

'Making three-piece sets of irons for the

fire. Where can I get some paint and a brush to finish them off?'

Arthur said, 'I've got some at home. I'll bring it in tomorrow for you.'

I finished the food and went back to the bench, cut all the long legs off the prongs and filed the ends smooth into a small spike. I measured the centre of the two-pronged bar across the top bar and hacksawed out a square. I did all five the same, and with the long handles measured the length to the fork, marked the distance and cut them out slightly so the bits matched together, with a little tweak here and there. I went back to the forge with all the parts and matched them together. I unwound the oxygen and acetylene pipes enough to reach, opened the valve on the bottle and adjusted the pressure to show on the gauges. Then someone came to me.

'What are you doing?' said Arthur.

'I'm going to weld these ends together.'

'How do you know about gas and oxygen, Pat?'

'I was taught at school.'

'I'll stand here and watch you. What are you going to use to weld those bits together?'

'I've got small iron rods here.'

He looked on as I replaced the burner nozzle with the brazing nozzle. I set the flame to glow, put on the goggles and started to get the ironwork glowing red hot. I placed the small rod onto the metal and it started to run and melt, filling up the cracks. I put the rod down, turned over the fork and put the heat back onto it, running the molten rod into the cracks. I completed all five, and when I finished and had shut everything down I had an audience looking on. Then the questions started. Who taught you to do that? School. And what about brazing? School. The last year I had stayed on because they got my age mixed up; when I had come up from Greenmere I was 10 years old and all my class were 11 years old, so I stayed with all the lads until the time came to leave at 15, and I was 14. Metalwork was my passion and main interest, so I learned everything, even welding with a torch and arc welding.

I wasn't colour coded. Arthur and Jim stood amazed. 'You are unbelievable!'

'Don't forget my paint tomorrow, please.'

The men started to dwindle away back to their work. I tidied the bottles away, then went back to the bench, got out a wire brush and scrubbed the metal flakes off the iron. I then got a file out of my locker and roughed up the edges and over the weld area. Finished now. I collected all the tools up and cleaned them down, and took what I had used of Jim's back to his tool locker and thanked him.

When I got home that evening I asked my Mum if she could help me as I was coming out with boils. I said that Jim Tyler had bandaged my arm up as I had done something stupid, and explained it to her. 'You silly boy!' she said. 'I'll make you drink cabbage water to purify your blood with salt and pepper. I did this for several months every time she cooked the greens, and noticed my spots had disappeared, with the boils also gone.

It was Thursday night, and Mick and I met as usual and wandered down to the town. We went to the White Hart first for a few pints, a couple of brown ales and a chat, then continued down to the Labour Club; this was a favourite haunt every Thursday. However, I felt that we had overstayed our welcome, and I favoured a coffee rather than beer, so I asked Mick what he felt – should we give it a miss for a few weeks? Dead opposite the White Hart was a café.

'Let's go in there as the weather is coming in cold. We could have a coffee and see what's going on.'

Didcot was a dead place at the best of times. When we went home I was asked into Mick's for an hour or so, so we played records, he spoke about Buddy Holly as there was nowhere he could purchase certain records. He said, 'What about we go to the smoke for a few days? Stay at Whitechapel at your Dad's sister.'

'I can ask. Would you go?'

On Friday morning my Mum had washed the bandage and ironed it, so I took it back and handed it over to Jim, thanking him.

19. Purley Hall

On Friday morning I walked to the forge and realised that the engine was gone. Jim said I could finish off my metal work, while he went to see Arthur to see what was happening.

I went back to my bench, retrieved my iron work from my locker and laid it out on the bench. I found some string stuffed in a corner behind the lathe, which was just the job as I had to hang the metal work off the bench while the paint dried. I started to paint each item and hung them up around the forge area, as that was the warmest place. It looked like Christmas with all the iron work hanging from every point.

Jim appeared. 'Right, we've an engine coming in with piston and rings to change. Have you finished painting, boyo? I can see they're everywhere!'

'Just around the forge keeping warm. I just have to clean the paint brush and take it back to Arthur.'

I found some dirty paraffin and washed the brush, cleaning it with the cotton waste that I had in my pocket. I pressed the lid back on the paint tin.

I noticed that the weather was getting cold and the nights were drawing in. That weekend the clocks would change, then I could have another hour in bed. However, the mornings would be darker still coming to work and darker again going home. The shed would have a different atmosphere and I would need lights on my bike, so I went to Bosley's shop on the Broadway on the way home.

The shed was cleared of engines, placed outside wherever there was a space for them. It took a while so I checked the iron work, which seemed to be dry, so I married up the three pieces together – poker, small shovel and toasting fork – wrapped them in newspaper and took them to the men. As I handed them to each person I received a dollar – five bob. Arthur Wheatley was very pleased with his and so was Archie Davies, and all the others.

Other men saw and wanted a poker, or a poker and a shovel. I took their names and asked them to be patient as I had to get on with being trained, but when I had some free time I would pursue their requirements. I put the list into my food locker for a later date.

I heard the engine coming into the shop with its steam cocks open. That sound never goes away – shhhhh shh shhhhh – with the piston pushing the air out through the steam cocks. I looked up to see this huge monster entering from the outer shed to the lifting shop close to the shop's doors and the front frame, its smokebox towering above me. What a sensation! The feeling went through me again.

It was No 4959 *Purley Hall*, my favourite engine. It was love at first sight! I know I was being silly but when I saw her I jumped for joy to hear drivers talk about the 'Halls' being all good engines, when the '69XX' 'Modified Halls' were all sluggish – except No 6952 *Kimberley Hall*, which was a good steamer and would be in the fitting shop to have her pistons and valve rings replaced within a few months.

Arthur came into the shop to talk to Jim. There was so much work to do on her, he asked if Jim would mind if he had a crew to get on with what Jack Dearlove had found on his inspection sheet; the records showed that many of the jobs had been left for another day and they had built up. Arthur showed us the list. All the brake blocks needed to be changed, on engine and tender, as well as superheater and a broken spring on the engine. Jack was our inspector at Didcot shed and was very good at his job; he had worked on all these Great Western engines, and would not allow anything to get by him. He was dedicated down to the last nut and bolt or piece of copper wire.

The engine had stopped in the correct position, slightly back on the stroke of the rigid wheel on both sides, allowing us to get a bigger stroke on the piston. Jim said that it might work and we would have to try it. We did one side at a time; I worked on the con-rod into the crosshead, and removed the castle nut and drove the spindle out of the crosshead with a leaded hammer so that the con-rod dropped onto the slide bar, while Jim took out the cotter pin and wedge. He knew exactly what he was doing. We now had some free movement at the rear end. I undid the gland nuts and pulled out the packing from the piston gland with the hand-held corkscrew tool. There was enough space to remove the gland from the shaft. I bent down to help Jim remove the piston casing, and he told me to go around the other side and do the same there. I undid the small bolts on the cover and removed it.

I went to see what was next. Jim had started to remove the piston cover, and told me to do the same as him. I went back to the piston gland, removed the nuts and pulled back the gland, taking out the packing, once more using the large corkscrew. There was such a racket going on at the rear of the engine in the pit, with Dave Davies and Jim Hale removing the rear tender brake blocks, and Matt Oglesby and Jimmy Holmar changing the engine's brake blocks, that it was impossible to hear what Jim was saying to me.

Jim had the nuts off the huge piston cover, which was now loose, and he wanted me there to help him lift it off. I went looking for the 3-foot-square wooden blocks to be placed just under where he worked at the piston. 'Keep away,' he said, as he used the crowbar to remove the cover from the studs on the cylinder, and it fell onto the wooden block. It was very heavy – it had to be to keep the piston in the cylinder.

Now with his crowbar Jim went to the rear of the shaft and edged out the shaft towards the gland. The piston was on the move towards the opening of the cylinder face and freedom. We removed the wooden block from under the frame, and Jim again told me to keep clear as he shot the shaft straight out of the cylinder in one heavy swoop. The piston head landed on the wooden floor, half in and half out. He came to the front and held the shaft up on the crowbar, with the end stuck in the bogie wheel spokes. I twisted the piston head around so it came out, still having enough clearance on the shaft in the cylinder.

Jim said that we should finish off this side then get on with the other side. I got a chisel from his tool locker and a hammer with a screwdriver and raised the leading end of the piston ring as it allowed me; I stuck a small crowbar in the half-moon loop, held the cold chisel to the face of the ring and whacked the hammer onto the face of the cold chisel as hard as I could. It shattered the cast iron ring away from me. I did the same with the others until they had been removed from their carbon channel. Jim had his micrometer measuring set out and was taking the sizes to get the new rings. The cylinder bore was 18½ inches. He knelt on the floor with some cotton waste under his knees looking into the cylinder and taking the measurements. Then it was dinnertime, and suddenly the whole shop was quiet. I made tea, and had a mouth full of dry bread with lard, and eating an onion, when Jim came into the shop with the rings over his shoulders, and a huge grin on his face.

'What are you laughing at?' I asked.

'It's nice to see everyone working in here, and not hiding around the shed.'

I replied, 'You are wicked – you shouldn't talk like that about your fellow workmates.'

'You haven't been here long enough yet to know about fellow workmates, my boy!'

I told him about my plans for the weekend – seeing Annie on Saturday and going to Oxford with her shopping, then the pictures, then Sunday morning going to Clifton Hampden where Alec Shand had a boat sunk in the mud, and wanted my help.

'You're a busy lad – into it all, aren't you?'

'I like to help people.'

The hour went quickly and the men started to come back into the shop, Jim Hale swaggering as if he was still in the Navy, rolling along the wooden floor with his big size 12 feet and long legs as if he was still at sea. He had a huge grin across his face from one ear to the other, and when he ate a toffee it got fouled up in his false teeth and he lost his rag. Dave took the Mickey out of him, and so did I.

I went back to do the piston channels, knelt down and scraped out the dirty black carbon using a small scraper that was just the width of the channel – it was tedious work, but I was making headway. Jim was on the other side of the engine undoing the nuts on the piston cover, as the two of us couldn't work together on one piston. Jim then took the piston rings to the bench, measured them and cut them to size with a whack of his hammer on a chisel. He then fitted them, and in another 30 minutes we would be ready to fit the piston back into the cylinder, having put some graphite manganese paste around the faces.

On the button with his timing, the shaft was pushed over to a 45-degree angle and went into the cylinder. Jim then lifted the piston with the crowbar stuck into the bogie wheel spokes as I slid the 3-foot wooden block under the head of the piston, and he lowered it down onto it. He eased the shaft into the gland port, knelt down, stuck two bars under the piston head and lifted it. I whacked his lead hammer on the face of the piston while he removed the wooden block, then I kept hitting the piston a few inches more. We were in the port now, and Jim said, 'Swap places.' The piston was in the leading edge ready to be pulled in. I kept squeezing the rings into the cylinder one by one, putting oil on each one and shooting some into the bore. Now we were on a roll as the rings reacted to the oil. I kept squeezing them until the last one shot in, and once again I looked down to see if I had my fingertips still on my hands!

'Help me with the other side, Wobble, and you can finish off here.'

I went round the other side, where the piston cover was barely on the cylinder. I took off the nut that held it on the face and quickly moved out of the way as it suddenly dropped off the studs, and rolled out into the shop. As it landed I said, 'Tails, I win,' and rolled it back towards the engine.

Jim shouted to me to move away as the piston shot out of the cylinder with great force. I looked at him and said, 'You little show-off!'

'Who's little?' he replied, towering above me. He was built with muscles in every part of his body. 'Right, go and finish off your side and I'll sort this side out.' But we had to get the cover back on.

'When you're ready, Jim.'

I wandered back to where I had left off the gland. It had to go on first while the shaft was free. I had the graphite packing already cut to size for the engine, but I had to put the tapered shaft back into the crosshead, which was to join up with the con-rod. With the help of the crowbar I edged the crosshead back to the shaft. The tapered cone pin slotted into the gap and the screw thread just showed nicely as I slipped over the metal bush Jim had made to show less thread. When I wound the nut down it pulled the cone through the hole. I whipped off the nut, took off the bush, replaced the washer and castle nut, and wound the nut up tight. Then I got my hammer and knocked the shaft head near the spokes and kept tapping the pin, winding the nut up even tighter till I saw half a hole. I put the spanner on the nut and whacked the spanner around till the hole appeared clearly, then with the cotter I tapped the eye hole and the legs sprang open. I fed the castle nut over the cotter pin and finished off by spreading the legs.

I was lucky as both pulled in together. Seeing half a hole I placed the small bar into it and pulled them totally together now. With the wedge I filed off the lead edge of the rough lumpy edges where it had been hit when it came out. Now nice and clean, it went back into its slot with great ease and a little grease to help it on its way and a whack from the 2½lb hammer. The rest was easy as the cotter pin was ready split with its legs wide open and sprung, and it entered the hole with no trouble.

There was just the gland packing to be rammed into place. 'Do the job properly, Patrick,' I said to myself. I was going mad – I was talking to myself now! Next I'll be looking for hairs in the palm of my hands! The packing went in like a clock-face: 12/3/8. Gland back into place, screw the nuts down equally and do not leave them loose – is Ted Powell about?

All that was left was the piston cylinder face. I went round the studs with graphite manganese paste, and the same with the piston cover. I shouted to Jim to give me a hand to lift the cover up. He came round with a crowbar and we both struggled to stand it upright on the edge of the bar, balancing it. I was pushing forward near the top while he was lifting it up to connect to a stud. We both prayed that it wouldn't fall, as we would both have been injured. We quickly placed a nut onto the stud jutting through the cover and as I screwed it on Jim let the pressure off the crowbar and the piston cover dropped, finding each hole. A wiggle on the small bar and the rest of the studs came through proud, some with graphite past over them. All the nuts were now wound onto the studs in tandem, opposite to each other, criss-crossing as the cover bedded itself onto the cylinder. Then with a hammer I hit each nut in turn till every one was tight.

The last job was to replace the metal cover back into position with the quarter-inch bolts and a small spanner from the tool box. Then I had the 'Wobble' call to go around and see what was going on.

'Come on, Wobble, I need you to help me put this side back in.'

We both twisted the piston shaft back into the cylinder, easing it towards the packing gland. Once more Jim stuck the crowbar into the wheel spokes near the back end of the piston as I pushed the assembly a little. The shaft entered the gland, and I got the wooden block again and pushed it under the piston assembly. Oil was sprayed over the rings and into the bore. Jim lifted up the piston and I whacked it with the wooden block as it edged into the cylinder. I leaned against it, keeping the weight on it, as Jim went around to the gland area and poked the tapered wedge into its hole. With the bar into the spokes of the wheel he started to push the shaft as I lifted either side with two small bars so the piston ran into the tapered cylinder. He was still heaving on the bar as the first ring went into the bore. One by one the rings went in, then there was a whoosh as the piston disappeared from the face right back to where he wanted it. By this time I was getting slower as my energy drained – I needed food and a hot drink.

As we made our tea I heard moaning under the engine. The other two gangs were still having trouble putting the brake blocks on. I couldn't help grinning – these were the men that kept leaving the brake blocks for someone else to do, thinking they might get away with it. But Arthur wasn't that silly.

We had our tea and grub, and funnily enough there was no Arthur. He must be shy, I guessed. He liked it when no one else was in the shop, and what he said stayed in the shop!

I felt great as we went back again to finished off what we had been doing. Five thirty wasn't far away. Using the same method we replaced the other piston cover, then I packed the gland with the new graphite rope that I had previously cut when I had done the other side, and placed it into the shaft in sequence as before. I explained to Jim that I had them stashed away ready.

'What are you like?' he said. 'Always ahead of yourself.'

Once the gland nuts were tightened down and the cover replaced, Jim wandered off to see Arthur in the office and I replaced all the tools, washed them, and put them away tidily. As I left for home, Jim said, 'Big job in the morning. The superheater.'

I rode home quite knackered with my RAF bag over my shoulder, wondering what was on the cards for tonight with Annie. Mum had cooked some cabbage and potatoes with boiled hock of bacon and white sauce, and she kept me the water from the cabbage to drink; I sprinkled a little salt and pepper into it and sipped it while eating my dinner. 'Where you off to tonight?' she asked.

'Just going down to Mick's and having a walk around town.' Another fib, but Mum didn't like her little boy meeting girls.

I asked Mick if he'd like to come with me to Clifton Hampden on Sunday morning, and we arranged to meet at 10 o'clock.

I met Annie outside the flicks and started to walk her back home. 'Why can't we go to the pictures?' she said.

'Well, we're going to Oxford tomorrow and I intend to make a good afternoon and evening out with you to make up for not having seen you over the last few weeks.'

It started to rain so I hailed a Priors taxi, otherwise we both would have been soaked to the skin. We made arrangements for the following day.

'Thanks for a nice evening,' I said. 'I love you with all my heart.' It was soaring!

Her father wanted to take me home, but I said no thanks, I would walk – the air would do me good!

In a way there was a romantic side to the railway within Didcot shed, climbing over steam engines, being a little cocky and sometimes too clever. I felt I was back at school, but don't get me wrong – I really enjoyed being at school. They were the best years of my life. But now I couldn't wait to start my new career, working for British Railways.

On Saturday morning I was up early and legged it out of my parents' home – I wasn't late, just wanted to be gone to play with my train set at the shed!

'Where are you off this afternoon?' Mum asked.

'I want to go to Oxford so I'll be home early I hope.'

Dad looked at me, but he never said much. I am sure he knew about Annie, but he kept it from Mum.

I shot out and cycled to work. There was no one about on Saturdays, only men coming off shift from the shed or station, some picking up litter from the night before, trying to keep the village tidy – they were dedicated railwaymen, as we all were.

I booked on with Arthur Leaworthy in the office, as the Swindon train hadn't come in yet with Mrs Bray on it. I walked down the side of No 1 road. There were loads of engines inside the shed, smoke pouring out with that sulphurous smell, some steaming, others just sat cold on No 3 and 4 roads getting ready for the washouts on Monday morning by my Dad and Trevor May. No one was in the cabin, but there was shouting from the men outside to help each other, as they were still replacing the brake blocks from the day before.

I hung up my coat on a peg and put on my boiler suit; after today I would put them in for cleaning. Clarky would take charge – that was his job, being a fitters' mate, smoking his Navy Cut ciggies. They will kill him in the end.

I wandered round the front of the engine – no sign of anyone.

'What you looking for?' came a shout.

'What you doing up there hiding?' I replied.

Jim said we would change the superheater, and told me to get myself wrapped up inside my overalls with a cloth, do up my overalls to my neck, and tie off the ends of my overall wrists so no soot would get into my clean clothes. I had a cap on my head.

We got the tools and oilcan with a mix of oil and paraffin, and I was given a wire brush to scrape off the rust around the nuts in the smokebox. Jim passed the oilcan to me and I squirted the nuts and threads, then he passed in the long socket iron bar (not the nice shiny sockets of today, but the old ones that were about at the time of Noah's Ark). With the iron bar rammed into the hole on the end of the bar socket we both heaved off the black nuts. Then I knew what the fuss was about – the screaming of the nuts on the rusted dried threads brought tears to my eyes. Now the other black nuts on the gland, accompanied by the same screaming noise. But we must have been lucky and someone was helping us from far away, in the land of dead engines, as the nuts came off with just a spanner, helped by oil squirted on the threads.

As we pulled the superheater just kept coming out of the tube. I had never ever seen anything like it – it just kept coming and coming. Suddenly the end was near, and Jim lifted it up in the air, pulling it the same time. I grabbed it as it fell out of the boiler tube.

I sat on the blast pipe with a piece of wood across the hole, sitting on cotton waste, and handed the superheater down to Jim on the ground. He then waited for me to climb down, then led the way out of the fitting shop to where the springs were held, but this time we went into the little corrugated tin shed and measured up the superheater against another one of the same size, 15 feet. I was told to go back and clean down the threads and oil them, try the nuts over the threads and see that they ran with just a spanner, then put some manganese graphite paste over them.

I helped Jim to carry the heater back to the engine, where he handed it up to me in the smokebox, telling me to hold it. It was heavy as I had to lean further out and hold onto something in case I overbalanced and fell off the front of the engine back into the pit. As I started to find the hole to fit it back into position I looked around and Jim was there pushing it back from the front of the engine, his arms being longer than mine. We fitted it into position so the studs ran through the superheater gland, then the nuts were tightened down tightly.

There was still more work to do, but Jim said that we had done enough. However, I had one more job to do, as Arthur had left me instructions. While the others cleared off for their breakfast I went under the engine to do the tyre measuring – and to check the brake blocks, being a little nosey.

The other job was taking the measurements of the thickness of the tyres of No 4959 *Purley Hall*. I made a drawing on a piece of scrap paper – Leading axle, Driving axle, Trailing axle – with a cross for the front of the engine. When I went back into the office after getting cleaned up and washing my hands I would pull out the brown card for No 4959 to write the measurements out. I kept my own records for these locomotives and their driving wheels and put them into a notebook small enough to fit into my top pocket.

While Jim and I had a break, the others being out of the shop, he asked what my plans were for the day

'I'm going to Oxford for the whole day, taking Annie with me and spoiling her a little.'

Our train was 1.20pm, but Jim said I could get myself away about 11 o'clock and he would drop my disc in. I thanked him – that would help.

20. Shunting – and Oxford again

I got home early, bathed and changed into my Wranglers jeans and a white shirt. Mum and Dad were out somewhere, so I rushed out and headed for the station. I saw them driving up the road before they saw me, so I hid behind a hedge – I knew that Mum would do her nut if she knew I was meeting Annie. Her little boy with a female enjoying himself at the station! Dad told me the following morning that she wanted to drive down the station and cause trouble, to see who I was with. (It was hard enough with her later in life, even before I got married.)

When Annie arrived in her father's car she looked a million dollars, and swept me off my feet. She was gorgeous with her long black hair, with twirls at either side, and a red outfit. My God, what a beauty!

I paid Annie's fare, then we went into the buffet and got two cups of tea. I said, 'O.C.S', which was 'On Company Service', a relic of the old GWR days, so got a penny off each cup, paying thruppence in total. We went into the waiting room to get out of the chill. There was a fire in the grate, so we shut the door to keep the heat in. I sat beside her with my heart bouncing in my ribs.

We left Oxford at 10.50pm on the last train, and were back in Didcot 20 minutes later. We got a taxi home to Annie's house, and then it took me home – well, up the road away from the house, then I walked the rest of the way.

On Sunday I called at Mick's about 10 o'clock and we biked out of Didcot down by the cop shop in Hagbourne Road, my second home, where I had my own room! Then down to the Lower Broadway, out through Marsh Bridge and up the Appleford Road heading for Clifton Hampden, 5 miles as the crow flies. We arrived around 10.30, and there was Alec Shand in a yellow two-seater sports car. I thought, 'What do these drivers earn?'

He said, 'I came into some money years ago and got that boat you see in the mud, Pat. What do you think I should do about it?'

I thought about it. 'Why not have a ride over to Wallingford and speak to the owner of the boathouse near the bridge? I'm sure he will help you out as I think you need a crane to get that out onto the bank. I couldn't do it even I had air tanks to lift it. I'm sure you will get a better response from them. Also nearby is Bushells – they might help you. Just pop in there and ask.'

He thanked me, got into his sports car and drove off. Mick and I went into a local pub and had a sarnie and a couple of beers. He asked how it had gone with Annie at Oxford.

'Getting serious,' he said.

'I was thinking of getting engaged,' I said.

'You're too young. Let's see life a little, then if you feel the same later when you're 20…'

We rode home a little the worse for wear. I couldn't find the pedals on my bike, and he was laughing and wobbling all over the road. We both got off and walked part of the way home.

*

There were named goods trains such as the 'Cocoa', which was a train of Cadbury's chocolate or cocoa beans, and 'Long Tom', which would be a 100-wagon coal train, but the 'fly' was far removed from those 'runners'. It was the goods equivalent of the stopping train, and would stop at all stations to shunt wagons in the shed and yard. The arrival of the 'fly' was the high spot in the day at some country stations, with the senior porter taking charge of shunting, and the lad porter assisting. The guard on the 'fly', if he was one of the old hands, would sit tight and let them get on with it because it was no good interfering, even with the best intentions.

When the 'fly' arrived it provided a chance to play trains, and they did, enough to make a real shunter weep. The train would

Shunting – and Oxford again

go back and forth with half a dozen wagons, first on one road then another, until the men passed the point of anger and frustration, and the job became laughable. The local coal merchant would have his wagons placed at a certain spot, as would the farmer, and so it would go on even if it was tipping down with rain until they said enough is enough, packed up and left.

They had their own engine prepared on the shed for use on the local 'fly' to Reading and Oxford, and usually they worked the round trip. They travelled as passengers to Swindon, then prepared the engine in Swindon shed and worked the 'fly' from there.

Sometimes a shunter would be brave enough to come up on the footplate while the driver was engaging him in conversation. The fireman would remove the outer gauge casing then gently tap the gauge glass with a spanner, ensuring that the roar of steam and boiling hot water escaping would cause the shunter to depart quickly, not even using the steps! They were a grand bunch of fellows who would give as good as they got, and it was a pleasure to work with a good head shunter and his mate.

Fly shunting was a good example of their skill, but before it was carried out the men on the footplate and on the ground had a little conference as to the exact requirements to facilitate this highly dangerous movement – there could be no slip-ups as it was completely against the Rule Book. But it was often the only way to get around a shunting problem without a lot of work. So each man had to be sure and have complete confidence in his mates. The engine would couple up to a string of wagons and start off at a good speed with the shunter running flat out beside them. At the appropriate spot he would give the signal to stop, and the driver would bang on the steam brake, then open up again. The first application of the brake brought the wagon buffers together and the shunter would uncouple with his shunting pole. By this time the engine with the front wagons was going like the clappers to clear the points ahead with the shunter still running. Then as soon as the last wagon attached to the engine had cleared the points they would be set for another line, allowing the second string to go rattling past on the their own with the under-shunters in attendance to brake them.

It was not often that it went wrong, but conditions had to be perfect. However, when it did go wrong there was the most unholy bang imaginable. If they happened to be coal wagons it produced the biggest dust ever seen. On those very rare occasions, when the big squaring-up took place, it was a case of closing ranks against the inevitable enquiry from both Traffic and Locomotive departments. Excuses given were such as, 'The sun was in my eyes,' 'I tripped over my shunting pole,' 'The steam brake seized on,' or 'My attention was diverted by the gauge glass breaking.' An answer for every incident was always ready, but everyone knew it was routine shunting movements that for once had gone wrong. As Bert recalled, as long as too much damage wasn't done, only a right old blowing and bellowing would be administrated to all concerned. Honour was satisfied by the heads of both departments and 'we all got down to running the railway again'.

All heavy shunting yards had young drivers or firemen passed for driving on the footplate. The older men had maybe just put down the shovel after many years, and one would think that they would be glad to be rid of it. However, this was not always the case, and they all encouraged the young fireman to have a go on the regulator, and it wasn't long before the youngster could handle the engine as skilfully as his mate. Maybe this is why the Great Western had such a success with their main-line trains, as the men loved the locomotive and each man knew the requirements of his mate. The shunting yard was the perfect place for an apprenticeship training ground for driving and firing, as from the first day men learned all about the steam locomotive. The same went for the young fitter's boy helping out in the fitting shop and waiting for the months to pass by so he could sign his apprenticeship papers and learn his trade as an apprentice fitter and turner – like me.

At Moreton yard the shunting operations required two engines, and Didcot yard four engines. The Ordnance Depot, with its 75 miles of roads, needed eight tankies; this was very different from the yards, as between each shed in that vast area were level crossings without protection by any gates or signals. It was the responsibility of the under-shunter to walk ahead of all movements over the crossings and the engineman's responsibility to sound the whistle. More steam was used through the whistle than though the valves!

A vast amount of stock was moved up to the top yard for marshalling into trains. The depot housed material for the entire British Army, and just about every item that could be used was there, some of it from the 1914-18 war, and in the days of tanks Bert still remembers passing great mountains of horseshoes stored between barbed wire and wheelbarrows, the latter stacked in their thousands.

Depot shunting had its moments of interest to a cleaner covering a firing duty, and to a junior fireman. The demand on the boiler and fire was light, so there was enough time to learn one's trade. It was the nursery of young firemen, and the drivers were all kind men, and still young enough at heart to practice the leg-pulls and practical jokes that seemed to be part and parcel of an

Tankies like No 3709 worked at the Ordnance Depot in the munitions section shunting wagons.
R. J. Russell collection

Shunting – and Oxford again

engineman's life. It was not unusual to spray a red-tabbed officer with the coal watering pipe as he stood at a crossing waiting to cross, or to open the cylinder drain cocks as they passed a detachment of ATS girls.

Someone working within the depot used to see the Supervisor every Friday to get a ticket to take some wood out in a wheelbarrow, showing the ticket to the sentry guard on the gate to be allowed out. Years later, while stocktaking, it was noticed that the wheelbarrows had dwindled away … and where was the wood stacked high? Bicester Depot!

When my Mum left the railway she went to work at the Ordnance Depot as an office cleaner. She got a bigger wage and it was cleaner work.

*

On the Monday morning No 4959 was still in the shop. Bill Clark was doing the overalls, and told me to get mine as he wanted to change them today. I swapped the dirties for the clean one – they smelled lovely and fresh and slightly warm, being all stacked together. As I wandered to the shop and towards the forge I struggled to put them on over my boots. No good, so I sat down, took the boots off, put the overalls on and replaced the boots!

I could hear a noise coming from under the engine, but couldn't see anything. I went into the pit and there he stood, having replaced the vacuum rubber gasket within the cylinder.

'You're joking!' I said. 'You said we were finished on Saturday.'

'What did I tell you last week?' said Jim. 'Don't trust anyone, even though you might think that they are friendly to you.'

Dick had also told me to keep my mouth shut. I can see why now.

We had a bit more room to stand under the footplate, and had all the tools required. Jim had already removed the coupling from the shaft and lever, now we had to undo the six clamping bolts and nuts that held the rubber within the cylinder.

'I see you have a new hat, Wobble.'

'Yes, I bought it on Saturday at the Army & Navy stores at Oxford.'

'Did you have a good time with Annie?'

'Actually I had a wonderful time.' I was still floating!

'Now go careful as we bring the rubber gasket downwards, and remember the way it came out, as it's going to be a pig of a job to get the new one back in, as the vacuum cylinder is 30 inches in diameter.'

We slid the whole rubber gasket down the shaft with the plate, placing it on the floor below us. Jim went to the stores to get the new rubber seal and positioned it in the pit under the tender. God, it was heavy and awkward! We both placed it into position just like the old one on the floor, pushing it onto the shaft and heaving it up towards the cylinder. We fitted it within the cylinder and replaced the cover, together with the nuts and bolts, criss-crossing them as we tightened then up so none of the rubber seal was rumpled.

'You go and make the tea, Wobble, and I'll finish off here with the coupling.'

'OK boyo,' I said as I crawled out at the rear of the tender and climbed the concrete steps. As I placed the kettle on the forge, suddenly Jimmy from Reading appeared.

'Hello mate,' I said. 'Do you want a cuppa?'

'Yes, please.'

I washed out a spare cup and got Jim's cup and did the same, washing the dried tea stains from the inside. He went mental! 'Bloody kid – who's upset you in these last few minutes?'

'I might drop your cup, then you can throttle me properly!' I replied.

Then Arthur inevitably appeared, also after a cup. 'What you got to eat? Looks like red union sarnies and a jar of pickled tomatoes and onions together.'

'Help yourself. Jimmy, do you want a sarnie?'

So we had a picnic, sitting around the open forge fire.

'How's the engine doing, Jim?' said Arthur.

Jim said we were about ready, then Jimmy from Reading said he also had some work to do on the engine, which shouldn't take long, but he needed a mate to help him, so asked me.

Just at that moment Alec Shand walked in the shop, and beckoned me over to him. Arthur looked at Jim inquisitively. Alec said, 'Can we talk?'

'Yes, let's go outside around the corner – it might be better.'

'I did what you suggested yesterday and went to the boathouse on the bridge. I spoke to the boss and he will arrange a crane to go to Clifton Hampden and pull out the boat and moor her on the bank to dry out. They will also put it on blocks, and secure it. If you're every over there you should see it sitting on the concrete slipway. Skip said you might help me or come up with something.' He stuffed a five quid note in my hand, but I gave it back to him.

'I didn't do it for money.'

'No,' he said, 'but you saved me a lot more money,' and handed me back the white £5 note, and wished me well. We shook hands, then he said, 'I've finished today with the railway. I've retired.'

'Thank you, Alec, and look after that boat. If ever I can help, just come and see me.' My eyes were wet, and I wiped them dry with some cotton waste from my pocket.

I went back in the shop and Arthur approached me. 'What was that about, Pat?'

'Nothing really… Right, where's Jimmy on the footplate?'

I climbed up onto the footplate and Jimmy had the AWS box stripped out, examining it.

'Can you put a crowbar under the slipper and heave it up so I can see what is happening, please?'

I got Jim's crowbar and went under the front of the engine, jammed the bar into a metal gap and lifted it upwards, resting it on my shoulder. I heard the AWS bell ringing. Jimmy said that was OK, so I dropped the weight off the slipper.

'Can you get me some spares and come down, and we can write out what you require?'

I was waiting for him with a pencil in my hand: a pepper pot valve and a new slipper shoe. I got Arthur to sign the chitty. As I stood in his office he asked again, 'What was that about, Pat?'

'Nothing. He wanted my help, that's all.'

I went back to the shop with the bits and gave the pepper pot valve to Jimmy. I went under the front again and changed the slipper shoe. I needed a small spanner and a coil of copper wire. I broke off the old wire from the bolts and pulled it away, undid the threaded bolts, took the slipper off and replaced all the parts, replacing the copper wire perfectly. I let Jim inspect it, and he was pleased.

Having sorted out the AWS problem, he said, 'I'm off back to Reading.' He signed off his card and I had to sign what I had done. We said our goodbyes to Jimmy, but he never came back and we never saw him again.

*

Dad received a letter from his sister, my Aunty Betty, for Mick and me to go to London after Christmas, in the New Year of 1961. I guessed Addie was courting or I wouldn't have been allowed back to Whitechapel, and I am sure my aunt wasn't like the halfwit brother and his wife, as they lived on the other side in the block of flats; my Dad and his sister were two of a kind.

I decided to open an account in the Post Office as I had so much money hidden away from Mum; if she found it she would claim it as hers. When my parents went to work that morning I came down for my breakfast, found a cloth bag, filled it with the money and stuffed it into my RAF bag with my food for the day.

When I got to work I placed the cloth bag at the back of the locker with my food bag and locked the locker – I normally I left it unlocked. Jim was having his usual cup of

Shunting – and Oxford again

black tea, and I asked him what was on for the day, as the engine had gone out.

'I think you're about to go to Oxford with a pipe to be brazed and they want it back a bit quick.'

'That's buggered up what I had planned,' I said.

'What's that, boyo?'

'I wanted to go to the main Post Office on the Broadway to open a new account. What time does the Post Office shut?'

He reckoned 5 o'clock, and I didn't get off till 5.30.

'I will go and see Arthur for you,' said Jim, 'and see if you can leave work at 4.30. Then you'll ride up there in plenty of time.'

'Thanks, mate,' I replied. 'You're not a bad old boy!'

'Not so much of the old, you cheeky little sod!' said Jim.

Arthur gave me the documents and workman's pass. The pipe was 8 feet long and had a white chalk mark where it needed brazing. Arthur said that he'd been on to Bill Miles. I decided to wear my overalls this time as it was getting colder, and I knew my trousers were OK, as they were new ones! I put my heavy donkey jacket on as well, and went to the station.

I caught the DMU stopper to Oxford. I saw the guard's van as the guard had got out onto the platform. 'May I put this into your van? I'm going with it to Oxford.'

'Who are you?'

I showed him my pass, and all was well. I found a seat near the window. Stopper all the way – Appleford, Culham and Radley, change for Abingdon. At the latter I saw the 'Abingdon flyer' standing at the platform – one little engine and one coach.

When the train drew into Oxford I retrieved the pipe from the guard's van and headed towards the wooden shed just over the iron bridge. I felt that I had wandered into another world, with engines everywhere. Reaching the offices I made my way towards the fitting shop, and went towards the welding bay. The welder greeted me and said, 'Leave it here and go up to Oxford and have a look around. Come back in 1½ hours.'

I didn't argue. I left the documents with Bill Miles and said I would wander towards the town and see what's about. Oxford was a lovely place to wander about in, but I went to the railway hostel, where I ordered tea and fish and chips, which cost me a bob. I sat there a while, hearing the trains thunder by and feeling the building moving.

A DMU at Didcot station in 1962.

The Abingdon branch train waits at Radley some time in the early 1950s. The loco is 0-4-2T No 1425.
Gerald Adams, Slip Coach Publishing Services collection via John Stretton

Later I walked out and headed towards the town and walked up to Carfax, the centre of the city, and down towards Jericho. I then headed back towards the station, and went back into the welding shop, but there was no one about. I saw the pipe lying by itself all cleaned up and brazed. I went into the small office and asked if I could take it. Bill said, 'OK, but next time can you ask Arthur to clean it up without the grease on it as it's not good for the welder to run after Didcot men.'

'I'll report back,' I said. 'Is Dick about?'

'No, he's on afternoons this week, but he might be out on the Thames fishing before coming in to work. Go and have a look.'

So I left the pipe where it was and wandered towards the River Thames, which ran parallel with the shed. There I saw him, sitting on the bank fishing. 'Hello, bruv,' he said. 'What you doing here?' I told him. 'Are you in any rush?'

'Not really – waiting for the train. I didn't know you fished out here.'

'I don't have anything to do with those in there,' he said. 'Rum lot. How are you getting on at Didcot? Who you working with?'

'Tyler.'

'Stay with him. He's the best.'

'I know, Dick – he went to see Arthur and said he wanted me with him all the time in the shop.'

'Good for you, Pat.'

'See you at home tonight?'

'No, I'm on afternoons.'

I left my brother to his fishing and went and got the pipe from the shop. As I came to the sleeper crossing at the station, a 'West Country' engine was coming into the station. I saw a man on the station with a grey long coat at my end of the platform. I took no notice of him, although he seemed jumpy. Then he went missing. The train came into the station and I waited to see if it was going to stop at the end of the platform. It did, then I heard one of the engine crews screaming. The fireman jumped off the footplate and ran down the platform shouting and screaming. His driver wondered what was going on and ran after him. Passengers stood in amazement as they allowed the engineman to run through them.

I walked across the front of the engine on the sleeper crossing and saw what looked like a pile of old grey coats bunched together in a heap near the front wheels.

The train that I wanted to catch had just pulled into the station. The guard's van was right at the rear of the DMU and I struggled up the platform and placed the pipe in it, out of the guard's way, and sat down waiting for the train to move. I now knew what the heap of coats were – it registered. A man had committed suicide by putting his head on the line as the train came into the station. I knew now how drivers felt when they ran over someone who had been hiding and had jumped out in front of the monster.

I got back to the shed about 2 o'clock and put the pipe in the shop. The men came in and asked where I had been. Arthur asked me too.

'The welder was very busy. And there's a message from Bill Miles for you – before any more pipes go to Oxford they must have the grease cleaned off them or whoever takes them will bring them back to be cleaned. He won't accept them. Ring him, Arthur, and he'll tell you the same.'

Arthur rang him, then he came back and got hold of my arm and walked me out of the shed. 'Did you see what happened at the station in Oxford.' I said I had. 'Are you OK with it?'

'No,' I said.

'Then get your overalls off and get home now. See you in the morning. Give me your disc, and get home.'

I went and got my food bag and walked out of the shed, then started crying as the tension was released. It affected me for many years after and sometimes I still remember and start to weep – it brought back the memories while I was writing this manuscript.

I rode my bike to the Post Office and opened an account, placing the money I had been saving into the book. I had enough to buy a motorbike!

I went home, had a hot bath and went to bed, still sobbing, and cried myself to sleep.

21. Christmas and New Year

The following morning was 21 December. We had nothing to do so I asked if I could do some forge work. Jim said OK, and asked how I felt. I felt a lot better now, and had slept well.

It was the same principle on the forge as when I worked in the metal shop at school, which I really enjoyed; the only thing different was the blower controls. The blower raged vertically upwards through the fire and sparks exploded outwards from the coals and other burnt offerings that people had thrown into the smouldering area.

I raked new coals into the burning area, and then took a pair of long-handled tongs from the rack, and squeezed the levers together over a spare hammer head I had in my tool locker. I placed this in the centre of the burning forge were the blower constantly blew air into the coals.

It was a 2½lb BR(W) ball-headed hammer dated 'Nov 60', and the head was soon glowing crimson as I brought it out of the fire and laid it at an angle with the tongs in my left hand, squeezing the handles tightly together. I brought the ball head of a new hammer down onto the hot hammer. The magic was just about to start, as I was a conscientious worker.

I hammered constantly, trying desperately to give the old hammer head the shape of an axe, by spreading the hot metal, squeezing the molten metal every time. The force of the hammer was hitting the right spot, then I replaced it in the fire again to raise the heat. With the blower still on the fire I pulled the head out and hit it once more in the right place.

Someone came and looked over my shoulder, whispering in my ear, 'It will never work for you – you're wasting your time.'

'We shall see!'

I hammered on with more determination – no one knew anything till it happened. An hour went by, and I was still working at the forge with sweat pouring from my brow and running down around my ears. Repeatedly I took the red-hot object from the heat of the forge and hit it with all my might, trying desperately to keep pushing the molten metal to either side, turning it over and hitting the other side to do the same thing. Slowly an axe was taking shape. Now I could see the finished object and the end was in sight now. When I pulled the metal from the fire I tempered it slowly in water, watching the water bubbling and turn to steam, before placing it back into the fire until it turned crimson. I then doused it into the water trough again slowly. I was finished, and turned off the blower.

I then went to the grindstone, put goggles on and pulled them down over my head. The grindstone was run on a belt system from a huge motor – the fitters saw to that, and it was new to me. The old-fashioned grinder thumped and groaned as it went round and round, with no guards to protect it, just this big rough-looking 12-inch-diameter wheel. It frightened me really to attempt to start grinding. Placing the axe on the wheel, sparks started to scatter off the metal, which gave me the inspiration to keep going and prove I could do this. Soon all the axe's rough edges had been removed. After a few moments I had a look at it – just a little more and it would be done. I was chuffed! It would go into action a few days later, chopping wood at home for the fire.

On Christmas Eve I went around to Mick's house, and showed him a letter that my Dad had received, arranging for us to go to London in the New Year. In the meantime his Mum was packing up a basket of food and a few bottles of beer, then Mick and I went down to the hostel by the staff club looking for a chap Mick worked with in the Parcels Depot. Tom lived like other men away from their homes all year round. Mick and I knocked on his door and went in. It was heartbreaking – a bed, a small side table and a few photos.

Mick wished him a happy Christmas, then Tom broke down in tears when he opened up the food. There was everything: all sorts of meats, turkey and chicken, with bread, pickled fruits, apples, oranges, and a small box of cigars.

He asked us to stay and have a drink, so we had a bottle of beer with him, wished him a happy Christmas again and pulled out a half bottle of whisky for him – Mick and I had gone halves with the cost. We both ended up in the Labour Club across the road, then the Railway Club, then we staggered home having done our good turn for the year.

The following day, Thursday the 22nd, I went to the stores with a chitty signed by Arthur as I required a wooden hammer shaft and wedge. He asked me how the axe had turned out – it was talked about round the shed. 'Why do you want more bits?'

'I haven't got a decent hammer.'

I brought the items back to the bench where I worked, and got straight into it. I used a rasp to shape the top of the handle so it fitted into the hammer's oval head and whacked it with another hammer with so much force that it came through the other side and wedged itself into the shoulder of the hammer head. Then I set about rasping away the wood at the top until I hit the metal. I drove the metal wedge into the wood, splitting the shaft within the metal head, and finished off by running a file round to stop any splinters getting into my hands.

I looked around the workshop for a bucket of the cleanest oil I could find, and placed the hammer in it overnight. Before I went home I tipped some over the handle, leaving it for a few minutes to allow the oil to penetrate. Oil was better than water, as it lasted longer.

On Friday the 23rd I slept in and was late for work, for the first time ever in my career. It never happened again.

It was a tradition to clean the fitters' tool boxes, getting them squeaky clean, so I went to the stores to get a clean bucket of paraffin and 2lb of cotton waste I cleaned Jim's tools right down to the crowbar and anything hiding in the area like he had never seen them before – I even had the trays out and washed them. I said to Jim, 'I'm here to keep you clean! Are you going to give that teacup a Christmas treat?'

'You cheeky sod!' I just grinned.

I removed my hammer from the bucket of oil, found some cotton waste, wiped the handle and head and locked it away in my tool locker.

I shouted up the shop to Jim, 'Have you put the kettle on?'

'No tea today,' he said. 'Off you go into the tea room and have yours there.'

I washed my hands of the smelly paraffin with Lifebuoy soap and wiped them with my towel, thinking that I'd better take it home as it might stand up by itself! I wandered towards the cabin and saw some men hanging around the door and talking to Arthur near his office. I said that I had been sent into the cabin.

It was one day before Christmas Eve and I knew nothing about what was about to happen. I had never seen so many men standing around and trying to hide in so small an area, even behind the thin chimney stack. They were fighting to look out of the window, thinking no one could see them. What was going on?

Then all of a sudden someone stood up in the corner of the room. It was Dave Davies. Another came behind me and pushed me towards the table. I felt his strong hairy arms and hands grab my arms. It was Jim Tyler. The men sitting on the bench parted like the waters of the Red Sea, and I was told to climb onto the bench and stand on the metal table. Arthur said it was tradition that the boy should sing Christmas carols for the men within the shed. I loved singing anyway and music didn't bother me as I had a good voice and I had sung in a chapel tent with hundreds of people joining in with the chorus with no music. So I sang 'Holy Night', 'We Three Kings' and 'Good King Wenceslas', ending with 'I wish you all a Merry Christmas'.

The cabin door was left open and the rest

of the shed staff were there – the boilersmiths Cyril Dawson, Frank Marshalll, Johnny Cooper and old Jack Dearlove, Trevor May and Chris Kelly, the boiler washers, Dick Bidmead, drivers and some firemen, and Jim Parsons the storeman as well as his assistant Arthur Wheatley and all the office staff. I started off and everyone joined in. What a good way to start Christmas! The fitters and mates put money on the table in a heap. I left a small package on Arthur's desk, but said nothing.

Afterwards I had an invitation to proceed to the Railway Club to collect my crate of Babycham, which I took home on my bike; I got them for Mum and the railway paid for them. As she had got enough Badgers Ale from the tallyman's club, on the quiet I drank some and Dick got the blame for it. I went home early.

On Christmas Eve I had a day off with pay. I had an invitation to go to all the fitters' homes for a glass of pop. I came home silly as normal. At Jim Holmar's house he introduced me to the family, then Jim Tyler's, then to Annie's house – now I was silly – then to Mick's. I crashed at his place till I woke up at nearly midnight.

Christmas Day I spent at home with my family, then in the evening I went to Mick's, and later walked up to Annie's. Monday and Tuesday I was off with pay because Christmas had landed on a weekend.

I went back to work on the Wednesday morning. It was going to be short week, and by the look of the shed not many people were about. I asked Cess about the ash building up and covering the rails – I wanted to earn a few bob. Cess said, 'Go and ask George East,' so I wandered up to his office door and knocked. He open the door, and it was very frightening as I had a premonition that I would be back in his office some time in the future.

'No, Pat, sorry. You're fitting staff. But thank you for offering.'

Jim asked me where I had been, and I told him that I'd been to see Mr East about some extra money for shovelling up ash at the coal stage. 'Come on,' he said. 'We've got a job.' Up in the corner of the shed was a 'Busby', a spark-arresting chimney fitting, so-named

No 5744 is fitted with a spark-arresting 'Busby' chimney. It is coupled to a 'chariot' and box van in the main marshalling yard at Didcot. *H. C. Casserley collection*

Christmas and New Year

from its shape. 'We've got to bring it into the fitting shop and place it on No 3751,' which was an 0-6-0 pannier tank.

We didn't struggle as we were the only crew in, besides the few others working on the front of the shed who were running about like blue-arse flies with Harry Buckel in charge again. We lifted the 'Busby' onto a two-wheeled barrow, and as I held it Jim went down towards the shop with his knees bent. I said, 'Wait a moment – let's just put it in as it is on the barrow,' and we held onto the 'top hat' and moved it that way. 'It saves on your back, old 'un.'

'Who are you calling old 'un?'

I looked around. 'I don't see any other person about – it must be you, boyo.'

'You're a cheeky little sod!'

'You like me really,' I said

'I can't wait to get rid of you,' he said.

'Shall I go and see Arthur and tell him on the way down towards the shop?' I replied.

'You would, an' all!'

'No,' I said, 'because you'd miss me. Tell me honest now!'

He went quiet.

We reached the inside of the shop at the same time as the tanky was shunted in. We shut the big wooden doors at either end and stuffed newspaper in all the cracks to keep out the cold, and put the latch on the small access door.

We stoked up the forge with extra coal from the shunter's coal box, breaking it up and scattering it over the fire, and for a bit more heat we put the blower on for a few minutes.

In the meantime we turned the 'Busby' over to look inside, taking out all the dirty cups and old bottles that had been stored inside, where shed staff had been too lazy to put them into a bin. We were going to lift it with the main crane to get it high enough, so we lowered the pulley block down onto the ground. Jim said, 'You go and operate the controls and I'll give you instruction and stand by you. You're confident now, Wobble, to help out, as I trust you. You won't do silly things.'

I felt really trusted, for the first time since I had started work there. 'This lever is the brake,' he said. 'Look inside the control box at the gearing cogs. The handle is broken that moves them, but you must not have your hand inside the box when operating the cogs, understand, Pat?'

'Yes Jim.'

'Good. Turn on the motor and press the button that says "LOWER". Pull the brake up and see the crane coming down. Gently lower the brake into the stop position. Now put your hand inside the box and move the small cog over. If it doesn't move just take off the brake slightly and lower the brake again to feel if the cog has moved together.'

'Yes, I felt it move into the other cog.'

'Now lift the handle up and see the pulley block lower downwards. Now let it lower down into the pit. Right, put the brake on, and help me lift off the chains. Go to the crane and push the button that says "UP".'

I did as I was instructed and the pulley block went upwards.

We put a pit board across the rails to position the 'Busby' in the centre of the pit, tied a rope around the smallest radius of the neck of the 'top hat', and hooked the rope over both hooks on the crane so they spread the load, then I lifted the hook upwards at a slow speed as instructed, just off the ground to see if it needed to be adjusted. Then it was lifted higher up, just sitting off the top of the engine's chimney. I shut the brake lever down.

We made sure the engine's handbrake was off and, using crowbars, edged the wheels forward to position the chimney below the 'Busby'. Then we scotched the wheels with angled blocks of wood on both sides.

I wound on the handbrake, Jim climbed up onto the boiler and I operated the crane by pushing the lower button. The motor started, I lifted the lever and the block on the crane lowered the 'Busby' onto the chimney. Jim wiggled it into position. He said, 'Just lower the crane down, Pat, then come up here and give me a hand.'

I shut off the motor, went across to the

engine, climbed up the front on to the tank and walked around to side opposite him. As we both heaved the 'Busby' sideways we felt it move down and rest into position, so we undid the rope and chucked it on the floor.

'Go and get some spanners from the tool cupboard, Wobble, please.'

I climbed down, sorted out a few spanners and chucked them up to him one at a time. As he caught them he sorted out which one to use, then tightened down the rough black nuts and bolts very tightly.

Jim signed off the brown card in Arthur's office and was given another card to complete a PPM yearly docket. He asked for the tanky to be taken out of the shop.

Next day – pay day – Jim again said, 'We've got a job on, Wobble. How are you with heights?'

'Are we going flying?'

'Don't be silly. You and me are going up the coal stage.'

We trudged across to the coal stage and walked up the bank's steps into the coaling part. I followed Jim, wondering where he was off to. We partially slipped down the embankment towards the steel ladder. 'Follow me up.' Jim started to climb the iron ladder, and I was five rungs behind him; I held onto the side of the metal frame and kept looking upwards; across the fields I could see the main road out towards Clifton Hampden, the Sinodun Hills and Wittenham Clumps. I changed hands and held onto the rungs; there was no support or resting place, and it started to get a bit fresh and windy as I continued up into the heavens, 50 to 60 feet to the top of the ladder. We had no ropes or safety harnesses.

'Come on, Wobble!' Jim shouted.

'I'm right behind you – don't worry.

He stood looking down at me as I came through the trap door on the platform and grabbed the handrail, slightly out of puff, and pulled myself up into a standing position. Now what a sight! I looked across to Didcot village, then to the Army camp; turning around I saw Appleford as clear as a bell. Looking down we saw Arthur looking up at us, as well as all the shed personnel, with George East standing by the shed clock. They all looked like ants running about, and the small steam engines looked like the models I played with at home.

Jim went to the inspection plate cover and pulled it open.

'There,' he said. 'Pat, look in there.'

I had never seen anything like it, a giant 10-inch ballcock, a hundred times bigger than a ordinary toilet ballcock! The copper ball was as big as four footballs all sewn together. Water was dribbling out of the ballcock, and the height of the water was at the correct level by the level indicator

The coal stage water tank was 44 by 36 by 8 feet in size, with a capacity, at 7ft 6in deep, of 74,250 gallons. On top was an inspection point, through which could be seen the biggest ballcock I had ever seen, when I went to the top and inspected it with Jim Tyler.

Christmas and New Year

that sat near the assembly unit – there was nothing overflowing. Jim shut the inspection plate. Happy with the situation, he said, 'Now let's go down. You go first, Wobble, then I can drop the platform down.'

I went down quicker than I had gone up. People still stood watching us as we came down safely, one after the other, onto the ground, holding onto the iron rail. Jim signed off the brown card and put me down as a witness.

I went round to Mick's at 6.30pm and had a quiet chat about how much money I paid my Mum for the housekeeping. I didn't get a lot each week, and seemed to be working to keep Mum in money – I worked for nothing. Mick asked if I had spoken to my Dad. I replied not yet, but thought I would wait till February as I would be 16 years old then and getting an extra quid a week, which would bring me up to £2 10s. To be honest I was thinking of leaving home, and finding somewhere else to live. Mick advised me to wait and see what the outcome was on my birthday.

'Let's go and have a pint down the Labour Club,' he said, so we set off walking and chattering and cracking jokes together, and eyeing up the crumpet, what there was – a couple of 80-year-olds walking home. They could've been on the pull…!

*

Beside the Provender Stores was a lake that held 3,326,000 gallons of water. During the 1950s two small children had lost their lives, a brother and sister, and were greatly missed by their family.

Near the West Curve stood the pumping station that fed all the water columns in the Didcot railway complex, and the water tank on top of the Provender Stores, for watering the 4,000 horses that had been accommodated in the building. The water tank on top of the coal stage held 74,250 gallons, and with the height of water in those two tanks the pressure increased the flow.

During the 1960s more men started to disappear, five in total. In 1965 Stefan went missing from the shed and the signalling department for a couple of days and no one knew where he was. Someone walking round the lake by the Provender Stores one Sunday morning found a stack of clothes folded neatly on the ground near the water's edge. He ran across the rails to the shed, and Jimmy Holmar grabbed a hook and rope and went back with a few other men and dragged the lake, but found nothing. As no one was found in the water I believe that the underground system sucked the bodies through the drainage pipes and into the pumping station.

The 'twins', Dave and Jim, made a model boat propelled by some clockwork that Dave had found at home. There couldn't have been a lot of work on at that time, as they were playing with a boat. Dave was good at making models and tools. Hiding behind an engine, these two chaps put in the clockwork and sealed the propeller, then balanced the boat with nuts for stability in the water. They sealed the whole of the boat, making a cabin and funnel, and set the rudder. Water tests were completed in only an hour.

Over at the Provender Stores reservoir they were ready, standing at the water's edge. Dave wound up the motor and Jim set the rudder. I mentioned that they should have put a string on it in case they could not get it back. I was told nicely to keep my nose out.

So off went the boat. The motion was wonderful, and it glided through the water right out to the middle and stopped! 'Oh God, it's stopped!' They looked around, then at each other, and Dave said that Jim must have set the rudder wrong, not allowing it to come back to them on the bank. I said, 'I told you so.'

It sank in minutes, by the stern just like a real ship. Cor, what a great sight! I stood to attention, saluted and sang 'God Save the Queen'. Dave and Jim didn't think this very funny, but I couldn't stop laughing.

I went to ask the boilersmith, as he used carbide, and obtained a large amount, keeping it dry in a sealed tin. Jim was not about and I wanted some fresh air, so I went on a walkabout, looking for the empty bottles in the carriage sidings – cider bottles were the best. When I reached the lake, standing at the water's edge I half-filled the bottles with iron nuts, then the carbide, then water, screwing the tops back on tight. I then threw them into the lake, where they sank. I gave the mixture time to work, then suddenly there was a huge explosion, the water erupting high into the air like a depth charge. I had had my fun and walked back, crossing the lines and looking all ways for railway traffic, as the marshalling yard was the most dangerous place ever.

The Provender Stores reservoir fed all the railway complex. The washout water from the shed came back near the West Curve and drained into a huge water tank. Water flowed from the Provender Stores tank via non-return valves. All the pipes ran underground, unless tapped into workshops and small sheds or outside as a water tap.

Twenty feet from the Oxford down main line from the station a fresh-water well was dug; this had a 6-inch ball valve and was connected via a 6-inch siphon pipe into the reservoir for its overflow, again connected to a non-return valve. Pipework ran underground towards the centre of the marshalling yard, where there was a branch to North Junction signal box as a mains fresh water feed.

Water pipes went to the carriage and wagon repair shed and were tapped off for fresh water, and on to the toilet block and fitting shop, where they also fed the 2¾-inch fire hydrant. From the toilet block a 1-inch pipe fed all the cabins, with a single tap over the Belfast sinks within the stores and shed.

The Provender Store and engine shed area, with some indication of the water pipework criss-crossing the area.

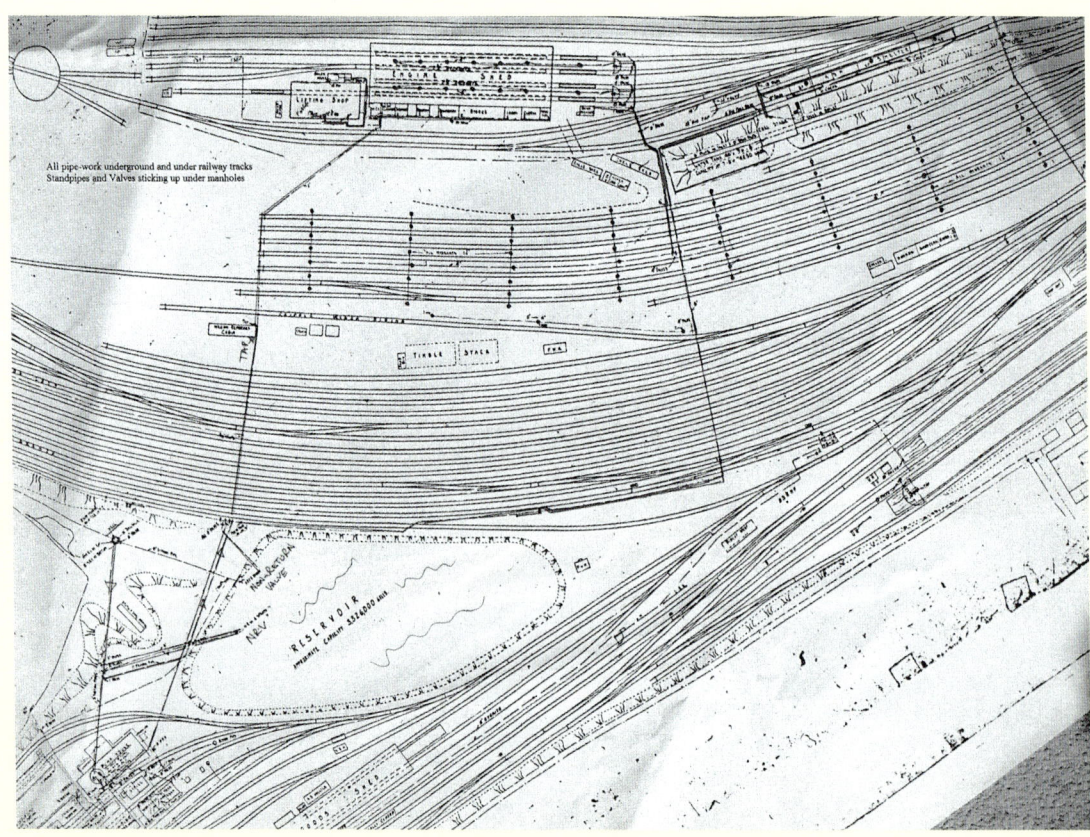

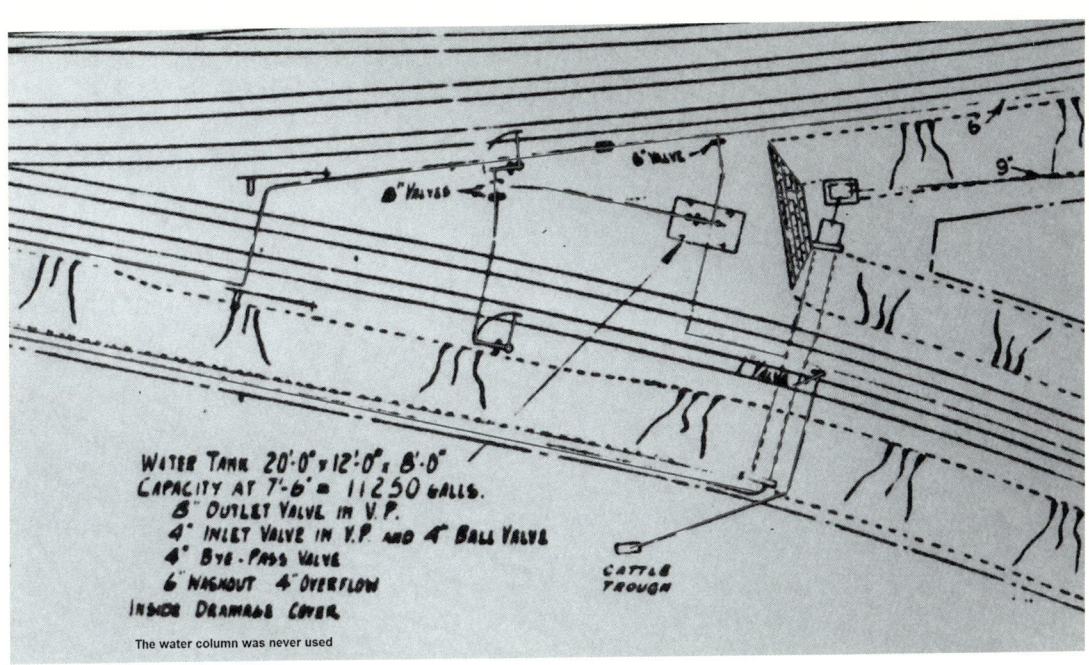

Detail of the water supply between the West Curve and Foxhall Junction lines. A 6-inch pipe ran parallel to the line underground towards the bank of the West Curve, where a brick wall was situated. The water column there was connected to the water system, but was never used.

This drawing shows waste water feeding catchment pits before flowing over a weir into a stream that ran into the River Thames at Appleford.

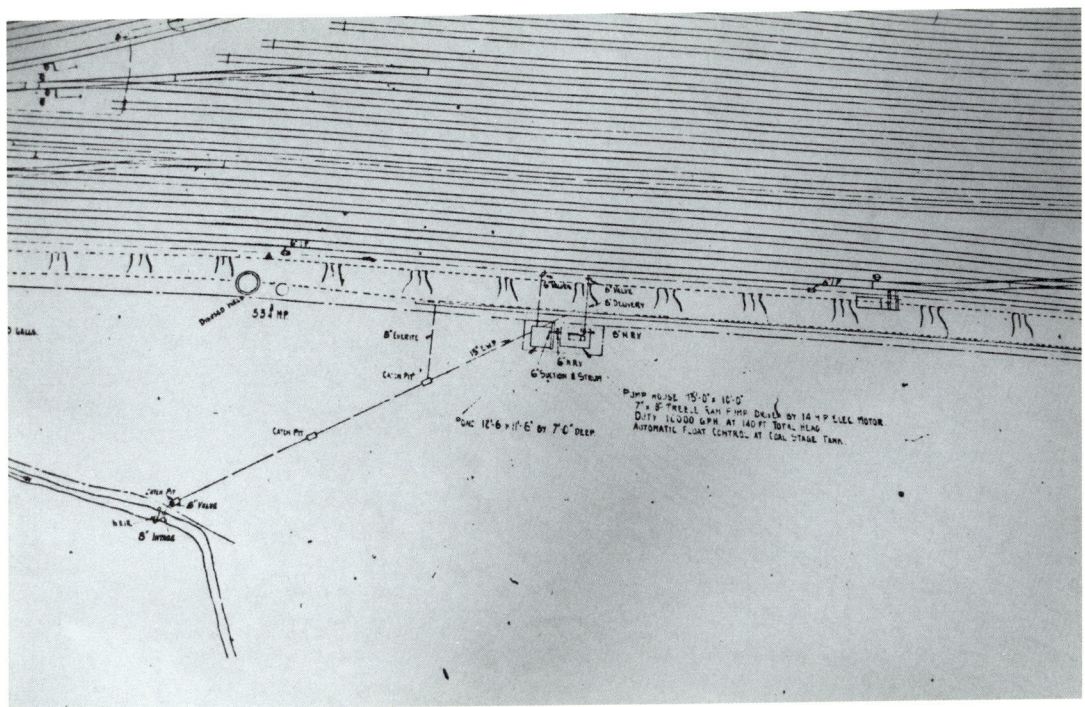

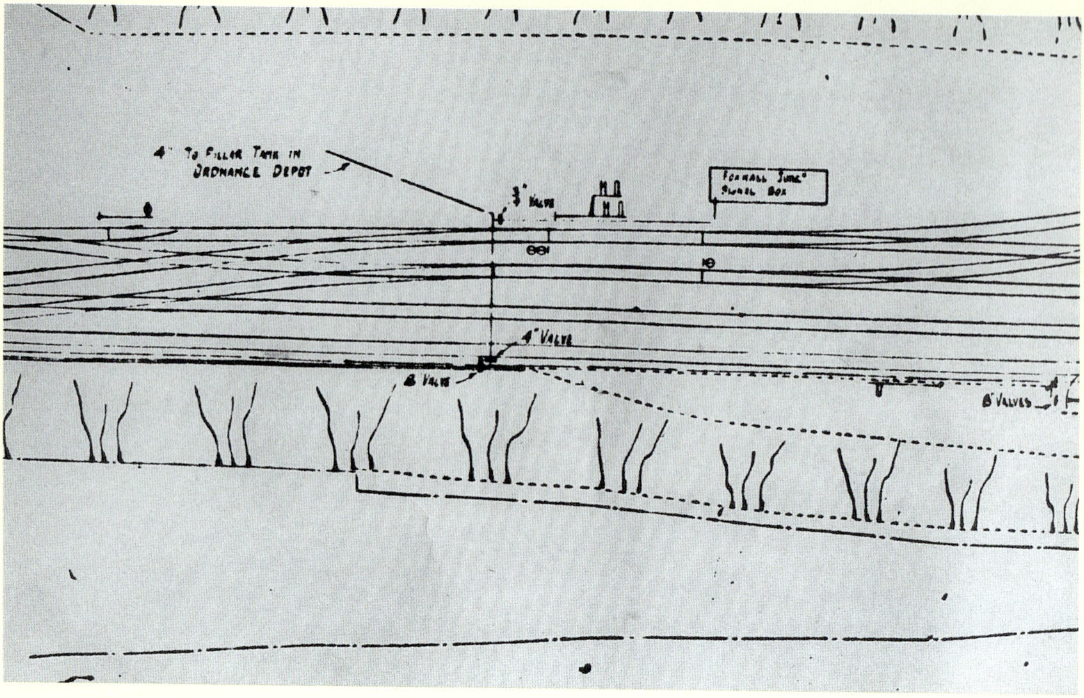

A water tank 20 by 16 by 8 feet, with a capacity at 7ft 6in of 22,500 gallons, fed water columns at Foxhall Junction.

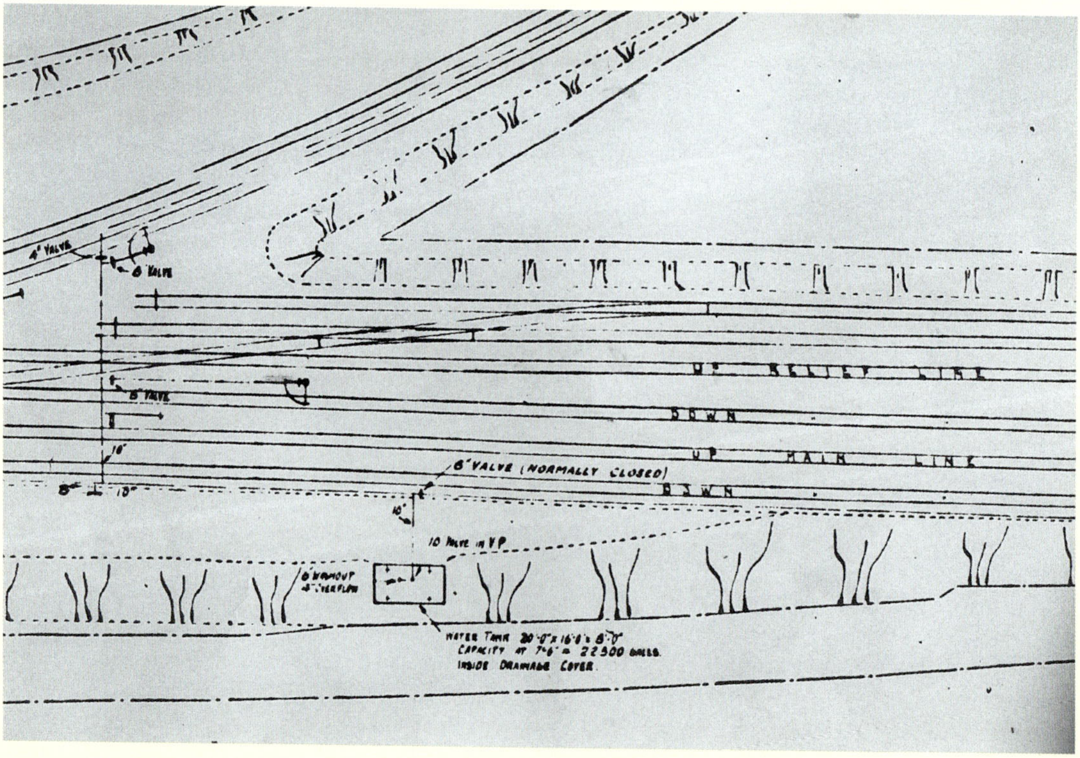

Four white tanks held fresh water within the Provender Stores and coal stage area.

It also fed the shed's steam engine boiler, and ran underground between the fitting shop and shed feeding the shed's 12 2½-inch hydrants for filling the boilers of engines.

It continued outside the front of the shed, with two more hydrants between Nos 1 and 2 roads and Nos 3 and 4 towards the water columns. There was another connection to the sand shed. Pipes also fed the ashpit area, branching off at several places to service appliances, as well as the coal stage. Beyond the ashpit shed it branched off towards Didcot station to supply that area.

A 6-inch pipe ran beneath the marshalling yard to the centre of the carriage sidings, feeding the water supply for refilling the coaches' tanks and washing down the outsides.

The Provender Stores complex once had its own pumping station at the rear of the building, feeding fresh water to the whole complex including Moreton marshalling yard, the Newbury line, Appleford signal box, Foxhall signal box, Didcot shed and the station area. The whole of the workshops and mess room had their own fresh water tanks 19 feet by 16ft 9in by 6 feet, with a capacity at a depth of 3ft 6in of 10,940 gallons. There was also a holding water tank 20 by 12 by 8 feet in size with a capacity at a depth of 7ft 6in of 11,250 gallons. On the very top of the building two tanks, spread equally apart, were 23 by 10 by 7 feet in size, with a capacity at a depth of 6ft 6in of 17,687 gallons each, with 3-inch control ball valves.

The West Curve pump house fed water by a 6-inch main to the Ordnance Depot and a water column. Water was also supplied to a Newbury line water tank and South Moreton marshalling yard.

The lake was the dumping area for return water from all the pipework within the vicinity, while dirty water from washouts went from the shed to a holding tank of 11,250 gallons between the West Curve and the down main line from the station. Another main fed a water tank opposite North Junction box.

As can be seen, even before the First World War Didcot's water system was vast, almost certainly bigger than that of Didcot itself at that time. The GWR built its own system, and that for Didcot town may very well have been, originally, an extension.

On Friday 30 December two workers came from Swindon to repair the glass in the windows and regrind the grinding wheel, completed by planned maintenance checks throughout the shop with the belts and safety guards on the belts. They worked round the shop writing things down as well as signing items off. They stayed with us for a week, and as they had to travel back and forwards to Swindon, each time they returned they had some spares in the work bags that they carried from the stores.

The oxygen and acetylene bottles ran empty and needed changing. We would then have to go to the stores about 50 yards away and see if there were some spares. Jim picked up the empty acetylene bottle on his shoulder, although it was very heavy, while I picked up the empty oxygen bottle in the same way, and we took them back to the stores, then brought the full ones back on a barrow.

I asked the Swindon men if they would like a cuppa. One had a flask with him, but the other said he would like one. We drank the tea and talked about the shop, and how long were they here for. When Jim came to the forge he said, 'Let the dog see the rabbit!, in order to get to the billycan and pour his black tea into his cup.

'We've got another job, Wobble,' he added. 'We're going up the station to inspect the lifts, so bring a grease gun out of my tool locker and some small spanners, and an oilcan. Make sure it's got some oil in it, please.'

I checked the oil and grease gun – all full – but when we came back everything would have to be replenished. We walked the cinder path to the station, and went though the undercroft to Platform 4. We walked back towards the Swindon end of the station, where the lift cage was, and found the steps leading to the roof. We climbed and found the door into the lift's operating shed. I was amazed at what I saw, with the wire drum and machinery. We greased the nipples around the drum and motor and checked the wire rope to see if any wires were coming away from the rope. I then climbed back down and headed for the lift, shut the cage door and pressed the button to go down. I heard that everything was OK, so went down to the cage in the undercroft and inspected the Constantia mesh doors there, pulling out some rubbish from the cage rail, then shut the cage doors together. I gave them a squirt of oil, pressed the button and the lift went up to the station platform; I inspected the underneath making sure everything was correct.

I then returned to the roof with the help of the ladder provided, and went into the wooden shed where Jim stood. 'All OK, boyo?' I had written down what I had done and gave the paper to him.

We then did the same for the other lift on Platform 6, except that Jim did all the running about while I stayed in the operating shed. He confirmed that all was OK. 'Come on,' he said, 'let's go and have a cuppa in the station tea rooms.' As usual we said, 'On Company Service,' and got tuppence off each cup.

'Got anything to do for Saturday afternoon, Jim?' I asked

'Digging my allotment up near you at the top of Sinodun Road, next to Reg Warr's house, and Archie Davies.'

'I hope the weather stays OK for you.'

'What are your plans? Are you taking Annie anywhere?'

'I won't know till tonight when we see each other.'

'What do your parents think of her?' he asked.

'We won't go there as Mum hates it, as I am her little boy. I have to fib to her if I'm going somewhere.'

'I feel sorry for you, lad.'

We walked back to the shed and Jim went into Arthur's office to sign off the brown card, writing out what we had found.

'Get washed up, Pat, and get home,' said Jim. 'There's nothing more to be done. See you on Tuesday morning, as we have Monday off with pay.

'I'm in tomorrow,' I said.

'No you're not – Arthur says so.'

So I wished Jim a Happy New Year, and called into Arthur's office to say the same.

I met Annie as arranged and we went

Christmas and New Year

to the pictures. Didcot was dead like a graveyard – there were no dances going on anywhere.

'How would you like to go to Oxford tomorrow, my darling?'

'No, we went there last week,' she replied.

'Shall we go to Reading then?'

'Yes. My grandparents live not far up the Oxford Road, and we could go and see them.'

I walked her home after seeing the film, and as we came out of the Coronet we bumped into Jim, as he had also been to see the film.

'Hello, Wob–' He hurriedly changed it to 'Pat'. Then he added, 'Hello, Annie. Did you like the film?'

I said, 'What film?'

He looked at me a bit old-fashioned, and said, 'Cheeky little sod!'

Annie giggled. 'Yes, it was OK, but I'm not into cowboys.'

Jim wished us both a Happy New Year, then left us to walk home with hands entwined and a kiss here and there. My heart was bouncing.

The following day, New Year's Eve, Dad drove me down to the station. I sat in the rear seat with Mum in the passenger seat, keeping her eyes peeled and looking for signs to have a moan about who she might see.

'What time are you coming home?'

'Haven't got a clue, so don't come to the station looking for me. I might run off with a black woman!'

'You're a comical little sod when you want to be,' she said.

'I have a life of my own.'

'Not till you're 16, my boy, and that's another thing we've got to talk about.' She stared daggers at me, but Dad just said, 'Have a good day, Pat.' I knew Dad had a rough time with her and she was sheer evil and two-bloody-faced, nice to some people but so jealous of others. I was her little boy, but when I went to the babies and toddlers school in Lydalls Road she dressed me up as a little girl every day until one of the little boys saw under my dress a dangly thing like he had, and said, 'You're a boy!' So I told her I was a boy not a little girl – I could have been dressed up as a girl all my life and never known the difference!

I went into the Ticket Office window and saw Mark Thomas. 'What you doing here? Are you moonlighting from the shed?' I asked.

'No, I have to cover both sides, Pat.'

'Tickets for Reading please, one with my privilege ticket return, and a return ticket.'

'Two shillings and sixpence, please.'

'See you next week. Happy New Year.'

We caught the 10.30 fast train stopping at Reading then Paddington. When we arrived at Reading we made our way towards Oxford Road and Reading West station. We had plenty of time as we walked, and I saw the viaduct and West station. When we got to Cannon Street we looked for the number of the terraced house. Annie knocked at the door and a little lady answered it. 'Hello, Gran! This is Pat. He is my boyfriend. Mum has sent you these items in a carrier bag.'

We had a cup of tea together but didn't stay long. After saying our goodbyes we wandered back to the town and went for a meal together. We went into a clothes shop and I bought Annie a frilly blouse. We really enjoyed our day out, then caught the last train, getting into Didcot at midnight. We left the train and walked down into the undercroft out into the fresh morning air of Sunday 1 January 1961. As we walked to the taxi rank I wished Annie a Happy New Year and told her that I loved her very much.

22. Table lamps and tantrums

When I got up on New Year's Day I had the third degree from Mum, looking at me with her screwed-up wicked eyes. 'What time did you get in?'

'Happy New Year to you too,' I said, and she gave me a huge slap across my face. I was at the end of my tether with her. Wait till I'm 16, I said under my breath.

After breakfast I went to see Mick. Mrs Howard invited me in and wished me a Happy New Year. We played some Buddy Holly records and he said, 'About London – when would you like to go?'

'I've got a letter back from Dad's sister and we can stay there in Whitechapel.'

'How about nearer your birthday?'

'OK, I'll get Dad to write back, and we can get our free passes sorted out, and a week's holiday. I'll tell Arthur nearer the time.'

Monday was a day off in lieu I went to stay with Annie all day.

On Tuesday I went to pick up my disc and out came Mark Thomas. He handed it to me, saying, 'Nice girl you have, Pat.'

'Yes I know, Mark,' I replied, and wished him a Happy New Year again.

The men in the cabin all said Happy New Year. I changed my overall for a clean set, and went back to the forge as usual. Jim was drinking black tea from his cup, with one foot on the base of the anvil. He said, 'You're off to Reading, Pat, with a pipe to be welded.'

The workers from Swindon were back and they brought some cardboard boxes with them with food bags inside, all the glass to repair the windows, and a replacement grinding stone, as the old wheel had worn away to nothing. After their day's work they completed PPM (Planned Maintenance) checks throughout the fitting shop. I was a bit confused and asked them if they were from the Didcot building firm of Blakes in Station Road. 'No,' came the answer. 'We are BR employees and go around different depots to do the work that is required.' That shut me up.

My brother Paul got demobbed from the Royal Navy, as he had done his three years National Service, and came down to see Arthur Brinkley to enquire if there was a position for him in the Running and Maintenance section. Arthur asked him to follow him outside and he showed him what the job was entailed on the engines. Arthur said, 'Do you think you could do the job?'

I was outside on No 3 road and saw Paul having a look round, then he went into the office with Arthur and came out with a huge smile on his face. He started on days a week after the interview. The whole family was now on BR's Western Region, although Paul was married and lived with his wife Joan in a flat above Jenkins's paper shop in Park Road; the agreement was that she had to work in the shop making up the papers and opening up at 6 every morning and closing at 6 in the evening.

I was off to Reading again. Arthur gave me my pass in his office, and Sam 'Donkey' Morgan was sitting very quietly behind his desk. I asked him how his Christmas had been. 'Quiet, in Sinodun Road, but Mr and Mrs James next door were rowdy over Christmas Day, and they brought the New Year in as well, standing outside watching everyone that came down Sinodun Road and shouting to everyone up the street and anyone who came by their house. They were loud.'

My errand this time was with another split vacuum pipe, approximately 10 feet long wrapped up in whatever they had available at the time, newspaper tied up with string. I headed towards the station and the waiting DMU, a stopper all the way to Reading. I placed the pipe in the guard's van, then found a seat in the carriage. I thought that I could walk down towards the signal box and across the points, but thought better of

Table lamps and tantrums

it with this long pipe, it being tricky with all the trains rushing about. So I decided to walk the safe way to the shed. I again reported to the fitting shop foreman, left the pipe and documents, and had a look round Reading. I looked in all the shop windows, and even went into the record shops to see the costs of vinyl records to build up my collection of Elvis. I was drawn to Reading and, after my day out with Annie, thought it was a better town by far. I wandered back to the shed 2 hours later and went back the way I had come, catching the train back to Didcot.

Vic Jarrot 'the Bishop' said that any time I left the pipe someone at that end would put it on a Didcot train early the next day so it could be picked up off the train. I said I would mention that to Arthur when I got back. Subsequently I got used to this, and even suggested that they could send it on the 6.00am Enparts train the next morning, but Arthur wouldn't allow it. A fitter's mate would pick it up from the station parcels office and take it to the shed.

I walked into the shed and handed over the pipe to Bert Paice, 'the Colonel', as he and Bob Looms were waiting for it. As they went under the engine to fit it, I went into the office. Jim was sitting in Bill Cox's seat.

'Hello, boyo!' he greeted me.

'Hello, Jim. Resting?'

'You're a cheeky sod!'

'Makes you happy,' I said.

I reported to Arthur about what 'The Bishop' had said.

'Who's that?'

'Vic Jarrot. That's what they all call him at Reading.' They laughed.

'Come on, we have work to do,' said Jim.

'I bet you've been waiting till I come back to say that to me.'

'So I can't sit down and have a cuppa for a few minutes? Come on, stop the silly talk and get outside down to the fitting shop.'

I was working under 4-6-0 No 4939 *Littleton Hall*, under the tender where the water scoop was bent. The fireman had been too late getting the scoop up and had caught a set of points, bending and buckling the scoop. So with the oxygen and acetylene and the biggest nozzle we had, we got the scoop red hot, then, while it was still connected, we hammered the metal straight from outside the tender, then set the measurement correct for the trough size from another engine's scoop.

There were three of us, one with a hammer and sledge and bars taking the strain, while I had the blow torch nozzle warming up, and Jim was swinging the 28lb sledge hammer. He soon put it back into shape. We then freed off all the pins with oil and grease, and oiled the threaded screws. We made sure the scoop fitted into its slot when wound up on the threaded screw on the footplate, moving it up and down to confirm that it fitted, with plenty of oil spread around the screw. It was like brand new when we'd finished.

Blimey, what a day! We never seemed to have stopped. As I walked past Dave Davies he said, 'How's your neck?'

I shook my head. 'Why, what's wrong?'

'Your neck – does it hurt?'

'No, why?'

'Well, while you were in Reading did you look up at all the tall buildings?'

'No, why?'

'That's how you get neck ache and a stiff neck, as we have no tall buildings in Didcot!'

'You silly sod!' I said to him. He was quite put out with that.

It had been a long day 'out in the sticks' looking round Reading, then coming back into the shed and starting work again. I got my wash stuff as I wanted to be clean and get rid of the dirt and grime. I washed my hands and dried them, and as I looked up I saw Jim wandering about. I shouted to him to put the kettle on so we could have a cuppa. I was so thirsty and the back of my throat was raw and dry as a chip. He walked across the rails and saw me waiting to pour the golden nectar. I swung the billycan round at arm's length. 'What's wrong with you, Jim?'

'Cheesed off as we have nothing to do and I am like a bull's head just wandering about.'

'Well, get some the nectar down you and

let me see a smile on your face.'

We stood a while chattering and supping the hot tea. I asked him if we were going to get another 'Hall' in for pistons, and what was the schedule for the next few months. He replied that No 6952 *Kimberley Hall* should be coming in for pistons and valves with some small repairs, and we always changed the steam cocks when we did the pistons; that was part of one of the schedules. I asked if we would be changing the brake blocks. 'I don't mind,' I said, 'if Arthur asked you, as the experience is needed if I ever come out of my time.'

'Are you happy with that then, Pat?'

'Also, Jim, I want us to do it as people are shouting about while we are working on the piston and valves, and I have a job to hear as they are so blinking noisy!'

That evening I called at Mick's to see what was going on at the weekend.

'How about we go down to the Labour Club on Thursday and go from there, mate?'

'Sounds good. And what about Saturday?'

'I would like to go to and see Merv and Jean at the Crispin in Harwell. We could get some food there and have a few pints. He's always game for a laugh, and to be honest I could do with a good laugh.'

'OK Pat, you're on!'

I then wandered up to see Annie for an hour. We sat on her stairs and chatted. 'If it's OK I'd like to see you on Friday, Annie. Shall we go to the pictures?'

She asked me what had happened on Sunday morning, and I told her about Mum slapping me.

'Is it because of me, Pat?'

'No, it's me. I'm her little boy and she wants me for herself.'

On the Wednesday morning Jim wasn't at the forge; I waited a while, but still nothing. Then I saw Dave and Jim Hale, and asked them if they'd seen Jim. 'He's about, Pat.'

'While I'm waiting, Dave, have you got the copper pipe in the drawer and the lamp shade and all the other parts? I might as well get into making that.'

Dave said, 'Go up to the stores and get two corks – take the pipe with you for size. Then go into the sand store and fill the pipe with dry sand, then put the other cork in and bring it back to me and I'll show you how to bend it.'

I did as I was told; a few shed staff looked on and were puzzled. When I returned, Dave said, 'Go and get the biggest iron bush from the cupboard and put it into the vice.' He held the pipe tight against the iron bush. 'Right, start feeding it around the bush steady.' As I fed it, it started to bend with no trouble. I was amazed – we went round the whole circle and the pipe was true to the bend. 'Now turn it round to create the start of the swan neck.' We both held onto it and kept bending with our hands with no heat applied. I stood it up on the bend, and with another little bend it came within its tolerance. I thought, this man knows what he is talking about. As I held the perfectly shaped lamp shade from one of the coaches, it looked good.

Dave said, 'Empty the sand out and then we'll feed the wire into the pipe.'

I said, 'We might have a job,' but hi-ho, nothing is impossible, just blinking awkward.

Dave and I went across to the carriage and wagon stores on the hunt. Dave tried the door and it opened. Mr Townsend was there, and asked if he could help us.

Dave said that we wanted some thin wire that would run easily around the inside of a copper pipe to feed in some cable. He rummaged around and found something that was just the job.

'We'll bring it back when we're finished.'

'No, keep it – it might come in handy again. What are you making?

'A table lamp,' I said.

'You're pretty clever, so I've heard. Pokers and shovels with toasting forks. How much are you selling them for?' I told him a dollar each. 'I'll have a set please. Pat.'

'I'll bring it home to you went I finish work in a couple of days,' I said.

As we started to walk away Dave said, 'You're a sly old dog! How do you know him?'

'We all live in Sinodun Road, and when

Table lamps and tantrums

his little boy had sand in his eyes I took the sand out, and took him home to his Mum.'

We walked back the fitting shop, looking both ways when we approached the tracks, as a few engines were on their travels towards the turntable. As they passed us a driver waved, and we put our hands up to acknowledge Ted Ireson.

As we walked back into the shop a voice said, 'Oh good morning! Nice of you to pop in, boyo! You're a cheeky little sod! We have a job on, so what are you doing making a lamp? We'll start after morning break.'

He said he would make the tea, and meanwhile Dave and I got on with the thin wire. He poked it through the pipe till it came out the other end, then tied the two-strand wire onto it. I held the lamp stand and he pulled the thin wire, keeping an even pressure on it when came to the tight curve at the base. We worked in tandem, me feeding and Dave pulling, then there it was right in front of us. Unbelievable – we were good! Jim shouted that tea was up.

Dave collected the coupling and tied off the connection point at one end of the pipe, placed the lamp shade into the slot provided then went to the locker and pulled out a bayonet bulb and fitted it. Then he put on a three-pin plug, wired it up and tested it in the socket on the wall. It came on – it was beautiful! He was amazed as well, and so were a few others in the department, then the silly banter. 'Is that all you got to do?'

I thanked Dave for helping me. 'You're OK, Wobble.'

Then, as usual, Arthur joined us. 'Got anything to eat, Pat?'

'You know where my grub is, Arthur.'

I didn't feel hungry as I was interested in doing work – maybe later when the hunger gets to me in the stomach.

Steam cocks were the worst job ever. I had to sit on the cold concrete floor with the fear of losing my legs if run over by the loco wheels. Lying down under the steam chest was the best way, but as men wandered by and looked down on the floor, they would say sarcastically, 'Having a sleep while you're down there?'

'Yes, well, trying to till you woke me!'

Next day, Thursday, was pay day again. When I arrived I heard all this banging coming from the engine closest to where I stood. I climbed up onto the footplate and still the noise sounded close, so I put my head into the firebox and met Jack Dearlove Senior inside it, hammering the burnt copper studs out of the side of the frame – at the age of 75 years young. I had to climb in backwards onto the firebars, as the drop was too much going in head first. Then the heat hit me, as the engine still had some 80lb of steam in the boiler. The fire had been dropped and Jack had swept the firebox clean; it was no good working with dust swirling about and coming up from the ashpan under the engine. I saw a face mask in the wooden carpenter's toolbox as he worked away by himself.

'Come in, boy, and see what I'm doing.'

He was sitting on a wooden box with a short clay pipe in his mouth, the bowl to one side just under his nose. His dress code wasn't standard: he was in his vest and his overalls turned down to his waist, as the heat in the box was terrible and the sweat dripped off my nose. When I looked at Jack's face he was the same. He puffed away on his old pipe, smoking some kind of baccy – it might have been old socks by the smell of it.

'Jack, have you a spare copper stud?'

'Yes, boy. Here, have one. What you going to make now?'

'A soldering iron.'

He pulled one out of his little box where he kept his tools, and I thanked him. My overalls were sticking to my body and sweat was running down my legs. I had to get out in the fresh air, so I pushed my head out of the firebox entrance and wriggled out, pulling with my hands and trying to grab something with my feet, pushing on the firebars to get a grip. I rolled out onto the wooden boards of the footplate and when I straightened up my hands and knees were covered in coal dust, which I brushed off.

When we had our cuppa Arthur appeared

as normal. 'What are you making?'

'Some more fire tools, and I've got a copper stud.'

'I will give you this, Pat – you're always busy and not messing about.'

'I like making things, Arthur, and seeing the end result.'

I went into the shop with the stud and Jim asked what I was going to make now.

'I thought a soldiering iron, but first I have to make a couple of fire irons for two people.'

'We have a couple of "22s" coming in to change brake blocks, Nos 2201 and 2221.'

They were designed by Collett, a miniature of a 'Castle' with a tender, but an 0-6-0 wheel arrangements. They were liked by the enginemen and the fitters who worked them – that is how I remembered them.

'Carry on with what you want to do,' said Jim, so I walked to the scrap area, found some metal and generally got stuck in to cutting and bending and making my own rivets. I partially built everything in the day as I was on a roll. When I came to weld the handle and shovel together, some men looked on in disbelief; one asked how I could weld with no flux, and I told then it was because I was taught correctly at school, and it had stuck in my brain.

Later that afternoon I took my table lamp home. I was as pleased as Punch with it, and when I got home I showed it to the family. Dick was a bit off with me over it – he must have been having one of his tantrums! I placed it on the sideboard and plugged it in. It worked a treat – I was so pleased with it.

I went into the bathroom to have a bath and just lay there soaking when the bathroom door flew open and Dick stood there, all cocky like, looking down at me with an evil eye. I shouted to him to get out.

'You going to make me, little boy?'

He slammed the door shut.

'Get out!' I shouted, but he fought me, punching me, hurting me. He even got my head and put me under the water, not allowing me to come up for air. I was gasping for air and took mouthfuls of the bathwater and went limp. He took the bait, and as I came up for air and he leaned over the edge of the bath I grabbed him with both hands and dragged him fully clothed into the water. He was fighting with a crocodile now as I pushed his head under the water and sat on his arms. Loads of bathwater flew up the walls and over the lino on the floor. Now I was ready – I'd had enough of him kicking my shins and punching me when I least expected it.

I heard Mum coming up the stairs, so just at that moment I allowed him to come up for air. Then I clenched my right fist and thumbed him one into his nose and eye. He didn't know what had hit him, and as he raised his fist to fight back the door flew open and Mum shouted out, 'Don't you dare, Dick! What's going on? Look at the mess! Patrick, get it cleaned up!'

I tried to defend myself but it was no good, as Dick was her favourite and I was nothing. He stood up in the water – there wasn't a dry spot on him.

'This isn't finished!' he said.

Mum said, 'Yes it is!' screaming at the top of her voice, 'or I shall start on you. You should know better – you are six years older than Patrick!'

He walked away to his bedroom with his soggy wet socks on the wooden floor and holding his nose where I had thumped him.

After getting dressed I went out again to see Mr Townsend, as he only lived up the road next door to Graham Wilde at No 40 – we were joined at the hip, friends for ever, him and me. I knocked at the door and his wife answered. When Mr Townsend appeared I gave him the bits I had made for him.

'You never hung about! How much do I owe you?'

'A dollar, please.'

'How much?'

'Sorry – 5 shillings.'

I walked back home down Sinodun Road, enjoying the dark of the evening. More money for the account, I said to myself.

As I sat eating my food with a cup of tea, my wet soggy brother wandered into the

Table lamps and tantrums

kitchen. Dad was sitting talking to me, and I grinned at Dick and nodded like a nodding donkey; wherever he walked I followed him with my gaze, nodding behind Dad's back, taking the Mickey out of him and poking out my tongue with a screwed-up face. He was getting angry!

Later Mick and I headed for the Labour Club as we had missed it last week and we both wanted a drink and a chat. I told him what had happened in the bath, and that it had been a hard few days working. We both planned to visit Merv at the Crispin in Harwell on Saturday night and buy some food from Jean his wife. We stayed in the club for a few hours playing darts and supping ale and having a laugh with the rest of the brothers. Upstairs we sat among them at one of the meetings, seeing what the crack was; there were some very interesting subjects and we took part in the vote. Mick got his bottle of pop and we walked home together. At the same place he opened the screw top and drank the rum down, leaving me the dregs, then threw the bottle into the undergrowth. They must have been mounting up, or the weeds were growing closer together to hide them.

On Friday No 2201 came in; the other would come in when we had finished this one, and Jim was intending to get it out straight away. I got the mix of thin oils and paraffin together in a dirty old bucket with an old 2-inch paint brush I found, cleaned up with a wire brush. Under the engine I went along the threaded adjusting screws, wire-brushing off the dirt and brushing on the oily mixture, then with some cotton waste in my other hand wiping off the drips. I hoped we would have an easy run with these heavy blocks.

Jim went outside with the two-wheeled barrow and brought in six brake blocks, leaving them near the wheels. He also chiselled off the rough edges so the blocks would go back into their original brackets more easily – we hoped. I wasn't looking forward to this as the blocks were very heavy and awkward and I hated blackened squashed finger nails, especially when the nail got caught in some clothing and started to edge away from the finger, flapping. I got the cringes then!

But I was sure I was not going to get into that position. Jim passed the huge brake spanner down to me, with which I hit the adjuster to shake out the dirt and grit. Both sides needed doing it this way – these large locking nuts were not finger tight. I placed the spanner over the nut and tried hitting it with the hammer. What a waste of time that was! I shouted to Jim to get the 7lb hammer, which was more my size; I had cut off the shaft 9 inches from the hammer, which would be better. I swung the hammer downwards with every ounce of strength in my body, and saw the spanner move. Again I hit the end of the spanner with all my might. I was on a roll now, and brushed more oily material over the thread and nut. As I ran the nut backwards I put more oil on the screw, then held the spanner and the nut started to run off the adjuster.

On the other side of the adjuster I had the same problem, as it was a left-hand thread and access to it was close to the front of the ashpan, with not much room to move. So I went to the main adjuster, a long tapered nut in the middle of two small nuts. As I heaved on the long nut I felt a slight movement. I asked Jim for a large cold chisel.

'What are you going to do?' he shouted.

'Knock hell out of the locking nut to shake it off the adjuster.'

He came down in the pit to watch what I was about to do. 'Go for it then, Wobble!'

I placed the chisel edge at a 45-degree angle and with the 7lb sledge I whacked it, and it moved. I had then undone the adjuster enough, but hi-ho I had the other side to do now.

As we rested a while Jim said, 'You can make me one of these hammers when we're finished. That's well balanced. What gave you the idea, Wobble?'

'I wanted something a bit heavier so I came up with idea.'

I went back to the other adjuster with a

spring in my step, thinking that he wanted me to make a hammer for him. Again I got the chisel on the outer nut, which gave me more room to move. I hit it with the 7lb hammer and the nut moved. With the wire brush I rubbed the threads and put some oil on them, then started to undo the nut clockwise, as this one had the left-hand thread. Now the other locking nut was treated the same way – I must have trodden in some dog shit! The nut unscrewed as I poured oil over the threads and started to undo the long nut, both sides equally. The brake blocks came off the wheels, with a bit of worn-down metal. The pins were knocked out and as I levered the rest out of the way the block fell to the ground. I went around the engine on the inside standing in the pit, as I had more room to move past the firebox. While I got the last block off Jim was replacing them, tightening them all up equally. I felt as if I was in hell, working underground. I shouted to Jim to put the kettle on, as I was as dry as a chip and my lips felt dry.

'Finish off in there and we'll have a cuppa,' said Jim.

'OK, uncle!'

'What's this bloody silly chat about uncle?'

'OK, Dad,' I replied. That got him biting. I had him on the end of the line, pulling him in!

I finished off the adjustments both sides, tightened down the locking nuts and pushed out the spanner and tools. Jim said, 'Leave the tools in there as we have another coming in after this one.

I said, 'Aren't we on piecework? I thought we would do that one tomorrow.'

'Nothing like the present,' he answered. 'We'll carry on and get these two finished today. Who's the boss?' he added. 'And who's the boy?'

'Yes, sir!'

I went and got two 7lb sledges with long handles. I held one upright in my right hand and outstretched my arm fully, still holding the sledge. I then gently lowered it down to my nose, with my arm still outstretched, so I had control of the last point of the handle as the hammer end touched my nose. Then I retracted the hammer in the same way by pulling the handle up with my thumb and hand. Arthur walked into the shop and looked at us both. Jim had a 14lb sledge doing the same. 'There – I told you I could beat you,' he said.

'OK, can you do this then?' I got one sledge in my left hand and another in my right hand, both arms outstretched level. I lowered both hammers to my nose from either side and held them there for a few minutes allowing them to put a black spot on my skin. Then I lifted them both back upright, never bending my arms. I cannot explain what he said in Welsh as I wasn't conversant with the language.

'Right, I'll sort out your new sledge soon, old mate,' I said, grinning.

Arthur joined us for our cuppa as usual, and Jim asked him to get the next '22' in, as the first was ready to pull out.

The shed shunter, No 8720, came into the shop and coupled up to No 2201, pulling her out and placing her on No 2 road to be fired up for the next day's shunting in the yard; Mick Gleason would refill the firebox with Welsh coal, and get a bundle of cotton waste and sticks soaked with paraffin. He would light this bundle on a No 8 shovel with his cigarette.

The shunter ran back up the slight incline towards the exit stop board. This incline was used to advantage by driving an engine past the points for the chosen road, then she ran down towards No 6 road where to No 2221 was standing. The engines were coupled up and the cold engine was brought into the shop where we stopped it in exactly the same place as before. Jim already had the brake blocks down on the floor. He had removed the rough edges with a hammer and chisel and filed out the holes.

We replaced the blocks in exactly the same way as on the other engine, but this one was not as dirty, as she worked on the shed or just ran to the station. Therefore over the last couple of years the brake blocks had been not been changed. I hit the chisel with the 7lb sledge as before to shake the locking nut from the adjusting screw, and I must have been lucky as the nut moved. Here I go again, and I started singing in a low voice to myself as I worked on. On the next side the gods were still with me, as that side was also loose. Who might have worked on this engine? Let me think. Ah, yes, he had left the company last month. Now all the locking nuts were off and I undid the main adjuster, seeing the bars working in tandem as the brakes come off the wheels. Blimey, I am good, even if I say so myself! Then I oiled up the threads for the adjustment when the blocks were back on.

I shouted to Jim, 'Hanging about, are you? What are you doing? Sat on your bum?'

Jim rushed around now, and I had got him with the same line and was pulling him in.

'Wind then on, Wobble, equally, and don't forget the locking nuts!'

Fifteen love, level pegging. 'OK, boyo!'

Job done. I threw out the tools near Jim's bench, and walked out with my extra hammer to my locker to stash it away. Jim was in Arthur's office getting the '22' moved for the morning.

Although it was nearly home time, I had a cuppa in peace on my own for a few minutes, contemplating what I should do about Annie that night. She was always on my mind and made me happy just thinking about her. I got washed up and went home, thinking it wouldn't be long before I signed my apprenticeship papers to be a fully fledged apprentice.

23. Something up

Annie and I had planned to go to the pictures but instead we walked and talked round Didcot, hands entwined together. She told me that her relations were coming over from America at the weekend for a month to see the family, and they would be having a special tea, arranged by Annie's mother; baking was her main interest, as well as looking after her other daughter and two sons.

On Saturday No 2221 had been pulled out overnight and placed on No 5 road outside the shed to be lit up, allowing the sulphurous smoke to drift over to the East Loop. I asked Jim what was happening with work, and he said, 'Please yourself, Wobble.'

'I'll start with your sledge hammer, then. Can you hold the handle where you would grip it best?'

He did so, I marked the wooden handle with a scriber, and borrowed a hacksaw from his tools, with his permission. I placed the sledge in the vice and sawed off the handle with a clean cut, then with a rough bastard file I roughed up the edges. I then changed the file to a smooth one and rounded off the edges and finished it off with an emery cloth, running around the edge, with no splinters found. I went to the stores and got 2 pints of clean light engine oil in a galvanized bucket, since I was allowed to sign the chitty and present it to Jim Parsons, the store keeper. I brought the bucket back to the shop and placed the cut-off sledge in the oil to soak till Monday morning.

Jim Hale had been annoying me to make some rubber fire mats to put out fires. I asked him where I should start, and he said, 'Right, Wobble, stores – three-quarter-inch-thick rubber sheeting and broom handles – say four, OK?' He signed the chitty and I went back to the stores.

'Back already, Pat?' said Jim as I handed over the chitty. He disappeared and came back with the broom handles and a sheet of rubber. God, it was heavy! I had a job to lift it, so walked along pulling the matting behind me until I reached my bench. I chucked all the stuff onto the bench, and went to the scrap area to see what had been dumped.

I sorted out some metal strip, enough for what I wanted to make these fire mats and keep Jim Hale quiet. I was shown how to cut the matting; it had string running through the middle of it so was very tough. Jim and Dave came to my rescue, one holding a cup of water and the other with a huge knife. They cut off one section 18 inches square. 'Now you can get on with the other three, Wobble.'

I must admit I did struggle, and using water to cut rubber was a new thing to me. However, it kept me quiet for a couple of hours, and I conquered it. I drilled out several holes and placed the flat metal on either side of the rubber to reinforce it firmly, then drilled the broom handle at the base. I cut out enough gaps to push the mat and metal together then bolted all the bits together with nuts and washers, allowing me to test one outside in the bracken and rough scrubland. I was pleased, and it was nearing home time.

'Hear you are, Mr Hale – all done, and the test one seems OK. I'm sure you'll test the others.'

I washed up and shouted out, 'Bye, see you Monday!'

A shout came back. 'Behave yourself!'

'No chance!' I replied.

'Where are you off to Saturday night?'

'Harwell – Crispin all night.'

'Does Arthur know?'

'He might when I knock at his door asking if his daughter is coming out to play.'

That got them going. I knew they would be off to his office to tell him.

I rode home as the rain started to pour down. All I wanted was a good soak in a hot bath, and to play some records in my bedroom loaded onto the record player. I

Something up

stacked the vinyl 45s high to serenade me while I slept in the hot water. As the water got chilly I turned on the hot tap with my toes, until that ran cold, then it had to be time to get out of the bath as my skin was wrinkly! I got dressed in my Wranglers, white shirt and pumps, had some food and a glass of milk to line my stomach before going out. Third degree again.

'Where are you going?'

'Out,' I replied. 'Mick's.'

We caught the local bus to see Merv in Harwell, as it stopped close to his pub.

'Hello boys!' he shouted. 'Welcome! First pint is on me!' He was jolly and playing spoof with a friend of his. 'Come and join in, you two!'

Mick and I looked at each other. Why not?

'Do you know how to play it? You have five coins in your hand and you must guess what the total is. With the four of us playing, whoever gets caught pays for the beers. I said, 'Game on!' and we both enjoyed the game. It didn't cost us much, as Merv got caught every time, and he was two sheets to the wind anyway.

I said, 'Have you got any food on, Merv?'

He called Jean, and we both gave her a list of what we would like to eat. When it came there was enough for the 5,000. We shared it with Merv and his mate Bob. We left about 1.00am – a lock-in again – and walked home the 3½ miles. It was spitting with snowflakes when we walked down the Broadway – we looked like two snowmen.

When we got home Mick drank his milk and I had a pint of cold tap water and sobered up. I went home to a nice welcome. 'Where have you been?' She was sitting waiting for me!

On Sunday, feeling refreshed after the night out together, I looked through the ice on the inside of the window, trying to scrape it off to see what the weather was like. A blanket of snow, and it was throwing it down. I decided to stay indoors for a while and see how it was later. In fact I stayed in all day as I wasn't going out in that; I hated snow at the best of times. Mum couldn't believe it, as I played records in my bedroom, and wrote out what I had seen on the railway while working as a fitter's boy. This story is taken from my notes. It was good to rest, anyway – I needed the peace, as I was so tired.

On Monday 9 January 1961 I walked to work in the snow. I had to walk in the tyre tracks where the coal lorry had been. At the shed the engines were snow-capped, and the coal picked out in black and white. The locomen looked freezing in their cabs as they drove out to their jobs. I didn't envy them, poor sods. I stood at the entrance to the shed, kicking off the white stuff on the side of the wall before I entered the Time Office.

Down at the forge all the big wooden doors were closed shut and bolted with newspaper stuffed into the cracks to keep the heat in the shop.

That day Paul, my eldest brother, reported to Shedmaster George East's office. All three of us had the same introduction when we started shed work with British Railways Western Region, on days for the first week. Word was spread by Ted Rock, and the three fitters were known as 'the Kelly family'.

Arthur was summoned to the Shedmaster's office to take Paul and show him around, introducing him to most of the staff and drivers. He came into the shop where Jim and I were working. Jim and he and shook hands, but he just nodded to me; he never had a lot to say to me and we never worked together all the time I was there.

Paul was introduced to Bill Clark, who opened the overall box and sized him up with a pair of blue overalls. He was going to be his new mate. Paul was a fitter and turner and had worked in the engine room of the destroyer HMS *Crossbow*, where he served his three years of National Service; he also served his time at Didcot Ordnance REME workshops. When he and his mate left HMS *Crossbow* they decided to row a boat around the ship singing to the Captain, whose name was James.

'Goodbye Jimmy, goodbye,
Don't cry, Jimmy, don't cry
We will see you again
But we don't know when.'

They were as drunk as skunks and had a bottle of rum in the boat, slurping it back. When the Captain saw them he told the Petty Officer, 'Get those two bloody idiots back on the ship!' When the destroyer docked in Portsmouth they were demobbed.

However, he was now here at Didcot for the duration, working three shifts on diesels and steam locomotives. He never did PPMs as he was on the front of the shed, and became quick in his responses and attitude. The drivers and firemen thought the world of him; he never once turned down any work or walked away from showing his skills, even when called out at night in all weathers on breakdown duties.

Paul and his wife Joan moved from the caravan site at Blewbury into Park Road, Didcot, above Mr Jenkins's paper shop. Joan worked in the shop.

My brother worked the day shift for two weeks, getting to know the lie of the land and the dos and don'ts. For anything else he went to Arthur's office to enquire, as he didn't feel right asking fellow members of staff, who had more faces than Big Ben! Work-wise he was on shift 12 hours the following day, his shift pattern starting at 6.00am till 6.00pm, and 4 hours on Saturday mornings. Then after the two weeks training he worked the complete shift pattern like the rest of the men. Jim Tyler was exempt from shifts, but he worked five days a week 6.00am to 6.00pm, and Saturday mornings for 4 hours.

The tool lockers were situated against the shed wall on the same side as the shed boiler, and Paul's was down near the entrance door; it had been Norman Brogden's originally. He got permission to move it up to the far wall closer to the brick house, but the same side as all the rest, so they were all in line. He was closer to the twins' lockers and next door was Jim Tyler's locker, then Jim Holmar's. Down past the 'A' frame of the crane were the lockers of Jack Dearlove, Ted Powell, then Bert Paice. All the lockers were made from wooden planks and stood 6 feet in height by 4 feet wide, and were very spacious, carrying everything that BR issued in 'Snail' brand tools and those that I made for them.

We had to open the big wooden doors to allow No 6952 *Kimberley Hall* to come into the shop, quietly as a mouse with the smokebox leading. I looked up at her – she was just like a woman, absolutely lovely, her

Me in the cab of No 6952 *Kimberley Hall* in 1961.

metal body beautifully round and shapely. She moved on past the crane frame and as the rear of her tender cleared the concrete steps I shouted 'Stop!'

'Spot on, Wobble,' said Jim.

Paul also stood and watched this huge lady as she sat in what would be her home for a few days, keeping out of the wet and cold while Jim and I worked on her. I felt honoured.

The shed engine closed up the buffers while 'Bronco', Cedric Ashmore, the fireman, uncoupled the two locomotives, then the driver gently opened the regulator to go back out of the shed on No 1 road. I shut the doors again to keep the warm in and bolted them. Only the small sprung door was open for entry.

Jim asked what I would like to do, and I said, 'Is it OK if we split? I would like to do one side while you do this side.'

'OK, boyo. Think you can manage her?'

'I hope to try.'

'Call me then if you get stuck,' said Jim.

I helped myself to the spanners required and started to undo the small quarter-inch set of screws around the front piston cowling, placing them in a tin to be safe. I added a drop of thin oil and paraffin to help the threads when putting them back together. I placed the long old socket on the nut at the bottom of the piston cover. When the bar went into the hole I had to pull upwards with all my might to undo the first nut; I felt a twinge down my back. I followed the same sequence on the ring of nuts holding the piston cover against the cylinder. The sweat ran down my back from the top of my head, and I felt sticky and cold when I had finished.

I helped myself to the crowbar with the flat chisel at the end and edged the bar into the face of the piston plate to grip and heave at the same time. I felt it move, so put the bar down and with Jim's soft metal hammer I whacked the cover with all my might – what I had left! Pulling off the nuts had really taken my strength away and I felt weak and exhausted – I needed some refreshment to get my sugar levels back!

I went round the other side and saw Jim talking to Paul; he hadn't started to strip out his side yet. I said, 'I'm making tea and the kettle is on.'

'OK, Wobble, replied Jim.

Paul looked a bit sideways. I said, 'It's my nickname.'

We had tea at the forge while Jim and Paul chatted. I sank the tea in one go as I wanted my sugar levels to rise.

Feeling much better now and refreshed, I left them chattering. Arthur joined them. I said, 'Help yourself,' and he nosed into my bag and pulled out a sarnie. Pouring himself a cuppa, he joined in the conversation with the other two.

I pressed on. I picked up the large bar again and conquered the piston cover plate. With a loud crash it flew off the cylinder. All three men looked at me in disbelief. I just said, 'Carry on – sorry to break the silence.' Jim looked at me with his head on one side, thinking twice before he spoke – I saw it in his eyes. I bent downwards to remove the piston casing away from the front of the engine.

I now worked on the con-rod where it joined the crosshead. I removed the cotter pin from the castle nut and drove the spindle out of the crosshead with Jim's lead hammer so that the con-rod dropped onto the slide bar. I then took out the cotter pin from the wedge that held the piston shaft into the crosshead. I knew exactly what I was doing. Having some free movement now at the rear end, I undid the gland nuts and pulled out the packing from the piston gland with the hand-held corkscrew. There wasn't enough space to remove the gland from the shaft yet, until I had pulled out the piston shaft with the large crowbar stuck into the wheel spokes. However, first I had to take out the wedge with my 7lb hammer and chisel and pull the crosshead off the shaft. With the con-rod removed from the crosshead I placed a block on the slide bar to lift it upwards. I was lucky – there was just enough space so the crosshead came off the shaft with a small crowbar. I edged it even further off the shaft, until I could remove the piston gland.

I placed my foot on the lower connecting rod and put the large crowbar behind the end of the shaft and pulled with all my might. I felt the piston slide forward. I had got another grip behind the shaft when someone put their hand on my shoulder and said, 'I'll do that please, Wobble. I don't think you've enough strength to pull the piston out.'

Jim took over, and I was sure he was right in his decision. I hadn't the strength to push the piston out of the cylinder quite yet. He placed the bar on the back of the shaft with the large crowbar stuck in the leading wheel's spokes and pulled the shaft out of the cylinder with all his might. It shot out of the cylinder in one easy swoop onto the ground.

He looked at me, and I said, 'I know I you made the right decision, and I'm pleased. Thank you, Jim.'

'You done well, boyo.'

It was now dinnertime and I stayed by the forge after putting some more coal on it from the tender of *Kimberley Hall*.

After dinner I placed some cotton waste over the piston rings and snapped them with two small crowbars. That's how I had been taught – the cotton waste stopped any flying objects. The rings were as sharp as a knife on the edges, and I picked them up cagily and chucked them in the rubbish bin. Now I went to my locker and got out the metal scraper that I had made, which just fitted inside the channel so that with a hammer I could scrape out the carbon. Arthur came to see what I was doing. 'I've never seen a tool like that, Pat,' he said. 'Did you make it?'

When I started on the next channel he wanted a go. 'That's quick and easy, Pat – you're clever,'

'I prefer an easy life, Arthur!'

'Did you go out Saturday anywhere nice?'

'Only to the Crispin. Did you wait for me at home, then, thinking I was coming to visit you?'

'No, what makes you think that?'

'Nothing.' I shook my head. I knew that the twins had said something on Saturday morning before I left for home. Blinking piss-takers!

'Spending a bit of time in Harwell,' continued Arthur. 'What time did you get home then?'

I hesitated a little while, trying to tease him. I was thinking what to say, whether I could wind him up and get him biting.

'Well,' I said, 'it was snowing when we got halfway home and we looked like two snowmen walking down the centre of the road.'

'What time then?'

'Why? It was too late to venture round your house, as I think you might have been in bed. Or maybe just getting up for your breakfast…' He walked away in disgust – I'd got him! I grinned and got on with scraping the carbon out of the channels.

Jim and Paul were still chattering at the forge. I went and got the box of tricks to measure the bore, which was 18½ inches with a stroke of 30 inches, adding the extension on the micrometer until it touched the bottom of the bore. There was just a few thou difference as the bore wasn't worn away. I told Jim the sizes and he logged them in his book. He told me to go to the stores and get six new rings. 'You can sign the chitty.'

On the way back Arthur was coming out of his office. 'Ah, Pat, got a minute?'

'What's wrong now, Arthur?

'Come into the office,' he said. 'You had me biting, you little sod, but I couldn't have shouted at you in front of those two at the forge.' I put my finger and thumb over my mouth, and with my elbow on the desk looked at him in disbelief. What was coming now? He was doing all the talking, and I sat quietly taking the fishing line and winding him in slowly.

'Spending a lot of time in our village. What's going on?'

'Why, Arthur, what have you got to worry about? We had a drink with Merv.'

'Someone told me you were coming to my house to ask my daughter out on a date.'

'No, sorry! Dave Davies and Jim Hale are winding you up and you can't see it, Arthur. I

Something up

can, as I told them Saturday morning before leaving work – and I bet you they ran in here after I left for home.'

'Those pair of bastards!'

'See, I was right!'

'Sorry, Pat. Anyway, what time did you leave the pub?'

'Nearly breakfast time Sunday morning – 1.00am.'

'Thank you for telling me. Now get back to what you're doing, Pat.'

It was getting near home time – the day had shot by. Jim had the rings and my side was ready to put back together; we had a chat before going home, and all I said was, 'See you in the morning.'

'What did Arthur want from you?' asked Jim.

'Tell you in the morning, mate. Good night.' I grinned a little.

The following morning, Tuesday, Jim asked me again about my chat with Arthur.

'Are you that desperate that you've been dreaming of me?' I replied, then told him about what the twins had said to Arthur and why he pulled me into his office. 'That's all. What's on today?'

'We'll finish off your side then you can help me do the other side.'

I said, 'Shall I go and get the steam cocks?'

'No, we're not changing any as they are short in the stores. I've already been to see if there are any.'

The piston rings were ready in the grooves of the piston, with the bore oiled. We both manoeuvred the piston into place and edged the shaft into the bore. Now with the crowbar Jim lifted the heavy end up, jamming the bar into the spokes of the bogie wheels, as I held the piston itself and pushed it right into the bore. I went and got the wooden block and laid it on the floor for Jim to rest a minute. He said, 'Leave it on the block for a few minutes, and measure the shaft's radius to see if we can get a tube and slide it over the shaft to help us. We've got plenty of time.'

I got my outside callipers, took the measurements and transferred the size to the inside callipers. 'I'll go and have a look for some pipe. Come with me, Jim.'

We both wandered over to the carriage and wagon area. When I knocked on the door one of the men opened it. 'Come in, Pat!'

Jim looked at me. 'Well known here, aren't you?'

I asked if they had any steel pipe or galvanised pipe, and they said to help ourselves. We had a look and found a small length that would do. As Jim walked out of the area I was pulled back inside by one of the men. All he said was, 'Come into the department if you need anything, as Mr Townsend said so, Pat.' I thanked him. 'And can you make four pokers for us?' he added. 'What's the cost?'

'Nothing,' I said, 'as you help me.'

By the time I got back to the shop Jim had cut off the amount he wanted and tried the pipe through the gland radius. There was just enough room. He put himself between the cylinder and the piston, while I sat on the wooden block and went to the gland to instruct him to move the piston one way or the other just a morsel – or a gnat's cock! I slid the tube over the shaft, and he got his large crowbar and jammed it into the spokes. He lifted up the assembly and I heaved it into the cylinder. It sat on the outer cover studs and I kept my weight against it. He removed the tube that we had just made, placed the key wedge into the slot and jammed his crowbar into the spokes of the leading wheel. I lifted the piston with another crowbar jammed in the bogie wheel spokes, and he pulled with all his might as the first ring shot into the cylinder. I shouted out for a rest. Then I got the flat bars to guide the rings into the cylinder by squeezing them together. The next ring went in, and Jim pulled the piston in. He put the gland over the shaft and pulled the crosshead and shaft together, looking for the line-up of the wedge. He replaced the con-rod connection, then the 7lb hammer went into action as he thumped the wedge into place and finished off that area.

'I've left the gland packing for you, Wobble.'

I got the magnesium graphite paste with the large saw blade from the locker, and once again out came my skills with make-up! I slapped the paste around the cover then around the face on the cylinder, then lifted the cover to align with the cylinder face. I felt as weak as a willy, as this cover weighed a ton and a half! Jim jammed his bar under the safety valve as I pulled the cover backwards at the top slightly. He lifted it up onto the studs and I pushed it into place, then I pulled from my pocket a nut and screwed it onto the protruding threaded stud.

'Come on, shall we have breakfast,' said Jim.

'No, I said, 'let's finish the cover as the paste will not stick.'

'You're a bloody stickler for being correct all the time!'

'Well, you brought me up to do the work correctly! Do you want me to work outside with the others then if you're whining and whinging at me, uncle?' He went quiet – I had hit a sore point.

We placed all the nuts on the ring of studs and tightened them criss-crosswise. Jim was on the bar as I changed it to the different positions around the cover, marking with chalk each one done, till we had done them all. I said to him, 'We're a professional pair!'

But Jim didn't grin. Something was up.

24. Revenge

Jim walked across the forge and put the kettle on, while I went down to the locker room and got my food bag. 'What's wrong with you, Jim?' I asked. 'Tell me. I've seen you like this once before. They're going to move me and you're not happy?'

He nodded. 'Yes, Pat. Next Monday morning.'

'Why?'

'They've been moaning again. I'll go and see Arthur and say you cannot as your agreement states.'

'I haven't signed the bloody thing yet.'

Arthur came into the shop just as I'd made the tea.

'Are you OK, Pat?

'No,' I said firmly.

'Look, you have to work with other men.'

'Maybe,' I said, 'but I enjoy working in here and I learn more with my fitter than all those others. Let's call a meeting and sort it out. The only other two or three I would work with are Jack, Dave, Jimmy and the Colonel. Tell me why, Arthur, please. This has all blown up since last night in your office, and what we said. This is Dave's doing – I know he has been whining because he wound you up on Saturday and it's gone from there. I remember he wanted me to work with him a couple of weeks back. I would prefer to stay here in the fitting shop, please.'

Jim and Arthur walked into his office together, as I cleared away and went back to the gland, packing the piston. As usual I cut the lengths of graphite packing across the slide bar, stuffed them into the shaft's gland and tightened the gland into place. Then I replaced the front cover and went around the other side to remove the other one, and started to remove the crosshead and con-rod connection. I had this horrible aggression building up inside me and I would take it out at the first person that came near me.

Unfortunately it was Dave Davies who started piss-taking as he walked by. I turned around and gave a full blast – all the thoughts came out as I gave him a mouthful, and told him he was a shit-stirrer and I would never work with him ever again. Christ, I was went bloody mad at him, and he stormed away straight down to Arthur's office. I was in the shit! Dick had told me to keep my mouth shut, but sorry, Dick, I had lost it.

Dinnertime came and I went outside to have my break in the brick shed. I shut the door and sat thinking about the job, whether it was worth it with all the backbiting going on, the whining, whinging and moaning. What a bloody lot of old women! The corrugated-iron door opened and in came Jim with his cup of tea.

'Found you,' he said. 'For God's sake, you can shout when you want to!'

'Have you sorted it, or am I up the road?' I asked.

'Sit quietly and I will fill you in. It was Davies – he told me he will never work with you ever again.'

'I told him that to his face.'

'He came into the office,' Jim continued, 'and raged over what you shouted to him.'

'Is he a man or a mouse?'

Jim squeaked like a mouse, and I laughed. 'You're staying with me, but you have made an enemy of him.'

'Tough!'

'He'll be after you now.'

'He'll get over it.'

We sat a while eating our sarnies and drinking tea. 'How did you know I was in here, Jim?'

'I looked in the cabin and it's raining outside. There was no one at the forge and I guessed you wanted some peace and quiet. Come on, let's get going again. I see you took off the crosshead.'

'I will finish off the top if you do the ring of nuts, uncle.'

Now he was happy as I saw him grin and nod his head. I undid the gland, removed the nuts and put them above me on the running plate. The wedge was next. I took out the split pin and leaned over the slide bar, placed cotton waste over the greasy area, then stood on a block of wood to get right over. I whacked the wedge with all my might, then changed to the 7lb hammer and whacked it again until it came out of its slot. I changed hammer size again and with a chisel placed at the top of the burr end to grip it, I whacked the chisel and the wedge shot out of its slot.

I picked up the large crowbar and split the shaft away from the crosshead. We were ready now to push out the piston. I replaced the wedge back into the open slot. There was enough space for me to pull on the bar, but I left that and went round to the front of the piston to help Jim. Just at that moment Davies walked by, keeping his head straight up and looking away from me. Jim grabbed my arm, shook his head and put his finger to his mouth. 'Get on with what you're doing,' he said, and pulled me into the piston cover area.

We both lifted off the piston cover, and as I held it back with help from the small crowbar, easing the top cover away from the studs, he told me to get out of the way. I was told to get out of the way quickly as he dropped the bar and the cover went down on the ground like tossing a penny in the air as it rolled around. I rolled it out of our way and placed it next to the wall. Jim told me afterwards not to encourage Davies as when he was angry I would come off worse and he would stick the knife in.

Arthur called me into the office and told me that on Thursday I had to go to Wallingford to have a company medical with the doctor. I was to catch the bus at the station. I asked who was paying for the bus ticket.

'You are.'

I'd lost out again. I realised I was working for free, paying British Railways to come here in my spare time!

'When you come back bring the documents to me in my office.'

'What's it all about then, Arthur?'

'You're going to be an apprentice in a couple of weeks. When you get confirmation you'll get free passes for your Dad and you to travel to Paddington and sign your papers, then you'll be contracted to British Railways for five years.'

We had a tea break and a quiet chat. 'Have you been in the office again, Wobble?' asked Jim.

I told him what was happening on Thursday, so I wouldn't be able to get my pay packet till I came back in the afternoon.

We got stuck in again and the piston shot out, nearly hitting Davies's tool box. That would have pleased him!

'You got some strength, haven't you?' said Jim. 'Are you still mad?' He went quiet again.

'Come on,' I said. 'Let's get on with what we're doing and shite to the lot of them! They're only bleeding kids and jealous!'

He grinned. 'You're right,' he said.

Davies's tool box was open and as I looked inside I saw my soldering iron lying with his tools. I took it out and put it into my food bag for safe keeping. I wondered where it had gone – he was getting a proper 'tea leaf'.

'What are you at?' I turned around and Davies was stood there looking at me.

'I just saw my iron so I have retrieved it.' I stood up to him.

'I was keeping it for you.'

'Yes, I guessed that,' came my sarky reply.

I got on with the rings on the piston, placing cotton waste over the ring while I heaved on the small crowbar and broke the hardened rings one at a time. Now I got my channel scraper and started to scrape away at the carbon around the channel edges to get them cleaner, and when they came out of the bore they were like solid concrete, with thick black carbon. But by home time I had cleared the channels and had fitted the new rings and oiled them together with the piston's bore.

'Come on, Jim, let's get this one back into the bore before I leave.'

He lifted the piston up on the large crowbar as I put the 3-foot-square block of wood under it. He edged the piston further into the bore and I went around the back end and shouted out the instructions, which way

Revenge

to place the shaft as I slipped the tube over it. He positioned the piston and the other end went through the gland. I took off the pipe and replaced the wedge in its slot, then took the weight, lifting the piston with the other crowbar. Jim pulled with all his might as the first ring went into the cylinder with a bang. I hoped he hadn't broken it. I got the small bars and squeezed the rings together. In went another, then finally the last ring as he pulled the piston right into the bore, then connected up the crosshead.

Because I went out of the shed a bit smartish, being slightly later than normal, I forgot my railwayman's cap. It started to drizzle and I realised I was going to get soaked – and I did. When I got home I was like a blinking drowned rat, with the cold running through my body. I had to get in the bath to warm up as we had no heating in the house, only a coal fire, and an electric immersion heater for the hot water. We were County Council people – we never had much, nor did the rest in the road. We were all in the same boat just after the war.

I couldn't wait to get out into the wide world so that I could be myself to have some fun as it had been a hard day at the play centre, which was the railway shed. Mick and I had a laugh and stayed in his house all evening playing records and drinking tea.

On Wednesday morning I went into the locker room and found my railwayman's cap with a 6-inch nail driven through the middle and into the wooden bench. I said nothing, but just left it there. I wondered for a moment who would have done such a thing, grinning at the same time. I had to think of the next move – something that would go down in history. I never told a soul what the plan was going to be. I would wait till 30 minutes after dinnertime, then I would put the plan into action when all would be quiet in the shed. The worm would turn!

I wandered up to the forge, same as every morning, and sat with a cuppa.

'Thanks for staying last night – that helped me a lot, Wobble,' said Jim. I shrugged my shoulders and said it was OK. 'I see you have the piston cover on and gland done; now we have to do the valves. We'd better get on.'

'I'll start to take off the top front covers if that's OK.' The oilcan was out ready as I soaked the blackened nuts under the frame on both sides of the engine. I retrieved Jim's spanners from the tool box, lowered myself under the frames and started to undo the nuts, some easy, others seemingly stuck on. I struggled, lifting the frame up slightly with the help from the small crowbar jammed into the frame's supports. I found my tin that I used to keep everything together, placing the rivets and nuts into the oil in the tin. I seemed to be on a roll. Must be getting used to it as it became easier – one side done, so I went around the other side. Jim wasn't there, but he'd removed the rear items on the valve. He must be in the toilet, so I started to undo the top frame on that side. When I looked up I saw him coming out of the locker room with something in his hand. He said that he had found this in the locker room with a 6-inch nail through it, and did I know? I said yes, I'd seen it there that morning.

'I told you he'll stick the knife in and turn it. Boys will be boys.'

'I am not worried about children,' I replied. 'Come on, let's get on, as I will not be here tomorrow, and I want to break the back of it to help you.'

Finally I had both front frame covers removed and all the rivets and nuts in the tin – it was bulging. I went back to the other side where I worked and started to remove the nuts from the front valve cover plate, placing them in another tin. I called to Jim for help.

'Just a minute, Pat, as I'm nearly done, then we can both get them out.'

We went for a cuppa. The twins strolled into the shop, went to their tool lockers, put away their tools and sniggered back towards the cabin for their break. I thought, 'It won't be long now, then the fun will start.'

I made the tea, and Jim said, 'You're very quiet. You're not worrying over the twins, are you?'

'Jim, leave it. I won't come between

you and them as you all go out together at weekends. But I think I've seen the other side of Davies just lately and I don't like what I've seen.' I had second thoughts about what was about to happen but, what the hell, he wasn't going to get the better of me. 'I'm just going to the toilet,' I added. I wandered off and saw some of tools on No 1 road, and tender brake blocks. I nodded.

I went back in the shop, drank some tea and had a sarnie – red onion between slices of bread.

'No Arthur today. Has he gone to ground?'

'I think Davies had something to say about him coming to the forge every morning. Seems we are getting all friendly. Probably a rift turning sour.'

'Ah well, he's the big boy and the boss.'

We went back to what we were doing, removing the piston valve. Jim started hitting the shaft and I felt the valve shudder out of its home. I pulled with all my might and it seemed to squeeze itself out of the frame. I took another hold and with his soft hammer Jim hit the valve and it came away free. He picked it up bodily like body-building weights. My God, he was strong. I was gobsmacked. I knew he was strong but nothing like I'd just seen.

We did the same at the other side, and again he lifted it straight up and brought it round near his bench. He marked the one we had taken out first with an X in chalk, and chalked the cylinder the same.

'You do one and I'll do the other,' said Jim.

We split them apart and started on the valves, stripping them out, cleaning off the carbon and chucking the rings away in the scrap area. While I was there I found a nice 4-inch-square block of rusty metal. Returning to the forge I threw it down near the water trough. Ammunition?

Jim said he had to go up town so he would see me after dinner. Everyone was coming in now for their dinnertime break. I chucked the metal block in the forge fire and put the blower on to heat it up. I saw men washing their hands in the ceramic sink and chattering as they walked back towards the cabin with their grub bags. The twins wandered off together into the cabin – another 15 minutes and the plan was ready. I removed the metal tongs from the rack and turned over the metal block to get it glowing. I shut down the blower, and with the metal tongs got hold of the square block and took it outside near the brick house and laid it on the floor. I undid the flies on my trousers and peed on the metal block – my God, it did stink! I did up my flies, picked up the block with the tongs, walked straight through the shop and dropped it between some dirt in the pit where they were working. Now the whole shed stank! I legged it back to the forge, replaced the tongs in the rack, then went outside to the brick house to have my dinner. I never said a word to anyone, and to this day no one knew it was me.

I got Davies for what he had done – he never said anything, nor did Jim to Arthur. However, in 1966 I met Davies coming out of the shed after it had closed and he called me a bastard. He still carried the grudge and knew it was me that had stunk out that pit where he was working. My Dad had a word in his ear when he caught up with him, and I understand he said he wasn't a bastard as he had a Mum and Dad. True story!

After dinner none of the men in the shed could quite understand what the smell was, as it was so powerful and especially under the engine where the twins were working on the brake blocks. The smell got down my throat and everyone's throat, come to that. Yet no one could find where it was coming from. Only one person knew!

Jim came into the shed and down to the shop. 'What's that smell?' It stunk to high heaven.

'I reckon the drains are blocked,' I said.

He got his overalls on and we started where we had left off. I scraped off the carbon while he went to the stores and got the rings, taking some more smells. The drivers wondered what the smell us. Jim saw the twins with cloth masks around their faces.

He laughed, and when he came back into the shop he told me. I burst out laughing. I reckon everyone in the shed heard me, but all I said was, 'Poor things!' But I couldn't stop laughing. I giggled all afternoon.

We carried on till afternoon break, when we got both valve assemblies back into their cylinders with the help of the tube fitted on the shaft. After the break I slapped the correct amount of manganese graphite paste onto the front of the plate, refitted it and screwed down the blackened nuts that held the cover on. I helped do the other side as Jim worked on the rear, tightening everything down criss-cross style so everything went down level. I didn't have to be asked. I got the front top plates on, fixing them down with the rivets and rough nuts, but these were oiled as they'd been in the tin soaking. Every nut went down tight – I had no trouble with them. I was about to do the other side when Jim said, 'Leave it – I'll finish off tomorrow as it will give me something to do. Get yourself home. You've worked hard again today, Pat.'

'I have a good teacher, Jim.

'Who?'

'You!'

I went to the locker room, got my things to wash up and had a good scrub. I took off my overalls, put everything into my locker and locked it all up. I didn't want another episode like today as I would be running out of ideas soon!

I called in to see Arthur and collect the paperwork for the medical tomorrow, and headed home. When I handed in my disc at the Time Office, the clerk, Lenny Head, said, 'What's that smell in the shed, Pat? Has someone shit themselves.'

'Guess so,' I replied. 'Night, Lenny.'

'See you, Pat.'

(The Kelly family did strike at the twins again later, as we shall see…)

25. Sal ... and Adolf

I rode away with my cap on my head and laughed all the way home. People must have thought I was having a fit, as they all looked at me a bit odd. Bath and bed – I was shattered.

On Thursday I had a day off with pay, and a lie-in. Later I rode down to the station and left my bike behind the parcels stores area, with Ernie Alder's permission. I caught the 10 o'clock local bus to Wallingford; not many got on in Didcot, but along the way, going through the different villages, the bus was crowded – everyone was going to Wallingford. Someone rang the bell and the bus stopped at the Cross Keys public house, not far from the surgery, using the directions that Arthur had given me with the documents.

I entered the surgery, the receptionist took my name and I explained that I had come to have a medical for British Railways. I gave her the letters for the doctor, saying that I would require them to be returned after the medical to take back to my foreman.

The receptionist gave me a card with a number on it – 25. She explained the system as it was all new to me. As I sat in the waiting room a lady sitting next to me said, 'You have the same number as lit up on the board – they are ready for you.'

I knocked on the door and someone shouted 'Enter.' I went in and the doctor said, 'You've come for a medical. Drop your trousers.'

Good job I had clean pants on – it made a change to have pants on at all, really. He felt down below and mumbled something, then wrote down what he had found. Then he checked my chest and back, telling me to cough each time. He got a rubber mallet and asked me to sit down while he checked my kneecaps for reflexes. Then he told me to take off my socks and with the other end of the mallet – the sharp wooden end – he scraped the bottom of my feet. I jumped.

'Sorry – too hard, was I?' He nearly had to scrape me off the ceiling. 'Get dressed and go back and sit down and wait for the documents when they call your name.'

I bet he got paid a load of money for giving me a going-over on behalf of the railway. I had to pay my own bus fare to and from the surgery as British Railways was that tight. Yet they took enough money off passengers for fares.

I caught the bus back to Didcot station and had a snooze. When it drew in at the end of the journey I was the only one on board. Getting off I thanked the driver – he was surprised as no one ever said anything – then walked via the undercroft towards the concrete steps. As I climbed up the steps I felt like a tourist, wandering about in the daylight smartly dressed. I walked to the open area of the carriage siding and across the oily, smelly sleepers, then along the cinder path with the ash breaking up with every footstep, just as countless enginemen had trodden before me.

As I entered the shed there were a few men standing at the window of the pay station. I got in line and waited my turn. I heard the same moans after the pay-packet had been ripped open to count the weekly money earned, and the swearing, but they still signed on and came to work. Go out and find another job if you don't get enough money! I can't do that. Why? Well, like I said, I get paid thruppence farthing per hour. Can you live on it? Is that all you get?

My turn came and I said my pay number, but was told that Arthur had it, so I wandered down to Arthur's office and knocked at the door, waiting. Then the handle moved. 'You silly sod, come in!' Arthur sat in his chair, and as I handed over the documents he handed over my pay packet. I said, 'Fair exchange is no robbery!'

He said, 'How did you get on?'

'Good, but I don't think I passed so I'm

not sure there will be a job for me.' I saw his face turn pale. 'They found I had three legs,' I continued, but he wasn't listening to me. He opened the sealed envelope and read the report.

'You passed one hundred per cent fit!'

Next stop then was to sign my life away to BR for five years.

'Next thing is nearer September,' he said, 'it's school for you.'

'Who's paying for it?'

'You are, and your exams.'

'You're joking!'

'No, you have to pay for the lot.'

'I won't go.'

'Then don't sign your apprenticeship papers.'

'I don't have a choice, do I?'

'No – work, or up the road, Pat. See you in the morning.'

I found Jim, and he asked how I'd got on.

'Passed one hundred per cent fit.'

'Good.'

I went back to the parcels stores, got my bike and went home. I had an hour to spare so I went to Annie's. Something was wrong – she ripped into me, and told me she was finished with me, saying I had been with another girl and someone had seen me with her.

'I haven't been with anyone, only you.'

'Well, I believe what Gill Andrews told me! She saw you out with a girl, kissing.'

'Not true – I swear it on my life.'

'How do you know this girl?' she said. 'She's older than you and lives up the top of Richmere Road.'

'Something is amiss here,' I said, 'and I intend to find out about it.'

'Do what you want, Pat. I've had it with you!'

Mick and I went to the Labour Club and had a few drinks. I was still mad about what had happened. I told him while we sat in the club, then Jim appeared and I put my hand in my pocket to buy him a drink, but he bought one for Mick and me.

'What's up?'

Mick told him. 'Plenty more fish in the sea, boyo,' he said.

Friday morning was freezing as I rode my bike down the cinder path. Arriving at the bike shed, I dropped my bag on the floor, climbed off my bike and pulled my trouser bottoms from my socks. I parked my bike in the rack, with the front wheel up in the air and held by a galvanized metal groove. There was no need to lock it as everybody was trusted – we few were a family concern!

Kimberley Hall had been shunted outside behind the fitting shop, and someone walked by taking pictures of the engines. I shouted out, 'Take one of us, please!' I ran in the shed and shop calling for all the men to come and stand by the engine as we were going to have our picture taken. Men came from everywhere and as we all stood still he took the shot. He came over to me and asked my name, saying that he would send a few copies to me. I was over the moon – the best picture ever taken. Famous at last!

I had a few jobs to get on with and kept out of the way for the rest of the day. On the Saturday 4 hours work was standard, and I washed the fitters' tools in paraffin and swept the shop out ready for the next engine. Jim gave me a hand as we pulled all the safety guards off the machines and gave it a right going over. We even took all the old coals out of the forge and replenished it with new coals. We wiped down the drilling machine and lathe with oily cotton waste. The water trough was emptied and filled with clean water from the tap above it. We didn't say much to each other as we cleaned everything down. He put the kettle on the new coals and we had a brew. Jim asked me what was happening at the weekend.

'I'll go out with Mick and enjoy myself.'

'I know you're aching over that girl.'

I told him it was a set-up, that someone wanted me out of the way so they could go with her. The best bit was that she bloody believed it, stupid girl! Anyway, circumstances might have to change as I didn't think either of us had finished yet.

They took out *Kimberley Hall* overnight and she was outside on No 5 road with a head of steam, and Lofty O'Connor keeping an eye on the fire through the night.

'Come on, let's get finished and we can get home.'

Mick and I went to Oxford to see what was on offer. We found a good pub, had a few drinks and stopped to talk to two nice young ladies who lived next door to each other. I said, 'Can I walk you home?'

Mick was Mick, and I started to enjoy myself. We caught the last train home, the 10.55pm. It was full to the brim with Didcot people out on the town, and only a three-car DMU. I got in early that night and nothing was said for a change.

On Sunday as normal I went down to Mick's for an early morning tea and we sat playing records. After dinner I went back down to my mate again and we went out for a walk around the town and called into the café of Mr and Mrs Eustace, dead opposite the White Hart pub. We had a coffee and chat to Eileen and Anne with their parents; it was becoming the best place to eat and get a decent coffee, before we went down to Jean's café, where most of the excitement was happening with girls shouting and screaming over the records they played. It was the 'in' place! Well, the only place… There was totally nothing to do in Didcot – it was as dead as a door nail, and a waste of space trying to get something done with the young people sitting around all day. I couldn't wait to get back to work next day and enjoy myself.

Monday was 13 February, and as usual I went into the cabin in the shed and wished everyone a good morning. The twins sat at the table, and I just got a grunt in reply. Still friendly then! I took no notice but to be honest I thought how silly grown-ups can be! I walked back into the shed and saw Jim up at the forge drinking black tea as usual. I went into the locker room, pulled out my overalls, wandered back to the happy atmosphere within the cabin and exchanged my dirty overalls for nice clean fresh ones.

No 4934 *Hindlip Hall* was the next engine coming in. Jim got hold of my arm, pulled out into the fresh air and pointed towards the turntable. 'See,' he said, 'that's our engine just going to turn and come in tender-first. We've got to split her and push the tender outside.'

'Rigid driving wheels, then?' I said.

'Yes – also con-rods rebushed, and maybe piston rings. That'll keep us busy for a day or so. How was the weekend for you?'

'Good. We went to Oxford and met a couple of girls who lived next door to each other. I asked one if I could walk her home. Mick was away with the other. I was as drunk as a skunk, first time ever. We caught the last train home.'

'You enjoyed yourself then?'

'Yes, Jim, a smashing time – free as a bird now Annie is out of the scene. No fault of mine – she has to win me back.'

He shook his head, then said, 'You're unbelievable.'

In came the 'Hall' tender-first, like an old worn-out steamer rattling all the way into the shop on her last legs. We could hear the con-rods slapping against the worn-out journals. Something was amiss, but I never said as I was only a boy and had to do what I was told; but this wasn't our shed's engine, as was clear from the oval shed code plate on the smokebox door.

Arthur must have been in touch with the engine's home shed to see if we could repair it as it had failed while out between stations. Jim stood by the 'A' frame to stop the engine in the correct place. I then climbed up on the tender and wound round the lever on the tender's brakes tight on the blocks as the shed engine stopped dead with its vacuum brakes. The fireman, Pat Walsh, came to the coupling point and shouted out to close up the buffers, then he dropped into the pit and reached up to uncouple the engines – he must have had strong arms. He then emerged from the pit and climbed back up on the engine. I heard him say they were clear and to pull out, so the driver opened the regulator gently and the engine moved quietly down and out into the open air.

Jim said, 'Shall we work together,

Sal ... and Adolf

No 4934 *Hindlip Hall* standing at Didcot station on a stopping train to Oxford in early 1961.

Wobble? We could share the workload. But let's have a cuppa before we both indulge, and you can tell how you got on Saturday night.'

I got everything ready, then said, 'No Arthur again?'

'No, it was noted he spent a lot of time up here with us instead of walking around the shed.'

'I'm just going to his office,' I said. 'Back in a moment.'

Arthur was on his own in his office. I said, 'I've just made the tea – are you coming?'

'Why not?'

'Get your cup,' I said, then we both walked into the shop. Some heads turned and looked at us in surprise as we headed for the forge.

Jim said, 'Hello, mate – where have you been?'

'Long story. I'd like a word later with you,' he said.

'I'll keep working then,' I said with a grin, and they both said at the same time, 'You little sod!'

'We had a brew and he ate my sarnies and we drank our tea. I asked the question that was bothering me – why this engine was here as it came from another shed. All he said was that some sheds were short of manpower, especially where this one came from – Oxford.

Jim wandered off with Arthur as I washed out the billycan and tidied and locked my locker. Then I walked back to Jim's tool locker and hung up his clean cup and took some tools that were needed to start.

I climbed up on the footplate and with Jim's small crowbar lifted the floorboards and put them tidy next to the boiler. Looking down I could see the huge pins that kept the tender connected to the engine. I squirted paraffin mixed with oil around the pins and tied some rope through the eyes of the pins. Now I swept off the footplate with the brush I had brought with me, then jammed the crowbar under the fallplate to get a grip and lifted it up on a block of wood before lifting it up on its hinge. By God, it was heavy – I felt like I'd done a day's work before I started.

Climbing down onto the floor I went and got the wooden pit board and placed it on top of the concrete steps, then struggled over it down into the pit. The filthy, dirty, smelly board was ingrained with years of oil. I struggled under the tender and positioned it for access to the three pins, with the rope tied ready to pull them out above me.

I climbed up on the board at an angle and pulled myself up sideways. I had to squash the huge cotter pins together and tap them out of their holding places. Good job I was still thin! I had my cap on my head to stop the dirt from going down my back and front. I got Jim's bent pin bar and with the hammer I knocked out the three cotter pins. I heard Jim return, and asked him to get up on the footplate and pull the pins out. He handed me the long crowbar through the gap between the engine and tender and, still standing on the pit board, I aimed the pointed end of the bar onto the bottom of the pin. I shoved the bar onto the pin with all my might and he pulled on the rope; I kept doing this until the pin shot out. Working on one of the others I felt some coal work its way down my neck. I thought I could take all this coal home for the fire, smuggling it out without letting anyone see it! I would be as black as the ace of spades soon! I hit the bottom of the pin and as the two metals struck together sparks flew, like a cluster bomb exploding. The pin shot clean out of its hole.

'That was easy-peasy,' I said. 'Now the middle for diddle!'

'What's up?' he asked.

'Nothing,' I said. 'I'm going silly.'

'We'll say no more about that…' he answered.

Again he took the strain as I hit the pin with the bar. It moved a smidgen. I squirted some oil on it, knocked it back in then had another go. I whacked the bar straight up under the pin with everything I had in my body, and it moved a little more.

'Knock it back down – we've got to get someone on the engine and take the strain on the wheels.'

'Is there anyone there that could help?'

We had to grovel as Dave Davies walked into the shop and past the engine. Jim asked him if he could help. He got a large crowbar, jammed it under the wheel and heaved. With that little bit of tension released the pin flew out of its hole.

'Thanks, mate,' said Jim.

Dave said, 'Where's your boy?'

'Between the engine and tender,' Jim said.

I spoke as quiet as a pansy, 'Thank you, David,' but I just got another grunt.

It was getting near dinnertime and I was still under the engine. We hadn't drained the tender yet, so I offered to open the valve to drain it. I had to play it cagey here as I might get wet. I stood the pit board upright so I could make a run to the front of the engine with no obstruction in my way – I had to do the 4-minute mile! I went back to the valve and started to undo it. The water seeped from the valve, then as I undid it more the water was gushing over my feet and they were getting wet. I ran out of the pit and climbed the concrete steps as the water ran into the drain in the centre of the pit. It had an hour to drain away while we had some dinner and chatted about life and the times that Jim had worked here in Didcot. He told me all sorts and how short Didcot was for spares as the engines ran on nothing.

'Come on, boyo, let's get on.'

The tools were laid out ready to undo the water services to the engine. I undid the nuts and bolts – they were rough and black and some water came out of the pipe I was working on. I placed the items in a tin so we knew where they were. I would have to remake the rubber gasket before replacing the pipe. Jim was doing all the others, and I sat watching him for a while, with his beret on his head, and dirt down his face.

'What you looking at, Wobble?'

'You.'

'Why?'

'I thought for a moment I was working with a Frenchman!'

'You bloody silly sod!'

'You have to laugh, Jim – you can't be

Sal ... and Adolf

miserable all your life!'

'Since you started I haven't had time to be bloody miserable!' A laugh went out from under the engine as some men came into the shop and I saw them peer through the engine's frame to see what was going on.

We climbed up out of the pit and looked around to see who could help with pushing the tender outside. Paul came into the shop with Bob Warwick, and we asked for their help. Jim told me to get up and unwind the brakes, while Bob opened the big wooden doors and secured them. Then they all started to roll the tender, just enough to get the doors back together. I wound the brakes on tight again, climbed down and went back into the shop through the small wooden door.

After the tea break Jim asked if I fancied getting stuck back in. I looked at him and was about to say, 'You're a slave driver,' when he said, 'I know what you're going to say – you were about to say, "You're a slave driver."'

'God, you can read my mind now!'

I told him I was game for it, and we'd get as far as we could before going home that night.

Arthur asked me to go to Swindon the next day and put the order in for new rigid driving wheels with axle bearings and other parts. 'Catch the 7.00am from Platform 3, and take your food bag with you. Collect the paperwork before leaving the shed, and your pass.'

I was up earlier than normal the next morning and went down to the station on my bike. It was 14 February, Valentine's Day, and a miserable morning, and as usual I put my bike around the back of the Parcels Department, leaving word with Ernie Alder that it was there for safe keeping. I went up the station steps at a rate of knots as the guard had his green flag at his side. I sped down to the end coach, leapt in though an open door and closed it behind me with a crash just as the guard waved his flag and blew the whistle. Right on time the train pulled out.

I knew exactly where I had to go as I had been backwards and forwards to Swindon ever since I started on the railway – I was getting to know the place like the back of my hand. However, I was still shy with the girls in the offices – one boy with a hundred girls typing and taking orders. I knocked at Phillip's door and went in; he was busy taking orders from someone on the phone and writing everything down. He looked up at me and beckoned me to sit down. Straight away this young lady came into the office and asked, 'Would you like some tea, Patrick?'

I said, 'It's like being at home!'

Sally brought the tea and I handed over the paperwork to Phillip, who walked away.

I asked Sally if she ever went out for her dinner, and she replied, 'Not often enough,' so I said, 'Can I invite you out to the nearest café or pub to have a chat and get to know you?'

'Why not, Patrick?'

'Call me Pat, please.'

'As long as you call me Sal.'

We shook hands and made the deal. Sal knew the area, and took me away from the works area safe from the prying eyes of people she knew. We found a nice café. We only had an hour but it seemed a lifetime. I said it was only occasionally that I had to come to Swindon, so I might not see her again. We walked back to where she worked, and said our goodbyes. I walked back into the office to see Phillip, and a few minutes later Sal came into the open office and went to her desk. The orders were the same – the order was to be pulled off the 6.00am Enparts train at Didcot.

'Pat, when you get back to the shed please get your foreman to ring me directly.' He then asked if I would like a cup of tea before I left. He knew that I had been out with Sal. 'She's a nice girl, isn't she?'

'Yes,' I replied as he called her over to get me a cup of tea. He then said he had somewhere to go, wished me a safe journey, and left. When Sal and I said our goodbyes again we kissed on the lips. Pity that Swindon was too far away!

I walked back to the station through the

works area and waved to the signalman to allow me to cross the tracks and walk up onto the station. The next train was 2 hours away, so I looked at the travel board and worked out the best way to get home to beat the slow train to Didcot. Over the station's Tannoy system came the announcement that the next train was to Paddington stopping at Reading only. When the 'Castle' came into the station and stopped I climbed aboard, found a seat and sat comfortably watching out of the window. As we pulled away the engine's whistle blew. You always knew it was Great Western whistle – a sound you would never forget! The 'Castle' started to pull away, slipping on the damp rail; some people ran up, opening the doors and jumping inside the coach while porters ran to shut the doors, and other people were stamping their feet because they had missed their train. The porters formed a line, standing in the way as people tried to get into the carriages.

I sat quietly taking no notice of what was happening around me until I heard the call 'Tickets please!' I got my pass out of my pocket and showed it to the Ticket Collector.

'You're on the wrong train. I'm sorry, we're not stopping at Didcot.'

'What shall I do then?' I asked him.

'Name,' he said. 'I'm going to report you.'

'Whatever makes you happy,' I said.

'It's a workman's pass. You can't get on any train when you feel like it.'

'You work for the railway, and so do I. What's the difference?'

He should have had a small black moustache under his nose, as these upstarts do. He took my shed number, 388, took my name again, as if it had changed – he even took the number from the workman's pass. I was grinning by this time.

'This is not funny, sonny!'

When we pulled into Reading I walked down the stairs and came up on the platform as a train for Didcot, Swindon, Bristol and South Wales was approaching. I climbed aboard, found a seat and sat down. In came the Ticket Collector. I showed him my workman's pass, he thanked me and 20 minutes later the train stopped at Didcot. I got off and walked down towards the shed. As I got across the sleepers at the carriage sidings I saw the stopper coming in from Swindon. I had saved 10 minutes, but I couldn't bear to have stood around on a station for 2 hours doing nothing – I had to be on the move! I never heard from Adolf, or the shedmaster.

I reported to Arthur. 'Please ring Phillip at Enparts as he would like to talk to you.' I handed over the pass. Then I went to the shop and told Jim that it was all coming in tomorrow in a covered wagon.

'Well done, Pat. Get yourself home – give me your disc.'

'Thanks, Jim.'

I walked back to the Parcels Department, went around the back to collect my bike and rode home. When I got home all was quiet in the house and no one spoke to me. Something was wrong, then Mum appeared with a Valentine card in her hand. I never had the chance to open it, as it was already ripped open and the envelope was in tatters. My mother wanted to know who had sent it – as if I knew! It was anonymous – all it said inside was 'This is no schoolgirl crush'. She threw the card at me and stormed out of the kitchen; her little boy was growing up, and she didn't like it. My God, how much more could I take?

That evening I went to see Mick, and his sister Jenny asked me if I had received any cards for Valentine's Day.

'Yes,' I said, 'I got the bits.'

I told her what had happened. 'Unbelievable,' she said. 'There's something wrong with your Mum.'

26. Happy birthday!

On the Wednesday morning the Enparts box wagon came into the shop at 7.30am; I saw it coming down on No 1 road when I came out of the Time Office after getting my disc from Lenny Head. It had been taken off the Enparts train at 6.00am by the fly and shunted down to the shed; engines had to be removed to allow it into the shop to be unloaded.

I opened the door on the box wagon and took the paperwork to Arthur's office.

'Good day at Swindon?'

'Yes thanks.'

'Phillip said you did. He likes you as you are quiet, and I hear you have a young lady there called Sal.'

'What else did he say?'

'Nothing.'

I wasn't sure. I called into the cabin to greet the men on duty. Jack Dearlove and Jimmy Holmar were reading their papers while Matt Oglesby had some snuff stuck up his nose, snorting it and leaving a brown mark round his nostrils.

'Want some, Pat?'

I took a pinch and tested it out. After that I couldn't stop sneezing all the way back to the shop; I had to blow my nose to get rid of it. Horrible stuff – never again!

Jim asked if I'd got any Valentine's cards. I said one, from my mate's sister Jenny, not Annie. 'She packed me up, remember?'

'You not heard from her then?'

'No, I'm not ready at the moment, and who cares?'

'Well, you have the right approach,' said Jim.

Arthur came into the shop singing out rather loud, 'Where's lover boy?'

My eyes dropped.

We emptied the wagon, being very careful how we took out the rigid driving wheel assembly. I suggested we put a rope on the axle to prevent the wheel from swinging around or hitting somebody and something; I'd learned from what happened when I worked with Dave Davies, when the wheels shot across the shop. So that's what we did. While I pulled on the pulley block and tackle and operated the chain, Jim held the rope, which he tied off on the 'A' frame of the crane. Just as before I raised the wheels slightly off the wooden planks of the van floor and held the axle as it swung around towards me. I jumped out of the way back against the corner of the box's framework, still holding the chains, raising it a little at a time till the axle took the strain and slid out of the box van, the rope holding it steady. I lowered the axle to the ground and Jim got some wooden wedges and placed them against the wheels while I lowered the pulley block and he removed the lifting bar. Now I pulled the chain back into the box van and tied off the axle boxes all together, pulled on the chain and lifted them off the floor just enough to take the weight as they slid out, then I lowered them down onto the floor. I handed Jim the chain and he pulled the lifting tackle away from area and tied it off.

I called over to 'Matt Munroe' – Arthur just glared. Jim asked him if he could get the box wagon moved as it was now empty.

We had to split the axle boxes and hammer letters on the side so we could recognise which one went where; my mate informed me that we would do it properly this time and measure everything against the bearing boxes and place them on the lathe to machine them out.

Out came the callipers from Jim's locker and I went with an old bucket to the stores for paraffin and 2lb of cotton waste. As usual there was a crowd of men at the window in the store area chattering; I asked them to excuse me, please, but not to let them stop chattering like a lot of old women. 'Got a lot of gob, Kelly, haven't you?' said one.

'At least I've got something to do!'

I moved between them all, and trod on some feet, apologising. Then they moved away from the stores window. I handed over the chitty and the empty galvanised bucket to Arthur Wheatley, and Jim Parsons came back with the cotton waste. I walked back towards to shop and heard the storemen saying, 'That's manners for you – take heed.'

As I headed for the shop I saw Dave talking to Jim near the lathe. I laid some dirty cotton waste on the floor and started to wash off the journal over the machined part. Then I dried the area with clean waste and now both journals were clean and ready. Jim took the measurements of the journals by using the outside callipers, then with a set of inside callipers he took off the measurements from the outer set. I saw the axle boxes clamped on the lathe and bolted together, and the cutting tool clamped into the vice of the lathe. I was intrigued by what was happening, and taking it all in.

Jim held the inside callipers to the face of the axle box, taking the measurement to get the correct size. Dave started the motor and I was told to stand back – it seemed to me this lathe had come out of the Ark! I would have loved to have a small manageable lathe in the shop, which I could have learned on, then I would have be proud as part of my training as an apprentice was turning and I never did any to speak of. Anyway, the lathe was now churning away with the noise from the belts slapping together as they raced away running over the pulleys.

Dave had a look at the tool on the vice as Jim put the lathe into gear so it moved forward to make the first cut; he then wound the machine pedestal back, and shut down the motor. He could take the true measurements and double-check what he was going to do. He fitted the inside callipers into the first cut to see if enough was cut out; he needed a little more, and again Dave put the motor back on as Jim did the deed with the lathe, gently winding the pedestal into the next cut. A little more came away from the bearing; he leaned over the vice and edged the callipers into the slot while the lathe was turning – spot on this time, so he wound the lathe a little into the bearing, set the speed and put the gearing into motion, then I saw the white metal bearing being cut away with the waste coming out like a slithering worm as the lathe was belting around. I felt like I was being drawn closer to that huge wheel, mesmerised. Then Dave knocked me and told me to stand away, as he could see what was happening. It wasn't long before the metal was removed inside the bearing, and he took the measurements again, then rewound the vice unit back to the length of the lathe.

In the meantime Dave had got the block and tackle and had brought it over and placed the chains and hook around the bearing block, while Jim took off the huge clamping bolts. They lifted the bearing block and swung it over near the axle, where Jim Hale had appeared with the spanners waiting with me to help lift each half of the bearing block onto the journal. We wound the long bolts and locking nuts down tight onto the rig that was made. One done.

We followed the same routine with the others, and in an hour or more everything was bolted onto the axle and tested. There was no play in any of the axle boxes.

I then put the kettle on for a cuppa. Jim said, 'That's better than you scraping out the white metal bearing and taking days to do it, and it saves on your muscles in your arms.'

Working on steam engines for British Railways could be the hardest career that anybody could imagine, with dirt and grime every hour of every day. However, times could change for a young apprentice if he trained as a fitter and tried to gain turning experience, if he was lucky enough to have a decent lathe in the fitting shop – not like the one we had in our workshop at Didcot. But to my surprise Reading, Oxford and most Western Region shops were all the same, it seems.

The following day, Thursday 16 February, we had 4-4-0 No 3440 *City of Truro* on No 1 road at the end of the shed next to the lifting shop doors. It was going to be a special day for the Royal Train to run down the branch line from Cholsey station to Wallingford. Young cleaners and firemen were put on it

Happy birthday!

to clean it up. First they cleaned off all the dirt with cotton waste and a steam hose, then there was a bucket of smelly soap to be washed all over the smokebox, boiler and cab. This was then wiped down and left to dry. *City of Truro* was shining when she left the shed to pull the Royal Train, with the Queen taking in the view of the beautiful Berkshire countryside! The breakdown van went out and had to be in position so that everyone could stand to attention on the ground outside the vans as the Queen passed the station.

Later, as I stood looking out towards the turntable and beyond towards the marshalling yard I caught sight of engine No 6136 moving within the yard, back and forth. It didn't seem like it was shunting, as no freight wagons came away from the buffers like other times when I had sat down and watched with interest. It had differently coloured carriages, and while everything around it had stopped, this train kept moving. It was the weedkilling train, and for the next hour it moved into places where it could spray its chemicals. I saw the vapour disperse from the pipes situated under the wooden frames on either side, front and rear. Someone was overlooking the operation, standing in the leading carriage and wearing a uniform.

Men with huge water cans and large spouts walked down the lines, spread evenly across the roads. They were wearing special suits and gloves to cover their bodies, and masks covering their mouths while they sprayed the weeds growing between the sleepers. They then brought the train into another area, continuing to spray all the lines that were away from the shed. George East, the Shedmaster, came out of his office and climbed into the guard's van as the train moved down to the next part to be dealt with. Meanwhile men came back to the leading carriage and placed the watering cans under the carriage to be refilled, queuing one behind the other, then walked away and spread weedkiller across the entire turntable area.

It was pay day so I looked up the shed to see what the queue of railwaymen was like, waiting for the pay clerk, Ernie Jones, to sign over their wages. It stretched towards the stores window, so I had plenty of time. I received my new pay structure – and never told my Mum.

I was getting deeper into the work I was doing each day, and it seemed as though there weren't enough hours in the day. I never really felt that I wanted to go home – all I wanted was just to work on these steam monsters. Everything around me was about railways, and what was happening within the Didcot complex. Was I having a nervous breakdown, or was I going crazy? Or was it the shock of getting a pay rise of £1 a week extra?

I went home that evening and stopped off at Mick's to see what the crack was about for the evening – should we do something different that night instead of the usual? 'Let's go for a walk and see the sights. What say you, Mick?'

We both agreed, as the same old thing was getting boring. Didcot was dead as a door nail, and we were both fed up.

'It's your birthday tomorrow, Pat,' said Mick. 'What about we go to Oxford tomorrow night for a change.' So that was the plan. I was home and in bed early that night.

Friday 17 February 1961 was my 16th birthday. When I got to work I heard something going on around the complex – a lot of noise with shunting and stopping of engines and screaming of brake shoes. There was open waste ground at the rear of the carriage and wagon works and between the marshalling yard and the turntable. This area had many fires spreading into the undergrowth and just below the surface, smouldering for days with the heat penetrating through the ground from the old fly ash from South Wales that had been spread over to form the shed's foundations in 1934. When the weather became very dry I would often see fires started by the sparks from a loco chimney stack, usually a tanky.

Young firemen were allowed to drive engines to the turntable to turn, sometimes opening the regulator with such force that the big driving wheels would spin, causing sparks to rise from the chimney and sparks from the rails, setting light to weeds growing among the wooden sleepers. This was the reason for the removal of the weeds, as well as the avoidance of stumbling or slipping on them.

As I was the only apprentice in the fitting department, I would go out with the rubber mats that I had made from the three-quarter-inch-thick rubber sheeting (used for gaskets) connected to a broom handle, beating the ground continually and trying to stop the fires getting out of control. There would be a signs across the rails stopping locomotives from coming down to the turntable, and notices on the Main Office noticeboard and the Shed Foreman being notified.

Jim Hale was the fire marshal, and his mate Dave Davies grabbed the rope that held the canvas hoses on the 'bosun's chair' hung up on the overhead crane support. They lowered them down to the ground and ran the empty dry fire hoses across the rails, out to and beyond the breakdown van. Smoke was appearing out of the ground all over the open area and it was getting close to the breakdown coaches. Then the flames caught the breeze and were whipped up, causing a vortex and spreading even further across the ground towards the shunting yards. It was out of control in some places.

Jim Hale panicked and strutted around, shouting and waving his arms. 'There's only me and Dave Davies!'

I said, 'Stick a broom up my bum and I'll run amok!'

Then he got serious. It was no joke so I was told to keep quiet and go and stand next to the fire hydrant, indicated by a metal notice on the wall, and operate that valve. 'The *red one!*' he said. Jets of water were sprayed while everybody pulled the water hose forward, like grabbing a long anaconda snake, fighting for their lives as the pressure whipped the canvas hose wherever it decided it wanted to be.

While I was on station at the fire hose valve situated on the main wall of the fitting shop, I was in control. I opened it fully and the two men at the front holding the nozzle were lifted off the ground, there was so much force. It was funny to see, and I think people would have paid good money to see the twins flying high in the sky while I sang 'Fly me to the Moon' in a loud voice!

Arthur came out of the shop and said, 'Thanks, Pat, I think I'd better take control now – you've had your fun.'

I bowed my head and replied, 'Yes, sir.'

For my birthday Mick gave me a present; when I opened it, it was a razor and brush with shaving soap. Actually, I never started to shave till I was 27 years old!

We cleared off to Oxford for the evening to get away from Didcot – at least Oxford had loads to do around the town. We caught the last train home.

On the Saturday morning I noticed that *Hindlip Hall* was back down on the rails and the rigid set of wheels was in place, but the underneath work still had to be replaced. Jim called me underneath. I was really tired after the night before and had a job to get going, but hi-ho, nothing stops for British Railways! We had to lift the engine's springs back into place, and they were not light. I went outside with a crowbar, jammed it through the wheel spokes onto the spring and lifted it while Jim pushed the pin through the centre hole under the axle box. Then he called me back under to help him. I threw a rope over the axle, tied the end to the spring, then pulled down with all my might. He slid a bolt down from the frame through the spring, placed a huge cup washer, flat washer and nut on it and screwed it up. I undid the rope, tied off the spring over the axle again and pulled down tight, swinging on the rope as other parts of the assembly were put on.

The we did the other side the same. Jim had everything ready. I roped up the spring and threw the rope over the axle, but first we had to lift it up off the ground. I pulled the spring upwards as Jim got hold of the other

Happy birthday!

end and lifted with me. We swung it onto the pit board, then pulled the pit board back under the axle.

The rope was in position so he turned the spring upright as I held the rope. I pulled again with all my might and the spring went straight up in the air under the frame. Jim dropped the bolt down through the frame and wiggled the spring till the bolt dropped into the hole. He put all the assemblies back onto the spring and told me to rest. My arms and shoulders ached. To finish off, tightening down the springs, first we needed to lift the engine. Jim told me to get the 4-inch metal blocks and put them on either side of the wheels before making the lift. I operated the crane and the engine went up just high enough so the metal blocks slid under the driving rigid wheels, then I lowered the crane until the frame came down onto the wheels just enough.

The springs were loose, so we tightened up the nuts. I held the bolt head while Jim wound the nuts up tight, and checked the pins in the centre of the frame where they hung in the centre of the springs. We then lifted the engine to take out the metal blocks, then lowered it down onto the rails. Cuppa time – the kettle was on and I drank some black tea with my old mate.

I told Jim that I was going to sign my apprenticeship papers the following Saturday in London.

'When are you 16 then?'

'Yesterday.'

'You kept that quiet, boy.'

'To be honest I didn't tell anyone in case I had to walk the line with my genitals hanging out again.'

Jim grinned. 'How do you feel about getting the tender back on before we go home?'

'OK. We'll get everything ready while the men are in the cabin, so they can help.'

We got everything ready and oiled up, upright pins ready and wire-brushed, and the same with the bars, wire-brushed to remove the rust.

I got up onto the tender and wound off the hand brake. As she rolled a little Jim straightened the tender bars, placing them in line. As the men came wandering in from the tea break, Jim shouted out for some help with the push. Some men left their bags on the bench and came to the rescue, while others walked into the locker room. With bars and hands they pushed the tender, and as it ran against the engine Jim dropped the two pins into the slots, then he shouted to keep the weight on, and the third pin dropped in as well. We shouted our thanks, then I noticed the men who hadn't helped come out of the locker room. I counted them out on my fingers – same old crew!

Jim replaced the footplate floorboards while I went underneath with a hammer and chisel, pulled the pit board underneath between the tender and engine, climbed up and replaced the cotter pins into the tender's large pins. Now I took away the pit board – heavy and soaked in old oil and dirt – and went back to the hoses, replacing the gaskets with new ones and fitting them back together. The worst one was the steam hose, with the wire twined around it. When I finished off it was nearing home time, and I'd done a good morning's work.

I got all Jim's tools together, cleaned them off and put them away, then went to the ceramic sink and got washed up, wondering where he had got to. I was just looking out for him to say 'See you Monday' when all the men came into the shop and sang 'Happy Birthday' to me, then cheered. Happy days!

Jim said, 'On Monday we can rebush the con-rods then we've got a great job replacing a tyre on a wheel.

We had to get on with the con-rods now as the wheels were back in place. We tested them while the engine was just off the track, and put them on the journals. We then lowered the engine – it seemed a double load of work, but we had to make sure that when they sat on the track they would be correct when it came to put everything back together, before the tender was connected up. We had several bars of white metal ingots spare in the cupboard but this was a big job as the con-rods on both sides needed bushes. We had taken off all the rods and they were ready to have the bushings removed, as most of the white metal bearings had rubbed out from the journals onto the wheels – we could see the tell-tale marks.

Jim told me to go to the stores and get eight ingots while he stoked the fire with some fresh coals from the tender – we had loads. 'We'll start by cutting out the old bushes as there isn't enough metal on the journals anyway.'

I took the barrow; its iron wheels were rickety and worn out with years of hard wear within the shed. When I got to the stores something must have happened as there were no enginemen standing about gassing. They were often a noisy lot; whenever I walked past I would hear the drivers shouting to each other and would open the door and look inside to see them sitting around the food table playing Solo. Who was doing the most shouting? It had to be Skip Morgan and Archie Davies as they were the main instigators and both seemed to always win the game. Their firemen would either be sitting near the window or standing around watching what was going on.

Then when the time came to leave the shed, all engine crews walked out together from the cabin. Some honest crews would go into the Time Office and read the glass-fronted notice boards to read any reports about where they might be travelling; they would make notes in their notebooks and keep them in their shoulder bags.

Skip always stated that there was a Green Card system at work. Only the top drivers put the system into place – no one knew about it in the offices. The code stated that if an engineman went off work for some reason or another while on duty another engineman would cover his position till the shift ended.

But today there were no enginemen hanging around. Then I looked up and saw someone in a bowler hat striding across the front of the shed. It was Arthur Leaworthy, a fair man and a good foreman; he had come up from ground level and fought at many union meetings in the Labour Club. When I was off work for three months in 1964 and had just got out of hospital he stood his ground and got me payment through the union's reserve funds, as I received no money from the Government for being crushed under a road coach on my way to work one morning.

Jim Parsons opened the stores door for me to go into the area at the top of the stores where I saw loads of ingots stacked in piles of ten; pity it wasn't gold bars, as we could have been rich! I loaded four ingots on the barrow and said I'd be back for the others. I asked Jim not to lift them as they were very heavy: 'Let the barrow do the work!'

'Thanks, Pat!

I trundled back to the shop and heard a noise that meant someone was working for a change. Jim he looked up.

'OK, boyo?'

'Yes, uncle!'

'I thought we'd got over that silly talk.'

'I am still a fitter's boy, I said, 'so I will continue being silly, uncle. But when I've signed my papers then I could change.'

Jim said, 'You'll always be silly.'

'Thank you, uncle!'

I offloaded the barrow onto the frame of the forge so the ingots could be placed into the ladle to melt down after we'd had a cuppa. Then I went back to the stores for the others. The door was left open so I shot in, laid the barrow down and loaded the last four blocks. I thanked Jim as I went by and he said, You're always welcome, Pat!' then he closed the door behind me a bit smartish – enginemen always wanted to get into the stores. I pushed the rickety old barrow back down to the shop where the engine stood waiting to be finished, with just the rebushing to carry out – unless Arthur came back into the shop and whispered in Jim's ear like he always did with some extra work.

Jim was still at it as I went around the front of the engine. The sweat was dripping from his face and off the end of his nose; he looked up at me, stood up straight, took some cotton waste from his pocket and wiped

Happy birthday!

the sweat away, leaving some cotton threads across his nose.

'What are you looking at?' he grumbled.

'You left some waste across your nose.'

He brushed off his face with his hand. 'Is that better?'

I put my hand on my hip, put on a camp voice and said, 'You look lovely!'

He shouted at me. 'What are you doing now? Go and put the kettle on.'

'Say pretty please, then!' I replied.

'Move before I throw this bloody hammer at you!'

I was gone like a shot. I made the tea then called, 'Are you coming as I'm ready to pour?'

I crept around the engine and, sure as eggs are eggs, there was Jim talking quietly to Arthur. I returned to the forge, but didn't pour his tea as something was on again, or maybe someone was going to get it in the neck. I poured mine, got a sarnie out of my bag with a red onion cut into quarters, then sat on a piece of wood on the anvil munching away, when the boys came round the tender, still whispering. I took no notice – just let them get on with it. I continued munching on the onion – it was sweet, but my mouth would stink for a week, as well as my rear!

The tea break was coming to a close. This was a bad omen – something big was going to happen. I left the forge, got a hammer and chisel and started to cut the old bushings out of the con-rods, throwing them in the corner of the forge, thinking I might use them to make a soft hammer when we'd finished this engine – but for now I had to get these bushes out and melt the ingots. In an hour and a half I was done.

Still no Jim. He had disappeared into the office. I just went on and did what was needed. I pulled the billycan from the fire, replacing it with the ladle. I pulled the prongs from the rack and placed an ingot into the ladle, went to the cupboard where we kept the round machined iron bushes and took them all to the journals on the wheels to get the correct size, and the size for the con-rods – three this side and three the other side, so six bushes were required. I went back to the ladle and lifted another ingot into the ladle with the prongs, got out the tin that held the powered clay and made the mix ready. I set the bushes at the correct size, sitting on the plate; the clay mix covered the bottoms and up at a right angle to stop any white metal escaping.

Now with the leather gauntlets I scraped off the waste from the ladle and threw it into the fire, as I had seen Jim do on many an occasion. I lifted up the ladle, the weight pulling my neck and shoulders, and heaved it over to the spot where I could pour the boiling hot lava over the gap, letting it flow into the ravine to make the bush. I replaced the ladle back into the fire and put two more ingots into it to melt down. Five more to do.

I pushed the bearing off onto the floor, knocked out the iron bushing and put it back on the plate. I got the bushing measurements correct again while the ingots were nearly melted down. I quickly picked up the bush I had made and placed it near the connecting rod, knocking the slag off.

Back at the forge I mixed more clay, pressing it around the base of the bush and into place. I put the leather gauntlets on again, scraped the dirt off the lava, picked up the ladle and made another bush, knocking it off the pedestal with the ladle and placing it back in the fire. Still no Jim.

Four to do.

Same again – back to the forge, mixed the clay, pressed it into place, put on the gauntlets, scraped the dirt off the lava, picked up the ladle, made another bush, knocked it off the pedestal with the ladle and placed back it in the fire.

Three to do. I was on a production line earning piecework rate.

Same again – back to the forge, mix the clay, press it around the bush, put on gauntlets, scrape the dirt off the lava, pick up the ladle, make another bush, knock it off the pedestal with the ladle and place it back in the fire.

Two to do.

Same process again.

One to do.

Same again, then I was done. I was lost for words. Jim was gone, but I was enjoying myself. He had taught me well and I got into it.

Then I went to make the driving rod bushes, but I wasn't sure until I had got all the con-rods done and put back onto the journals. I had to knock all the rough white metal off the bushes that I had made as I went around the engine, filing a lead around the leading edge, then walked around the other way back to where I started. I was getting more engrossed in what I was achieving, working alone. I was still only a fitter's boy till 25 February, and a gofer – gofer this, gofer that – a young boy in a mechanical world.

Still no Jim. I reckoned he had got lost. Something was amiss, and I hoped it was nothing to do with me, as I was very insecure; it seemed everyone wanted me to work with them and I couldn't do with the hassle.

At dinnertime I was starving. The kettle was on, and I saw the shift men coming back into the shop, most of them washing up in the ceramic sink with the boiling water. They waved to me and I put up my hand in response. The shed's stationary boiler was working overtime; it hadn't gone wrong since my mate and I had fixed it.

I went outside and sat in the brick house for comfort and to keep me sane. I poured my tea. The sun was trying to get through the clouds, so I left the door open for a few minutes, and could look out across the open ground and watch the steam engines racing past on the East Loop line – a magical moment for a fitter's boy. Not long now before the apprenticeship started, and to be honest I was missing Annie. She was the love of my life but the silly girl listened to others.

I sat on the yellow arched firebricks, as they kept the warmth in my bum. Reading my *Daily Sketch* and drinking my tea with a sarnie and the sun coming through the open door, I felt I was in heaven until the silence was broken by the sound of chattering coming from outside. Gently I closed the door, as I didn't want to get involved with any silly chatter, as I had had enough of that when I was at school.

I guessed who it was – Davies and his mate Hale, 'the twins'. They were ripping into someone, I didn't know who, but I was sure it was about Jim. I sat motionless, hardly breathing. I heard everything. Thank God I was left out of it! Bloody kids, they wanted to get their arses kicked! Davies was the instigator of all that went on in the shed, yet stood back when it came down to it – he was trouble. But as Dick said, keep your mouth shut!

They were standing between the brick house and the shop in the passageway; they would soon stop talking if someone came round the corner. I thought they had gone back into the shop, as it went very quiet, so I opened the squeaky door with a good push and it flew back with a crash. Blinking hell, they stood there, gawking at me with their mouths open wide. I just looked at them, grinned and went back in the shop. They crept in like two old women hunched together – it didn't matter with 'the Toad', as he had no neck, and Hale looked like he had shit himself.

The ladle went back on the edge of the fire as I went back to what I was doing, running a file edge round the bushes to give a lead, and again I worked around the engine till I got to the other side.

Suddenly someone tapped me on the shoulder. 'How are you doing?'

'Hello stranger!'

'Make some tea,' said Jim, 'and let's go into the brick house out of the way, and I can tell you what's going to happen, Wobble.'

We took our drinking utensils outside into the brick house and closed the door behind us.

'Sit down, Pat,' Jim began, then went on to tell me everything that was about to happen. Paul was having Bob Warwick as a mate and he would stay on the front of the shed, and do no services. Bill Clark was retiring soon, and I was to stay in the shop

Happy birthday!

with Jim. Paul wanted to put his locker up near the door next to the twins.

'I know. I heard,' I said. 'I heard Davies and Hale moaning about it. It was suppose to be confidential. Bloody Arthur, you can't trust him. Carrying on listening to what he was saying, I heard some more, then we can tell each other what's true.'

Jim went quiet. Then I said, 'You're going to be chargehand and shop fitter.'

He glared at me. I knew I was right. Anyway, I shook Jim's hand and said, 'Congratulations – you deserve it. I'd rather have you than "the Toad". It would be a torture working with him.'

We sat awhile chewing over what the fuss was and how long he had been in there with Arthur. I could understand it, as he knew his job inside out as well as all the work loads of the men running the maintenance department. Some of the men respected Jim but others thought themselves high and mighty and too good, but I was surprised when Bob Looms came up to see Jim to shake his hand, saying 'Congratulations' in his Belgian accent, as well as Jimmy Holmar in his Hungarian accent, Jack Dearlove, my brother Paul and Bob Warwick. We were the chosen few.

It never went to his head having the power of a chargehand; however, all the position meant was that he was to take over when Arthur was on holiday or sick, a fallback person, and would get the rate for the job.

'How you getting on with the job?' said Jim finally.

'Have a look. I've done the connecting rod bushes and was about to put them in, but I went for dinner.'

We turned the rods over and started to drive the bushes in with a piece of hard wood and a sledge hammer. We had to do all six bushes. I wanted to know whether we were going to strip the pistons and valves out.

'I'll check with Arthur when he comes in for his tea break,' said Jim. By this time he was waiting by the anvil. 'All right, boyo?'

'Yes thanks.'

He looked at me waiting for me to say his name. 'Well, I said, seeing as you're chargehand I'd better call you Jim.

'Yes,' he said, 'you'd better.'

'OK – this will be a new start then.'

27. Moving out

Paul started nights on 19 February 1961 till the 26th; he was the fitter during that week on nights with Bill Clark, his fitter's mate. The two men were part of Arthur Brinkley's team of mechanical staff in the shed. The shift pattern and routine maintenance would be six nights at 8.00pm to 6.00am, starting on Sunday and finishing on Saturday morning.

Paul had completed his apprenticeship in the Royal Air Force in the Ordnance Depot at Didcot with Bill Clark, an ex-Royal Naval Petty Officer during the Second World War. He was Chairman of the Labour Club.

Close to the entrance to the fitting shop, with the doors closed, stood a tanky, No 3751, with the smokebox door facing the shed. The last job of the night was to replace the piston glands with new packing; the old was worn out, allowing steam to escape and loss of compression.

On this last night, and what was left from the day shift, this would be the last job before Paul and Bill could get their heads down before the morning shift arrived at 6.00am. Bill carried the tools in a sack while Paul brought along the 'Smokey Joe' paraffin lamp (this was part of the engineman's equipment used on the footplate), cotton waste and a small bucket of paraffin from his high wooden cupboard, the toolbox secured to the wall in the fitting shop.

The shed was in complete darkness, just a glimmer of light showing between the smoke exhaust chutes from the lamps high in the roof, their metal shades and bulbs covered with years of soot and ash.

Bill collected a 'Not to be Moved' board from the side of the shed where they were stored, and placed it on the oil lamp bracket under the water tank on the front buffer, sticking it out for safety so that it could be seen from another oncoming locomotive.

Paul emptied the tools onto the frame of the tanky, while Bill picked them up and laid them in sequence, sorting what sizes would be required. Paul held the empty sack in one hand, crawling over the piston slide rods within the engine's frames. He then positioned the sack over the crosshead slides under the boiler in the dark. Swinging himself into motion, he crawled on his knees and got into position to drop his legs on each side of the piston crosshead, dangling his legs down near the axle. He sat on the sack to stop the oil and dirt becoming embedded in his trousers through his overalls.

Bill struck a match, lighting the wick on the 'Aladdin's lamp' from the same box of matches that he used to light his Players Navy Cut cigarettes; he then passed the lamp to Paul. However, not looking what he was doing, the smoke from the cigarette getting in his eyes, he lowered the lamp at a tilt with the open flame sparkling and the flow of oil coming from the spout onto the sacking. Then suddenly the sacking caught fire.

Paul looked around and, suddenly feeling the heat from the fire out of control, shouted to Bill, 'Get that sack, and pull it out quick!' The fire started to take hold, spreading towards Paul. Bill was hesitating and dithering about, and Paul was still shouting to him, until he realised he must climb onto the frame, get hold of the sacking and pull it. But it was being held by the split pins on the crosshead. With one huge pull while Paul lifted his bum into the air, he finally pulled the sack out, tearing it to pieces. It flew into the air, landing in No 2 pit and left to smoulder.

In the meantime, while Bill walked down to the stores and found a new sack, Paul sat on some cotton waste. Bill arrived back at the scene and passed the sack over to Paul, who placed it under his bum. Paul had by now removed the nuts on both the gland covers by the light of the lamp and, with his 'rat-tail' corkscrew, pulled out the old flattened graphite packing, with not much room to spare.

Placing the new graphite packing around

Moving out

the piston rod, to gauge the size, he cut it by knocking the hammer onto it, making six separated pieces. Joining the split ends at '12 o'clock', he pushed them into place, then tapped it forward with a hammer and flat bar onto the face of the gland. Another was placed at '3 o'clock', using the same routine, then '6 o'clock', and so on. He then placed the gland cover back into its slot, replaced the nuts and tightened them down.

Crawling out from his cramped position, he made sure that he kept his head down, as the metal boiler might crack his head, while at the same time making sure not to fall onto the ground, as there was not much room to move between these tankies' frames.

Once free, he washed his hands in fresh paraffin, dried them with cotton waste and went back to the fitting shop. There he washed the tools in paraffin, drying them with cotton waste and placing them away back into his cupboard. They both washed their hands in the workshop ceramic sink with Lifebuoy soap. Then having got their mugs and grub bags from the tin lockers, Bill got the teapot and went into the fitters' cabin to have a brew and a rest.

The potbelly stove was keeping the room warm and they both got their heads down for the rest of the night. Resting his head in his arms and fast asleep, Paul woke suddenly, oblivious of anything until his instinct brought him out of a dream. It was 5.00am when he went back into the fitting shop.

Stripping to his waist, he washed his body, taking away the smell of paraffin and oil from that night's work, took his shaving kit out of the locker and had a shave before heading home.

He wrote out that night's report cards and made sure that they were in order, with the times correctly in place for the work carried out. He handed the reports to Jack Dearlove, the day shift fitter, and chatted about what had happened that night before calling into the Time Office and handing his brass disc over to the office clerk. Looking back into the shed, he saw that green and yellow sulphurous smoke was coming from the chimney of No 3751, and remembered how he was nearly burned; he would be in hospital now in the Burns Department in Oxford. He never forgot it.

*

On Saturday morning 25 February 1961, having completed my period of probation, I signed my Apprenticeship Agreement. Then Dad and I travelled to Whitechapel to see my grandparents.

My Grandfather was a commissionaire, and he took me and his eldest son, my Dad, out for a drink at a local bar, and we sat talking. He told me that he was mentioned in despatches in the Khyber Pass when he went for reinforcements under a barrage of bullets. While we were talking in came a woman and man with a huge Alsatian dog. While the man went to the bar, my Grandfather reached across to the lady and asked her if she was busy today. She replied that her husband was at the bar. Grandfather said, 'That's a shame – I wanted you to have sex with my grandson as he is 16 years old today and I wanted him to experience a woman.'

She replied, 'He certainly is a good-looking lad and I would have given him my whole body!'

I lost out again!

Dad asked me not to get married while doing my apprenticeship. 'Wait till you're out of your time.' I agreed, and he was over the moon and couldn't thank me enough.

I also spoke to Dad on the way home in the train about my money and Mum – I didn't get a lot each week as I seem to be working to keep Mum in money, and I was working for nothing.

'But your mother runs the household, Pat.'

'I know, Dad, but I am working for nothing and she is taking all my money, and leaving me with 12 shillings and a tanner a week. As I'm working for nothing, I might as well go on the dole!'

'You're not doing that – you've just signed

your apprenticeship papers!'

'I'll leave then and find somewhere else to live. You can tell her if you like.'

'No, you'd better tell her, Pat.'

'Right – wait for the shout when you're out of the house, because World War 3 is about to happen tonight!'

'Oh my God, bejesus, Holy Mother of God!' he said.

Getting away to London with Mick never happened; we had to postpone it until further notice, but he was OK with this as he knew what I was going through.

26 February was payday, and I got a pay rise – £2 10s. To be honest, I was thinking of leaving home, and finding somewhere else to live. Mick said wait and see what the outcome was on my birthday, but I couldn't wait until I got it off my chest. I had a word with Mum.

'I'm not paying you £1 17s 6d per week and leaving me 12s 6d per week, as I might as well work for nothing, and you take all my hard-earned money for yourself.'

World War 3 did erupt in Sinodun Road, but I stood my ground.

'Get out then!'

'OK, I'll be happy, that will do me – I'll be gone by the weekend.'

'*Get out now!*' she roared.

So I went upstairs, put some clothes into a box, walked out of the door, got my bike and rode away.

Dad went crazy. 'For heaven's sake, Kathleen, you cannot put him out!'

'Then I shall have his wages.'

'No!' he said. 'I can understand what he is saying. He is working for nothing and it's not fair on him.'

'I do not want him back!' she said.

Dad went to Mick's house to ask if I was there. 'No, Mr Kelly. Why?'

'He's gone, and I'm at my wit's end with worry.'

'I bet it's about his money,' Mick said. 'I knew he said it was unfair what Mrs Kelly was taking from him.

My Apprenticeship Agreement, signed on 25 February 1961.

'Do you know where he might have gone, please?'

'He used to have a girlfriend that lived in Norreys Road – he could be there. Please don't say anything to his Mum, as she'll do her nut.'

'Oh God, what else?'

I was told about all this later. Dad went and got his car and drove to Norreys Road. A member of the family opened the door and Dad said, 'Do you know Pat Kelly?

'Yes.'

'Is he here, please?'

'No, sorry. Annie, do you know where Pat is?'

'No,' came the answer. Her mother asked Dad to come in and she would put the kettle

Moving out

on.

'I'm at my wit's end,' said Dad.

He needn't have gone to Annie's house really as she had chucked me in, and when her mother found out she went ballistic, as she knew nothing about it, as at the time she was going out with a different boy. Dad thanked her Mum for the tea and went home worried sick, back to the atmosphere within the house. He was as angry as hell.

'Did you find him?' asked Mum.

'What do you care?' he shouted back at her. 'I'll bloody swing for you, Kathleen!'

Meanwhile I had gone down to the Polar Star, the railway hostel, and asked if they could let me have a bed for the night. The manager, Mr Sullivan, arranged a room and said that when I go to work next day to report to the shedmaster with my intensions.

*

No 4934 *Hindlip Hall* was completed on time and left the shop on Sunday 26 February. That night I didn't sleep too well, being in a small room, although it was comfortable and warm. The whole of the Polar Star block was moving with men all night long, in and out, all on different shifts – there was no peace. Seven o'clock Monday morning came around quickly enough, and I got up and dressed after the longest and loneliest night of my life. I sat in my new room in the hostel crying. This is what it had come down too, because my mother wanted me to be treated as a child! But I was no idiot or being silly, as I knew exactly what I was doing, having wanted to get away from Mum as she was dragging me down, taking all my wages off me.

I rode my bike down to Midwinter's, climbed the wooden stairs into his lovely shop and asked for six eggs, some bacon, a loaf of white bread, half a pound of butter and half a pound of cheese. I handed over the cash, put the food in my RAF bag and went to work.

As I entered the shed and got my disc Dad was waiting for me. 'Where have you been all night?'

'Don't worry, Dad – I'm OK.'

'Where did you sleep?'

'I found somewhere. Look, I love you dearly, Dad, but I can't tell you for fear of Mum. I need my own life and I'm not going home to be bullied by her.'

'I'll see you later,' I said, 'and we'll talk.'

Entering the cabin, Bob Looms looked at me and said something about the Polar Star.

'Please say nothing, Bob, even to my Dad.' I said. 'Please keep schtum.'

'OK, Pat, I understand.'

Back in the shop I put the frying pan in the sink and gave it a good scrub and soak, washing all the muck away, even the little bobbles of mice droppings. I went up to the forge with the groceries in my food bag.

Jim said, 'What's on, boyo?'

'I'm hungry. If it's OK may I have a fry-up?'

'Why not go in the breakdown van, then no one will see you.'

That was a good idea, so he went and got the key and I walked across to the van, pulled myself up to unlock the door and slid in just enough between the pillar and door, closing it behind me. I went into the tiny kitchen, found matches and the stove ready to be lit, put in paper and kindling, and opened the damper to draw the smoke up the chimney.

I scooped some butter into the pan and placed it on the stove. The fire was now well alight so I cracked a couple of eggs and placed the bacon in the pan as well, sizzling away. I put the kettle on; the water came from a tank in the roof, and it was fresh. I rummaged for the tea caddy, but had forgotten to get milk, so I had black tea. I cut the loaf, buttered the bread, then sat down in the coach area and ate my heart out.

Jim had gone to get Arthur, and they both appeared at the base of the breakdown van. Jim climbed up, opened the door and put the steps down for Arthur. They walked to the kitchen, which felt warm and cosy, and found me crashed out, sound asleep. They came back later, but by then I had gone. When I woke up I cleared away the dishes and frying pan, remade the fire, tidied up, pulled the steps back into the van and locked up.

I went to see Mr East, the Shedmaster, about boarding at the Polar Star for a few days until I could sort out my problem with life at home. He phoned the Polar Star and spoke to the manager, Mr Sullivan, asking if I could be accommodated for a few days. He said I would pay in cash, but the reply came back that there was no need to pay. I was very grateful.

I met Dad later, and we went into Arthur's office. I asked if I could talk to my Dad, and everyone left so we could have some privacy.

'Right, where are you staying?' asked Dad.

'Not far, but do you really want to know? If I tell, you'll go and say something to her.'

'I'll keep it to myself,' he said.

'Promise me, Dad. Just keep schtum.'

'I promise, Pat.'

'Polar Star.'

'Well,' he said, 'at least you've got a head on your shoulders.'

'I've just come out of Mr East's office and they will let me have accommodation for a few days.'

'What's it costing you?'

'Nothing – they said I can have it free.'

'Have you any money?'

'I have a few bob on me, but I really need you to help me. Go into the bedroom, open the bottom drawer of the dressing table, pull it right out and put your hand underneath. You'll feel a book taped to the wood. Bring it to me tomorrow morning, please. Don't let her see you, as she'll go mad and claim it as hers.'

Dad asked if I had enough food, and I told him about going to Midwinter's shop, and what I had planned. I just didn't care any more, and started to cry with sheer anger at what I had gone through last night at home. I wasn't going to stand for it. I'd made my mind up. All the rotten things went through my head, but I had decided that enough was enough. Either she comes around or I would leave England for good!

I told Dad that I had seen an advert in the *Daily Sketch* for the British Army, and had filled in the advert with my age and address.

'No, you're not going to join no bloody Army!' said Dad.

'We'll see,' I replied

He went out of the office crying, as I did in the office. Something had to be done. He went home to sort out the mess, as it was the end of his shift.

Arthur asked Jim and me into his office, as he was concerned at what was going on. 'Sit down, both of you,' he said. 'Now, Pat, what's going on, as I heard you and your Dad having words. I'd like to know please – are you going to give up your apprenticeship and leave?'

'No, but I don't live at home any more.'

They were both taken aback. 'You kept that quiet.'

I shrugged my shoulders. 'I have to stand on my own two feet now. Look, I don't want you to say anything to anybody, please. I don't want to fall out with you and quit the job I enjoy.
And I've signed the papers to carry on the apprenticeship on Saturday.'

Next day Dad arrived with my account book. 'Pat, where did you get all this money from?'

'I worked for it, Dad.'

We went into the shedmen's cabin and he pulled a 10-shilling note from his pocket. 'This should keep you going, son.'

I thanked him. 'She hasn't come around?'

'Not said a word. And I found out it's a shilling a night bed – that's 7 shillings a week. But you've got to eat.'

'I will, Dad – don't worry!'

'But I do, son, as you are my youngest, and have just signed your apprenticeship papers.'

'Look on the bright side – if I'm not living at home I'm saving my money as she is not getting it.'

I told Dad that I believed Dick had never paid Mum any housekeeping money, as he was her blue-eyed boy. To be honest, he wasn't like Paul or me – he even brought a prostitute home one day and introduced her

Moving out

to Mum, who thought she was wonderful. Who would do a thing like that? Dad couldn't believe it. Dick was earning top fitter's money at Oxford, and extra with overtime. Later, when Dick left home he was sheer evil – he didn't care about who he hurt or what he did. He hurt me in a big way, trying to get his own way with a girl I was going out with, when I was at another shed. I never spoke to him for 15 years for what he had done.

The Polar Star building had an 'H' block, the same as those at most railway junctions, and like the others it attracted railway employees with its accommodation. It was 300 yards from the station, and men were coming and going 24/7. It had two floors and on each there were two washing facilities, both with locks on for private bathing, so I didn't need to go downstairs half naked to get a bath. As I walked in through the main door there was a sign indicating the staff accommodation block, which took the whole of the wing. The rest of the building seemed to be a maze of corridors and more than 100 rooms. I was on the upper floor in room 58. It was a bit like a depressing prison block, but the manager Mr Sullivan was a pleasant enough person.

He showed me around, and as we walked he asked me how long I would be there. I said I thought a month – it depended on my mother. He said he would set up an account for me. There was also a 24-hour canteen, which came in handy, as I was getting hungry by this time.

Then I visited the games room downstairs, which had a full-sized snooker table, table tennis, and dartboard – everything was thought about for comfort and relaxation. Still wandering around I found the TV room with eight armchairs for comfort, but the place stank of stale cigarette smoke, which turned me off straight away. There was a drying room down opposite the porter's office with a call board; someone would knock the door if you required to get up at a particular time. I wrote my room number and Monday till Saturday 6 o'clock early morning, which would give me time to get some breakfast and sort myself out before leaving for work.

I went back to my room, which was about 7 feet by 6, and someone had come in and laid my bed ready for use. I found clean fresh sheets and pillow with pillow cases, and several blankets. I saw a lady leaving the room I was about to occupy and she explained to me that the bed would be made every morning, and at the weekend the sheets would be changed with pillow cases and two towels. I gratefully thanked her for her help.

The room contained a single bed, a two-drawer chest and a single wardrobe that was 2 feet wide. The walls were of breeze blocks just painted magnolia, with a 60-watt bulb for illumination hung from the ceiling; there was no shade, making the room seem grimmer and more miserable. Below the window a 4-inch steel pipe ran from room to room, providing the heating. The room overlooked the British Railways buildings at the bottom of Station Road and, across the road from them, Don Avery's paper shop.

I found out later that Tom Edwards looked after the new members and stopped anyone bitching before things went too far.

I made a list of items that were required; a light shade was one of them, and bath salts, soap … the list started to get long.

I washed in the communal sinks, bringing my towel from my locker at work to dry myself, but this was really hard until I had been shopping to buy the things I needed.

*

A letter arrived from Dad's sister saying that we could stay in Whitechapel. I got Dad to write back and say that we would both get our free passes sorted out for London, and a week's holiday. I informed Arthur and filled in my holiday roster, booking my free pass from Saturday 5 till 12 March.

Not long after that Dick received a brown envelope from the War Office instructing him to do his National Service. For his three-year conscription he applied to join the Irish Fusiliers in Northern Ireland, then he shipped out to Tripoli, where he caused trouble. Mum and Dad had to send him money. He drove the Captain's personal car with his mates, knocking off water jugs carried by some women; they thought it was a big laugh, till they were threatened with jail for the duration.

After I left work at Saturday dinnertime I had a visitor at the station, waiting for me near the Parcels Department. Annie wanted to talk to me, about a reunion. I said I would think about it, as I wasn't very pleased about what she had done, believing another person rather than me, when I told her the truth all the time. I rode to the Polar Star, leaving her to walk home on her own. I wasn't interested, as time had moved on, but I was sorry to see her walk off on her own.

I subsequently went to see Annie and her parents. I sat there quietly while they made me a sarnie and gave me a mug of tea, which kept me going for a while. They asked what I was doing for Sunday lunch, and I said that I guessed I would have my dinner at the hostel, like the rest of the men living there, but thanked them anyway. I was still hurting from being thrown out of my father's home.

On Friday 4 March I collected my free pass bound for 'the Smoke' for a week's holiday with Mick, starting the following day. We both had to work Saturday morning. I wrote on the porter's board for a call at 6.00am. On waking I pulled all the covers off the bed and left the towels and sheets in a heap on the floor, as it was changeover day. Then I dressed and went down to the canteen for breakfast – full English and a mug of tea for 1s 3d.

The sun was breaking though the clouds but it looked like showers again and was very humid and thundery. When I reached the shed it was pouring down, then stopped. Inside the shed I saw Dick Bidmead shovelling ash out of all the pits. He was on No 4 road with his old wheelbarrow when it rained, but he was a dedicated person and loved what he did; he never once shouted at anyone, just got on and enjoyed life.

I heard a rumble coming across from the Appleford direction. I went out towards the turntable and watched the lightning storm shooting across the sky. I stood up on the metal frame looking around watching and waiting for another electrical crack to shoot across the dark sky. A huge thunderstorm was raging around Didcot and each lightning strike was spectacular. I held out my arms as if I was flying, feeling the warmth in the air. Suddenly it got very cold and the wind started to blow, with the storm following. I knew it was dangerous, but at that time I just didn't care as I walked back down the slope of the turntable frame and stood next to the turntable on the ash, watching the lightning shooting across the sky. However, suddenly I saw a flash come straight down from the sky, the forked lightning striking the rails with blue flashes jumping across them. It went away as quick as it had come. I only saw this twice in my career.

I didn't have a care in the world, but hearing a shout I looked towards the back of the shop and there was Jim shouting to me to get out of the rain as it was pouring down, but I was still in a daydream. It was tipping down now, and the lightning struck the shop's conductor on the roof and the whole building shook and rattled as we bowed our heads with the noise. Then the wind blew the storm out, the thunderstorm fizzled out, the temperature got cooler and the humidity dropped.

'What time are you away today, Pat?' asked Jim.

'I have be at the station for 2 o'clock.'

'Get something to eat and change, and put something on the post board. I'll see you on the 13th. Give me your disc.'

'Thanks, Dad. Sorry, I mean thanks, Jim.'

'Have a good week. You will come back, won't you? Please.' He was unsure.

28. A 'Castle' in trouble

I made my way to the hostel for dinner – full roast and a mug of tea. I sat in my corner out of everyone's way, eating quietly, taking no notice of what was going on around me. Then I went out and got my bike and took it to my room for safe keeping while I was away. I had a shower in the communal area, went back to my room, dried off and got dressed. I left my dirty clothes folded on the chair, ready for me to wash them on my return.

I put on my best suit and shoes, wrote on the board that I would be away on holiday from 5 to 12 March, picked up my holdall and walked to the station to meet my mate at the ticket office, where he was waiting. Then I heard a shout from outside the station: 'Pat, wait!'

Dad came over from his car. 'Come and speak to your Mum.'

'No, sorry, Dad, we're off. The train's pulling in.' I turned to Mick. 'Come on, we'd better not miss this.'

'What about your family?' said Mick.

'Hard luck,' I replied.

We made it to the platform and got into the first door that came near. The guard blew his whistle and waved the green flag and the train pulled out of the station on time. We found a seat.

'Mick,' I said, 'we're going away for a bloody good week together. Please don't bring up anything, as I'm sick to death with it.'

From Paddington we took the Underground to Whitechapel, and walked the rest of the way. I introduced Mick to Aunty Betty and Uncle Michael. We were told that we would be sleeping together, if that was OK.

'Don't worry about food,' I said, 'as we will get something out. We're not going to be around the area much, only in London.'

Mick had to inject himself every day, and asked me to carry some sugar lumps in my pocket, and I bought a Mars bar for standby.

We asked Betty and Michael to come out with us for the evening, and did they know a good pub? Michael went mad: 'Yes, we'll go to the bar where I work as a drayman!' He had been a foreman at the Whitbread Brewery, but had to leave as he had an affair with the boss's wife, and ended up as a BBC messenger.

My aunt was a lovely lady and I thought the world of her. She was real broad Southern Irish, the youngest child and only sister – she was so spoilt. She worked hard to keep the family together. Mick and I had a cup of tea and a few sarnies before going out, just to keep the stomach in check for when the beer started to flow!

Every day we toured around London, seeing the sights and using the Underground, even walking between stations to look around. We found a local pub and spent some time there, as the food was good as well as the ale.

Midweek I had a letter from Dad asking to me to come home and see Mum on the Monday evening to talk about going back home to live. I showed it to Mick, and he showed it to Betty, then we had 20 'God, bejesus, Holy Mother of God'! She wanted me to go home; she said to talk to my mother when we got back, and Mick said the same.

On the Saturday morning we decided to walk around Whitechapel and found a little record shop; Mick went mad, as he found loads of Buddy Holly records. He was so excited he bought four and went back to Betty's to look at them.

Sunday morning we set off to Paddington. We thanked them both and left a present in the bedroom for them. We made our way towards Whitechapel Underground station; I was pleased to have learned such a lot about the Underground and how to use it properly, as when in the future I went to another depot in Acton it came easy for me to get around; also I came back to Whitechapel to live for six months while working on the railway at Old Oak Common – that was my plan in the future.

On the Monday morning Dad was waiting for me at the Time Office when I got to work. 'You got my letter, son – what was your decision?'

'Well, to be honest, Dad, I got it in the neck from your sister, Aunty Betty, and my mate Mick to go home and sort it out tonight.'

'Are you going to need something to eat? I might as well tell Mum to cook something for us.'

'I'm not promising anything at the moment,' I said, 'as I have to come to some agreement with Mum. I'm fed up with her mollycoddling me.

I went home from work that evening and was welcomed in. My Dad was waiting by the back door; Mum was sat at the kitchen table with her arms folded, and not a friendly or pleasant face on her. She looked like a wrestler waiting to pounce!

Mum had to come and talk to me about coming back home, as I was stubborn and I wouldn't lower myself to go to her. I told her I was going to prioritise my money and I would make the rules about paying her weekly housekeeping money as she took a pound off me when I started on the railway, but she was so domineering and wanted every penny I earned. When I first started work it left me with nothing. Yes, I had agreed to it but as time went on it became hard – I felt I was working for her life and not mine. She didn't like what I said to her. Dad went to say something, but Mum shouted, 'Stay out of it! I'm talking to him!' I think Dad was standing there amazed and couldn't believe what was going on.

'I want the money you owe me for the weeks you've not been here,' she said.

I looked at her in amazement – I couldn't take it in. 'No,' I said quietly. 'I'm going to say I will give you 5 shillings plus the one pound only for housekeeping and no more money.' I also told her never to ask me for any more money, as she was wasting her time, as I was hardening up now – I would not allow another woman to step in and demand money off me ever again while being an apprentice.

I had the same £1 5s, and told her that since she had never paid Currys for the bike money each month I would pay that, and with the suit I bought from Reeds of Reading, I would pay that, after sorting out who I must pay off first.

'And I will not be mollycoddled by you any more,' I continued. 'If a go with a girl I do not want you spying on me everywhere I go and trying to cause trouble. And while we are at it,' I shouted, 'you *do not* open my letters! Also you didn't take housekeeping off Dick when he was home. Why? And you let him bring home a prostitute for Sunday lunch and you thought the world of her – she was a slag!'

By this time Dad had disappeared, as the room temperature started to rise as World War 3 was about to erupt.

'So what's it to be, Mum?'

'I will think about it,' she said.

Well, I'm off back to the hostel. When you've made your mind up you come and tell me, as at the moment the ball is in your court. I've finished with you.'

I went to Mick's down the road and was invited in for a cup of tea and a sarnie.

'How did you get on?' he asked.

'She will not have me back, and the ghoul wanted three weeks' housekeeping off me.'

'What's wrong with your Mum?'

'I told her what I was happy the give her – £1 5s a week – and she never paid for my suit or my bike. I don't know what she's done with the money. Dick never gave her housekeeping.'

'Come to us on Saturday, Pat, and stay till Sunday night and we'll feed you,' said Mick. Mrs Howard came into the room from the kitchen. 'You will come, as Mick told you, and stay with us?'

'Yes, Mrs Howard.'

I asked Mick if he would like to come to Reading on Saturday afternoon as I wanted to go and sort out some business.

A 'Castle' in trouble

I rode back to the hostel, had a shower, went to the notice board to write out the time for next morning's call, and went to bed.

*

After a few weeks of completing several shifts working days and nights on a temporary basis, my brother Paul was ready for permanent shift work: seven days on, or seven nights on 10-hour shifts, 8 in the evening until 6 in the morning, starting on Saturday night first shift, ending Saturday morning – he was paid 112½ hours, worked out as double time, time and one half, and time and a third.

All fitters and mates had to do these shifts, with the exception of Jim Tyler, as he was the only one who did a day shift, and with being made up to chargehand brought in extra payment.

There was a telephone call to the shed from Foxhall signal box early that morning, before 5.30am, for the duty fitter to report to the station. The Fishguard boat train was limping into Didcot station, and could someone proceed to the station as the locomotive, No 7008 *Swansea Castle*, was in trouble. People where looking out of the carriage windows wondering why the express passenger train was moving so slowly into the station, which was not a regular stop.

Paul was waiting with his mate Bob at the London end of the correct platform as the locomotive coasted in. They saw that the piston had shattered and steam was rising all around the boiler from the piston on the left-hand side. They climbed onto the footplate to ask the driver what had gone wrong.

The South Wales driver told them that when he was between Steventon station and Foxhall signal box an explosion of steam had erupted out in front of the locomotive. The driver had said he heard a loud explosion like a bomb going off from the left-hand side front near the piston area, and next thing steam was gushing from the cylinder and coming back over the engine's cab in waves as the engine had a full head of steam at 225lb per square inch.

He had immediately shut the regulator to slow the locomotive down and applied the vacuum brake gently. The fireman had to lean right out of the cab window while his driver held onto him for safety's sake, and in between the waves of steam he saw with great shock that the con-rod had broken; it had come away from the crosshead and was flopping about, although it was still in the slide bar and had not dropped. Both enginemen became very scared as they thought the engine was about to crash. Had the con-rod dropped onto the ground, the 'Castle' would have turn over on her side, causing a major incident.

Suddenly the driver went a bit shaky and fell to his knees, knocking his head, before fainting from sheer exhaustion, Paul grabbed him while his fireman came to the rescue; the two men had worked together for many years.

The station master was also on hand on the footplate, and shouted to his second-in-command to ring for an ambulance at once. The locomotive would have to be swapped, with a new driver who knew the road. The piston was hanging out of the cylinder and the piston cover was gone, broken away from the studs and nuts – it was never found between Steventon and Didcot.

When Jim Tyler came on duty at 6 in the morning he was asked to go to the station immediately to see what had happened. He inspected the area of the piston, or what was left of it. The con-rod had sheared at the crosshead, and the piston rod was still connected to the crosshead. When the con-rod had come back with the next revolution it pushed the crosshead forward into the piston gland, and with force the piston had flown against the cover inside the cylinder, causing it to blow out onto the line in splinters.

The 'Castle' was uncoupled from the passenger train and went to the shed. Paul arranged with the station master to ring the signalman at the East signal box to get the

A 'Castle' crosshead and slide bars, showing where *Swansea Castle*'s con-rod had fractured.

station pilot, No 6952 *Kimberley Hall*, on standby to take over the train.

While all this was happening a spare driver was brought from the enginemen's cabin. This was Bert 'Skip' Morgan, who knew the road; he replaced the existing driver, but the fireman went with the train, as he had some business in London.

The 'Castle' was slowly taken off the main line. Jim met the locomotive at the entrance to the shed and walked back beside it, making sure nothing fell off. Paul and Bob rode back on the footplate into the ashpan area near the coal stage to have the fire removed. As I approached the area I saw Jim walking beside the engine and Paul and Bob waving to me like two crazy schoolboys out for a ride.

Everybody went to the coal stage to have a look at what had happened. Jim and I were getting ready to receive the 'Castle' into the lifting shop, as we had all the tools ready.

In the meantime the station pilot was taking the passenger train out of the station for London with a main-line Didcot driver and the South Wales fireman aboard.

Swansea Castle was shunted into the shop and uncoupled. We needed piston rings and cylinder head studs, a new piston cover with safety valve, a new piston head, con-rod and crosshead with all the gudgeon pins.

'Don't change into your overalls, Pat – here's your pass. Get to Swindon now, please. I've rung Phillip and all he needs is the order. Come back with what you can carry in a sack.'

So I caught the fast train to Swindon, and now on arrival I knew exactly where to go to the Enparts department. When I got there I looked around the door and went as red as a beetroot again. The same thing had happened – all the girls in the office had stopped working to see who was walking in.

Phillip invited me to sit down and offered me a cup of tea. He sent Sal, the typing girl, to get it. He said why I was in a hurry, as I made her laugh, but I told him it was a rush job and described the 'Castle' incident. He read the spares list and saw how rushed the shed was for the parts, being required for the next day. Sal came back to the office, upon which Phillip winked at her and left me in the office with her. She said, 'You spent a lot of time up at Swindon – three times now.'

A 'Castle' in trouble

'The way things are going it could be more,' I said.

'Pat, are you counting then?'

'Sal, I seem to be coming to see you more than Phillip – as you wear the skirt and he wears the trousers.'

She giggled. 'I must go,' she said. 'I'm getting black looks from the typing pool.'

'Where are we going to eat at dinner hour as my train doesn't leave for 2 hours. And thanks for the tea – you did it too perfectly!'

I reached across and gave her a peck on the cheek. 'Go downstairs and I'll meet you across the road at the entrance to the tunnel.'

'Wait for me, Pat – I'll be there.'

Just as she left Phillip came back into his office with some paperwork. 'OK, Pat, the Enparts will be on the train tomorrow morning. Here are the cylinder studs to take back. Everything is being loaded as we speak into a box van with the paperwork inside; the delivery note will be on the outside of the van. I will ask the foreman to give your instructions for the station fly to collect it off the train at 6 in the morning. How did you get on with Sally?'

'She's nice and pleasant. It's a pity, really.'

'Why?' he said.

'You spoke to my foreman and he took the Mickey out of me. He came into the fitting shop singing "Where is lover boy?" the other day when I was up here last.'

I saw Sal go out of the office, and thanked Phillip for his help. 'What's up?' he said. 'Are you going back?'

'No, not yet,' I said. 'I have to go somewhere.'

I ran to the tunnel entrance and found Sal waiting for me. I gave her a kiss and she responded. I looked around to see if any traffic was coming and saw Phillip at the outer office door. Again I thanked him with a wave, and we went off under the tunnel and out of the works to her favourite place, where we enjoyed each other's company once more.

I caught an early train and got into Didcot at 2 o'clock, carrying the sack of studs – that was really all I could have carried. I went down to the shop and left them by the engine.

'Cheers, Wobble,' said Jim. 'You were a long time.'

'It's not me, it's the trains…'

We refitted the new studs and kept the new nuts and washers together. Arthur came into the shop with a message for me. 'When you've fitted all the new components put the old bits back into the box van and send them back to Enparts, reference Phillip, as Swindon would like to see what happened.'

I washed up and went back to the hostel to shower and change my clothes, then went to the canteen and afterwards to see Annie; I had been away longer than expected.

Back at the hostel I was out for the count, and before I knew it I heard a knock at the door. Time to get up.

The spares arrived from Swindon and came into the shop in a box van. We had to fit the new rings in the new piston, which had a 16-inch bore with a 26-inch stroke. This engine had three other pistons, so Jim measured the inside diameter with a micrometer with a small extension. I put the rings back into the cylinder, marked the size and checked if there were score marks. Everything was OK. Taking the rings to the bench, I measured to my new mark of three-eighths of an inch, then secured them into the vice on the bench and smacked them with a hammer and chisel to break away the excess. There was no way to file the ends as they were case-hardened steel.

Now we refitted the new piston, guiding the shaft through the piston gland. With the soft metal hammer we whacked the piston head against the cylinder face using thin small bars, edging together the rings while the piston was lifted up on the crowbar. We again knocked the piston until it hit the outer ring on the face of the cylinder. I had to guide the bars to close the ring and hit the piston four times; this had to be done. When the piston finally went into the cylinder it went with a whoosh, and as usual I looked down at my hands to see if I still had my fingers! Everything had to be lifted on crowbars driven into the wheel spokes, but the best was to come. The cylinder cover weighed a couple of hundredweight as well as being located under the running plate of the locomotive. After smearing the cylinder face with manganese graphite paste around all the studs, Jim and I lifted the cover onto a wooden block with the help of two crowbars. Balancing the cover, it went straight onto the studs, a nut was quickly screwed on one stud, then we had a breather. For a few minutes the sweat ran down our faces and backs and steam rose upwards towards the shop's ceiling.

Still very hot and bothered and sweating like pigs, Jim was on the cylinder, and I was connecting the piston shaft into the crosshead on the engine, then packing the gland, the last job. *Swansea Castle* left Didcot the following day back to its own shed.

The box van came back into the shop, we packed everything onto the floor and secured it, with letters to Phillip and, with thanks from me, I slipped a letter in an envelope for someone special.

I walked past the enginemen's cabin and heard a terrific laugh. John Pritchard was relating the time that a gang of platelayers shouted to him as he was passing, 'Drop us off some coal, mate!' This happened from time to time because they needed it for use in their lineside cabins.

John was working a goods train from Newbury to Reading and the request came near Aldermaston. 'We were travelling at about 30 miles per hour. I checked the tender and found a rather large oval-shaped lump of coal – it must have weighed about 100lb. As we drew near to the lineside hut I noticed that the door was wide open, so I decided to throw the coal as close to the hut as possible, thinking it would smash into small pieces as it hit the ground. One good heave and the lump of coal flew out, hitting the footpath and bouncing forward like a Dambusters' bouncing bomb, straight into the open doorway. As we passed there was an enormous bang as the coal smashed through the back of the hut, splinters of wood and coal showering everywhere. The hole was about 3 feet across!

'My driver at the time was Billy Brown,' John continued. 'He witnessed what had happened. Billy suffered with a stutter and said, "F-F-F-Flipping hell, don't mention this to anyone." Luckily we never did receive a "please explain" memo.' The cabin erupted with laughter, and the men came out into the shed still laughing.

I was between jobs until No 7327 came into the shop. I asked Jim if I could make a soft hammer for myself. 'Yes, you can do one for me also,' he said. I said that he had one already. 'Well, make me another.'

'OK!' Stung again.

I went outside where a line of engines were sitting ready for the scrapyard. I climbed up onto all the footplates to see if anyone had left tools lying about. On the first engine I was lucky, finding what I was looking for. Still sorting though the footplates I found another item; I didn't need any more but decided to rummage about on all the engines, finding more of the same. I found an old sack to put the items in as they were getting very heavy to carry.

I went back to the shop and emptied the items on the floor.

'What you got there, Wobble? What do you want those hammer heads for?' Jim asked.

'I'm going to make a better hammer and a more secure handle, rather than the tube that you got – these will be made with a shaft handle.'

'Off you go then.'

I got the blow torch and set the pressures to cut the head away, and the ball end the same, leaving an oval hole where the shaft would fit. The first one was a test run, as Jim looked on, amazed and bewildered.

I put the ladle on the fire and placed the old metal white bearings that were collected over the months into it to melt them down. I got out the biggest iron bush that we had in the cupboard, put the plate on the anvil, made up a clay base solution and ran it around the base of the bush. I then placed

A 'Castle' in trouble

the old hammer head into the centre of the bush. I heard a voice say, 'It won't work.' Jim and some others were standing watching. After thinking a while, I took out the head and stuffed the oval hole with some clay at either end to stop the white metal from filling it, then put the head back into the bush. It was a trial-and-error job, always the first one. If it went wrong then I would modify it.

I put on the gauntlets, scraped the waste from the ladle and poured the lava into the hole of the bush, realising now that it might not work, but I kept pouring. I looked around, and more men had come to see what I was doing. Then Arthur arrived on the scene, asking Jim what I was doing. 'Just look and watch,' he said.

I placed the ladle back onto the forge away from the fire, knocked the bush onto the ground and let it cool. Now was the time to see if the proof was in the pudding, as I knocked out the white metal from the bush – and out came a perfectly round hammer head. I then punched a rod into the oval head, and having a wooden shaft handy I tried it in the oval slot. Picking it up, I checked the balance – it just wanted a tweak. Jim said, 'Let me try.' I said it wasn't finished, but he said, 'That's bloody good – you can start making mine now.' Then I heard 'I want one,' and so it all kicked off.

I had six hammer heads, and said that, if anyone wanted one, to bring me the hammer shafts. 'It'll cost you.'

'Sod off!' they all said. OK.

Arthur said that I was always making something. 'Well, I'm an apprentice now,' I said, 'as I signed the deeds and my life away. I'm signed up with the railway for five years.'

While I was at the forge I made four pokers for Mr Townsend's crew, taking them into the carriage and wagon shed and leaving them in the corner with a note.

29. A fishy tale

The next job was two new tyres for the 5ft 8in rigid driving wheel on 2-6-0 'Mogul' No 7327. I was sent to Swindon the day before we started to order the parts from Enparts the next day. I caught the 7.05am stopper from Didcot, and was told not to hang around talking to the women in the office and to get back to the shed. However, there were fast trains to Reading and London only, and only every 2 hours did a stopper appear. Arthur told me to get a fast train to Reading, change there and come back on a stopper. I explained that I couldn't do that, as I had done it a couple of weeks before and had been reported by the Ticket Inspector. 'I could walk and thumb a lift,' I suggested.

'You're being silly, now.'

'Yes, sir.'

So I arrived in Phillip's office again. He said, 'You might as well move in as you're the only shed ever doing anything!' He disappeared, but before he went Sal appeared with a mug of tea.

'Is it OK if I come and see where you get it from?' I asked.

We walked out of the office area into a tea room and a cubby hole. 'It's nice in here,' I said. I was on my best behaviour as I hung on and kissed her. 'Are you free dinnertime?'

'I have to go into town. Would you like to come with me?'

Phillip came back into the office and said that the parts will be on the Enparts van for tomorrow morning same as usual. 'Is there anything else you would like or want.'

I said, 'Tools,' so he said, 'Come with me,' and led me to a stores area. We climbed the steps and, after a large number of locks had been undone, we went into an Aladdin's cave of tools!

'What do you need?'

I couldn't believe the amount of tools that sat within this small area. I was given a Britool socket set, a set of screwdrivers, hammer, micrometer, adjustable tape – the biggest there was – and a sack to carry the small items. 'The large items will be your responsibility.'

'How do I book these?'

'You're good for it, Pat.'

I thanked him, and he said I was always polite and very friendly. We shook hands.

'Have you a handkerchief in your pocket?' he asked. I pulled one out. 'Spit on it,' he said, then wiped the lipstick from the corner of my mouth. 'It's the same colour as Sal wears…'

When I got back to the station I went to see Ernie Alder in the Parcels Department and asked him to look after the tools for me while I went down the shed, as I didn't want anybody to know.

I went into the shed and handed over the paperwork.

'I see you're early,' said Arthur.

'I caught the 2.30pm, and it's 3.15 now. If you're going to have me timed I would rather not go any more, Arthur – please get someone else to do it.'

I went into the shop and Jim said that we needed another set of oxygen and acetylene bottles, and the only place to get them was the carriage and wagon department. We walked across the back end of the shed past the old oil tanks and through the coach cleaning area, where a gang of cleaners was shouting; the man in the middle was Taffy Williams, who was the foreman, and Dick's father-in-law. I stopped and watched. He had a piece of flat shiny wood with just enough space for two old pennies to be placed flat on it. The shout went up and money was thrown down on the ground, even old £1 notes – there was a wad of them. I saw the flat wood being thrown into the air and the pennies coming off it and landing on the ground. There was an uproar as someone had backed the pitch odds and evens; whoever won got the cash and was loaded, counting out his wad of notes. Gambling was rife in those days

A fishy tale

when I was an apprentice on the railway, and lots of money was won and lost.

Jim was waiting for me as I came to the door, and he said that no one was in and the door was locked – where were are going to get the burning gear from? I pointed up towards the yard and he turned to see; as he did so I found the key, opened the door and walked inside. He glared at me: 'You little sod! Where was the key stashed?'

'We're in and here are the bottles,' I replied. He made me pull the trolley with the bottles on and he picked up the pipes and the biggest blowtorch nozzle. We struggled back to the shop, then I returned and left a note, locking up and putting the key back where I found it. My secret.

The huge wooden fitting shop doors were wide open at both ends, allowing fresh air to flow through (it was summer now, and very hot). The tender of the 'Mogul' had been disconnected from the engine, and stood outside in the yard on the same road. The engine's con-rods were removed from the loco frame for access to the rigid driving wheel, which had to have its iron tyre removed as it was worn away with a flat.

The engine was hanging in the air, attached to the overhead crane, and a chain pulley block securing the axle vertically to stop it from falling to the ground. Support for the wheel was provided by two of the 3-foot-square wooden blocks underneath the spokes, which would prevent the journal from being damaged.

Railwaymen were looking inside the fitting shop and not daring to venture inside to see what all the noise was. The noise was hammering, which could be heard up at the station and beyond. Fitters and their mates were swinging heavy sledgehammers onto the iron rim of the wheel. It was a dreadful sound within the shed complex, and outside the doors the men would scream with the pain in their ears, their faces contorted! It was the same, of course, for the men doing the job, as we had no ear defenders in those days.

I held the huge heavy blowtorch with the biggest size nozzle to help maintain the maximum heat from the mixture of oxygen and acetylene from two sets of bottles. Men stood opposite each other heating the metal tyre, running the heat around the rim, the sweat rolling down every face, keeping the heat on the tyre, making it glow red, then turning a crimson red. While Jim Hale had the other set of bottles on the other side of the wheel, Matt Oglesby poured water onto cotton waste which spread over the axle, keeping it cool. Jim thought, 'This is winter work, not now, in the midsummer months.'

Standing opposite each other at the four quarters were Jimmy Tyler, Dave Davies, Jimmy Holmar and Bert Paice. The four men held 14lb sledgehammers. These were very heavy to grip and to raise level with the shoulders, aimed towards the top of the tyre rim. The blow torch crew were told 'move now, out of the way' as all four men stepped forward and started swinging their sledges. Men outside the fitting shop held their hands over their ears, as did all the men walking by the shop and in the shed.

Jim shouted, 'It's started to move!' so we were brought back on the scene, heating the rim to get it back up to temperature, running the heat around the tyre and not allowing it on the axle and wheel. While the men rested a while, wiping the sweat that ran down their wet faces and necks with cotton waste, more measurements were taken and areas marked with chalk, showing what and where to hit the most, so that the tyre would leave the steel wheel equally.

The tyres were separate from the wheel, and every six to 12 months there would be an inspection, measuring them with a tyre gauge and checking for wear, which was one of my jobs while working here.

To fit tyres in Swindon Works there was a ring embedded in the floor with firebricks and blocks the shape of a wheel, all connected up to pipes running below the floor containing a mixture of oxygen and acetylene. I had been shown this shop when Phillip showed me around the site. The men in that area had the axle attached to metal slings on a hook from a crane. Slowly lowering the axle, they applied the newly turned and heated tyre (which came from the lathes in AE Shop) onto the rim.

Fallen leaves on the rail often caused tyre wear, causing the wheel to slip on the rail. The wheel would then leave a flat in the rail, and when another train passed the same spot again the same thing happened. In the end the tyre had a flat spot and the rail the same.

*

I had to report to Mr Sullivan at the hostel when I got back to my room and tell him to arrange my money to pay for the room. He asked me what was happening and I told him that I thought I would be going home in two weeks as Mum had thrown in the towel. He said that I had been paying for my food and keeping my room tidy: 'You pull off the sheets and fold everything on a Saturday morning for when the girls come into the room. To be honest, Pat, we will not charge you anything, but keep doing what you do and please do not repeat what we have said – keep this arrangement between the two of us.' I thanked him.

*

A long line of coaches and parcel vans blocked the way over the crossing and the passenger pilot was waiting for a coal train to pass East Junction. I stood there in the driving rain coming across the open fields from Appleford, with a north-east wind driving through my clothes. The coaches started to slide forward, then it was safe to cross. There was no sharp smell of creosote coming off the sleepers, just oil and grease, which covered every patch of the wooden walkway. I trudged along, trying not to slip or get my feet in the gap between the rail and the walkway – then along the cinder path, head down to stop the wind driving down my neck, and my shoulders hunched. There was no crunch of the cinders underfoot, just a dirty quagmire of muck to slosh through.

I was cold, wet and miserable with this weather and I hadn't even started work yet. When I reached the inside of the shed and out of the rain, it seemed a little warmer, especially after yesterday when the sun had beaten down and the weather was red hot outside. Didcot never had the same two days of weather on the trot!

When firemen like John Pritchard came into the ashpit from the main line the first thing most of the enginemen did was to find an old long-handled broom, tie some cotton waste around the handle, open the smokebox door wide, then shout to the driver that he was ready. The driver then opened the regulator one notch, having made sure he had wound the tender handbrake full down and with the vacuum brake fully on, to stop the engine moving. The engine felt the pull of the steam, but couldn't move. John lit the cotton waste with his lighter, then held the broom handle at the brush end and inserted it into each superheater element to see if the flame was drawn into the tube; he then proceeded along the next tubes. Finally he pulled the cotton waste from the broom handle and threw the broom down onto the path, where he would pick it up later, after showing me what the procedure was.

Shouting to the driver to close the regulator, John climbed into the smokebox and marked any superheater that needed to be changed with a piece of chalk. The driver put this on his inspection card, which he passed to the shed foreman, who in turn passed it to the fitting staff foreman, then onto the fitters and apprentices to replace the superheater elements.

*

My brother Paul and his wife Joan lived in a flat above Mr Jenkins's paper shop in Park Road. Joan worked in the shop, opening it up at 6 every morning, six days a week, while the other assistant closed up at the end of the day and put the keys though the letterbox. Her job consisted of getting the papers ready for the regular customers every morning,

A fishy tale

sorting out the magazines and papers for the paperboys to be delivered locally around the top end of Didcot.

Next door was Moxon's fish and chip shop. Paul became very friendly with Mr Moxon. One day Mr Moxon was going though his schedule of what needed to be ordered from the fishmonger. However, he had some old fish stored in his back garden shed, where his freezers were situated, which hadn't been used and he needed to get rid of it.

Paul, being nosy, asked to see what he had, and Mr Moxon brought out the biggest cod Paul had ever seen. 'Can I pay you for it?' asked Paul, even though he was a Kelly and never paid for anything in his life! 'I know I have a cheek,' he continued, 'but can you wrap it up for me please and I'll get rid of it tonight when I go on nights.' The deed was done.

Paul was a fitter and turner, but only did fitting work in and around the shed, and also went out on breakdowns. I kept clear because as I couldn't be with my brother – there was a little friction between us, and I had to watch my Ps and Qs with him. Funnily enough, we never worked together, ever.

Paul and all the fitters had their tool cupboards in the lifting shop along one side of the wall on the right-hand side as you walked in. Bob Looms was with Paul as his new mate; he had a dry sense of humour, and his jokes were very funny – we needed something to cheer the place up.

Paul and Bob were having a bit of a problem from Dave Davies and Jim Hale, 'the twins'. So that night Paul brought a certain package into the fitting shop in the middle of the night when it was quiet; the entire shed was like a ghost ship. They got to work, lifting Dave's tool locker out without letting anything fall inside, as all hell would break loose. These cupboards were very heavy, tall and wide, and had been built to last by Swindon Works and fitted into the shop when the shed had been finished in 1934.

The next operation was to nail the huge cod to a baton on the wall. They then lifted the cupboard back into place in its slot. Very slyly, both men covered their tracks, sprinkling dust collected from the shop on the floor.

The weather had turned very warm and dry again, and a few flies started buzzing around the shop. Normally we just swotted them, but then we started to notice that the small flies became the big bluebottles that carried germs. After two weeks it got very hot and more and more flies had spread along the wall, as if there was an outbreak coming up through the floor.

Dave Davies and Jim Hale became concerned, and went to the stores to get 5 gallons of Jeyes fluid. This they sprayed around the area for several days; I did hear them say that something must have died, as the smell really was gross. I did not know what was going on – it wasn't my concern and I kept out of it – but I knew that the twins were trouble anyway.

Paul and Bob were back on afternoons from nights, and the smell was outrageous. They came into the shop for tools for a job they had to do at the front of the shed, where an engine was waiting. Dave and Jim, hovering nearby, ask if they could smell anything. Bob was smoking at the time and just blew out some smoke and said, no, he couldn't smell anything!

It got so bad that even Paul and Bob felt sick, so Davies and Hale pulled out the cupboard and there were flies and maggots everywhere. They were shocked to see who had done this to two such nice friendly men! The twins went mad, and so did Jim Tyler, as the fitting shop chargehand. Arthur Brinkley was away at the time on holiday. They sprayed Jeyes fluid everywhere. Paul just looked innocent, but after that he and Bob were left alone.

*

On Saturday morning, as usual, after I got up I took the sheets off the bed and folded them together, doing the same with the towels, so everything was ready for the cleaners when they came into the room. After my full English breakfast I met Dad at the Time Office, and he asked me to come home as I had been away too long now. I agreed, and said that I would like to come home on Monday evening. Dad said, 'Will you want any food, son? I'll get something. I'm so pleased you're coming home, son, as I have missed you.'

'Thanks, Dad!'

There wasn't anything to do in the shop as we had caught up with the repairs, and I wanted to get the soft hammers sorted, with Jim's permission. I got the blowtorch, place the hammer heads on the anvil, set the pressure on the bottles and changed the nozzle to a cutting size, put the goggles on, lit the gas and set the controls to away half of every hammer head. Then I turned them around and cut off the other half. There were five to do. The handles were left with Jim in his locker.

I left the heads to cool and with the gauntlets on I went to the grinder and started the belt system up. I ground both ends of all five, happy to get stuck in, and also very happy that I was going home. Jim put the ladle on the fire and put some old white metal bearings in it, while I made a mix of clay, got the iron plate from under the forge and found the biggest iron bush in the cupboard. I spread the clay around the bush and put some in the oval hole of the hammer head. Meanwhile I went to my tool locker and found a tube the same size as the oval hole in the hammer head, just wedging it in place to test it. At that moment. Jim had the gauntlets on and poured the lava into the bush around the hammer head and up to the top of the iron bush. With a pair of heavy pliers I pulled out the tube quickly so it could be replaced by the hammer shaft. We heaved the iron bush onto the floor, and knocked it away, leaving just the soft hammer. All five were done in the same way. Then I hammered a shaft into each of the oval holes and hammered in wedges to split the wood and secure the head.

I tested one and the balance seem good. Jim took one and really put it through its paces, hitting the side of the anvil with all his might.

I said we should leave them in a bucket of oil till Monday to soak the shafts, then we could hand them out to the men who had asked for them.

We then had a cuppa and a chat, and Jim asked me about me going home to live. I told him Monday evening, and he said that was good, as he had been getting worried about me. He asked about Annie. I said that we were back together, but I hadn't seen her so much lately, till I sorted myself when I got back home. I told him that Mick and I were off to Reading at 2 that afternoon to sort something out.

Back at the hostel I wrote on the board for a 6 o'clock early call for Monday, and had a shower – I was really dirty and oily, so I had to scrub myself raw. After getting dressed I left the building and made my way towards the station where I met Mick, and we caught the 2 o'clock fast train to Reading.

'Where are we going, Pat?'

'Up the Oxford Road,' I replied. 'It's not far – we can walk it.' I wanted to go and sort some business out. I told him I was going back home to live on Monday evening, and he was very happy.

We had a good day in Reading. We went to the pictures, then we went down to the Majestic ballrooms in the evening, pulled a couple of nice girls and jived with them until we decided to make our way back home. I had to call into my room at the hostel to pick up my bag and found that my dirty clothes had been washed and dried, and a note had been left to say that they had done them. I was choked. I would have to sort something out tomorrow for them all. I told Mick and he said he would help me.

It was nice walking towards Sinodun Road again, and nearly home. But I was staying at Mick's that night and Sunday. Mrs Howard looked after me like her own son, and I was so welcomed into the family.

On the Monday morning, before going to

A fishy tale

work, I left a big card for the girls who had looked after me while I stayed at the hostel, together with a big basket of fresh fruit, a couple of bottles of sherry and a envelope with some cash inside. I went into the canteen and spoke to the girl who had done my room, handing over the keys to her. I asked her to look into the room. I explained to Mr Sullivan that I was leaving and going back home that night, then I took a bottle of whisky from my RAF bag and handed it over, with my thanks. We shook hands. I was just about to leave with my bike when the girl that had looked after my room came down and thanked me, and I thanked her once again.

A few weeks later there was anger in both hostels as the prices went up from 7 shillings a week to 15s 6d, as the cost of living had risen. There was much shouting around the shed: 'What we should do is stand together!' The food allowance also shot up with everything else. All the young men staying in the hostels refused to pay and called on everyone to walk out, but they never considered where men were going to stay. It all started with two or three boys raging, then got out of hand. They all ended up crawling back with their heads hung low, went to their rooms and shouted from behind their room doors, having been scolded like little boys with a smack from their parents! When they were paid that next week, 15s 6d was taken out of their pay packets. Hurray for democracy!

Trevor May began to appear at the forge every morning in his wet old overalls to have a cup of black tea with Jim Tyler. The two men chattered and laughed together, and I saw Trevor open his snuffbox and offer Jim a pinch. He took it and stuffed it up his nose, leaving a brown stain under his nose. I remembered that I had taken some from Matt Oglesby and couldn't stop sneezing.

Suddenly Trevor took out his false teeth and looked at them. I felt sick, as the next thing he did was to lick the top plate where there was some cabbage, and swallowed it back down as if he was having a second helping of food! It was not a pretty sight, but he felt no indignity in what he had done. Then the shout went out for him to go back to the washouts with my Dad.

I checked the bucket of hammers, wiped the shafts with cotton waste and handed them out to the men that wanted them.

30. A lesson learned

Firemen who had nothing to do would be brought into the shop to help with the engines. Labour shortage was a problem and rife within the shed – too many firemen and not enough drivers. They would act as a fitter's mate, the pay scale being roughly the same. Because firemen knew how to pack spindle glands out on the road, that's what some were put on to, standing on the cold footplate in the shed while the engines were on washout. The washout crew splashed them with the cold water hoses to clear them out of the way so they would finish the pannier tanks, as there wasn't enough room on the footplate for men working on the engines, and they were on piecework.

This arrangement gave the fitters a chance to get on with the other repairs, rather than sitting under the engine on the slide bars with the boiler pressing down on their necks while packing piston glands, and without Ted Powell glaring inside and telling them to leave the gland off a little. But no such luck – these firemen had more balls about them and would answer back in some choice language.

When they removed the nuts they always dropped one or two into the dirty pit, with scale and water rushing down the drains. Then they would ask a passing fitter to pass the items up through the frames to them, or get off the frame into the pit and find the rough black nuts before they were washed away with the boiling hot water from the steam hoses. The firemen new nothing of what was expected of them by the fitting staff; we were all brothers, and dedicated men.

When a fireman sat on the slide valve and crosshead bar, his main job was taking out the old packing. They had never seen half the tools we used, like the 'corkscrew' tool to pull out the old graphite packing, and didn't know about refitting the new packing in sections, trying desperately to knock the whole length back into the gland – it didn't work that way. It was like teaching a six-year-old and very difficult for them to understand – they still had dummies in their mouths, as well as bad language! I knew few of the words – must have been footplate slang!

So I had to explain, measure the packing around the shaft, hold it with your finger, lay it across the slide bar and with the hammer – not your finger, as it might hurt – hit the packing and it will cut off. It won't do any damage to the slidebar. Now do that two more times. Then pack the gland so the ends meet together. Now with the other packing dead opposite do the same – do not leave the slits in the same line. Why? Because the steam will escape through the slits, and lose pressure in the steam chest. Clever person? Yes, I'm an apprentice.

It was a pleasant surprise when we had another fireman come into the shop, a new member of the team for two weeks to help me, as my fitter was doing other things with his boss, Arthur Brinkley, in his office. I had become fed up being left alone after a couple of hours working, and would wander out of the shop to get some carbide from the stores. I dropped it into some water in a bucket and left it in the corner of the room where the boilermen had their lunch. It stank to high heaven. The boilersmiths used some choice language, and some rude gestures. I had never heard such words come out of a man's mouth – I wasn't taught at school to speak like that!

When I got home after a hard day's work, Mum was at the door with her right hand held out flat, so I put my right hand in hers and said, 'How do you do?'

'You funny little boy,' she said. 'I want my money from when you left home – all of it!'

'If you wait till Dad comes home we could have another row,' I replied, 'and I will leave again, but this time I will never come home, as I intend to leave England. I won't tell you where I would go, as I want to make a life of it away from you!'

Two weeks later when I came home one

A lesson learned

evening I found the lamp that I had made was missing. Looking around for it, I found it in the shed sawn in half. Dick! I stood my ground, threatened him and went for him. I swore that if I had a chance I would drop him in it!

After a month I had a visit by a British Army Land-Rover and a Sergeant and Corporal from the Royal Berkshire Regiment at Reading. They had come to pick me to join the Army. Dad shouted at me: 'You're an apprentice – you can't go and leave!'

'I told you, Dad – I want out and away from her, as she is doing my bloody head in!'

'I will never allow you to join the Army,' he replied. 'I had enough when I was interned in the Irish Army as a boy soldier, and I'm not allowing you to go!'

I was adamant that I wanted to get away from home. I went to the Fire Brigade in the Broadway to see if I could join up as a firefighter. Again Dad went hairless at me, and wild.

'This is all about what's happened over the last couple of months,' I said. 'I don't care. I'll tell you this much – if she doesn't stop I will go, and you will never find me.'

'Please, son, let's stop!'

'Well, you married her – deal with it! I cannot go through life with her on my back moaning about money, not leaving me alone to live my life, and enjoy female company!'

As I was just turned 16 years old, I applied for a provisional driving licence, as I wanted to ride a Lambretta scooter, or even later drive a car. I waited each day for the post.

*

Dad left the railway in 1962 and moved to British Leyland at Oxford as a driver in special turning – a drier position, and he was happy. He retired in October 1978 and in March 1979 he died of cancer. I had also left the railway by this time, and I had his car. One day when I finished work at Grove Cranes, Cowley, Oxford, I entered the works car park and saw him sitting in the car waving to me. I was so excited I ran to the car, and he disappeared. I sat in the car crying.

Before he died he gave me an Irish 50p piece, and I kept it in the pocket of my coat, but it moved to my wife's coat pocket. I put it back in my overcoat, but then it went back into my wife's coat. We had to get a vicar in to do a séance as Dad was disturbing my two daughters – they kept seeing him, and so did I and my wife Jennifer.

*

The next Saturday afternoon I was given a silk shirt by Bob Warwick. He said, 'I bet you any money you won't wear this shirt down the Broadway on a Saturday afternoon!' It was so flashy! He had bought it in Singapore when he served in the forces.

So we made a bet. I told Bob I would wear it the following Saturday at 2 o'clock, if he wanted to come down the Broadway and have a look – I would be around. The next week I saw him on his bike, sitting watching me and waving as I wore the silk shirt with an open neck, a pair of blue Wrangler jeans and my two-tone winklepickers, carrying my leather jacket slung over my shoulder. I swaggered down the Broadway from Smallbones to the Post Office. I won the bet and kept the shirt. Everybody I walked past turned their heads to look at the shirt; it was lovely and I kept it for a couple of years till I grew out of it.

On Sunday I had a day out with Annie at her parents' home, and she told me what had happened about her last love affair. He had tried his luck but never got anywhere, as she was never like that; she was a pleasant person and I always enjoyed my time with her. I asked her that next time would she please believe me when I said that I had not been with anyone else. Her mother asked me to stay for tea; she made some cracking teas and there was plenty of food, and a homely atmosphere. There wasn't much of that at our house around that time, as I was walking on egg shells.

On Monday morning when I got to work

the cabin was empty. There was no one about, and it was the same in the lifting shop and in the shed. I went outside and the breakdown van was gone. So I got my overalls on, went to the forge and built the fire up with coal taken from a tender out in the shed. Going to the shedmen's cabin, I asked Micky Gleason for blocks of firelighters as I had to get the forge alight in case we had to smelt ingots to make castings.

The emergency was that in the early hours No 7912 *Little Linford Hall* had jumped the rails at Vauxhall Bridge, west of Didcot, and both cranes were out, one from Swindon and the other from Old Oak Common; she had come off the road all wheels. The Didcot lads were out all night. Someone was sent to get hot food for the men, as all three breakdown vans needed replenishing.

I could hear the steam cranes working in tandem, the safety catches on the safety drum rising and falling, holding the drum in case something slipped. The cranes could be seen from the station, and the main lines between London and Bristol were closed both ways, so traffic was re-routed back as far as Reading. Oxford wasn't blocked, so trains ran normally on that route. Eventually they lifted the locomotive back on the road and I was going home at 5.30 when the breakdown van came back in; the cranes had gone back to their sheds.

They gave me some lip and I retaliated all in good fun. I found out next day that they had been knocked up that night by a shed man who went out on his pushbike with all the emergency men's addresses.

The locomotive had been working a parcels train and went through Didcot until at Foxhall signal box it hit a set of catch points and jumped the line. No one was hurt. All the men said they were shattered after working all night and the following day. They came in the day after in dribs and drabs whenever they had had enough sleep.

After the area had been cleared of the debris the permanent way gang had to put the road back together, fit new sleepers and lines and repack the ballast to get the main line open again. Before I left for home the forge was going a treat, as I kept the coals on the fire.

Next day I sat in the brick house away from everybody reading the paper and drinking tea. I didn't want to work with Ted Powell, then Jack Dearlove came to work on the afternoon shift and asked me to work with him. I said that it would be an honour.

*

Jim Hale was a pain in my arse. I offered him a toffee as he had a sweet tooth, but he had false teeth and they got tangled up in his mouth and he shouted out that he was choking. Dave Davies stood behind him making faces and taking the piss out of him. It was funny at the time but I paid for my mistake big time; I turned on the fire hose and soaked Jim Hale from head the foot. He was dripping with water and stood there just looking at me, shocked at what I had done. Dave went to Jim Tyler who was chargehand and reported me. Arthur was on holiday, thank God, as he would have sacked me for sure. I was bloody stupid!

Nonetheless, a big hand came down on my shoulder and marched me towards the office of Mr East, the Shedmaster. Jim stood his ground, but 10 yards from the office I stopped dead. 'Jim, do you realise that if I go in there it will be on your mind for the rest of your life that you got me sack?'

With that he stood still. Then he said, 'Will you do what I give you and take your punishment?'

'Anything, Jim. I swear I will do what you want.'

'Come back to the shop and stand by your bench.'

By now I was shaking, frightened, shocked, having come that close to being sacked. Tears started to flow. I thought of all the things I done with Jim workwise, going to his house at Christmas time, having a drink together, and the beer he bought in the Labour Club. The money I won at the Chequers at Harwell – happy times – the

A lesson learned

laughs we had under the engines. But if that's what being a supervisor does I thought you can stick it where the sun don't shine.

I stood next to my tool bench for the next few minutes, then he appeared with a flat block of plain rusty metal plate 9 inches by 6 inches by 4 inches. He put it on the bench, then went and got his 2½lb hammer and drove the ball end into the plain flat plate, denting it in several places, on both sides. He glared at me, straight into my face, in sheer anger. I guess I had upset him as well as I had upset myself – such a foolish thing I had done.

'I want that plate smooth and squared off, both sides – do you hear me, Pat?' he shouted.

'Yes, Jim.'

'You will stand at that tool bench as long as it takes.'

I said, 'Sorry.'

'It's all gone by the wayside – we're finished,' he said.

My heart hit the floor, then I walked away and cried in the locker room. I really sobbed. My life was in tatters. I had been thrown out of the shop, and the work.

When Arthur came back off holiday I was at the bench, filing. I couldn't speak to him. He went to Jim and had words, then told Jim that he done right. Jim never came near me for six weeks; he was as angry as a raging bull. Eventually the plate was smooth. Dave Davies stood next to me showing me how to water-test the block, and I was sure he went to Jim and said that I had finished it. I squared it off at the four corners, both sides were completely smooth as I had emery-clothed them, and used every file I had to work with.

Jim came to me on the last day of that six weeks. 'Have you learned your lesson, Pat?'

'Yes, Jim.'

He had his hammer in his hand and drove the ball head into the plate on both sides. I should have kept it to keep me in check.

'Right, let's go and do some work. Now you can file you will never ever forget how to file anything.' He was right – I was damn good at filing and making things by filing, but what a lesson in being strict.

*

I was called back under No 6159 in the shop, which had broken springs at both ends of the rigid wheel axle. The crane was hooked up at the rear, just lifting the engine off the track. I had to hand the 4-inch-square metal blocks to Jim to put under the wheels before lowering the crane. He put his hand out but I dropped them onto his fingers and squashed them. I felt really bad, but somehow couldn't say sorry to him. His face was very serious, staring at me as if he wanted to come out of the pit and clout me. I felt bad for years after as I couldn't go back and say that little word, 'sorry'. He gave an anguished cry, which echoed through the fitting shop.

'Bloody well *get out*! And before you go, I want to know did you go the pictures at Didcot on Friday night to watch that new cowboy film?'

'Yes,' I replied.

'So I suppose it was you who did it!'

'What?'

'I had a brand new coat and you threw an ice-cream tub at me and it landed on my new coat. I just bought that day.'

'Yes, go and blame me because we had a fall-out!'

He was awkward as bloody hell, but I stood my ground. I wasn't going to be accused of something I didn't do. But he was still very angry, because I was sitting in my usual seat with the yobs and my girlfriend Annie.

'Course I blinking didn't! Anyway, how was I to know you were in the flicks that night?' I boiled with temper. 'You can't blame me for any little thing that might happen! What did I do – go up to the top balcony, sort out where you were and throw a tub of ice-cream at you with people looking at me? Bloody grow up, Jim! Have some sense!'

Then he shouted again, 'Get out of my shop! I've finished with you! I've had enough!'

I stormed off and went to see Arthur to get myself moved.

Arthur came into the shop. 'What's going on, Jim?'

Jim told Arthur about the row we'd had. 'The trouble with you Jim,' said Arthur, 'is that you've brought your troubles into work from home, and blamed the boy. It's not his fault. If you want Pat out, you're going to miss him, as he'll never come back – he'll refuse. Don't be like the rest of the men. Right, Pat,' he said to me, 'go with Jack on inspection till I sort this problem out. Please say nothing to anyone else.'

*

On Saturday afternoon I asked Dad to take me to Abingdon to buy a scooter. He took me in his Ford, and he had to be present with me to buy it as I was under the age of 18, and it was going to be a hire purchase agreement. They sent me a payment book, with stubs that came out every month. Now I was 16 years old I was getting a pay rise of a pound and I worked out the payments to a pound per month. It was a second-hand scooter and I had to put down a deposit of 3 quid, and the total cost was 18 quid, so I had 18 months to pay.

'What do you think, Dad?'

'If you're happy, boy.'

So we went for it. I had applied for my licence and received it before we bought the scooter. I saved half a dollar a week in a jar hidden away from Mum in one of the cupboards, then when I had enough I took it to the Post Office and put it into my account.

After a year went I went back to the seller to get the scooter MOT'd. When I arrived a copper in uniform was talking to him. The bloke asked how he could help me, and I explained that I needed an MOT certificate. He looked in at the battery casing and failed me! I asked why.

'Because you have no battery.'

'But that's how you sold it to me last year when I came to buy it, and you never put a battery in it! When I asked you said "no". You said it would be OK.'

The copper looked at him. 'You'd better honour the hire purchase agreement and give that lad an MOT certificate, and put a battery in the box while I stand here and watch.'

That was the first time a copper helped me – my lucky day. I squared away the bike purchase agreement and paid it off with cash from my Post Office savings book.

On Sunday I was at Mick's again and we stayed in chatting, playing records and talking about the scooter I had just bought. 'I've got L-plates on it – shall we go out for a ride, Mick?'

'What about the L-plates?'

'Take them off – who's going to tell?'

'Have you got insurance?'

'Yes, I got a cover note from Mr Jeffries of Prudential Insurance, third party.'

'OK, let's go to Wallingford and eye up the crumpet!'

We had a good day out, but when I got home Dad went for my throat. 'You're a learner! Drive properly or I'll take the bike away from you!'

'Yes, Dad.'

On Monday I worked with Jack, as he was on days. Sam came into the cabin. 'Arthur wants to see you, Pat.'

I knocked at Arthur's door and walked in. 'Are you OK, Pat?' he asked. I nodded. 'Stay with Jack all week, OK? I want you to book into night school in September. Go and see what courses you want to do, and bring the information back to me so I can get in touch with Paddington, who'll paying for the courses. That's part of the agreement you signed.'

'And the evening fees?'

'You.'

'British Railways are as tight as a rat's arse!' I told him.

'Yes, but you'll get the money back when you pass the courses.'

'I don't want to go to school,' I said. 'All I want is to be a fitter and turner.'

'You will go to school or *leave*,' insisted Arthur.

A lesson learned

So I went to school and booked the courses: Monday, Engineering Drawing, 7 till 9 o'clock, and Wednesday, Arithmetic, 7 till 8, then Science, 8 till 9. I came back with the report sheet and handed it over to Arthur.

*

I was sitting in the cabin when my brother Paul asked Bob Looms if he could have a roll-up. Bob handed over his tobacco tin and Paul started to roll a cigarette. It got bigger and bigger, and Paul had to put two to three papers together to accommodate all the tobacco. He used all the baccy in Bob's tin, but turned to Bob and said he was only joking – he would put it all back. But Bob said, 'No, you bloody will not! You'd better smoke it!'

'I was only joking Bob!'

'Hard bloody luck! You'd better smoke it or I'm going to get cross.'

So Paul ended up smoking it, and the last laugh was on him. He never did it again.

*

When I went into the classroom on the Monday evening each of us had to pay a bob into a pot, and we had a tea break and biscuits. This would be for six months. I enjoyed as the tutor, who was after our ideas on how to build an electric car.

Wednesday evening was worse. I couldn't get used to the equations and how the teacher laid them out on the blackboard. I loved doing sums, but this was terrible. Every time I had to ask as I couldn't see how it was worked out – I'd left school too long ago. But I thought it's only an hour then tea break will be here, then Science with a lady teacher. Christ, she was strict and bolshie! Anyway, I did the course but was getting nowhere, so one Wednesday Annie and me went to the pictures – then World War 3 erupted. Read on…

Someone said, 'Hello, Pat!' I never thought any more about it, but was at work a few days later and Arthur, the foreman, was talking to me outside his office near No 1 road when Ted Ireson, a fireman, walked up to us and said. 'What a nice-looking girl that was on your arm last Wednesday.'

I realised that I had seen this twat, and had to make up an excuse a bit quick. 'Not me,' I said. 'I was at night school.'

'It was a good film, wasn't it?' said Ted.

I walked off quickly, but 'Brink' asked Ted some questions. Then I heard a shout: 'In my office – *now*!'

Arthur told Sam, the office clerk, to get out and stay out. Then all hell broke loose in his office. He went mad and ripped into me. I tried to say that I was still going to Monday's class, but I couldn't get a word out as he was shouting at me. I felt sorry for his own children when he went crazy like this. Even my Dad didn't shout at me like this – he only belted me across my backside.

On Saturday 21 September another locomotive and a few wagons came off the road near Steventon bridge. The locomotive, No 6800 *Arlington Grange*, fell over onto the railway bank and took some wagons with it. Swindon and Old Oak Common were summoned out to help lift the locomotive and wagons back onto the line.

Meanwhile Arthur had reported to Paddington, and some top Paddington managers came down to see me in Mr East's office and read me the apprenticeship agreement papers, threatening me with the sack. That was the fourth and last time I visited his office.

Dad's Army belt bloody *hurt* as he held my hair and whacked me with so much force that I had the marks across the skin of my backside for weeks afterwards. I couldn't sit down; as one side got better I kept my bum on it, then the other side got better. I was eventually able to sit on both cheeks. I was scared for ever! (Today my parents could have been put away for life!)

31. Snowbound!

Again I was on the move to Reading, this time with another split vacuum pipe. I had to find my own way down to the shed; I left the station, turned right and went down to where the cattle market was in Great Knollys Street, then down Hodsoll Lane, under the bridge and over the tracks to the steam shed. I again reported to the fitting shop foreman, left the pipe with him and had a look around the town. I went back 2 hours later, then caught the train back to Didcot. I got used to this; I would even leave the item there and ask them to send it on the 6 o'clock Enparts service the next morning. A fitter's mate would pick it up from the station parcels office and bring it to the shed. But today there was no way I could have left the pipe, as I would have been hauled over the coals and reprimanded.

Jack Dearlove said, 'Go off and do what you want, Pat,' so I went into the shop, got the two-wheeled truck, went to the stores and asked Jim Parsons for the box of old steam cocks he had stored. He had loads – they should have been sent back to Swindon. I put the box on the truck, went into the fitting shop, put the box on the floor and set up the lathe.

Dave Davies appeared and helped me. I started to take off a thou off the face of the steam cock, then gently using fine emery cloth finished each one off. Then I refurbished another, and that kept me busy for ages. Again, no one really showed me; I got stuck in by myself.

I saw Arthur walk in and speak to Jim. 'What's he at? Did you tell him to do those?'

'No,' came the answer. 'All I know from Dave is that he set the work load up himself.'

I did about 20 and took them back to the stores. My day's work was up, so I washed up and cleared off home.

I had to be at school that night, being Monday, and every Monday evening I met an old schoolfriend. I was a little late so walked on when suddenly I saw someone entering the front door and kissing. Who else but Gill Andrews, with her tongue down his throat. So I trundled off for the night school class, engineering drawing, and thought no more about it till 7.30, when I said, 'Packed her up, then, Dicky?'

'No. Why?'

'I was there and you came late, and I saw she was over someone else's, snogging her in the doorway.'

'You're taking the piss out of me, Pat!'

I put my hands up together and said nothing. He raced out of the classroom, then came back after 8, blamed me and stormed off. An elephant never forgets, and what comes around goes around. My wish came true. It took me some months, but it made my day!

Next morning Jim asked if I had any work to do, so I told him I was machining the steam cocks. 'I'll come in and get you when I'm ready, Pat,' he said. I went to the lathe and ignored him; I didn't speak to him after the row, but just carried on doing what I was doing.

I had a steam cock in the jaws of the lathe ready to skim a thou off when Arthur appeared. 'You OK, Pat?'

'Yes thanks.'

'Who told you to use the lathe?'

'I did, as the steam cocks were mounting in the stores.'

'You're suppose to ask,' he said.

Stopping the lathe, I took out the job, shut off the motor, put the job back into the box, put it on the truck and walked away back to the stores. Then I went into the cabin and sat and waited for Jack.

I had turned. I felt I was doing no good there. They had beaten me. Jack was in the cabin and said, 'Come on, let's get out and do some work.'

I spoke to Dad about what was happening and how shirty they had got with me. He said, 'Put in for a transfer to get out of the shed.'

Snowbound!

I wrote one every week and presented it to Arthur. I had become very stubborn and felt as if I was being got at. Now I was being brought into the office for more tellings-off, and all I kept telling him was that I wanted a transfer out of the shed, and away from dirty steam engines. The worm had turned.

I never got paid back the money I had spent on the night schools doing engineering drawing and science on Mondays and Wednesdays – I think the railway thought I should pay them to work in their establishment

I couldn't wait to get out of Didcot shed. You could cut the atmosphere with a knife – it got worse and the back-biting was hell. I didn't realise that this is how it was when I came to the shed, but the instigators were the same old clique who could get their own way some of the time, but not all of the time.

*

A third friend, Graham Wilde, joined us in our adventures, not to the dances but when we all went to London. Most Saturday mornings we caught the train from Didcot; Graham was the only one who paid to travel, as Mick and I had free passes that took us straight to the Whitechapel. I introduced my friends to my Aunt Betty and Uncle Michael. and from there we hit the high time at the pub in Whitechapel, amongst the local Jewish population.

I recall there was a song out at that time by Bobby Vee – *Rubber Ball*. The pub pianist said, 'You sing it and I'll play it!' We had one hell of a night and were thrown out after closing time. We caught the Underground back to Paddington and the last train was about to leave – the milk train. So all three of us ran like hell and caught the train by a scruff's hair as it started to pull out of the platform. We got to Didcot at 3 in the morning, just as the sun was rising, stoned out of our minds! We walked home, trying to sober Mick up, while me and Graham were laughing. When we got to Mick's back door, he told us to be quiet, or his Dad would hear us. So Graham and I stood him up leaning on the back door just as his Dad opened the door, and he fell inwards. His Dad went mad – we ran away!

*

On Wednesday 28 June 1961 a driver walked to the Time Office at Reading shed and asked the shed foreman to be taken off his train because he didn't know the road ahead – he only knew the way to his shed in Reading. He had signed the 'Knowledge of the Road' book following several duties running to Reading and returning to his own shed. He felt better that he had been honest, as he had a train behind him with two other men whose safety he had to consider.

Reading had several men who knew the road, and one had been on duty since the early morning. Pulling the records out of the office, the foreman found that the driver had signed the 'Knowledge of the Road' book following several duties running to Reading and returning to Didcot, then on to Oxford, learning the loop lines and procedures on runs with freight trains on both the day and night shift. He had made several runs through the new Goods Loop line at Didcot during daytime in sole charge of his train, and had proceeded along the Down Goods Loop towards Appleford on shunting duties within the Baltic Yards, Dardanelles Sidings and Centre Yard, as well as the Carriage Sidings.

He had been allocated to 'Zone Relief duties', mostly working freight trains from point to point, increasing his knowledge and road learning by working freight trains to Oxford, running through the Down Goods Loop and noticing the position of catch points and signals. He was therefore a very experienced driver; he always read the notice boards for route changes and special notices when he booked on shift, and helped the firemen working with him. A sight test, due after 12 months at the shed, found his eyesight normal, including his colour vision; all was tested and passed, and the paperwork signed off and placed in his file in the office.

A general view of Reading shed in 1959. *L. W. Ibbotson, Slip Coach Publishing Services collection*

He was therefore signed on for the westbound newspaper train, all stations to Swindon. He was shown where it was waiting in the sidings opposite the shed. The original driver walked back to the engine with him so he could explain to the fireman what was happening; the guard was also on the footplate, and wrote the new driver's name in the book, and why the original driver was leaving the train. Everything was above board. The new pilot driver knew the road, and blew the whistle to let the signalman know he wanted to get out onto the main line.

When they reached the West End signal box just beyond the station at Didcot, the signalman rang ahead to Foxhall Junction to see if the signalman there would accept a train into his block section with a pilot driver supplied from Reading shed, as he knew the road towards Swindon. The signalman agreed to accept the train, but only as far as his home signal. The West End signalman gave the driver a verbal warning of the situation, and again as he left the signal box and returned to his train standing at the Down Relief starting signal before entering the Foxhall Junction block section.

The signalman then 'set the road', taking his cloth from his shoulder and pulling the appropriate levers. Everything was going to plan.

Waiting on the West Curve was the Ipswich freight. The driver blew his whistle twice, raising his arm to the signalman, who acknowledged with a wave back. Because there was a small hump in the track, the driver couldn't get the locomotive to move, so he applied sand to the rails, while the fireman attended to the fire to make sure there was sufficient steam to get the heavy train on the move. The locomotive started to grip and they moved away.

The fireman was still shovelling away when the driver noticed another locomotive coming slowly towards the junction, but he saw that the Down Relief home signal was in the stop position, so knew he would be OK.

The Ipswich locomotive was now over onto the Down Main line heading for

Snowbound!

Swindon, and picking up speed – then all hell broke loose. The pilot on the newspaper train failed to stop at the home signal, and ploughed into the eight box vans at the rear of the freight, derailing them. The driver of the Ipswich train felt the shock wave as the other locomotive pushed the wagons across the rails, and heard wood splintering and metal crashing through the train. He immediately applied the vacuum brake while the fireman wound the tender brake on, and the train came to a halt.

The fireman climbed down off the footplate and ran back to see what had happened, and saw that the other locomotive had crashed through several of the Ipswich freight's wagons. Happily the guard was not hurt. He then ran back to tell his driver what had happened, and they made a decision to uncouple the front of the train away from the derailed wagons. As was standard practice, detonators were paid on the rails away from the crash site to warn any oncoming trains.

In the meantime, the Foxhall Junction signalman had sent the 'Obstruction' bell signal down the line to Milton signal box and up to West End box. He then went to his Train Register Book and wrote up the incident as he saw it, with the Ipswich train spread over the two roads near the signal box. He wondered what the London Division would do and what action they might take, but he had done everything by the book, as he had been taught over the years.

The call went out to collect all the Didcot fitting crews. The breakdown van was ready with the kettle on, so tea and sandwiches could be provided for the early risers from home. The breakdown crew took orders from Arthur Brinkley, as he was in overall command.

No one had been hurt, but the Swindon crane attended to lift the wreckage onto flat 'Macaw' wagons to be taken away. Both main lines were soon open to traffic between London and Bristol; only local traffic was affected.

*

The local dentist had his surgery near the engine shed, and he was very keen on stories about the Great Western Railway that the drivers and firemen told him while he was dealing with their teeth. He would give free treatment in return for railway tales, but then came the time for him to retire; he moved to North Wales and everything came to the end.

The shed staff wanted to show their appreciation. A 'Manor' was working an express train through the dentist's new home station, and he was told to be there when the train came through as they had something for him; he still did a little postal false teeth business and was expecting some materials he had ordered. The shed foreman looked the other way while someone loosened the bolts from behind one of the nameplates before leaving the shed to couple up to the coaches. As the express approached the station, the fireman climbed out and walked along the side of the 'Manor', holding on for dear life. The driver slowed the train slightly,

At Foxhall Junction foreman Arthur Brinkley stands on a block of wood as Jim Tyler picks up material.

the fireman removed the nameplate then climbed back into the cab, handing it to the driver.

They wrapped the nameplate in sacking, tied it with string and labelled it with the dentist's name. As the train approached the station the driver slowed the train right down. The gentleman was expecting teeth, but the fireman threw the nameplate into a bush next to him, then the driver opened up the regular to gather speed again.

The shed foreman demanded to know what had become of the nameplate, and the crew said it had become loose and had fallen off somewhere during the journey. But he knew perfectly well what had happened and what had been done.

The name of the 'Manor' is not known.

*

Working conditions changed on 13 June 1962 from a 48-hour week to 44 hours – no more Saturday mornings.

Then in the winter of 1962/63 came the snow. Throughout the country frost and cold weather brought many trains to a halt. The freezing conditions took men from their normal work to help, and we were all called in during the crisis as we were all dedicated railwaymen.

A railwayman's worst enemy and fear is snow, as the cold weather gets into a man's bones when working day and night to keep the lines open to traffic in often blizzard conditions. The cold weather started in the early part in December 1962 and lasted till April 1963.

Men kept the points from freezing by pouring an oil/paraffin mixture over every joint, knocking the ice away with pickaxes, then shouting to the signalman to operate the points to free them. As the points moved, they poured their oily mixture onto the exposed sliding surfaces.

Walking to work and back home, everyone was wrapped up, trying to keep the cold away from their bodies. Nothing was moving; cars were covered with snow, stuck where they lay beside the road. High mountains of snow on the roads were pushed aside by tractors with buckets. There was no sand or salt available; everyone had to help and do their bit for each other. People walked on the road in the ruts and trenches of snow, and fresh ice formed every night as the temperatures plummeted well below freezing. On the pavements the pristine covering of snow sparkled in the glow of the street lights. In Sinodun Road we had no water for over a month, and the Water Board sent up a road tanker.

Railwaymen hardly went home. They had a few hours' sleep on the benches in cabins, curled up with overcoats thrown over them, and the potbelly stoves burning constantly, and the smell of stale food and dampness from the weather conditions outside.

The temperature dropped over night to -25°C and the men often wrapped newspaper around their bodies, tied with string, before pulling on their outdoor clothes. Newspapers were also stuffed around the legs to keep the cold out, and to prevent chapping that would lead to stinging red sores. The wet went through the stitching on our leather boots, so newspaper would be used again to keep the feet warm.

To free up the engines, men made torches with cotton waste and paraffin and, starting at the piston cylinder cocks, tried to thaw the ice. They told the driver to move and keep the engine rolling while they placed the burning torches around every moving part, laying sand on the line to get the wheels to grip. When they finally got everything moving, two of the four men had to stay on the engine while they went back to the shed

Snow fell over Berkshire on 1 January 1963, and again on the 3rd and the 5th – 15 inches on that Sunday. Blizzard conditions prevailed and all roads were cut off. There were long delays on the railways. On 10 January we had more snow and plenty of it, with 6-foot snowdrifts all around.

Temperatures dropped to -35°C on 17 January and all the roads were impassable for wheeled vehicles, so people walked

Snowbound!

everywhere. Locomotives froze up 30 minutes after coming into the shed, and everyone was helping out to defrost them; the ground was so cold that a drop of water froze straight away.

When the locomotives were brought into the shed the doors were closed – that was the first time I had seen them closed. 'Fire devils' were alight in the shed as well as outside, but the shed stank with the fumes. Inside the lifting shop the forge was kept going day and night, with all the doors closed; rags and newspapers were stuffed into the cracks to keep us warm. Buckets of ash from the ashpans were left near the engines to keep the fitters' tools warm, so that when you picked up a spanner the skin didn't tear from your hands.

On Thursday 24 January we had more snow and blizzard conditions – the whole country was in a state!

Arthur came rushing into the shed and pulled everyone off what work they were doing. Someone was sent out collecting all the boilersmiths' rodding and metal skewers, which were wrapped in cotton waste and rags, and buckets of paraffin were placed around the shed. The men lit their skewers and place them under the steam cocks to free the cylinders of ice. Snow was falling every day, bringing blizzard conditions. Everyone could see two black lines running through the snow, but each set of points had to be oiled to stop it freezing, using iron rods with old waste wrapped around them.

Arthur told us to get over to the main line as a engine on a freight train couldn't release its steam cocks, as they were frozen. While the twins worked on one side of the engine, I stood next to Jim on the other side. Suddenly there was a huge bang and the cylinders seemed to explode as steam issued from the cocks and the engine stated to move away. The engine crew thanked us with a wave.

The Army Ordnance depot sent over 40 men from 521 Company to the marshalling yard to help clear the snow from the tracks; these chaps were from the Pioneer Corps.

The River Thames froze at Abingdon and people walked across from one side to the other; they even roasted an ox on the ice in the middle of the river. Even the sea froze.

At Reading the snowplough was called out. The mechanical foreman of the section was Vic Jarrot, nicknamed 'The Bishop.' He walked into the fitting shop and saw Allan Brown and two others, Brian Wheeler and Johnny Mack (real name McNamara), a Didcot man. They had to get No 2251, an 0-6-0 tender engine, and fit the snowplough to the front frame. The shed foreman asked the shed pilot to bring the '22' into the fitting shop to have the front buffers removed, together with the coupling hook and chain. I went out into the shed to collect the cradle trolley; this had four small wheels so it could fit onto the rails. They positioned it in front of the buffer beam.

Eric Hall, the workshop fitter, asked someone to go to the oil stores to get some light engine oil, cotton waste and paraffin. They mixed the ingredients together in a shiny galvanised bucket, and using the cotton waste they had to soak the area around the nuts holding the buffer; the other two men did their own thing with the other buffer.

Then Johnny got under the beam with a socket, knuckle bar and metal tube and I had to stand in the pit, pulling down with all my might, praying that the nut would crack loose, and it did. The rest of the nuts were not so easy. They had to get the oxygen and acetylene bottles to torch the nuts hot, then undo them, as the studs were needed again, being round-headed and bevelled.

The buffer cradle trolley was then placed in position and, winding the screw jack under the buffer block and pulling it away from the frame, with the help of the other two men pulling and heaving on crowbars the buffer was lifted completely off the front beam. They lowered it to the ground with the help of the block and tackle. The coupling came off easier than the buffers, with two men undoing the huge nut at the back of the buffer beam.

The shed driver went under the coal stage

and filled the tender with coal. Then he brought the '22' around the side of the shed, near the turntable on No 6 road where the lamp house was situated. This was where the snowplough was left after the last time it had been used, covered in dirty ash and sooty snow. Under it were old broken teacups, milk cartons and rubbish that had frozen.

The team beckoned to the driver to come slowly onto the plough, stopping him at the right place, as any further movement would have meant the plough dropping onto the ground. It was cold enough working out there in the freezing conditions – we didn't want any more work. At our side we had a metal brazier full of coal and wood burning to keep us warm, and we put our tools in the fire so they were warm when we came to use them. Nothing was worse than having cold metal in your hands.

Using a small hydraulic jack on a block we slowly eased up the plough; Brian was in charge of this. Oxygen and acetylene were brought to warm the bolts to ease them off. Johnny had a small rat-tail crowbar; he pushed it into the hole in the plough, and it found its way into the beam where the buffers had been situated. He pushed the first bolt through, and placed the nut on the threaded screw, winding it up with a spanner. The plough started to come together when all the bolts were in place, and we screwed them down with a socket, knuckle bar and metal tube, heaving and pulling them tight. It had started to snow again, and we were glad that the job was finished. We checked the distance between the rail and the lower frame of the plough, and the rest was up to 'The Bishop'.

The snow continued to fall over the whole country that night and into the next day. It was a total whiteout, with freezing conditions down to -20°C; many railwaymen never went home from their depots. Large shovels, pickaxes and crowbars were used to clear the ice and snow from engines' motions and wheels. Several sacks of cotton waste, plenty of paraffin and iron rods were stored on tenders, with the steam lance and an extra length of pipe.

A call came through on the 'omnibus' telephone system from Control that the Didcot to Oxford and Newbury lines were blocked. However, Reading shed's No 2251 had a full head of steam and on the footplate were 'The Bishop' with Eric Hall, the driver and the fireman, all wrapped up in coats, hats, gloves and scarves, with their Wellington boots and extra socks. Across the engine's roof was a fitted 'Zeppelin sheet' of canvas pulled down and tied to the tender to try to keep the snow and ice away, and keep the men warm on the footplate. The locomen who had volunteered were Bill Peirce, the driver, and Charlie Caulkett, the fireman, as they both knew the road.

As they left the yard they blew the whistle to acknowledge the signalman giving them the right of way. The road ahead was clear heading east towards Reading. The area was only clear because the snow had blown across the rails and drifted across open ground. The regulator was wide open as they headed on, and they seemed to be doing well as there were no phone calls to return to Reading shed, which was a good sign.

Coming into the gorge of the Downs with the cutting at Goring & Streatley ahead, nothing could be seen as the railway lines were buried under heaps of snow, which was blowing out each side of the plough; looking back, two black lines could be seen again. They were making headway, on through the chalk cutting as No 2251 hit the laying snow, with the snowplough staying firmly on the track. Charlie was shattered from shovelling coal into the firebox, so Eric, taking hold of the shovel, gave him a rest. He opened the injector to allow water to be pumped into the boiler from the tender; this kept the steam pressure up and they could see the water bobbing up and down in the gauge glass. Meanwhile the locomotive started to glisten with frost and the sprinkling of snow blowing back over the boiler, and ice was forming.

Goring & Streatley was cleared after running up and down a couple of times, then they headed back towards Cholsey

& Moulsford. The wind had whipped the snow across the line, as this was another area that was open to the elements, but they drove on and went straight through it. After more shovelling of coal, Bill the driver noticed that they had started to get a little low on water. They stopped near Cholsey & Moulsford station, and 'The Bishop' went across the rails to a phone to see if they could return to Didcot shed to refill with coal and water; they notified the signalman in the East box.

Proceeding into Moreton cutting, there were drifts everywhere, as this was also an open area. With Didcot in sight – or at least a black spot on the horizon – all the men were cold, hungry and sick to death of the white stuff. The signals were set to allow them straight into the shed area, but first they had to go to the coal stage to fill up with good Welsh coal.

Loaded to the hilt and more besides, they went down to the turntable and reversed into the entrance of the shed. Standing near a water column, with a brazier burning to stop it freezing, all they saw were men walking about with cotton waste on fire, heating the steam cocks on the cylinders and the water pipes between tender and engine to keep the water flowing. The shed's big front doors were closed to try and keep the heat in.

Vic Jarrot and Eric Hall went and saw Arthur Brinkley in his office, reporting to him and finding out what was to happen next. Charlie and Bill went to the Time Office to explain their next move and asked the men to keep their eye on the loco to keep her stoked up, as they had to go out again later that day. But first they needed something hot inside them. All four walked through the snow to the Polar Star hostel to get something to eat and drink, and to get out of the cold.

The next phase, their locomotive with a full head of steam and steam blowing through the cylinder cocks, was to go out onto the main line to Oxford, running past the North signal box, Appleford and out into the open fields. The snow had drifted up the banks, giving an alpine appearance – it covered everything in sight. There was no traffic on the roads – the scene was just like a Christmas cake. No bridge or railway lines could be seen and the hedges were just covered bumps.

As they went into Culham station the snow was banked high in the cutting, drifting with the wind that was blowing it up into the air. It took several attempts to travel through the wet snow; it was hard reversing, then gathering speed again to crash into the drifts. Charlie was still shovelling the black stuff into the firebox, making as much steam as possible to drive the monster forward to open the line for passenger trains. With the exhaust pouring into the air from the chimney, dirty grey and white, they bore on into the next drift.

The day was getting bad and the weather started to get into their bones. They couldn't wait to get to Oxford. Just one more station to go – Radley. They tore straight through, leaving a trail of snow sprayed over the platforms.

Now they were all hungry, thirsty and tired, but Oxford wasn't far away. Through open fields with no cuttings, they just carried on the best way they could, passing several points that were just black blocks in the snow.

At Oxford station they had a hot meal at the hostel, while No 2251 was at the shed having a refill of coal and water. The shed foreman also knocked the ice and snow from her wheels. When the men returned, she was free of the frozen stuff and looking clean. The return trip to Didcot was much the same, keeping the steam up with Charlie and Eric working together in tandem, shovelling coal. In the distance, on the horizon, there was a break in the sky; the clouds were allowing the sun to shine a little, but it was still terribly cold. The wind started to pick up and the 'Zeppelin sheet' started to shake and crackle. The wind was picking up the snow particles and blowing them through the slits onto the men on the footplate.

The signalman at East box set the road

to allow the snowplough to change course towards the Newbury branch. Bill noticed men digging furiously into the deep snow on the line, so he gave three blasts on the whistle to warn them to take cover for their own safety. As the plough struck the heaped snow, it shuddered and the men on the footplate hung on to anything they could find. They were going like hell in the night, straight through this white enemy with the chimney pumping out ash, soot and white smoke into the atmosphere, like a volcano erupting.

Snow was spraying in all directions, even coming over the roof of the engine as they tore up the Newbury branch line, driving through another cutting near Hagbourne, along the back of Sinodun Road, and out into the country towards Upton & Blewbury station across the Ponderosa. As they started the approach to the Churn Estate, all they could see was snow across the fields, no railway lines anywhere, and the station was just an open mass of snow. No 2251 bore into the snow but then shuddered to a standstill. They tried to reverse, but the wheels were stuck solid. They were in deep trouble. Bill and 'The Bishop' tried everything in the book; they even got the steam lance out and tried to force steam into the spokes of the wheels while Eric and Charlie broke the ice away. However, nothing was happening and after a couple of hours they gave up.

The fire in the box started to go out, and looking through all they could see was snow embedded in the damper. Nothing was going to move her now, so they decided to leave her there. Charlie got the tube of detonators and laid them on both sides of the line, and they put a red flag on top of the rear of the tender. Then they gathered their belongings and walked back 2½ miles along the line that they had cleared to the last station at Upton & Blewbury. Vic, using the 'omnibus' telephone, called Control to say that they were stuck and could someone come and pull them, as they were waiting in the signal box near the station.

Control telephoned the signal box at Moreton Cutting and spoke to the signalman there, Alex Membury, asking him to pass on a message to tell the shunters to uncouple a freight train in the marshalling yard. An 'Austerity' engine was given orders to travel towards the Churn Estate to help pull out the snowplough, pick up the enginemen and return them to Didcot shed.

They had a clear road ahead to Didcot, then went up the Newbury branch to Upton & Blewbury. Waiting for them were Bill, Charlie, Eric and Vic. They all climbed up on the footplate and rode on towards their engine. When they saw the red flag, they slowed down so that Charlie could pick up the detonators from the line.

The engine travelled towards the rear of the tender slowly until the buffers met, then Charlie coupled up. The rest of the men got off the footplate and started to clear away the snow and ice from No 2251, as she was stone dead and frozen to the rail. Then the driver of the 'Austerity' started the pull the snow-stricken engine out of the mass of snow, but the wheels were frozen stiff and just slid along the track.

Each man made a torch with cotton waste and paraffin and started on the cylinder cocks, trying to thaw the frozen water. Heating the piston rod gland, they told the driver to keep her rolling while they placed the burning torches around every moving part of the engine, laying sand onto the line to help the wheels grip. Finally the wheels started to move, but two of the four men had to stay on the dead engine as they travelled back to Didcot shed.

32. Reading transfer

I never went back into the shop. For a while I stayed outside on shed duties. I could see Jim struggling on his own, but sometimes he got the twins to help out. I never again went to any other shed taking pipes, or to Swindon – I refused. I noticed that Jim Hale had to do the running about – as I told Arthur, I was an apprentice, not a skivvy, and I had no time to go to the sheds owing to being late for night school twice a week.

Life changed as 1963 changed into 1964. Loads of transfer letters went in every week, just to get my own back – I had become a little immature. However, in May 1963 I received my transfer to Reading Diesel Depot at last. I was to report to Eric Chard on Monday morning, having caught the 7.20 from Didcot. Paddington issued me with a free workman's pass for my journey back and forth. On occasions I also used it for my nights out at Reading. One of my companions was Michael Russell from Sinodun Road. On night we went to Reading Town Hall and saw some scruffy-looking yobs wearing hobnail boots and rough clothes getting out of a taxi. When we asked someone who were they, we were told they were the Rolling Stones. At the time I didn't care, but as time went on I bought all their LPs.

My learning curve started with being put with different fitters every other week, to be put through the basic practices and procedures with service sheets. There were Monthly, Quarterly, Half Yearly and Yearly services, as well as repairs, such as station faults with windscreen wipers and exhaust troubles, or trouble-shooting other problems. Mostly the work was on diesel multiple units (DMUs), removing tappet covers from the engines and setting the tappets up with feeler gauges.

On my first week at the depot I was send up to the town to get a supply of 5-amp fuses. I asked whether I would need a two-wheeled barrow – would they be heavy?

'Yes, take a barrow,' they said, but I was stopped at the door and had the piss taken out of me. Very funny! Everyone was laughing, pointing and cheering. Thank you, one and all!

If I wanted to get into the cab of a DMU steps had to be provided. I was put in the driver's seat in the cab. First of all I was shown and instructed on the controls, and the fitter told me to move the gear handle till it clicked into drive. I pushed the gear lever through all the gears in one straight swoop – the first telling-off came quicker than normal! The fitter then stopped the diesel engine, and I was told to get underneath, climb up and over the torque converter to the gearbox and remove all the nuts from the gearbox cover plate, in which the driving sprockets for the transmission were housed. Then I had to inspect inside the gearbox with the fitter. I was lucky nothing was broken, or I would have been in trouble and sacked.

The engines were made by AEC at Southall in west London. Checking tappets, belts, drives and gears was mostly done on yearly services; one gang worked nights at one end of the railcar and the second gang worked the other end on day work. There were two AEC engines on one car, with four engines on a three-car set; they were side-valve engines.

The DMU drove in above you, so working on them was easy. A three-car set was the full length of the new shed. I even had to assist in removing the engines with the help of a forklift, and refit new engines to get the car out back on the line.

At break time we went into the locker room downstairs and washed our hands at a fountain and round washbasin in the middle of the floor. After washing I went upstairs to the break room overlooking the marshalling yards and main-line trains.

I got friendly with a gentleman who didn't speak perfect English – I think he was a cleaner. He was a nice guy and pleasant, we got talking and I remember he said he was constipated. So I wrote out what he should take and how to take it – I recommended Ex-Lax chocolate. Just take a little – but he enjoyed it so much he ate the bar. I didn't see him for a week, and when he did come back to work he looked as though he had lost a lot of weight. The Ex-Lax had solved his problem, but he couldn't get off the throne for a week! I couldn't stop laughing, and he did join in after a while when he saw the funny side. He couldn't sit down for the week and his second home was the toilet.

We had 'Warship' diesel-hydraulic No D827 come in to be worked on. It was a job to sit on the driver's seat and look over the bonnet. Between the driver's and fireman's seats was a small door into the nose of the loco. The engine room was behind the driver's seat, and there was a small door leading through a partition to a walkway in the engine compartment, in which there was also a boiler for heating when hauling a train. You could walk from one cab through to the other cab.

I recall that myself and a few other apprentices were sitting in the cab of this 'Warship', having a laugh; I was reading the paper. Suddenly a man came up the ladder and shouted at us, and did he let rip! He was only the Chief Mechanical Engineer, standing there in his white overalls! He shouted at all of us, and we stood to attention. He never caught me doing that again. The trouble was that he picked on me to explain the diesel horsepower and what kind of engine was in the compartment, seeing as I was the intelligent one, reading the *Daily Sketch*!

All the lads from Didcot caught the 7.20am train and we sat together in the same compartment each day, playing cards or talking. When we got into Reading station we went to the end of the platform and walked across the lines to get to the path on the far side. We walked down past the West signal box and crossed over the main line towards the steam shed. There were eight roads, and the signalman shouted from his box when all was clear, but we never hung about as it was a very busy area. We looked

Diesel-hydraulic 'Warship' No D829 *Magpie*. *British Railways*

Reading transfer

The London end of what was then known as Reading General station in November 1965. In the background is 9F 2-10-0 No 92007 on a goods train. *Ray Ruffell, Slip Coach Publishing Services collection*

all ways, as this was the main line from Paddington to Cornwall, and many a time we heard a whistle blow. We were also careful not to step on the points in case they moved.

Once when we all came off the train and went over to the path on the west side, Dennis Tyler from Didcot just turned around, walked back to the station, got onto the Didcot train and waved at us as the train went by.

On Saturday night I went to Reading by train with Annie. It was a stopper, and on this one occasion when we got to Tilehurst station someone pulled the communication cord. I touched it, and the vacuum brake came on – the train wouldn't move. The station master had to instruct the signalman to stop a main-line train to get the passengers to Reading. In the meantime I was asked to try to find the fault, but I couldn't. A fitter came out from the depot to fix the problem. I was told on Monday morning what it was, so if it happened again I would know next time to leave the chain alone.

My regular routine on Sundays was going to see Annie and staying for tea with her family.

On Monday I was back at work. in a clean area and a different environment. Walking up to the station with a fitter, he showed me how to carry out repairs on the windscreen wipers, a common fault. Many a time I had to go up to the station at Reading and fix windscreen wipers with the fitter, or crawl between the car sets and fix something or other. I poked my head up between the platform and the car – just a small gap. If anyone was to look down they would be surprised to see a face looking up at them!

At dinnertime I hung around in the rest room playing cards or went up town with Dennis for an hour. We would walk into a store where a young girl was serving, and make her blush, or have a laugh by picking up a pair of knickers and spreading them apart between our hands. Or we might ask the young girl what size cup for a woman of a 36 bust size, trying to clip the bra at the back, until being shown the door by the manager and escorted out of the shop.

On Friday nights on the way home from work, on occasions when the train came into Reading Didcot men would be driving a 'Hymek' down from Paddington. It was often No D7078 driven by 'Skip' Morgan, and he would shout out of the window, 'Come up front and ride in the cab with me to Didcot.' To stand up front and watch the other trains coming at you on the up line was thrilling. As we came into Didcot station I was allowed to sound the horn, and there waiting for me was Annie. As I went by I sounded the horn and everyone jumped out of their skins – very amusing for those watching. When I climbed down from the cab she would give me a right telling off as she was frightened, and I saw her jump! ('Skip' was a damn good friend, and when he died in 2014 All Saints Church in Old Didcot and the streets around Lydalls were packed to capacity as men came from all over the country to see him off.)

On arrival I would go down to Didcot shed and swap my dirty overalls for clean ones. I asked Annie to wait for me at the station as I would not be long, telling her not to talk to strange men.

'What, you and all?' she would reply. Funny girl! But she was lovely and I thought the world of her. I loved her so dearly.

Back at the diesel depot something was amiss, as no one could get the antifreeze mixture correct; everyone had a try, even the fitters. They must have been bad, as the task came down to me – or more likely they had cocked it up deliberately to get out of doing the antifreeze.

So I pulled the short straw. Eric Chard came to see me personally and spoke to me on the QT; he asked me into his office, and said that he had read my report about how clever I was! Here we go again – same silly talk! I was given a huge apron, covering my overalls, and had to wear wellington boots, leather gloves and goggles. He showed me the basics and the hydrometer, and I read the instructions about how to mix it, and the operation of the hydrometer.

There were several 45-gallon barrels

Brand-new 'Hymek' diesel-hydraulic No D7082 in about 1963.
Slip Coach Publishing Services collection via John Stretton

about, mostly empty. I cleared the area for what I needed – the dirty, filthy, blinking fitters had left water and antifreeze mixed on the floor, which made it slippery and dodgy to walk on. I cleaned the area and washed the floor. Now it looked presentable. There was a wooden bench with tools spread across it, so I put these into place correctly. There was a small overhead electric crane to lift the barrels safely.

Now I was organised and ready. I got in three empty barrels and used the crane to lift two full barrels. With a pump I drew antifreeze down into an empty barrel till it was about half full – 20 gallons – leaving a 5-gallon 'float'. I now added 20 gallons of water, making 40 in total, and gave it a stir. I took out a sample, put it into the hydrometer and took the reading. A little more antifreeze was needed, so I added more a gallon at a time till it was on the button. I'd saved 2 gallons for every 45 gallons. Two 45-gallon barrels were now ready, and I placed them in an area to be taken away and labelled them 'READY TO BE USED'.

By the end of the day ten 45-gallon barrels were ready. I put up a notice reading 'Please Keep Area Clean', hand-written on a board to which was attached a pencil on some string with which to write the DMU number and sign.

Eric came into the area and was amazed. 'We should name this room after you, Pat!'

The main thing was that I was now the best thing since sliced bread, and could do no wrong in his eyes!

I was now good at mixing the antifreeze by using the hydrometer and using mathematics to work out the quantity of water that gave the correct measure. It was a task I really enjoyed and was left alone to get on with it; the chargehand in that section always called on me to help out, completing the measurements with accuracy.

In the same area were crates of injectors for the DMUs to be changed, and the returns went into a wooden box that was suitably labelled.

One day, waiting to go on and be turned on the turntable, was No 4910 *Blaisdon Hall*, and I knew the Didcot driver, Harry Merrick, and his fireman Roland James. He asked me if I would like to balance the engine on the table; he knew that the table wasn't balanced like the one at Didcot. Of course I jumped at the chance. Well, I kept winding it into forward gear and opening the regulator slightly, then shutting it and applying the vacuum brake, but missed the balance. Then I wound it into the reverse gear, let off the vacuum brake and missed the balance again.

The sweat dripped off me. I climbed off the locomotive and Harry laughed at me. I was with a few lads I knew and worked with at the depot, and all my mates teased me and slapped me on the back. When the locomotive came back down the road Harry and Roland waved and laughed and blew the whistle again. I was laughed off the locomotive, and it has always stuck in my mind. I remember all the good times, grinning as I write them down.

While working at Reading depot I met some good apprentices. There was Dennis Tyler of course, Mick Quartermaine, mechanical apprentice from Tilehurst, and Dave Smith from Reading, an electrical apprentice. At weekends Mick played double bass in a group around Reading. On one occasion I went on a blind date with him. His girlfriend brought her mate – she was a smasher and very good looking. We used to meet up at Old Oak Common with another apprentice from Reading depot called Allan Brown, who came from Newbury.

Mick Quartermaine was a skinny kid and we enjoyed life together. He rode an old scooter, a German Zundapp Bella, and we used to ride it from the depot down the side of the track, falling off a few times, then across to Hodsoll Lane and out into Great Knollys Street to the corner shop where we brought food, then rode back again. We were both silly idiots!

Once Dennis, Mick and I all went out to Dave's house. We were a bit late coming back at lunchtime, so we parked Dave's van at Reading station and cut through the station.

If anyone was to ask us why we were late, we would say that we had been working on the DMU at the station.

On the way into the front of the station a little Navy Wren was lugging her kit bags up the stairs to Platform 1. As we ran by, I shouted, 'Carry your bags, lady?' and ran up the stairs. She grabbed Mick and said, 'Here, then, carry these,' and Mick had the lot of them. He called out, 'You said that, Pat! Come back here and give me a hand!'

So Dave, Dennis and I ran back down the stairs and picked up a bag each from Mick. We ran back up the stairs and dropped them on the platform, then ran down to the West signal box pathway to the depot. The Wren gave Mick some cigarettes, so he was happy.

As we all ran down past the signal box a train came round the bend, and we found ourselves standing between two trains, frozen, not moving, not even a cough, as the doors shot past in a swirl of dust. Then we legged it down to the depot, jumping over the points on the main line that would move for the next train as the first one went past. We just made it into the depot back door and went under the DMU, making out we had been there all the time.

I was called into the office one Friday afternoon and told that my six months was up, and I was being transferred back to Didcot the following Friday, which would be my last day. So the following week we all had some good times together.

We met up with John Crocker, an apprentice who had just come back to his home depot from a transfer. He had a motorbike and sidecar, a BSA 650cc Road Rocket. So Dave, Mick, Dennis and I got on it with the owner and went up to Reading for a ride – Dave, Mick and Dennis were in the sidecar and I was on the bike. Five of us – it was all good fun!

That week I was asked to go down to the Huntley & Palmers biscuit factory, where there was an 0-6-0 diesel shunter having trouble with the vacuum brake. It was an English Electric 350hp shunter – very powerful. Huntley & Palmers also had their own steam engine, a fireless locomotive. It was filled up with steam before each shift, but if you drove it too far it used up its fill of steam and just stopped; then it had to be pulled back into the factory to be filled up again. When I went down that day it was standing across a set of points, dead as a doornail.

Huntley & Palmers 0-4-0 fireless loco No 1 (built by Bagnall in 1932) was photographed at the Reading factory in June 1969, the year that the system closed. *Ray Ruffell, Slip Coach Publishing Services collection*

33. Old Oak Common

So in November 1963 I had to go back to Didcot. Reading had been good, clean and tidy. We all said our goodbyes, then come Monday morning I was back.

I came into work one Thursday and was told to get together oil, rags, tools and some sacks as we were going out early the following morning on a shunter, English Electric 350hp 0-6-0 No D3974. We had more shunters being allocated to our shed.

We set off to Moreton Marshalling yard, where a wagon with a hot axlebox had been brought in by a train from the main line; oil was unable to get to the metal bearing as the oil holes were blocked up. We strapped and tied our jacks and bars, oil and tools onto the side of the shunter, then Jim Tyler, Bob Warwick and I climbed up into the cab with the driver and second man (fireman) – there was not much room to move about, and we had not been given any footplate passes! Moreton was about 4 or 5 miles away towards Reading, and the carriage and wagon breaker's yard was closed so there was no one there to do the work, which was why the shed fitters had been told to do it. Men were leaving the railway in droves, going into the car factories, earning much more money for cleaner work, and with less strain.

We were dropped near the wagon and took our tools to the job. I was sent up to the shunter's cabin to make the tea and we had it on the job. We jacked up the wagon, stripped out the bearings, fitted new ones, oiled up, dropped the jacks, cleaned all the tools and had an afternoon watching the shunters go up and down with their trains.

We had to wait for a ride back to Didcot so were told to get our tools and equipment into the guard's van of a freight train that was going back with a train around the East Loop at Didcot towards Oxford. It stopped outside the shed and we dropped off with our equipment. We waved to the driver and thanked the guard. His van was comfortable with seats and a stove, side windows to look out at an angle, and its own balcony on which to stand; I felt like royalty waving to the railway people that I knew as they waved back to me!

During December I had to work in the shed removing superheaters from loco smokeboxes. The smokebox door had to be wide open, and the smokebox itself was full of soot and ash. Jim Holmar, Matt and I wrapped towels around our necks and heads, buttoned up our overalls to the neck and tied our sleeves and trouser legs with string to stop the soot getting into our clothes.

We climbed into the smokebox over the blastpipe, put a socket box spanner onto the studs and tried to undo the nuts by pulling down on a crowbar after soaking them with paraffin and oil mixed together. As they came undone the nuts screamed against the threads. Then we pulled out the superheater that was split and got a new one the same length, which was about 12 to 15 feet. Then we washed the studs in a mixture of oil and paraffin again, passed up the superheater between the three of us and slid it back into position, replaced the clamp, then put the nuts back onto the studs using the socket box spanner and bar, pulling down tight.

When we climbed out of the smokebox we were as black as the ace of spades with sweat and soot. I washed myself off in the lifting shop hand basin, or got a bucket of boiling water from a locomotive, stripped down to my inner overall trousers and just washed as clean as I could.

*

In January 1964 came another transfer, to Old Oak Common. This one came automatically as apprentices were being moved as sheds started to close and BR wanted new fitters for their workshops. It was unfair really as the best fitters and old hands

Interior of one of the Old Oak Common roundhouses. *Ted Abear collection*

had to leave and be put out to grass, and I really felt for them.

I was still meeting up with Mick Quartermain and Allan Brown, the Reading apprentices. Allan came from Newbury, so they rang me up at Didcot to say what train they were going to catch. On Monday morning we all sat together and went to Old Oak. Allan stayed in Hendon and I went to live in Whitechapel. I kept falling asleep on the train home, jumping off just as it moved out of Didcot, otherwise I would have been carried off to Bristol Temple Meads, which was a bit far from Didcot, and I never had a ticket. Mick Quartermain went home to Tilehurst every night, and we caught the same train every morning until he began to ride on the back of Blondie's motorbike and

I never saw him again. Blondie was a mad sort of guy, but he had a good nature, and would help anyone. He was an apprentice fitter and built motorbikes from scratch; the bike he rode had parts from many different machines!

At Old Oak Common I did lots of jobs, running around for the electrical foremen checking diesel shunter numbers and their hours. I travelled all day with the help of the van driver, as he knew London like the back of his hand – Battersea Power Station, Acton Marshalling Yard, Ranelagh Road, Paddington station and the Post Office area there, Ealing, Slough, Willesden Junction, Greenford and more. I was out for a week, and returned with everything written down – station, engine number and hours. Perhaps

No 7015 *Carn Brea Castle* on the traverser at Old Oak Common in 1957. *Ted Abear collection*

they saw something else in me, as more jobs came in for me to do.

The works mechanical boss was Wilf Diamond, who was nicknamed 'Legs' after the American gangster. My mate Derek Everson recalled what happened to 'Legs'. Derek worked on the breakdown gang, and one evening the crew came together at the depot and the crane was getting up steam – a DMU had run up the station platform at Newbury and become derailed.

Only one person was missing, and that was the manager, 'Legs'. They set off behind a 'Warship' diesel, D846 or D847, Derek can't remember which. They headed for Southall to meet Mr Diamond, who had driven from Greenford, where Derek believes he lived; the arrangement was to pick him up at the station. As the breakdown train pulled into the station he was waiting, and the crew had a mug of tea ready for him as he gave the OK to proceed to Newbury.

When they arrived at Newbury they walked up the platform towards the derailed DMU, and when they got alongside the 'Warship' Wilf dropped down dead.

Halfway through the transfer to Old Oak Common when there was nothing to do I was out on my travels away from the shed on walkabout with Mick Quartermain, John Langston and Barry Hughes. We disappeared after 10.30 every morning and walked off site, sightseeing in Windsor and out on a jolly down to Acton to the swimming baths; I was also shown where they went to school. We wandered off and went around London

No 6002 *King William IV* at Old Oak Common, backing into the bottom shed. *Ted Abear collection*

riding the Underground for free.

Barry Hughes introduced me to Fred Lazby, a machinist on a lathe. Near the old shed's workshop there was a picture on the wall of a pretty girl with her legs open catching birds and putting them up her skirt. Fred drove a three-wheeled Reliant Robin and he would look out for me when I come out of Willesden Underground station, or if I was walking to work at Old Oak Common up near the Walls sausage factory; I would hear a beep on the horn and he would pull over to the kerb.

When I arrived at Old Oak I was asked if I had visited 'Abear's Corner' in the factory, which I did eventually. It got its name from Ted Abear's great-grandfather, who was a coppersmith there in the early days; he used to make you billycans if you wanted one for half-a-crown, and for a bit more you could have a copper tin lined.

I caught the 6.05am from Didcot, which had left Penzance at 9 o'clock the night before. There were two sets of engine crews, one pair on the footplate and the other set sleeping; they changed over at Swindon. The Old Oak Common crew started out from Penzance, so when we got to the signal box opposite Old Oak at 7.30 the train slowed down to let the London men get off and go across the tracks to the shed; I did the same.

'Who might you be, son?' they asked

I replied, 'I work at the shed too.'

But when I came back next morning, attached to my clocking-in card was a note to report to Tony Coles, the Supervisor Foreman.

'Where were you yesterday?' he asked.

Very frightened, I said I couldn't remember.

'Well, get your gear together. You're out for a month travelling around the Western Region with a chap called John.' I had to travel to Reading and be at the diesel depot

No 6007 *King William III* at Old Oak Common factory in 1957. *Ted Abear collection*

for 9.00am sharp. I was told that my wages would be sent on to me, but I said I would rather they be kept for me there for the month. I travelled back to Reading the same day, catching the 8.00am train!

Thursday was pay day at Old Oak. The pay was delivered in one of those large square railway security boxes in the morning. The pay clerk was Joe Robbins, and two others would be there to deal with it and get the pay packets filled. If I remember right it was a 2.00pm start, and there was always a queue waiting. One morning in 1957 or 1958 the pay office got robbed just after the delivery of the cash box. It caused a bit of a rumpus, and they had to get a fresh delivery from the bank.

The 8.00am train from Paddington was first stop Reading. On arrival I went straight down to the shed, crossing the lines next to the huge signal box. I waved to the signalman to ask for clearance to cross; someone looked out of the sash window and waved me over. I put up my thumb and stepped over all the points – I didn't fancy getting my foot caught between them. At the diesel depot I went to see the foreman.

'Welcome back, Pat!' said Eric, the mechanical foreman. 'We're waiting for you to come back and show the young apprentices how to mix the antifreeze as you were the best one who knew what he was doing.' I was honoured! 'John is waiting for you in the canteen,' continued Eric. 'He hasn't been here long. Where were you at Old Oak Common? Did you not get the message till this morning?'

'Not till 7 this morning.'

'But they knew yesterday.'

The factory traverser at Old Oak Common in 1958. *Ted Abear collection*

for one month's work, five days a week.'

'That'll keep me out of trouble!' I said, and he looked sideways at me.

So I had a month's work getting about and seeing the sights, instead of going out on a jolly.

*

Didcot was raining, cold and miserable – nothing changes! Anyway, the DMU that we wanted came into the station with Archie Davies driving it. We had a 3-hour slot and we had the coach set booked.

The day before I had rung the shed for permission to put the DMU into the fitting shop on No 1 road, but I asked Arthur not to say anything about it. The East Junction signalman knew what the score was and it was arranged to shunt the DMU back into

Ray Simms and Billy Gibbs with No 4073 *Caerphilly Castle* at Old Oak Common in June 1961.
Ted Abear collection

'Yes, my fault,' I admitted. I couldn't say where I had been as the rest of the boys would have got into trouble, so I took the blame, and laughed it off.

I went into the canteen and met John. We shook hands and I apologised for coming in late.

'You only live in Didcot.'

'Yes, but I work at Old Oak Common, and I didn't know till this morning when I got to work.'

'Well, you're here now. Let me explain what the job consists of and why we do it. We are going around the whole of the Western Region doing ultrasonic fatigue testing for cracks in axles, and the reports will be sent to Swindon. We have three DMUs here today to get on with, then tomorrow Didcot. We've been commissioned

Working on the valves of 'Britannia' No 70020 *Mercury* at Old Oak Common factory in 1955.
Ted Abear collection

the shed. Archie asked me if I wanted to drive her into the shed area. Well, I couldn't turn it down – that would have been silly! He said he would stand with me as we went into the shed.

John was in the rear cab, and he would sound the horn when he wanted it to stop. Arthur came out of his office and stood watching; no one knew anything about what was going on. As the front cab came into the shed entrance I blew the two-tone horn, and we came in slowly; men came out of the woodwork, seeing me at the controls and bringing the DMU into the shop. The fitting crew stood amazed. Then I heard the horn sounded at the other end, so I applied the vacuum brakes and stopped. I shut everything down, pulled out the key and handed it to Archie.

'You did well there, Pat,' he said.
'Cheers, Arch!'

I opened the door and dropped down to the ground, with Archie following. I walked back to see John, and he was pleased to say the least – we were in the dry to do the test and report the findings. He handed down the test equipment and I placed it on the floor carefully.

'Before we start, would you like a cuppa?'
'That would be a good idea, Pat!'

Archie went into the enginemen's cabin and a few minutes later brought out three cups of tea. John and I started work, and the men in the shed looked on, standing around to see what was happening.

I removed one side of the wheel's cap and put the set screws under the car's wheels. Then I cleaned off the grease from the area, and John came to my side and set up his scope machine, spreading the wires across the front on either side the axle. I removed the other end caps and laid the set screws together. Then I fixed the two sets of wires onto the axle ends in the same position as yesterday, as John had taught me.

Arthur came around the front of the cab and asked me what I was doing – he thought I was still at Old Oak Common. I introduced him to John as I got ready, then while they spoke I ran the extension lead into the Time Office as there was a plug behind the door. We were now ready to do the ultrasonic fatigue testing. Jim Tyler came up and asked me how I was doing.

'Hello, Jim – nice to see you again!'

He told me that he missed me and I told him that I would be back in Didcot in three months. He asked what we were doing, and I asked John if it was OK to show my fitter.

'Go ahead, Pat – you know what you're doing.'

I turned on the scope box, which sat in a round globe glass. If you looked into the glass you would see lines going straight. 'You have to imagine those lines indicate the axle and the metal of the axle,' I explained. 'If there is a break in those lines, like there is here, we have a fatigue in the axle and John has to report the findings and send the report to Swindon, where they will strip out and repair it.'

John heard what I said and looked down

The Time Office window at Old Oak Common in 1962. *Ted Abear collection*

No 7036 *Taunton Castle* with driver Arthur Evans with fireman Ted Abear, both Old Oak Common men. K. Leech fired the engine from Bath to Bristol, then Ted carried on to Chippenham. Mr Leech rode on the locomotive and took this picture, offering each engineman a copy. *K. Leech*

to see the break in the line. 'Well done, Pat – I only taught you yesterday.'

Jim asked if this was the only DMU we had to do, but I said I must have got lucky as we had to work across the whole of the Western Region. Arthur looked down at the scope and saw the same wiggly lines, with a few broken bits in the middle, showing where the fatigue and cracks were. He was intrigued.

'But you might be different at the other end. It might be OK. I'll give you a shout when we're ready.'

John and I worked down all the axles of the three-car set, ending at the cab at the other end, from where I had driven it into the shed. The findings were not good. Five axles had fatigue in them, so John decided to go into Arthur's office and ring Swindon straight away, explaining his concerns. He was told to stay where he was, and they would ring back. He stayed in the office speaking to Arthur, telling him how I had volunteered in my dinner hour as Eric Chard, the mechanical foreman, wanted to have four apprentices trained to mix the antifreeze the way I had done it the previous year. He told them the room had been named after me, and I was honoured!

I came into the office and said that it was all done and put back together. Arthur said, 'How's night school going, Pat?'

'I failed the course.'

'Are you going to resit it?'

'No,' I said, 'I just want to be a fitter and turner and enjoy my life.'

The report came back from Swindon to arrange for the three-car set to travel there tomorrow at the very earliest opportunity. John was to go with it and take me with him, as they wanted to meet me. John said that I had better go home and come back in the morning, as we were going to Swindon first thing – he would sort out the arrangements.

I hung about and went into the shop to speak to Jim. He said, 'We haven't done much since you left.'

'Missed me then, uncle?'

'Here we go again – silly talk.'

'You got to laugh,' I said.

'Yes, boyo. When are you coming back – three months? How did you hook up with this job?'

'I was chosen. I didn't know anything about it till two days ago as I was out on a jolly with some mates.'

'Do you travel daily?' he asked.

'Yes, but it's so tiring, and I have to rush to get the train every night at Paddington.' I told him I got the 6.05am, so had to be up at 4.30 to get down to Livings' Bakery for some grub and make my way to the station. Sometimes I was lucky if there were Old Oak men riding the train as they stopped at the signal opposite the shed, so I could get out of the coach and walk across with them to the shed.

'On Friday nights I get out early,' I continued, 'with permission from the foreman, as "Skip" Morgan comes into the canteen looking for me to go back to Paddington and I ride home in the cab with him, as he's the driver of the 5 o'clock in the evening.'

'No wonder you're thin and fit,' said Jim. 'Are you seeing Annie?'

'Only weekends. If I decide to come home from London I spend a lot more time up with the Scotch boys from Glasgow and the lads from Acton.'

'Where do you sleep?' he asked.

'In the hostel, in their rooms while they're at work doing nights.'

I told him that I had got into a league darts match in Richmond with Barry and a few of his mates, and we all met at the club. 'Best out of three. Last round I was pulled in as I was the reserve and someone went off sick. I was three sheets to the wind. They shouted out the score – they wanted two singles and a double, and they erupted when we won the league, with only three darts. We all went back to their place in Acton and I was offered some purple hearts. I said, "No thanks," and had a bottle of whisky, sharing it with Barry Hughes. We sat on the floor behind the settee.'

Then John came into the shop with Arthur and asked me to be at the station for 5.00 tomorrow morning on Platform 3; Archie would be the driver and would take me.

'I live in Swindon,' John explained, 'and you can you pick me up at Swindon station at 5.40, then we'll transfer over to the works. We'll take the DMU into the replacement shop. I'm afraid we shall have a day at Swindon.'

Arthur piped up, 'He'll be happy as he has a girl in the Enparts department!'

I walked home that afternoon and Mum was surprised. I had a bath and tea, then got changed and went to Annie's house, but she wasn't at home. I talked to her Dad and asked him if I could get engaged to his daughter. I pulled a small box from my pocket and showed it to Annie's Mum.

I stayed a while till Annie wandered in with her make-up smeared. 'Who have you been out with?' I asked. We had words, then I left, saying goodbye to her Mum and Dad. It was over. As I went out I heard screaming and shouting!

Mick saw Annie with a signalman's son during the week, and they were all over each other. He told me who it was.

34. Ultrasonic fatigue testing from Reading

I caught the DMU next morning and sat with Archie in the cab as we went to Swindon. As we entered the station we picked up John as arranged, and had permission from Control to drive into the factory. Archie took instructions from John as to where we had to go, as a new fitting shop had just opened.

We followed hand signals from one of the men who worked in the department. He put his hands above his head to indicate stop, then drew his hand sideways under his throat to tell us to shut down. We left the three-car set to have the axles removed. Outside was another three-car set ready to go back to Reading, and it looked as though we were going back to Reading in it, but first I was introduced to the foreman and the manager of the department and shown how they strip out the axles, and deal with minor incidents. It was all very interesting, and clean – the working conditions were just right. They thanked me for helping John, who had taken me under his wing!

We had an hour spare, so John asked if there was anywhere I wanted to go. 'Arthur said something about the Enparts department!' he said. 'Come back here in an hour and a half, as we must be away.'

I found my way up the stairs and knocked at the door of Phillip's office. 'Hello, Pat!' he said. 'Do you want a cuppa?'

'Yes, please.'

'Here she comes!' Sal opened the door and nearly fell over. I told her I was working at Old Oak Common for six months training, and had been chosen to work for the new department doing ultrasonic fatigue testing of axles, and we had found five axles yesterday at Didcot on a DMU. I had a couple of hours till I had to go back to Reading, but all I got to say to her was to ask her if she was courting.

'No,' she replied.

'Can I court you?'

She smiled, and we arranged to meet on Saturday morning, at the station at 8.40. Then she kissed me, but I had to run. 'See you Saturday!'

I was as free as a bird and a new life was starting.

Archie and I took the other DMU back, first stop Didcot, where I had to get off, then Arch travelled on to Reading diesel depot.

I was to meet John at Didcot next morning at 9.00, as we were going to Oxford to look at the three-car set we were travelling on in the siding, which would be a couple of hours' work. We stayed on the DMU as the passengers got off, and the guard approached us to enquire who we were. John explained to him that we had 2 hours to get the front wheels checked over with our equipment.

Once in the siding John handed me the ultrasonic fatigue testing gear, which I put in a safe place on the ground, and his tool box. He then climbed down with me, and we got stuck in. I got the covers off the ends of the axles and ran a long extension lead under the rails to the welding shop area, where I found a 13-amp plug. John got the wires together and straightened them out, and with luck the equipment sat right over a wooden sleeper.

As he was testing this front axles I went down to the rear and started to take off the end caps and wipe off the grease ready. Then I went back to where he stood and he showed me the scope. I viewed the wiggles going across the inner axle. 'Spot on!' I said. 'I've set everything down the other end.'

As John got on I followed him, finishing off by replacing the caps. Then he called me. 'Come and look, Pat.' The axle was fractured, and we both agreed this one was in a dangerous state. We located a phone and told the driver of the DMU to stay where he was till we returned with instructions. I took John into the Oxford workshop and introduced him to Bill Miles. I sat outside with the welder and he made me a cuppa, then a while later John came out and said they wanted the DMU at Swindon straight away, and that the other three-car set we sent down yesterday had to make its way here, urgently. I left the arrangements to the powers that be, as I was only the boy, but I was looking forward to the ride to Swindon!

We had to wait as the drivers had to swop over. We had an hour to kill, then it would be tight. We spoke to the driver and explained the situation, asking him if he would like to go to Swindon or back to Reading – we gave him the choice. He chose Swindon.

'Tomorrow we're going back to Reading, Pat,' said John, 'as we have three sets to investigate, which should take an easy three days. That should take us up to Friday. We'll be at that depot for a week, as that is going to be our repair depot for a while.'

I rang wages at Old Oak Common to have my pay sent to Reading.

'Haven't you had any money since you've been with me?' asked John. 'Why didn't they sent it to your home address?'

'My Mum would take the lot.'

'Oh, I see…'

We saw the three-car set come into the station, passengers waiting as it stopped. But the driver shut down and locked the outer doors, then walked through the train, and that was the last time we saw him. The guard blew his whistle, waved his green flag and stepped back inside his door as we took the DMU out of the station.

We got the signal and drew out onto the middle line. The driver sounded the horn and waved to the signalman; we were only minutes behind another DMU, so our driver had to slow down as we didn't want to race away and catch him up. Twenty minutes later we came to Didcot North Junction signal box and were transferred over the West Curve, which was new to me. Passing Foxhall Junction box we took the main line to Swindon. I waved to the signalman as he looked out of his sash window with his duster in his hand – he was shocked to see me waving at him, as I knew him! Forty minutes later we would be in Swindon.

John said that he enjoyed what we were achieving, and we were making progress – twice in one week to Swindon and the new workshop.

We were to be in Reading at 8.00am the following day. John said, 'I guess you'll want to go to Enparts when we reach Swindon!'

'If it's OK with you.'

'Wait till we get in and we'll sort it out and see how we are. Have you got a young lady in Didcot?'

'Three years,' I answered, 'and I was going to ask her to get engaged this week. I even asked her parents for their permission. But it never materialised.'

At Swindon the DMU went into the new part of the factory, the fitters guiding us into the shop. The driver was fascinated by what was happening. We climbed down onto the new steps and John told me that we had hour. 'We're going back to the station, you're going back to Didcot and the three-car will be going back to Reading.'

I legged it over to Enparts and gingerly knocked on the door. 'Hello, Pat!' said Phillip. 'Twice in one week!'

Sal appeared. I asked if we were still OK for Saturday, but she wasn't too keen. 'Sorry – best that we don't, as I've found someone local to go out with.'

'OK, thanks for being honest with me,' I said. I said my goodbyes to them both, and walked out into the unknown, back to the new shop.

The management gave us repair cards for checking three more DMUs, so we climbed aboard the set, Control gave us the signal and we drew away from the factory to Swindon station. John got off, leaving the testing gear equipment in the car. 'We'll start again in the morning at Reading. You'd better ring them to take the equipment off the car when it gets back to its own depot.'

'I'll mention it to the driver while we are going back,' I said.

*

I got up at normal time, had some breakfast and left home 6.45 to catch the 7.20am, with

The fuelling point at Reading depot.
Michael Russell collection

a couple of the lads. The train was a stopper, all stations to Reading. Out came the cards and we played three-card brag in our own compartment; if anyone tried the sliding door to get in we told them it was a private party. We started to get excited as the pot got bigger, but Dennis Tyler won it, jammy sod!

At Reading we all bundled out of the carriage onto the platform and made our way towards the giant signal box; with the signalman's permission we legged it over the rails and points and ran down towards the diesel depot.

I went upstairs and made a cuppa, waiting for John. The first three-car sets started to come into the service bay, and looking at the amount I guess we had at least a week's work, checking every detail on all the double axles and writing out the reports. We even had to go to the fuelling point and fatigue-test two three-car sets up there. The units would come in from all over the Western Region, as Reading was the main depot.

Eric Chard, the mechanical foreman, came to see me and handed me a package. 'Here, you'd better sign for it,' he said.

'Ah, yes, my wages,' I said. 'I told them to leave it till I got back to Old Oak. I should be back in three weeks, but seeing as I'm stationed here, I could get it here if, that's OK with you, Eric.'

'Why didn't they send it to your home address?' he asked.

'Mother would have spent it all. "What's mine is hers." I worked for nothing while she took the lot!'

John had received a phone call from Swindon to say there was a six-car set coming from Paddington to Didcot direct, and was there any chance we could travel to Didcot today and do the necessaries. John replied that it would mean working overtime and travelling time for the two of us. 'Stay on the phone,' they said, 'and I'll asked the management.' Then John said to me, 'What are you doing now, Pat?'

'I'm about to get the end caps off that three-car set outside.'

'Wait a moment as something is going on.' Then John got the OK; Control would organise a driver. He asked if it would be possible to shunt it into Didcot shed. 'Ask them to take it in,' he said, 'and if nothing is in the fitting shop run it straight through and out the other side. Ask them to talk to Arthur Brinkley, the workshop foreman.' I told John to please ask Swindon to contact Old Oak to pay my overtime and send it to me at Reading, when my wages were due.

I asked Eric if he could ask for a van and driver to take us to the station with our gear, so we could catch the 9.00am. John said that we would be back tomorrow.

When we reached Didcot John handed me the equipment on the platform as the guard scrutinised us. As soon as the door was shut behind us the guard waved his flag and blew his whistle, and the train drew out with so much speed – these new diesels were on fire, and couldn't wait to get to the next station!

We carried the equipment down to the shed between us. I looked around the shed and sidings – nothing had changed. As we walked past the shedmaster's office area I saw the big clock, noting the time – 10.15. My arms ached.

'A cuppa, I think, John, before we start.'

Ultrasonic fatigue testing from Reading

He agreed, and we walked down the concrete path alongside No 1 road, down the length of the DMU. It seem funny seeing a diesel sitting inside the shed, with no sulphurous smoke and steam!

The shop looked good – we had the whole road right into the shop and out the other end. We left the equipment on the floor near the crane's 'A' frame, out of everyone's way. Jim and Arthur were standing at the forge, and beckoned us over. I said, 'Do you mind if I make some tea as we're both parched?'

I put the kettle on, and Arthur said that he had some milk in the office, and went and got it. I went to my locker and brought out the tea things. John was taking it all in.

'What time are you two working till?' asked Arthur.

'At the moment 9, maybe 10. We have Swindon's permission – it's got to be done tonight.'

I asked John how he was getting home, and said he could stay at my house, but he said he'd better go home.

'Jim is offering to help you both,' said Arthur.

'Sounds good. What say you, John?'

So it was agreed, but 'Just one thing,' I said. 'I'm starving and have got no grub. How about we all go to the hostel later and get some cooked food and come back and square this job away?' We all agreed on 1pm.

Jim asked John what the plan was. 'Pat, and you Jim split up and take off all the end caps and wipe out the grease.'

Then Arthur said, 'I can help too. What can I do?'

'Would you like to help me fit the wiring?' John replied. 'Then I can show you what to look for.'

At 1 o'clock we all got washed up and went to the Polar Star for some grub. I could have eaten a scabby cat! We all had a full-blown dinner and pud. I saw Mr Sullivan and we exchanged pleasantries; he told me he missed me, and asked where I was working. When I told him he said, 'Seems like you've gone up in the world, Pat!'

'I can't say that,' I replied, 'as I'm still an apprentice fitter.'

I treated them to the meal – it was a couple of quid, and I was on good money with London weighting. We walked back with full stomachs, and I went to Midwinter's and bought a pint of milk for tea later on.

My brother Paul came in, as he was on nights again, then Bob followed; they stood watching, and couldn't believe the length of the train. They had two options, to get to their tool box and go outside, or walk around the front of the DMU. Arthur had gone home, but Jim was still there working side by side with me. There was an awkward moment when he paused, then he reached out and told me that when he left work one Saturday lunchtime there was someone waiting at the entrance of the station asking where I was.

'What did you tell her?'

'I didn't know where you were.'

'That's good enough, mate,' I said, then I told him about nearly getting engaged. He was shocked.

As I made the tea at the forge I asked John how things were going. 'Found any?'

'None.'

'That's good – now I'll grease and refit the covers as I go.'

I loved working in the shed when night time came; it was eerie with the ghosts of old enginemen with cleaners from years past. I imagined ghostly figures walking between the engines and down near the enginemen's cabin, seeing them wander through the walls of years past.

Time went on and we had just a few covers to finish off; it was just passed 9.25 when we finished. John said that nothing had been found. 'Now you get yourself away and we'll get the driver to take these cars out of the shed.'

'What if we put the gear into the compartment,' I suggested, 'then he can take the car to Reading depot and maybe unload it there for when we come back in the morning.'

John agreed. 'I'll meet you at Reading in the morning,' he said, 'say about 8.'

I walked home with Jim. He pushed his bicycle and I walked with him till we parted up near St Birinus School; he lived up Queensway and I was off into Sinodun Road. He apologised to me over our falling-out, saying how sorry he was, and I felt the same. I felt really bad about dropping that 4-inch metal block on his fingers.

'I can't wait for you to come back as you're a good fitter, Pat.'

'Only three more months Jim. How is Davies doing?'

'I think he's missing you,' said Jim.

'I'll tell you a secret,' I said. 'That smell was my doing.'

'See you when you come back home, mate.'

'I'll look forward to it!'

*

It was back to Reading next morning. I caught the same train as all the apprentices and slept all the way – I was dead to the world. The boys shook me as we came into Reading station – I could have slept through an earthquake, I was so tired. It was an effort to walk down towards the diesel depot, putting one foot in front of the other.

At the depot stood the six-car set. I helped to unload the ultrasonic fatigue testing equipment from the compartment and took it into the depot, as it was raining. I told Eric it was clear, the first one since we started testing. They must have been a bad batch.

When John arrived he went directly to Eric's office, while the driver of a waiting van went and got the rest of the equipment. John told me that we were off to Paddington and Ranelagh Road. 'We've got to catch the fast train to London, and try to get back to Ranelagh Road. If we talk to the driver of this train he might be going back into the sidings.'

We caught the fast train to Paddington, leaving the equipment out in the corridor, as London was only 20 minutes away. As we drew up to 'the Lawn' at the terminus we got our stuff and I left John looking after it while I walked down towards the buffers where the diesel was humming away. I knocked on the cab door and one of the crew members opened it.

'Hello mate,' I said. 'Is there any chance you are backing out into Ranelagh Road?' I explained who we were, and that we would like a ride with our equipment. I showed him my travel pass.

'Yes,' came the reply. 'We have to fuel up.'

I waved to John, and we got our stuff loaded into the rear cab. The coaches were pulled back to Old Oak Common to be cleaned, then the diesel started to pull out of the station, gently running to Ranelagh Road. On arrival I got down and John handed me the equipment. An old guy who looked after the engine crews came from nowhere, and we saw the three cars standing over in a corner next to the wall. We had to be very quiet as we didn't want piss thrown all over us!

There was a coal-shoveller in residence at Ranelagh Road. We only knew him as 'China'. He always had a clay pipe in his mouth, and his job was to shovel the coal forward in the tenders for all the steam crews on return jobs. There was an old 'MOGO' wagon body on the ground against the far wall, and this was his cabin and his home – he lived there all the time. He was a small man but always dirty; when he wanted to wash he got a bucket of hot water from one of the locos.

I told John about the times when loco safety valves blew off and the women in the buildings adjacent to the sidings would throw piss pots over onto the crews – or so the stories went. The locos all round the turntable brought back memories, especially of the bad-tempered old dear whose first name was 'Ginger' living in the buildings with the extended backs. If your engine started blowing off and making a noise she used to come out cursing and swearing, and throw milk bottles down at the enginemen if they were in the tender shovelling coal forward. One Old Oak Common fireman

As steam declined Ranelagh Road, outside Paddington, became a fuelling point for the new diesels.

named Harry Odd was there in the tender one day and his engine, a 'Britannia', blew off with a huge bang. Out she came and started throwing bottles – she hit Harry on the back of his shoulders. So Harry grabs the next bottle, lets fly and hits her with it. By the time the law arrived Harry had gone and nobody had seen anything – we railwaymen stick together.

Part of No 5 link here was the Ranelagh Bridge Pilot turn, which booked on at 3.55am to prepare a 'Castle' Class loco (1hr 20min prep time), then ran light engine to Ranelagh Bridge to be stabled in the Pilot siding in front of the signal box. It was not unknown for the loco to stand there all day. It would be relieved by a set of men about 10 in the morning. The early men would then go Paddington station and return on empty carriage stock to Old Oak Common. The late turn Ranelagh Bridge men would bring the loco light to the shed around midnight and stable it there ready for the job again next morning.

John and I got stuck in. I went around taking off the end caps and wiping the grease away while John set up the scope machine. We now had a routine: he would take off his end caps and I would do the same, test the axle, put the caps back on, then onto the next, and so on. It worked well, a good system, but last night it had been a doddle as we had so many pairs of hands helping at Didcot shed.

We swapped places and I was allowed to use the scope. We were soon squared away and sat looking at each other for a while, debating the next plan of action, as this three-car set was OK and recorded on John's list.

'Back to Reading,' I said. 'I suppose I'll be going back to Old Oak soon then, seeing that I've been out only two weeks of the month's work.'

'We might have to go into Old Oak tomorrow,' said John.

'Can't we leave it till a few days and see if there are any more? What if you spoke to HQ when we get back to Reading – and you could also ask Swindon to get in touch with Old Oak to have my overtime sent to the pay office.' I gave him my pay number, and he did the deed.

The diesel that had brought us to Ranelagh Road took us back up to Paddington. The driver said, 'Stay in the cab as we are stopping at Reading.' That saved us the lifting of the gear and struggling out with it onto the ground.

35. Fireball

I had to book a day off on the Friday as I was having my scooter test at Newbury, the nearest test centre, at 11.00am. I rode the scooter there as I had 'L' plates. Before going out on the road I informed the test person that I had heard a knocking from my front wheel, and it sounded like the wheel bearing, but I was informed that would not matter.

The tester said, 'Now, I will walk around Newbury and look at you doing everything correctly. I want to see hand signals and stopping at the correct distances. When you see me jump out from behind a car I would like you to stop straight away. Off you go then.'

I rode out of the test area and proceeded on my way around the town. I never saw anyone but kept my eyes straight in front of me. After an hour I wondered where he was until I looked ahead and saw someone laid out on the road covered with a blanket.

I stopped my scooter, made it secure at the kerbside and went back to where the person lay.

'Are you OK?' I asked.

The figure replied, 'I've signed your certificate.' I had passed the test!

'But why are you laid out on the floor,' I asked him.

He replied, 'I thought it was you coming down the road so I jumped out in front of you, but it was another motorbike and he nearly ran me over!'

I took the paperwork and went back home to Didcot, laughing all the way. People must have thought I was crazy, with tears of laughter running down my face. I had to pull into a layby to wipe away the tears!

I went down to the shed, but not via the station. I followed the dirt road between the sewage farm and the East Loop and left the scooter near the railway embankment. I scrambled up the grass bank and stood near the main line, looking both ways before crossing over, then ran to the back end of the shed.

I peeped into the shop, saw Jim and waved. I went down towards the cabin and opened the door. No one was about so I left two pairs of dirty overalls on the floor, and took two clean pairs from the tin box. Clarky wasn't about – he must have retired by now. I wondered who had taken over the job. Suddenly Paul stepped into the cabin, and said that he was doing the overalls now. 'What do you need?'

'I'd better take three pairs – I don't know where I might be trained,' explaining about the ultrasonic testing. 'How are you getting on at home with Mum?'

'We won't go there, bruv! Do you know, when I came back into the house one pay day I showed her a white £5 note. Joan was with me, but Mum demanded it.'

I told him about Dick, as he never gave her any housekeeping money at all, but she demanded all my pay, so I was working for nothing.

'You left home I heard, Pat.'

'Yes, Paul, I went down to the Polar Star and stayed there for several weeks. She went crazy – she even shouted at Dad.'

Then he said he had been offered a place at Reading Diesel Depot, 'But to be honest I'm not sure, Pat. I might be better looking at the private sector, something to get my teeth into. Maybe William Press at Abingdon, who operate crawler equipment. It might do for you when you come out of your time, but keep this to ourselves, bruv. Here are your overalls. Go careful, Pat.'

I went to the shop to see Jim, and Arthur appeared and we had a chat. Then I asked him if I could use the phone to find out what was happening on Monday. Arthur rang through to Reading depot and handed the receiver to me. Eric went and got John, who said that first thing we were going to Old Oak carriage sidings, as there was a six-car set there to be fatigue-tested. He asked me how I had got on with my test. 'Passed. I'll tell you on Monday – it will make you laugh!'

'Have a good weekend,' he said. 'By the way, I missed you today.'

'Behave yourself, Pat,' said Arthur. 'See you in a couple of months.' I waved goodbye to Jim and rode home.

*

I went down to Mick's over the weekend and we went to Harwell, where there was a dance at the Atomic Research Establishment. The singer was John William 'Long John' Baldry. There was a coach from the Post Office, and we went to the dance, and on the pull. Everyone we knew was there, and we both pulled.

We caught the bus back to Harwell and asked the driver to let us off in the village. The bar at the Crispin was open to private members only.

We stayed for breakfast this time as we were not going to walk home in the rain. I asked for a Mars bar and stuck it in my pocket – as I didn't want my mate to pass out on me. We called for a taxi from Didcot and got home some time before 10 o'clock, so Mick had to take his insulin. I made an excuse about staying at Mick's overnight, telling Mum and Dad that we had missed the bus at Harwell.

Mick subsequently applied for a position at the Atomic Research Establishment and got it. He left the railway in 1964, just after that dance. He had liked what he'd seen.

On the Monday morning I caught the Reading stopper with all the apprentices, talking about seeing Long John Baldry, what they had got up to over the weekend, and what records they had bought. Then I mentioned that I had passed my bike test, and what had happened with the instructor, and they roared with laughter. I felt sorry for the tester really – he was a decent man, and it was just unfortunate that he had jumped out into the road. Silly person!

The following month I part-exchanged my scooter for a red 250cc BSA from Trevor Goodall's in Lower Broadway, Didcot.

*

John and I caught the fast train from Reading to Paddington. On arrival the train engine was uncoupled and a steam engine coupled at the other end. We sat in the same compartment and rode the empty carriage stock back to Old Oak Common, with the ultrasonic fatigue testing gear ready in one of the corridors. I told John about my scooter test incident and he also couldn't stop laughing. Some cleaners rode the empty carriages back to the depot with us, clearing up the waste paper and rubbish.

Suddenly it went dark as the carriages ran into the carriage shed. Looking out of the window all that could be seen was carriage stock, including the Royal Train coaches, being guarded by Railway Police, on their own line. I knew someone who tried to enter the end coach to help himself, but he had to leg it straight out of the back end and run for his life, ducking and diving under the carriages with the cops after him.

The ultrasonic equipment was unloaded and we found the six-car set on its own track under the shed roof. We reported to the chargehand and explained the situation; we also wanted to know what time the unit would be used, which was early the following morning.

We got stuck into the project and got it clear later than normal, finding that six axles were bad with fatigue. John went to the foreman's office and reported the situation, explaining that we would have to contact Swindon. After phoning, John said that we were off to Swindon later, to the factory. We loaded the equipment back into the DMU, locked the driver's door and wandered over to the factory. I showed John where 'Legs' Diamond's office was, and went off for a cuppa, but was called back. 'Where were you off to?' asked 'Legs'. He called his gofer into the office and asked him to make tea for the three of us.

John explained the situation about the help I had given Swindon factory and, when asked how long I would be away from my normal job, John said, 'Another week at the most depending on the DMUs and if they decide to check main-line diesels.'

The tea came and I slurped mine down.

'Thirsty are you? Would you like another?'

'Yes please,' I said. 'A bigger mug this time, please!'

'You'll have what you're given.'

'Yes, sir, Mr Diamond.'

You can't take him anywhere – only a second time, to apologise!

We had to get back to the six-car set as it was getting close to the time. I said to John, 'Why don't we ring Reading to pick up the equipment from the train and take it to the depot, which will save us having to carry it on to Swindon?'

Mr Diamond arranged this with Control, and meanwhile I went and collected my wages. When I opened my wage packet, my, what a few hours extra overtime can do to help an apprentice! I was rolling in the green paper stuff – someone might think I had robbed the Bank of England! I would have to hide this when I got home…

As arranged, we stopped at Reading, unloaded the equipment, got the signal and shot off to Swindon. At the works we entered the factory, and management was waiting for us. John explained everything and handed over his reports for their inspection. There was another six-car set waiting outside.

I said, 'See you at Reading in the morning.'

'Thanks, Pat. We have to have a serious talk in the morning.'

I felt a little down, as I knew I was going back to Old Oak Common, sooner rather than later.

I returned to Didcot; the driver slowed down at the station enough for me to hop off

Next morning came the serious talk with John. 'I can keep you a couple of days but you need to go back to your temporary depot, Pat, as Mr Diamond wants you back.'

I reported back to Old Oak the very next morning. I had two months left out of the six months. I was choked – however, I had learned the basis of ultrasonic fatigue testing.

When I got home that night I told my parents not to bother coming down to the station on Friday nights as I would not be coming home for the next two months. London in the 1960s was the 'in' place to be and I felt like enjoying myself, walking around Oxford Street, going to the parties at Acton, and sleeping rough in the hostel – I was becoming used to sleeping in hostels.

I wondered whether there would be any awkwardness between me and Annie, having not seen each other for a few months as my life started to change for the better. As a result of our prolonged estrangement Annie told me that she had come down to the station every Friday night and waited for the train to come in from Paddington, then, seeing I was wasn't on it, she wandered off home upset. Later I went to see her and we patched it up – but were we both back on track?

Because I would not be around much longer, being between depots training, with roughly 18 months to two years left before coming out of my apprenticeship, Arthur suggested that I go with Jim Hale to Swindon to show him my contacts and who to report to when ordering spares. However, I didn't show him my usual contacts, but instead took him somewhere else and into another office area to point out the procedures. He already knew the way to Reading and Oxford to take the pipes for welding, as he had done that before I came on the scene. If Arthur found out he would have had my guts for garters – the worm had turned.

*

In the early hours of Friday 14 August 1964, while Didcot slept, a fireball came near to destroying the town when an 8F struck a loaded oil train. Ex-LMS 8F 2-8-0 No 48734 came into the marshalling yard at Didcot tender-first from the Oxford area and stopped outside the North Junction signal box window. Gerald 'Golly' Collins was working the night shift at North Junction, and the 8F's driver, Mr Hitchcock, and his fireman,

Ron Duke, both Oxford engine crew, were having a joke and enjoying the laughter and banter and not paying proper regard as to where they were. When the driver got the word from 'Golly', 'OK, off you go,' he should have reversed into the yard to pick up his freight train.

However, at 2.17am the Fawley (Southampton) Esso petroleum freight train was passing North Junction on its way to Bromford Bridge in Birmingham. While the residents of the Berkshire town lay fast asleep in their beds the Stanier 8F ran out of the marshalling yard and straight into the side of the passing train of fuel tankers, splitting open one of the 12 full petrol tankers with its buffers as if it was a tin can.

The signalman sent 6 bells – 'Obstruction Danger' – to Appleford, East Junction, Foxhall Junction and West End signal boxes, then took control, ringing Didcot fire brigade. He then rang the shed at Didcot to report what had happened.

The Bromford Bridge oil train was always a shift turn for the top link Didcot locomen. The driver was Stan Wheeler, and felt that dreaded shockwave through the train. Knowing that something had happened, he slowed the train as quickly as he could, bringing it to a standstill. Fireman Matt Fitzgerald climbed down from the diesel engine and ran back to see what had happened. Seeing the damage, he ran back to report to his driver and Cyril Tolley, the guard, who worked to the book and wouldn't let anything go amiss.

Eleven tankers crashed over onto their sides with the force of the collision and erupted in flames. Crude oil spilled out, running like water under the ashpan of the 8F, where fire and ashes lay over the sleepers from the impact of the crash. The oil burst into a fireball, fusing the locomotive to the steel railway line and engulfing it in flames.

The driver, fireman and guard of the petrol train went back to help the Oxford enginemen, Driver Hitchcock and Fireman Duke, who had caused the damage, to help uncouple the rear of the train, with the heat from the flames burning around them.

There was argument and shouting between the men, with the fire getting closer as the tankers were being uncoupled. The heat was terrible and their clothes were smouldering. However, they got hold of themselves and stopped arguing – if they had left it to burn, lower Didcot would have been destroyed, together with the North Junction signal box and the locomotive shed.

The signalman came to find the driver of the diesel and, having received direct instructions, he gave the order for the front of the Fawley petrol train to go ahead and get clear of the area, before the fire started to get out of control. The flames did get worse, shooting up into the air, with more tanks exploding – the heat was unbearable. What was left of the petrol train was burning out of control with the steam locomotive locked and entangled within it, and the coal in the tender burning!

Waiting at Appleford station was the District Inspector, to give the all clear. After speaking with the signalman, the Didcot crew were given instructions to proceed with caution to Hinksey yard in Oxford, where an Inspector would check the train before it travelled on to Bromford.

Meanwhile at the rear of the fuel train the tanks were uncoupled, but the vacuum pipe had to be released by the men, who then tried desperately to push the full tankers back away from the fire with crowbars under their wheels. That left 12 tankers burning out of control, the heat engulfing each tanker in turn; the pressure built up inside the tank, forcing the metal to expand to breaking point, than an explosion spurted crude oil over the rest of the area, onto the wooden sleepers, each side of the grass bank, until the whole area was engulfed with flames. Even when the fire was out, crude oil had soaked into the earth, leaving a terrible smell.

That morning as I went to work all I could smell was crude oil, and all we could see was black smoke rising into the air. Didcot was lucky that day. As I rode my pushbike down towards the station I was stopped by a gentleman from Maidenhead, who told me how he had seen an orange ball and a cloud of black smoke filling the sky, as if a volcano had erupted. He did not know where or what had happened – he had just got into his car and followed the glow. He asked me how he could get closer to have a look, and I gave him instructions; he thanked me and drove off.

Signalman Harold Radway saw the blaze from his box in Westbury at 2.40am.

After logging on at the office, I walked down as far as the Fire Brigade allowed, checking that I was not wearing metal studs or carrying matches. It was too dangerous to proceed, so I had to walk back to the safe zone within the shed perimeter.

A small footbridge crossed the main Oxford lines near Appleford, and the heat of the burning crude oil twisting the ironwork; the breakdown crews had to remove the footbridge with the help of the steam cranes before the main lifts to remove the Esso petrol tankers. The footbridge was scrapped.

*

Cyril was a Didcot guard working on freight trains, and I had often spoken to him about several incidents that had happened while travelling in the guard's van from Kidlington to the Oxford area. One night the engine crew left Banbury with a freight train. Cyril, sitting in his van, suddenly felt a vibration through the wagons near Kidlington. He thought a wagon had jumped off the road and was running along on the chairs. Looking out from the canopy towards the locomotive, he strained his eyes in the darkness looking for sparks coming from the wheels, but the train travelled on towards Oxford. Stopping at their destination at Hinksey yard, the Didcot engine crew, consisting of Driver Tom White and Fireman Arthur Fenn, uncoupled

The burned-out tankers of the oil train.

the freight from the locomotive. Meanwhile Cyril inspected the freight with his lamp where he remembered that vibration came from, but there was nothing wrong; no wagons had left the road. He walked up to the loco, still baffled by what had happened, climbed onto the footplate and got himself to Didcot shed and home to bed.

The following week the same thing happened again – same place, same thing. This time, when the freight train had drawn into Hinksey yard he walked slowly, checking each wagon, noting where it was in the train and what sort it was. It turned out that empty Esso fuel tanks had caused the problem running over the uneven ballast below the sleepers. Cyril reported it to the Controller at Reading, and wrote it up in his logbook – incident, time, place, and tank number. However, Control reported back saying that Esso were testing experimental tankers on many of the freight trains.

*

Eventually the badly burned LMS 8F locomotive was dragged from the turntable into the lifting shop, its screaming rusty wheels and sticking con-rods looking as though they would never turn again, and grinding noises coming from the engine and tender axle boxes.

The crew involved consisted of Dave Davies, his fitter's mate Jim Hale, then Jimmy Tyler and me. The big double doors were closed at both ends, then we started work on her. We stripped the con-rods off both sides and with the small chain pulley crane lifted all the parts into the tender and roped them together. Then, clearing out the axle box oil holes, we refilled them with oil, and even got a hand drill and drilled through the molten white metal bush to get to the journal.

Jimmy found some wooden planks, cut them to size and refitted them on the burned footplate. We drained the tender of water – what was left of it, for it had partly boiled dry. We took off the piston covers on both sides and anything that was hanging off, such

The 8F 2-8-0 locomotive engine that caused the fire on the crude oil train stands outside the fitting shop ready to be removed to be cut up for scrap. *John Stretton collection*

as broken pipes. Then we removed the valve guides so there wasn't any movement when the wheels went round. This all took weeks to do, and the main tasks were to free off the wheels and axle boxes underneath the rusted, burnt engine.

Once the task was complete we brought another locomotive in on No 1 road and coupled it up to pull the 8F out of the shed to see how freely she ran. We oiled all the ports as she went along, then back into the fitting shop she went; we had to spread sand on the wooden block floor to gather the spilt oil after we soaked every point again; we had to get the wheels turning. Then the dead engine was shunted outside the shop once more.

Several weeks later came the order to move the engine to Tyseley shed. Before I signed off that day I had to go to the oil stores and fill up all oil containers and get a load of cotton waste. We lifted all the oil and waste into the tender, just in case the locomotive should seize up again while travelling to Birmingham, from where she would be scrapped. There would be no more steam mixed with oil to give this locomotive that distinctive smell.

It was a premature end to 19-year-old No 48734, one of the newest of its class, having been completed at the LNER's Darlington Works at the end of 1945. As LNER No 3129 its first shed was Dunfermline, where it entered traffic on 1 November 1945. It became No 3529 in March 1947 to make way for the mass arrival of repatriated 'WD' 2-8-0s, which in turn meant that the Stanier design was concentrated on the LMS routes. Our engine went to Crewe South on loan on 16 September 1947, but the date of its the next identity change to No 8734 was not recorded. It became a permanent resident upon nationalisation on 1 January 1948. Sixteen days later, it was off to Buxton LNW, and was officially renumbered 48734 on 20 September 1948. It went to Lancaster on 15 September 1956 for a single week, then it went back to Buxton, Crewe South again in November of that year, and its final shed was Bescot, reaching there on 7 January 1961, just before its final intermediate overhaul at Crewe. Its official withdrawal date was 3 October 1964. There was no hope whatsoever of a reprieve, and it had been broken up at Crewe by the first week of November.

When the big day came I was asked to go with the other three, wearing plenty of warm clothes and taking food together with a flask, as we would be riding the 8F, all four of us in the cab. The locomotive that pulled her was another Tyseley engine.

It was an early start and a very cold day as I remember. There had been a frost and every part of the ironwork was white. Coupled up on No 1 road, we got the go ahead from the main office; the driver had read the notice boards for any stops on the way, but we had a clear road. As we went past North Junction signal box the driver of the leading engine sounded the whistle a few times and we hung out over the side and waved. As we went over the Appleford iron bridge across the Thames I threw some coal eggs into the water, not realising how close the ironwork was to the engine.

We went through the centre road at Oxford, then Banbury, and finally Birmingham Snow Hill and Tyseley, where we dropped her off. We then walked back to Snow Hill and caught a train to Oxford, changing for Didcot and getting in late. The most upsetting thing was that I felt dirty travelling in a passenger train in my railway clothes. But what a different world out there! I only knew my part of the old Great Western Railway, and was very biased.

Wantage Road station on the main line to Swindon was closed to passengers, and someone working at BR thought of a good use for its redundant footbridge, which was the same design as the one destroyed in the fire. The bridge was carefully dismantled and transported on flat 'Macaw' wagons to the site of the original, and re-erected.

36. A brush with death

It was a bad start to the day on Thursday 15 December 1964. I went to work on my pushbike, and when I got near to the Kynaston Road and Mereland Road junction I encountered a work coach containing Compton employees picked up from Didcot and surrounding villages; Compton was a company that built mobile cranes.

I was riding my bicycle on the left-hand side of the road coming towards the junction, and still some 20 yards away, when the coach came across the centre of the road and couldn't get back to its own side of the road. It seemed that the driver was struggling to control the vehicle at the speed he was doing, and he hit me full on in the centre of the radiator. My bicycle went one way towards the left front wheel and I fell towards the right wheel arch and in front of the wheel, with my body trapped from my left pelvis to the top of my chest. The coach was still moving along and I felt the wheel running around my ribs and stomach. I hammered on the bus's frame, shouting for the driver to stop for heaven's sake. I really felt like a wooden tapered block stuck under the tyre. I was pushed along Kynaston Road on my back for 6 metres, with the front wheel crushing my chest. To this day I don't know how that front wheel never ran over me – my guardian angel was with me all the time.

My hands were free, and I was banging on the side of the coach, shouting 'Stop!' Eventually it did. The driver went missing and another man got into the driver's seat and reversed the coach off me. (Allan Trinder was on the bus at the time and he told me the story in 1984. I rang my wife and said I was going to be late home, and took the guy on a pub crawl, stopping at every pub on the way home from the Oxford Crane Company to Didcot. I couldn't thank the guy himself – Morris was his first name.)

I was cold laid on the ground and thought I was going to die. My injuries were severe, and the ambulance men said that they didn't know how I stayed alive. I was conscious all the time until I ended up in hospital. When I arrived into the Oxford Infirmary in Woodstock Road I was transferred from the ambulance to a recovery bed. This was the worst part. I remember that when the hospital staff lifted me up and over onto the bed I prayed that they wouldn't drop me – I felt like a bag of loose bones.

My Mum and Dad came into the hospital and I heard the doctor say, 'Have you signed the paper?' My Dad said he had. I saw someone cut my right arm, but I never felt anything, then a tube was fitted into the cut. Then I saw the blood fill the tube. I was given an injection, and was told to count to ten. I got to five.

When I was being operated on in theatre I died. I understand that the staff resuscitated me, and when I came out of the theatre's doors I died again. I was resuscitated again, and was taken into the recovery room to rest, where they could keep an eye on me. I knew nothing of what was going on; my parents came to my bedside but I was out of this world.

When I woke a few days later I looked around the room, seeing everyone walking behind glass. It was an enclosed area with glass surrounds, and again I died. The priest was summoned to give me the last rites. I seemed to leave my body above the room, and saw the priest at my bedside; I saw the doctor and nurses trying to revive me, and saw myself lying in the bed. I had two angels holding me up in the air; I felt the feather and wing of one of the angels that touched my shoulder. The room was light blue, and it was so peaceful and quiet.

Then with a jolt I came back into the world of the living.

I was told of my injuries: one punctured lung, a broken left pelvis, and all the ribs in my chest broken. I had carbon monoxide in my chest, together with other internal injuries. I had a tube in my throat, and when they took it out the nurse put a tube inside the trachea just to clean the area. They washed the outer tube with surgical spirit, and sometimes a drop travelled down my throat. God, I did drink a gallon of water! It was there to remove the carbon monoxide from my chest, with the help of a tube and the hospital's vacuum system.

I couldn't talk. When I woke up one morning and tried to say something no sound came out, so the nurse put her hand over my throat, then the sound came. I asked for some water. I couldn't understand what this thing stuck in my windpipe was there for. The nurse made a plug from rubber, and put it into the hole in the middle of the trachea so I could talk. The nurses wanted to hear me say something, so they gathered round my bed, and when I finally said a few words they clapped and cheered.

I had to have 30 injections each day to keep me alive, and the doctors said that if I had smoked I would not have lived.

My Dad and two brothers came and visited me as I lay in bed, and Mum came when possible, catching the train to Oxford.

At night and sometimes in the early morning I saw a man with half his face blown off, with only half a nose and one eye, walking by the annex. That frightened me considerably.

Then for some unknown reason, because of my body and what I had gone through, I messed the bed, and I was ashamed, but the nurses were good and told me not to worry.

I was also a human guinea pig, as the path lab kept coming into my room and trying out drugs. I had a tube embedded in my back that went into my body, into my stomach. It was taped down across my shoulder and down my back; every time the technical staff put a drug down the tube I had to tell them the effects of what was happening, if it worked or not. I guess really I was dying, and while I was still breathing they used me.

Then the day came when I was transferred out of the annex into a corner room, before being allowed to enter the ward. I had constant supervision 24/7, with seven people looking after me. One day the doctor said I was going to be taken for a walk to see how I was adjusting. I had a my jimjams on and the nurse put a dressing gown on me, tied the belt up and put my slippers on my feet. 'Here we go then.' Sitting on the side of the bed, I touched the floor and with help I got to the other side of the room, turned round, went to walk back, and fell to the ground, crumpled up on the floor. I had lost the use of my legs. Several people got me back into bed, out for the count – my days of walking seemed to have come to an end.

The next move came when sister came into the room with a wheelchair. I was helped into it and the staff moved me into Cronshaw Ward, for broken limbs.

*

Arthur Brinkley kept in touch with the hospital daily, and had to report to Paddington. I was in a bad way, and asked Dad on the QT to go and see Annie and tell her where I was, as she might not know. I said to him, 'You know where she lives.'

I had a surprise on Christmas Eve when this gorgeous beauty with long black hair and wearing a two-piece mini skirt in red and high heels came into the ward. Everyone jumped for joy! I asked her to slow down and come and sit with me, with her make-up and bright red lipstick. I asked for the curtains around the bed to be pulled as I wanted her to myself. She had booked a taxi from Didcot to the hospital and return. God, I loved her!

One night I lay in bed and suddenly I felt a pain so severe that it seemed to rip out my stomach. I had never had pain like it, and was doubled up into a ball. The doctors were called straight away and next day I was wheeled down to a clinic on a stretcher and given tests with a barium meal; I constantly drank loads from a beaker while the bed I was strapped to was twisted hydraulically to view what was travelling through my system, seen on an X-ray machine, until the meal hit my gut, then the doctor saw what was inside my stomach and giving me the pain. They found that I had an duodenal ulcer brought on by the operations after the crash, and also from eating greasy fry-ups. They put me on tablets straight away for the foreseeable future, and I had the barium meal test every six months until 1971, when I was so ill I brought up blood. I went to the hospital next day, but it had disappeared.

My Mum and Dad and family came to visit me regularly with other friends from the street. I also had several visits from Annie.

There were no Christmas carols in the shed that year.

In January 1965 I was released, and I think I had been lucky. I saw some amputated fingers and broken bones, and many years later I found that I had only one kidney, and had to have a new replacement hip where the bus's wheel had crushed me. I lived from day to day, really feeling better in myself – I had certainly 'been there and got the T-shirt'!

The morning before I was off home the sister came into the ward and removed the tube from my throat while I sat on the edge of the bed; it seemed funny having it removed, as now I could breathe much more easily through my windpipe.

Mum and Dad brought in my clothes for me to change into; those I was wearing at the time of the accident were thrown away. I put on my jacket, stuck my hand into the pocket and pulled out 15 quid that I had drawn from the Post Office after the accident. Mum demanded that I give it to her, 'No,' I said to her very quietly, as it was to pay a bill before I got run over.

That New Year, 1965, I had been courting Annie for three years. One morning, when I was still off work following the accident, but getting better, she told me that her parents were going to the hospital the next day, and she would be at home by herself. I turned up on my 250cc BSA motorbike, but seemed to have got the time wrong. When I knocked at the back door her father appeared and asked me what I was doing there. 'Come in,' said his wife. 'We must be gone – we're late.'

'But what about him?' Annie's father said again. Could they trust him being alone with their daughter? His wife said, 'Yes, let's go.'

Annie appeared and smiled. 'We'll wait a while,' she said, then came to me and kissed me full on my mouth. Then she got hold of my hand and led me up the stairs.

Later that same day, when I got back home I had the fright of my life – my Mum was home from work and demanded to know where I had been. My Mum hated girls, especially when her little boy was growing up and not allowed to see the world.

So I sang to her 'Home on the Range', a song she hated. She walked from the kitchen sink, pulled out the kitchen drawer, put her hand in and threw whatever was in her hand. I just got out of the back door. We used to have glass in the door, but it was now fitted with hardboard, and the blade of a knife, with my name on it, went 2 inches through the hardboard. As I opened the back door the handle of the 16-inch-long bread knife swayed back and forth. She never found out about Annie that day. I called to see Annie that night and we went out on my motorbike.

I told Mike about what happened, and he said, 'That got the muck off your chest, then, and made you feel better.'

He was right, it did, after what I had been through with my accident.

*

I went back to work in the first week of March 1965. I looked across the front of the shed; there were no engines but on No 5 road was No 6937 *Conyngham Hall*, with long benches laid out evenly. I wondered what was going on.

I went into the shed to sign on. The Time Office staff and pay clerks welcomed me back, asking how I felt. I was better, but I had a feeling of fear about getting under anything metal…

I was told by Jim that everyone in the

shed was going to have their picture taken that day out front. 'Seeing that you've been off, Pat, we're closing down, and the men will have to find out what they intend to do.'

I asked him, 'What about you, mate?'

'I might have a job lined up. Just waiting to hear from the powers that be.' That same day I saw someone talking to him at the forge, a big man in a suit, and I heard him say, 'You'll be the driver and operator.' But Jim kept everything close his chest and never told a soul.

For something to do I took a walk along the wooden boards provided on the roof of the shed. Seeing men working on the roof further along, I asked if I could come up. I was told to stay on the boards and not to step over onto the roof. I did as I was told.

Years of dirt encrusted the asbestos roof as I climbed further up to the very top, looking at the smoke chutes. It was a joy to see the whole of Didcot and the surrounding countryside.

Fitter Ted Powell and his fitter's mate Frank Dowding were on inspections as the engines came in off the main line and had their fires dropped. They worked over at the coal stage before each engine went down to the turntable. Fitter Jimmy Holmar and his fitter's mate Matt Oglesby were out on the front of the shed completing faults on the locomotives ready to leave on all four roads, fixing broken boiler gauge glasses or making adjustments to the vacuum brakes, sand pipes or tender brakes. The shed foreman on duty that day was either Bernard Barlow, Harry Buckel or Reg Warr, strutting up and down with his bowler hat on, trying to get the engines out on time.

Fitter Jack Dearlove worked on inspections and was tip-top at what he did; he was a dedicated railwayman and would never allow anything to get past him. However, in 1965 I once saw him get angry with an Indian fitter who came to work in our department. His name was Ali Patel, and he kept saying, 'In my country we do this' and 'In my country we do that.' Jack had been out in India during the Second World War and saw many things, and one of them was the filth and dirt. Jack told him to shut his mouth, but he didn't, and Jack had a violent attack of anger – he grabbed him, dragged him out and, after opening the cabin door, threw him in the pit. Ali came to work with flat leather flip-flops on his feet and no socks, and wore an 'Aladdin'-type overshirt and baggy pants as if he was still in India. This did not go down very well with the rest of the fitting crew. He was told by Arthur Brinkley to get heavy boots and overalls a bit quick!

Ali told me that he had a letter from the Government saying that if his family came to England they would receive £50 each. In my opinion that was a kick up the arse for the English people, seeing that I would only get

Foreman Reg Warr is on the left, and next to him looks like Jack Hancock, Chief Loco Inspector. The other two on the right I think are boiler inspectors for the insurance company involved – No 4079 *Pendennis Castle* was withdrawn in 1964 and bought privately for preservation.

£8 a week when I was a fully fledged fitter! Where was the justice?

Anyway, steam was on the way out, taking with it some of the best men I was proud to have worked with – which is why I made sure they appeared in this book.

*

In 1965 I started at Swindon. Until I got there I knew nothing about what was going to happen – the railway left me in the dark, again.

I had to report to the manager of the site. As I sat in his office the room temperature was freezing, like an icebox. It was as if he was afraid to add a little coal to the fire. He asked me if I was on day release, but I explained that I had not been to school as I had just came out of hospital after an accident, and had lost the will for school. He wrote down everything I said. I was given an address where I had to stay in Swindon, on Farringdon Road. He directed me back out onto the street with a drawing on a notepad, and I had to report to Mrs Curtis. I left his office, turned right and walked down every road but found nothing, so I turned around and walked back up towards some cottages near the railway museum; I found it after an hour. I knocked at the door a little lady appeared. I was welcomed in, and Mrs Curtis explained the rules. I said I had to return to Didcot that night and put everything in order at home. The I went back towards the works heading for 'AE' shop. I had with me the telephone number for Annie's place of work – she worked on the switchboard in Jobs Dairy – so when I saw a phone box I rang her. I had to meet her that night at our usual metal seat in the corner at Edmonds Park around 7 o'clock.

In the meantime I made my way to my place of work and reported to the foreman, who asked where I had been.

'With the manager setting up my residence and putting myself into order for tomorrow,' I said, explaining that I had to go home and sort out my situation that night and come back next day. He gave me my wage disc and a key to my new locker, in which I put my overalls and day clothes. I was introduced to my new fitter, and worked for the time I was there until finishing time, when I had to leg it back to the station to catch the 5 o'clock stopper to Didcot.

I had to explain to my parents that I had to stay over at Swindon, so Mum and Dad got an overnight bag ready with a week's clothes inside. I also had to go and see Mike down the road to tell him I would see him on Friday night to sort out what was on for the weekend. I then walked up to the park and saw Annie sitting on our seat waiting. When I got to her she knew something was on; I told her that, because of what had gone on over the last few months, I was going to leave her, because I'd had reports back that she had not been true to me.

'You've been seen out with other boys,' I told her.

She burst out crying and said she was sorry and would not do it again.

'No, the trust has gone, and to be honest to us both I have totally finished with you, and women,' I told her. 'I wanted to get engaged to you and still you went out with someone else.'

I got up and walked off, while she walked away towards Park Road, crying. I headed back to Sinodun Road, also crying. I shouted out into the air, 'I bloody well loved you!'

Next morning another apprentice fitter, known as 'Blondie' – who built motorbikes from scratch, and rode a bike made up from different parts from many other bikes – came to my house in Sinodun Road from Harrow in London and took me to Swindon and my lodgings in Farringdon Road.

For three months I never went with another girl, until 8 May 1965 when I met up with Jenny in the Buccaneer Café on the Broadway. One Saturday morning I asked someone to ask her out. She replied I had to ask her myself. So despite having been hurt in love, I stood up and went to this girl and asked her out that afternoon. My life changed drastically, and after a few years we got engaged, and we would love each other forever.

'Blondie' would bring me over to Blewbury, where Jenny lived, on a Wednesday evening, seeing that it wasn't very far from Swindon. There I got myself a new bike of my own, a second-hand Tiger 90, a white ex-police machine with 'cowhorn' handlebars, which I part-exchanged with the BSA. We both went back to Swindon that evening, ready for work the next day.

I found myself in an environment full with all sorts of trades and men – some could take a joke, while others had lost the plot! One day I was working in the nose of a D800 'Warship' diesel-hydraulic, undoing pipework with my head down a hole. I never felt what was going on behind me, when suddenly I felt my bum go cold and some twat had set off a fire extinguisher, spreading cold foam. As I climbed out of the nose I saw everyone laughing their heads off. I said nothing, but just grinned, pointed my finger and told the guy responsible – a skilled electrical man from the RAF – that it would be my turn next. 'Be on your guard because I take no prisoners!'

A few months later my opportunity arose, and seeing the guy down the same hole head first, bottom stuck up in the air – a prime shot – I got out of the cab quietly and went on the hunt around the diesel locos looking for a full fire extinguisher – they hung in the cabs. I found one with the tag still intact, walked back to where the old RAF guy was working and pulled the red tag from the unit. Now I knew what was going to come out of it before I started, but hey-ho, a laugh is a laugh, and when someone does something to you, you expect the person to honour the deed. I couldn't resist it. I stuck the spout up his rear and pulled the trigger. A full blast of icy air shot out of the nozzle – he was soaked. He went raving mad, screaming and shouting, and we came to blows in the cab. I couldn't stop laughing, but he had me by the

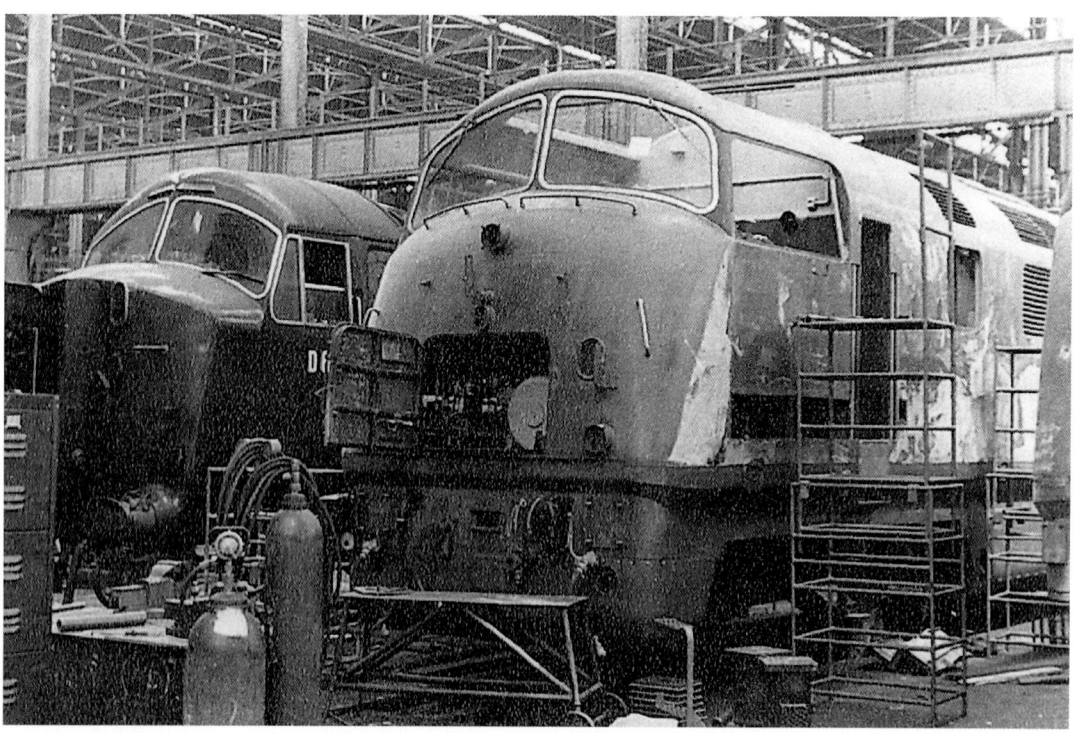

Inside Swindon Works. I was busy inside the nose of a 'Warship' like the one seen here when I was attacked with a fire extinguisher. *Jim Russell collection*

A brush with death

throat, and when the line foreman climbed up the steps into the cab we were both frog-marched up the stairs to the mezzanine floor, and the office of the factory's General Manager.

He said to the RAF guy, 'I've been waiting for you to come to me as I have heard stories about you, and what I have heard I do not like. You are on remand, and I shall take further steps to have you dismissed. Now get out of my office!'

Then he said, 'Mr Kelly, come in and shut the door! You are a dead lucky person, Mr Kelly, because you are an apprentice, or you would be up the road behind him. But I understand he had done this to you when you arrived.'

'Yes, sir.'

'But you had to get your own back, am I correct?'

'Yes, sir.'

'Just get on with what you have to do and in six months you are out of here – and do not get into more trouble!'

'No, sir.'

'Off you go. Shut the door on the way out. Any more trouble and you will be sacked.'

I went back to the AE workshop under the mezzanine floor and everyone wanted to know what had happened. 'We heard the manager scream at the other guy – he's gone, as they sacked him on the spot.'

I kept low and did as I was told, but saw many others get into trouble. One even had the police brought in for pinching bronze, a sackable offence. I saw them take the culprit away, handcuffed, and so did everyone that Thursday evening when we were collecting our wages. Then 'Blondie' and I rode our bikes to Blewbury where Jennifer lived; we stayed for a few hours, then we rode back to Swindon. He was a good sort.

During the five months I worked in the factory I went out on road tests towards Bristol, returning doing 'dead-man's' stops. Later I was transferred to the welding school up above the factory, 'in the heavens'; many men worked in the school getting their coding as welders with British Railways.

At the time comments started to be fed back from conversations among the welding staff, things we had said to each other while welding, niggly things. So we laid a trap for the person who we thought it might be, and sure enough we caught the culprit; something I said went back and came out of the teacher's mouth, and we all looked at each other in amazement, and nodded. The time had come to teach the teacher and his stooge a lesson in physics and sociology, as we now knew the snitch who was running back to the teacher telling tales. He thought we knew nothing about him, but alas we knew, and he came off worse, as did the teacher.

The snitch always got a motorbike magazine, probably paid for from the teacher's own benevolent pocket fund, as he got all the perks. What a sad day for them as he went out and forgot his magazine, leaving it on the bench. Four of us carefully welded metal plates into a block, leaving a little gap through which to post the magazine, then finishing off the weld perfectly. We carried the block to the hydraulic pressure-testing gauge, placed it on the testing block, closed the door and made it secure. We had just finished when both the teacher and the snitch walked into the classroom together, laughing and joking. 'Have you seen my magazine?' One of the welding crew members pointed towards the testing rig.

The best bit was yet to come, as the welded block needed to be pressed down to split the weld and reveal the weld strip. I must have done well when I welded that block, as I had a 100% pass – the weld was the best ever, but the boy never thought it funny as he tried desperately to get his magazine out, but having nothing between his ears he found there was only ashes.

The teacher demanded who had done this. I stood up, but unbeknown to me behind my back everyone stood and said in unison, 'I did!'

The following week we had a different teacher who thought we were the best crew he had ever had, and we treated him like he treated us. The next three weeks went well and some came out better than others. I was pleased with what I had achieved, and went back into the AE factory to finish off some projects I was doing with the fitters.

I then had a transfer to Reading, which was a silly move really, as I wanted to go back to Old Oak Common. When I arrived at Reading in 1965 the steam shed was gone. It had been rebuilt to carry out strip-out repairs, with a low-level entrance so that men could walk straight under the diesels. But we had to have huge steps to climb into the diesels' cabs. At that time I worked on the engines and engine compartments, and never drew the short straw that meant working on the traction bogies – that was a filthy job. I even went out on road tests to check out the diesel engines, heading towards the Bicester line.

The six months shot by, and towards the end of my apprenticeship I felt very down and unsure as to where to transfer for the best. I was easily led, and should have stayed where I was, but Mr Diamond offered me a position at Old Oak. The truth of the matter is that I should have stayed.

On 14 February 1966 I was fully fledged apprentice fitter, and ended up at Oxford. What a tip it was, and run down – nothing like Didcot shed, which had been spotlessly clean. However, that was my fault, listening to other people. In the end I left the railway with great sorrow roughly six months later.

*

Steam came to an end on the Western Region in 1966.

Mum had left the railway as I started work, and six months later she went to work at the Army Ordnance Depot. When Dad died she moved to the Blue Mountain old peoples' home at Wallingford, passing away on 24 August 1993 at the age of 87. By then I was working at the Heyford USAAF base in the boiler house on nights. One night she came to me wearing a hood and cloak and floated away over the boilers. I cried my eyes out that night and some American airmen came in to look after me. God, how I missed them both!

However, I was brought up and taught to work hard and play hard. After leaving British Railways in 1966 I went to work in construction, but the company closed down, with redundancies, in 1973.

I went to see Arthur Brinkley at his home in Harwell and he arranged an interview at Reading Diesel Depot, putting in a good word with the manager, but they turned me down. Arthur went mad and tore into

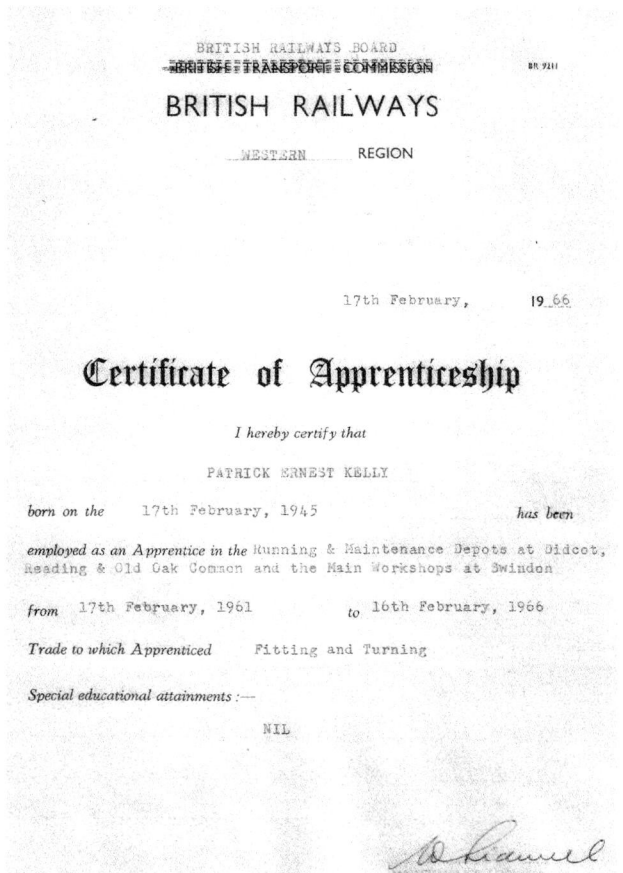

The completion of my apprenticeship, 16 February 1966.

The Mark I Type RM62 ballast-cleaning machine is seen here at Didcot station in September 1966. These machines were hauled to the site, then worked under their own power.

the manager, Reggie Hanks, and that was the last time I saw him. Tragically he died on 24 September 1985 at the age of only 64, and was buried in Harwell village cemetery, Oxfordshire. I would often visit his grave 'just to say hello' when in the neighbourhood. I had worshipped the ground he walked on, and throughout the rest of my career I followed his ways and methods of work when I was made up to a supervisor position.

I only knew three men to go to Reading: Arthur Brinkley, Bob Looms and none other than Dave Davies. Jim Holmar went as a fitter to the Samor canning factory in Didcot Park Road.

Meanwhile Jim Tyler, having been made redundant, was offered a job in the Permanent Way department driving a Plasser & Theurer Type RM62 Ballast Cleaner. Research by British Rail found compacted trackbeds full of irregular stones, steam engine ash and often material from the construction of the line, none of which were conducive to tamping or maintaining good track geometry as lines got faster. The answer was to remove at least 9 inches of sub-track material and replace it with regular-sized 70mm railway ballast. BR ordered a number of ballast-cleaning machines to mechanise this process, and in the mid-1950s these machines were built to two designs by the Swiss Matisa SA Company. As the concept was developed, Plasser & Theurer from Linz in Austria developed the larger self-propelled RM62 ballast cleaners. BR ordered 20 of these machines between 1966 and 1974, across four versions. As the spoil conveyor extended beyond the machine, BR converted some redundant parcel vans as runner wagons.

Epilogue

I subsequently married Jenny, and in 2001 we moved to Norfolk to retire together. I phoned Jim regularly, and sent him the proof copy of my earlier book, *Didcot Steam Apprentice*; when it was published I posted him a copy. On 13 June 2006 I decided to pay him a visit. I found his name and address in the phone book, went up to the front door and knocked. I heard all the bolts and locks being undone, then the door opened; it seemed that it hadn't been opened for a long time. A little man stood looking at me. I asked him if Mr Tyler lived there. He then spoke, and I knew it was him from his Monmouthshire accent. We said our hellos, then chatted about the times when we were on the railway and the memories of when I was at Didcot shed. I turned my head to the side slightly and he said, 'You just look like your Dad – you're the image of him.' That brought back memories to me.

Jim said that he would be 91 the following year, but he still had all his marbles and was quick with it. He remembered when he was my fitter and how through the years I had worked with him and how he had put me right. 'Well, I tried,' he said, 'but you always went your own way.' I stood there, my mind working, and, yes, he was right. If only we could go back again and do things differently! He told me that I was the only one who ever got in touch over the years.

We shook hands, and Jim put his other hand over mine; it was as hard as a rock through all those years doing heavy work. Then as we said our goodbyes the tears rolled down both our faces.

I was grateful for the help he had given me in putting this book together, as I still had all the paperwork, which I kept. I can still see him today, my fitter at Didcot lifting shop on the old Great Western Railway.

A few years later he died and Jenny and I went to the funeral at Newlands Avenue, Didcot. I cried my eyes out, before driving home back to Norfolk.

Goodbye, my friend and my mentor.

Appendix 1: The fitting crew at Didcot Running and Maintenance Department

Shedmaster
George East

Time Office
Mrs Bray (also PA to Shedmaster)
Lenny Head
Mark Thomas

Pay Clerks
Ernie Jones
Stan Barten

Office Clerk
Sam Morgan

Running and Maintenance Foreman
Arthur Brinkley

Shed Foremen
Arthur Leaworthy
Alfie Jones
Harry Buckel
Bernard Barlow
Reg Warr

These shed foremen were also daily drivers; when coming off duty they fitted into the slot for their status. Many a time I would be in contact with them regarding their driving. Reg Warr was the only member of staff who worked in the shed as foreman and on shift work.

Boilersmith Foreman
Bill Cox

Stores
Jim Parsons
Arthur Wheatley

Inspections
Ted Powell

Junior Inspections
Jack Dearlove

Fitters
Jim Tyler — Lifting Shop Fitter
Dave Davies — 12,000/24,000 mileage servicing brown cards/repairs
Bert Paice — 12,000/24,000 mileage servicing brown cards/repairs
Norman Brogden — 12,000/24,000 mileage servicing brown cards (DMUs)
Jimmy Holmar — 12,000 mileage servicing brown cards/front of shed repairs
Bob Looms — 12,000/24,000 mileage servicing brown cards

Fitter's mate	Fitter
Jim Hale	Dave Davies
Frank Dowding	Ted Powell
Matt Oglesby	Jimmy Holmar
Ted Gallagher (resigned 1960)	Norman Brogden (resigned 1960)
Bob Warwick	Bob Looms

Boilersmith	Boilersmith's mate
Alan Membury	John Cooper
Jack Dearlove Snr (76)	Cyril Dawson

Overall keeper
Bill Clark

Apprentices
Patrick Kelly, from February 1960 ('Wobble')
Paul Kelly, from the Royal Navy, 1961
Charlie Clanfield, transferred from the engine department, 1964

Shed Cleaner
Dick Bidmead

Fire-droppers and coal stage attendants
Chris Kelly
Lofty O' Connor

Fire-raisers
Mick Gleason

Lofty Davies
Frank Marshalll

Boiler Washouts
Trevor May
Chris Kelly (transferred from coal stage)

Appendix 2: Didcot's locomotive allocation in October 1959, October 1960, November 1960 and 1961

October 1959

0-6-0

2214
2221
2234
2240
2252
3210
3211

0-6-0PT

1502[1]
3622
3653
3709
3721[2]
3751
4649
5744
5746[3]
5783
7772
8435[4]
8458[5]
9407[3]

0-6-2T

5639
5647

2-6-0

5326
5337
5351
5380
7308
7324

2-6-2T

6109
6113
6120
6124
6136
6139
6156
6159

2-8-0

2819
2836
2844

4-6-0 'Hall'

4913 Baglan Hall[6]
4939 Littleton Hall[7]
4959 Purley Hall
4965 Rood Ashton Hall
4969 Shugborough Hall
4994 Downton Hall[8]
5943 Elmdon Hall
6910 Gossington Hall
6915 Mursley Hall
6952 Kimberley Hall

4-6-0 'Modified Hall'

6969 Wraysbury Hall
6983 Otterington Hall[9]
6996 Blackwell Hall

October 1960

0-6-0

2214
2221
2234
2240
2252
3210
3211
5744
5746[3]
5783
7772
8435[4]
8458[5]
9407[3]

0-6-0PT

1502
3622
3653
3709
3721[2]
3751
4649

0-6-2T

5639
5647

2-6-0

5326
5337
5351
5380
7308
7324

2-6-2T

6109
6113
6120
6124
6136
6139
6156
6159

2-8-0

2819
2836
2844

4-6-0 'Hall'

4913 Baglan Hall[6]
4939 Littleton Hall
4959 Purley Hall
4965 Rood Ashton Hall
4969 Shugborough Hall
4994 Downton Hall[8]
5943 Elmdon Hall
6910 Gossington Hall
6915 Mursley Hall
6952 Kimberley Hall

4-6-0 'Modified Hall'

6969 Wraysbury Hall
6983 Otterington Hall[9]
6996 Blackwell Hall

November 1960

0-6-0

2201
2221
2230
2240
3211

0-6-0PT

1502[1]
3622
3653
3751
4649
5746[3]
8720[10]

2-6-0

5351
5380

6302
6363
6379
7324
7327

2-6-2T

6109
6113
6120
6124
6136
6139
6156
6159

2-8-0

2819
2836
2839
2849

4-6-0 'Hall'

4902 Aldenham Hall
4915 Condover Hall
4939 Littleton Hall[7]
4950 Patshull Hall
4965 Rood Ashton Hall
4959 Purley Hall
4969 Shugborough Hall
4976 Warfield Hall
5918 Walton Hall
5943 Elmdon Hall
5987 Brocket Hall
6910 Gossington Hall
6915 Mursley Hall
6937 Conyngham Hall

4-6-0 'Modified Hall'

6969 Wraysbury Hall
6983 Otterington Hall[7]

November 1961

0-6-0

2221
2230

0-6-0PT

3665[12]
3751
5746[3]
8494[11]
8720[10]
9450[11]

2-6-0

5380[13]
6302
6313
6350
6363
7324
7327

2-6-2T

6109
6120
6124[14]
6130
6136
6139
6145[15]
6159

2-8-0

2836
2849
2893
2898
3819
3820
3840

Appendix 2

4-6-0 'Hall'

4902 *Aldenham Hall*
4910 *Blaisdon Hall*
4915 *Condover Hall*
4939 *Littleton Hall*
4950 *Patshull Hall*
4959 *Purley Hall*
4965 *Rood Ashton Hall*
4969 *Shugborough Hall*
4976 *Warfield Hall*[16]
5987 *Brocket Hall*
6910 *Gossington Hall*
6937 *Conyngham Hall*

4-6-0 'Modified Hall'

6969 *Wraysbury Hall* 1
6983 *Otterington Hall* 2
6996 *Blackwell Hall* 3

4-6-0 'County' – stockpile from Old Oak Common

1002 *County of Berks*
1007 *County of Brecknock*
1015 *County of Gloucester*
1018 *County of Leicester*

Notes

All locos built at Swindon unless otherwise stated

[1] Stored from 16 June 1960
[2] Moved to Lydney on 4 November 1960
[3] Built by North British Locomotive Co
[4] Built by W. B. Bagnall Ltd
[5] Built by Yorkshire Engine Co Ltd
[6] Came to Didcot from Reading on 4 November 1959
[7] Went to Swindon for repairs in November 1960
[8] Left Didcot in October 1959
[9] Went to Swindon for repairs in October 1959
[10] Built by Beyer Peacock
[11] Built by Robert Stephenson & Hawthorns Ltd
[12] Arrived 24 October 1961
[13] Arrived 26 October 1961
[14] Arrived from Slough 24 October 1961
[15] Stayed at Didcot until 19 October 1961
[16] Left for Swindon 4 October 1961

Index

Abear, Ted 250, 254
Abingdon branch 155, 156
Addie (cousin) 110-11, 154
Alder, Ernie 24-25, 77, 79, 190, 195, 220
Andrews, Harry 81
'Annie' (girlfriend) 13, 80, 83, 92, 104, 108, 109, 111, 123, 124, 125, 126, 136, 138, 148, 150, 168-69, 172, 177, 178, 191, 192, 197, 204, 212, 227, 243, 255, 264, 270, 271, 272
Ashmore, Cedric 181
Automatic Warning System (AWS) 126, 154
Avery, Don 13, 34, 211
Axle boxes, bearings and springs, work on 22, 30, 37, 38, 71-72, 198, 200-01

Barclay, Len 9
Barlow, Bernard 272
Barten, Stan 76, 142
Betteridge, Bert 81
Bidmead, Dick 39-40, 87, 112, 160, 212
'Blondie', apprentice fitter 248, 273, 274, 275
Boiler wash-outs 24, 117, 226
Bosley, Mike 96
Brake blocks 32-33, 66-67, 85, 175-77
Bray, Mrs 15, 22, 23, 43, 148
Breakdown train 61-62, 114, 134
Breakfast, cooked in firebox 92
Brinkley, Arthur (foreman) 13, 15-16, 18, 22, 25, 28, 37, 43, 47, 48, 62, 65, 74, 75, 76-77, 79, 81, 83-84, 85, 86, 88, 90, 100-01, 109, 114, 120, 122, 127, 131, 133-34, 140, 142-43, 144, 157, 170, 173, 176, 182, 185, 186, 190-91, 193, 197, 200, 206, 209-10, 219, 226, 229, 230, 231, 232-33, 235, 237, 253-54, 258-59, 262, 264, 270, 272, 276
British Railways Staff Club, Didcot 42, 64
Brogden, Norman 25-26, 27, 39-40, 65, 66, 69, 75, 88, 89, 109, 180
Brown, Allan 237, 245, 248
Brown, Bert 9
Brown, Billy 218
Brown, Pete 80-82, 110
Brown, Ted 118
Buckel, Harry 36, 86, 87, 88, 272
'Busby' loco chimney 160-62
Butler, Wilf 52
Butters, Bob 11

Call boys 34-35
Callipers, making 46, 51, 64-65
Caulkett, Charlie 51ff, 238-40
Chard, Eric 241, 244-45, 251, 258, 262
Clark, Bill 22, 63, 66, 113, 115, 148, 153, 179, 206-07, 262
Cleaners 57-58
Coles, Tony 250
Collett, Len 107
Collins, Gerald 'Golly' 264
Connecting rods 27, 37-39, 67, 68, 69, 139-41, 145, 201-02
Cooper, Johnny 89, 102-03, 160
Cox, Bill 103
Crawford, Bert 138
Crispin, The, Harwell (Mervin and Jean) 113, 125, 172, 175, 263
Crocker, John 246
Crossheads 37-38, 44, 120, 185-86
Curtis, Mrs 273

Davies, Archie 52, 202, 252-53, 255, 256
Davies, Dave 18, 22, 29, 40, 43ff, 51, 57, 61-62, 63, 65ff, 81, 89, 106, 109, 116, 125, 126, 138, 145, 159, 163, 171, 172, 182, 185, 186-88, 194, 197-98, 200, 204, 205, 221, 223, 228, 229, 232, 267, 277
Davies, Taffy 11
Dawson, Cyril 160
Dearlove, Jack 48, 144, 160, 173, 180, 197, 205, 207, 228, 232, 272
Diamond, Wilf 'Legs' 249, 263-64, 276
Didcot, Labour Club 59, 63, 102, 116, 143, 163, 175, 191
    Mereland Road 7, 9, 13, 19, 42, 64
    Newlands Road/Avenue 8, 25
    St Birinus School 9-11, 13, 42

Index

Didcot, Newbury & Southampton line 7-8, 11, 52, 68, 75
Didcot loco shed 14ff, 17, 25, 35, 49, 94, 101
    ash road 20-21
    coal stage 20, 162-63
    enginemen's cabin 58
    fire in yard 199-200
    fitters' cabin 18, 19, 45, 139
    fitting shop 17, 21
    forge 17, 33, 35, 68, 141-42, 158, 218-19
    hours and pay 15, 52, 63, 96, 190, 199, 236
    initiation ceremony 57, 58
    lifting shop and crane 16, 33-34, 161
    North Junction, collision at 264ff
    'Polar Star' hostel 112, 209-11, 213, 223-24, 225, 259
    Provender Stores and lake 76, 163-64, 167
    stationary boiler 95-96, 115
    stores 18-19, 58, 61, 178
    toilets 39
    washing and washing facilities 39, 139
    water supply to shed and yards 164-67
    Didcot Ordnance Depot 39, 52, 114, 152, 153, 167, 179
Didcot station 14, 59-60, 116, 193
    platform lifts 168
    station pilot 92;
Diesel multiple units (DMUs) 75, 76, 155, 170
    at Reading 241ff
    ultrasonic fatigue testing 252-54, 256ff, 263ff
Dowding, Frank 29, 34, 35, 63, 131, 272
Duke, Ron 264-65
Durman, Ron 52

East, George (shedmaster) 13, 14, 15, 32, 160, 179, 210, 228, 231
Edmonds, Bert 92-93
Edwards, Tommy 75, 106, 211
'Enparts' 78, 79, 80, 171, 196, 197, 216, 220, 232, 257
Evans, Arthur 254
Evans, Roger 'Parrot' 9, 10, 11
Fairford branch 56

Firebox, working in 173
Fitzgerald, Matt 265
'Fly' turns from Didcot 52, 92, 150-51
Foxhall Junction 165, 166, 234-35

Gallagher, Ted 25, 26, 27
Galloway, Chris 114
Gauge glasses 35-36
Gibbs, Billy 252
Gibbs, Les 34, 77, 102, 116
Gibson, Bill 107
Gleason, Mick 24, 112, 176, 228
Goodall, Jack 97-100
Goring & Streatley 238-39

Hale, Jim 18, 22, 29, 39, 57, 61, 63, 89, 116, 117, 125, 126, 137, 142, 145, 163, 178, 182, 200, 204, 205, 221, 223, 228, 241, 264, 267
Hall, Eric 138, 237, 238-40
Hancock, Jack 272
Hanks, Reggie 277
Head, Lenny 25, 71, 189, `97
Hitchcock (driver) 264-65
Holmar, Jimmy 30, 31, 36, 65, 74, 88, 109, 145, 160, 163, 180, 197, 205, 221, 247, 272, 277
Howard, Jenny 42, 73, 192, 197
Howard, Mick 12, 42-43, 46-47, 59, 63-64, 71, 73-74, 76, 80-82, 97, 102, 110, 113, 116, 125-26, 136, 138, 143, 150, 158-59, 160, 163, 175, 179, 191, 199, 208, 212, 213, 214, 224, 230, 233, 263, 271
Hughes, Barry 249, 250, 255
Huntley & Palmer, Reading, fireless loco 246

Ireson, Ted 173, 231

James, Roland 10, 245
Jarrot, Vic 'the Bishop' 171, 237-40
Jones, Ernie 39, 63, 116

Kelly, Chris (father) 8, 12, 13, 19, 22, 24, 88-89, 102, 117, 148, 150, 158, 160, 169, 207, 208-10, 213, 214, 224, 226-27, 230, 231, 269-71, 276
Kelly, Jennifer (wife) 273-75, 278

Kelly, Kathleen (mother) 8, 12-13, 16, 23, 24, 71, 72, 81, 102, 125, 143, 148, 150, 153, 158, 163, 168, 170, 174, 196, 208-09, 213, 214, 222, 226-27, 269-71, 276
Kelly, Paul (brother) 12-13, 16, 170, 179, 180, 181, 182, 195, 204, 205, 206-07, 215, 216, 222-23, 231, 259, 262
Kelly, Richard (brother) 12-13, 15, 16, 18, 23, 27, 36, 39, 47, 156, 174, 210, 211, 212, 214, 220, 262

Langston, John 249
Lazby, Fred 250
Leaworthy, Arthur 148, 202
Lighting up steam locos 24, 112, 176

Locomotives, diesel
'Hymek' 113, 114, 244
Shunters 247, 248
'Warship' 113, 138, 242, 249, 274-75

Locomotives, steam
'22XX' 0-6-0 103, 106, 107, 174, 175-76, 178, 237ff
'28XX' 2-8-0 35, 55, 114, 118, 119
'4300' 2-6-0 11, 84, 86, 139, 220
'57XX' 0-6-0PT 44, 152, 160, 161, 206-07
'61XX' 2-6-2T 107, 108, 229
'94XX' 0-6-0PT 21
9F 2-10-0 108, 243
'Castle' 4-6-0 25, 215-16, 217-19, 254, 261, 272
City of Truro 4-4-0 198-99
'County' 4-6-0 52
'Grange' 4-6-0 27, 30, 31, 52, 85, 231
'Hall' 4-6-0 17-18, 43, 47, 48, 52, 65, 67, 74-75, 86, 88, 90, 93, 108, 114, 117, 144, 153, 171, 172, 180-82, 191, 192, 193, 200, 209, 228, 245, 271
'Manor' 4-6-0 235-36
'ROD' 2-8-0 52, 105
USA Transportation Corps 2-8-0 93

Looms, 'Belgian Bob' 22, 27, 29, 31, 32, 43, 51, 65, 89, 109, 171, 205, 209, 223, 231, 259, 277

McNamara, Johnny 138
Maintenance manual 89-90

Marshall, Frank 24, 32, 36, 65, 112, 160
May, Trevor 18, 24, 88, 117, 148, 160, 225
Medical examination (BR) 190
Membury, Alan 89
Membury, Alex 240
Merrick, Harry 245
Midwinter's shop 25, 101, 121, 209, 210, 259
Miles, Bill 91, 155, 171, 256
Morgan, Bert 'Skip' 25, 103, 141, 202, 216, 244, 255
Morgan, Sam 74, 76, 170
Moulsford, Louis 9, 10, 11, 42
Moxon's fish and chip shop 223

Neal, Tony 63
Nutt, Albert 9

O'Brien, Pat 71, 73-74, 82
O'Connor, Lofty 24, 192
Odd, Harry 261
Oglesby, Matt 36, 65, 88, 89, 90, 145, 197, 221, 225, 247, 272
Old Oak Common shed 247ff, 264
Oxford 90-91, 155-57, 192, 200, 239

Paddington 54, 55, 260; Ranelagh Road 260-61
Page, Mr (schoolmaster) 9
Paice, Bert 83-85, 89, 109, 171, 180, 221
Parsons, Jim 61, 131, 160, 178, 198, 202
Patel, Ali 272
Paul, Ernie 118
Peirce, Bill 238-40
Pistons and cylinders, work on 26, 27, 28, 44, 85-86, 118ff, 127ff, 132ff, 145ff, 153, 181ff, 186ff, 226
Powell, Ted 29, 34, 35-36, 44, 47, 50, 65, 87, 88, 131, 180, 226, 228, 272
Pritchard, John 218, 222

Quartermaine, Mick 245, 246, 248, 249

Radway, Harold 266
Reading 53, 90, 137, 169, 170-71, 224, 233-34, 242, 243, 276
    Diesel Depot 241ff, 251, 258, 276
    Oxford Ballrooms 71, 73, 82, 108, 109, 126

Index

SR loco shed 53
Regulator gland, repacking 45
Report sheets 88
Rock, Ted 179
Russell, Michael 241

Safety valves, work on 47-50, 84-85, 115
Sally (Swindon stores) 195, 216-17, 256, 257
Sand boxes 35, 86
Shand, Alec 141, 145, 150, 154
Shorter, Ken 9
Shunting work 135, 151-52
Simms, Ray 252
Skinner, Charlie 97
Slade, Mick 52
Smith, Albert 81
Smith, Dave 245, 246
Smith, Tom 97
Snow and snowploughs (winter 1962-63) 236ff
Suicides on the railway 24-25, 43-44
Sullivan, Mr, hostel manager 209, 211, 222, 225
Summers, Les 10
Superheaters, work on 87, 148-49, 222, 247
Swindon 77ff, 195-96, 273ff

Tenders, work on 40-41, 69-70, 71, 171, 193-94, 201
Thomas, Mark 19, 27, 169, 170
Tolley, Cyril 265, 266-67
Tyler, Dennis 243, 245, 246, 258
Tyler, Jim 16ff, 28ff, 30, 31, 32ff, 36ff, 43ff, 68ff, 71ff, 85-87, 106, 109, 112, 115-16, 118, 125, 127ff, 131ff, 137ff, 144ff, 153ff, 159, 160-61, 168, 169, 171, 175ff, 178, 180ff, 185, 192ff, 197ff, 201ff, 209, 212, 215ff, 224, 228-30, 235, 247, 253, 255, 259-60, 262, 267, 272, 277, 278
Tyres, measuring wear of 77, 93-94

Upton & Blewbury 11, 81, 82, 83, 110, 240

Vacuum pipes 90

Wallingford 11, 190; branch 74, 199
Walsh, Pat 108, 192
Warr, Reg 30, 272
Warwick, Bob 27, 28, 29, 31, 32, 88, 125, 126, 195, 204, 205, 227, 247
Water tank, working within 131-32
Weedkilling train 199
Welding 143
Wells, Walter 99-100
Wheatley, Arthur 139, 160, 198
Wheeler, Brian 237, 238
Wheeler, Stan 265
White metal, use of 26, 27, 68-69, 139-41, 202-04, 218-19
White, Tom 57
Wilde, Graham 46, 47, 233
Williams, Taffy 220